D0141946

DANIEL

THE KEY TO PROPHETIC REVELATION

DANIEL

THE KEY TO PROPHETIC REVELATION

A Commentary

by

JOHN F. WALVOORD

MOODY PRESS • CHICAGO

© 1971 by
THE MOODY BIBLE INSTITUTE
OF CHICAGO

ISBN: 0-8024-1752-3

Library of Congress Catalog Card Number: 75-123161

13 14 15 16 17 Printing/BB/Year 87 86 85 84 83

Printed in the United States of America

CONTENTS

PREFACE

AMONG THE GREAT PROPHETIC BOOKS of Scripture, none provides a more comprehensive and chronological prophetic view of the broad movement of history than the book of Daniel. Of the three prophetic programs revealed in Scripture, outlining the course of the nations, Israel, and the church, Daniel alone reveals the details of God's plan for both the nations and Israel. Although other prophets like Jeremiah had much to say to the nations and Israel, Daniel brings together and interrelates these great themes of prophecy as does no other portion of Scripture. For this reason, the book of Daniel is essential to the structure of prophecy and is the key to the entire Old Testament prophetic revelation. A study of this book is, therefore, not only important from the standpoint of determining the revelation of one of the great books of the Old Testament but is an indispensable preliminary investigation to any complete eschatological system.

In the twentieth century, comparatively few important commentaries on the book of Daniel have been published. Twentieth century scholars, to be sure, have the heritage of some of the great commentaries of the past, beginning with Jerome and John Calvin, and including later works such as the commentaries by Moses Stuart, E. B. Pusey, and Otto Zöckler. To these can be added the commentaries by S. P. Tregelles, Nathaniel West, Joseph A. Seiss, and William Kelly. One of the old giants is the commentary by C. F. Keil, still a standard work. Critical scholarship, assuming that the book of Daniel was a pious forgery of the second century, has in later years greatly influenced treatment of the book of Daniel. Works by Robert H. Charles, S. R. Driver, F. W. Farrar, and the monumental work of James A. Montgomery in the *International Critical Commentaries* have dominated the field. Later liberal critics such as Arthur Jeffery in the *Interpreter's Bible* and Norman W. Porteous in his recent work have brought liberal scholarship up to date.

The exposition of the book of Daniel has been enriched by reverent, conservative scholars who have produced popular works such as the expositions of H. A. Ironside, Arno C. Gaebelein, and Louis Talbot; and many similar volumes have served as homiletical treatments of the book.

7

Robert Culver has contributed a theological treatment of Daniel relating to prophetic interpretation. Specialized studies such as those by H. H. Rowley and Robert Dick Wilson have led the way in scholarly debate in the twentieth century relative to the authenticity of the book of Daniel. Among all these works, however, no thorough commentary from the premillennial conservative point of view has appeared. The important works of H. C. Leupold and Edward Young, standard commentaries on Daniel, present only the amillennial view and are now twenty years old.

Taken as a whole no complete commentary on Daniel from the conservative point of view has been written since Leupold and Young's work. In the light of recent scholarly discussions and considerable additional archeological evidence, the findings of both conservative and liberal scholarship published in the first half of the twentieth century must now be thoroughly reviewed and reevaluated. The Qumran scrolls still await publication as they relate to Daniel, but there are indications that they will support rather than weaken the conservative interpretation regarding Daniel as a genuine book. The clarification of details surrounding the capture of Jerusalem in 605 B.C., the reign of Belshazzar, and the fall of Babylon as embodied in recent discoveries cast new light upon any exposition of the book of Daniel. The research of D. J. Wiseman and the recent study of Darius the Mede by John C. Whitcomb are important contributions. The studies in the field of introduction by Merrill Unger, Raymond Harrison, and Gleason Archer are also invaluable. Thus, a verse-by-verse commentary written from the conservative point of view, presenting the premillennial interpretation but including the consideration of all alternative views, is long overdue. It is hoped that this present study will make a contribution of a constructive nature toward the understanding of Daniel as one of the most important prophetic books in the Scriptures. The present work is an effort to provide a commentary which will give all the essential information necessary for a detailed exposition of the text in the light of extant literature, recent biblical scholarship, and the expanding field of archeological discovery.

In attempting an interpretation of the book of Daniel, the principle has been followed of interpreting prophecy in its normal sense while, at the same time, recognizing the apocalyptic character of its revelation. Full attention is given to the critical theories which regard Daniel as a forgery. The denial of the authenticity of the book of Daniel is refuted by internal evidence and archeological discoveries which support the genuineness of the prophecies of Daniel.

To avoid constant repetition of the English translation, the Authorized Version is quoted at the beginning of each section. Where the Authorized Version requires revision to bring out the precise meaning, attention is called to such variations. The *Hebrew and English Lexicon of the Old Testament* by Brown, Driver, and Briggs was used as a standard dictionary, although others are quoted. Principal sources include the commentaries by Montgomery, representing the modern critical view, Keil, expounding the old conservative view, and Edward Young and Leupold who support conservative amillennial scholarship. All students of Daniel must confess their debt to these monumental works. Acknowledgement is made to all publishers of copyrighted material for their gracious permission to quote representative portions.

Invaluable assistance has been offered by Dr. Bruce K. Waltke, Professor of Semitic Languages and Old Testament Exegesis, of Dallas Theological Seminary. His careful review of the manuscript and suggestions for its improvement have immeasurably improved the work as a whole. His intimate acquaintance with the Hebrew and the Aramaic text, as well as his wide reading and contemporary scholarship, has enriched this study.

In preparation of this commentary, the author has been guided by the objective to prepare a companion volume to his earlier commentary on the book of Revelation. In this new commentary on the book of Daniel, an attempt has been made to provide the careful student of the Word of God with the necessary tools and information to ascertain accurately the revelation of this important book and to relate it to systematic theology and specifically to eschatology as a whole. In the light of contemporary world events, which fit so well into the foreview of history provided in the book of Daniel, a study of this kind is most relevant to the issues of our day and, supported by other Scriptures, offers the hope that the consummation is not too distant. If the reader, through the study of this volume, has greater understanding of the divine prophetic program, more insight into contemporary events, and a brighter hope concerning things to come, the intention of the author will have been realized.

INTRODUCTION

THE BOOK OF DANIEL, according to its own testimony, is the record of the life and prophetic revelations given to Daniel, a captive Jew carried off to Babylon after the first conquest of Jerusalem by Nebuchadnezzar in 605 B.C. The record of events extends to the third year of Cyrus, 536 B.C., and, accordingly, covers a span of about seventy years. Daniel himself may well have lived on to about 530 B.C., and the book of Daniel was probably completed in the last decade of his life.

Although Daniel does not speak of himself in the first person until chapter 7, there is little question that the book presents Daniel as its author. This is assumed in the latter portion of the book and mentioned especially in 12:4. ·The use of the first person with the name Daniel is found repeatedly in the last half of the book (7:2, 15, 28; 8:1, 15, 27; 9:2, 22; 10:2, 7, 11, 12; 12:5). As most expositors, whether liberal or conservative, consider the book a unit, the claim of Daniel to have written this book is recognized even by those who reject it.[1]

Except for the attack of the pagan Porphyry (third century A.D.), no question was raised concerning the traditional sixth century B.C. date, the authorship of Daniel the prophet, or the genuineness of the book until the rise of higher criticism in the seventeenth century, more than two thousand years after the book was written. Important confirmation of the historicity of Daniel himself is found in three passages in Ezekiel (Eze 14:14, 20; 28:3), written after Daniel had assumed an important post in the king's court at Babylon.[2] Convincing also to conservative scholars is the reference to "Daniel the prophet" by Christ in the Olivet Discourse (Mt 24:15; Mk 13:14).

Higher critics normally question the traditional authorship and dates of books in both the Old and New Testaments, and therefore disallow the testimony of the book of Daniel itself, dispute the mention of Daniel by Ezekiel, and discount the support by Christ in the New Testament. But conservative scholars have given almost universal recognition to the book of Daniel as an authentic sixth century B.C. composition of Daniel, the captive of Nebuchadnezzar. Consideration of the arguments of higher

11

critics is given in the later discussion of the genuineness of the book of Daniel, upon which the conservative opinion rests.

PLACE IN THE SCRIPTURES

The book of Daniel, written last of all the major prophets, appears in this order among the major prophets in the English Bible. In the Hebrew Old Testament—divided into three divisions consisting of the Law, the Prophets, and the Writings, which is also called Kethubim (Hebrew) or Hagiographa (Greek)—Daniel is included in the third section, the Writings. In the Septuagint, Vulgate, and Luther, however, it is placed with the major prophets. Josephus also includes it in the second division of the Jewish canon, the Prophets, rather than in the Hagiographa. There is, therefore, general recognition of the prophetic character of the book.

Although the ministry of Daniel was prophetic, it was of different character than the other major prophets; and apparently for this reason, the Jews included Daniel in the Writings. As Robert Dick Wilson has pointed out, the reason for this was not that the Jews regarded Daniel as inferior nor because the prophetic section of the canon had already been closed, but as Wilson states, "It is more probable, that the book was placed in this part of the Heb Canon, because Daniel is not called a *nābhi'* ('prophet'), but was rather a *hōzeh* ('seer') and a *hākhām* ('wise man'). None but the works of the *nebhi'im* were put in the second part of the Jewish Canon, the third being reserved for the heterogeneous works of seers, wisemen, and priests, or for those that do not mention the name or work of a prophet, or that are poetical in form."[3]

J. B. Payne observes, "For though Christ spoke of Daniel's *function* as prophetic (Matt. 24:15), his *position* was that of governmental official and inspired writer, rather than ministering prophet (cf. Acts 2:29-30)."[4]

In any case, the Jews did not regard the third division as less inspired, but only different in character. This is clearly demonstrated by the fact that they included in it such venerable writings as Job, Psalms and Proverbs, the historical books of 1 and 2 Chronicles, Ezra, Nehemiah, and Esther, along with others not considered either the Law or the Prophets. There is no hint anywhere in ancient literature that the Jews regarded Daniel as a pious forgery.

PURPOSE

In the dark hour of Israel's captivity, with the tragic destruction of Jerusalem and its temple, there was need for a new testimony to the mighty and providential power of God. Such is afforded by the book of Daniel. It is obviously not the purpose of the book to give a detailed account of Daniel's life, as important details such as his lineage, age, and death are not mentioned, and only scattered incidents in his long life are recounted. Little is said about the history of Israel or the lot of the Jewish captives in Babylon. The book of Daniel, like Esther, reveals God continuing to work in His people Israel even in the time of their chastening. In this framework the tremendous revelation concerning the times of the Gentiles and the program of God for Israel was unfolded. While it is doubtful whether these prophecies were sufficiently known in Daniel's lifetime to be much of an encouragement to the captives themselves, the book of Daniel undoubtedly gave hope to the Jews who returned to restore the temple and the city, and it was particularly helpful during the Maccabean persecutions. It was clearly the purpose of God to give to Daniel a comprehensive revelation of His program culminating in the second advent. As such, its prophetic revelation is the key to understanding the Olivet Discourse (Mt 24-25) as well as the book of Revelation, which is to the New Testament what Daniel was to the Old.

APOCALYPTICAL CHARACTER

The book of Daniel is rightly classified as an apocalyptic writing, because of its series of supernatural visions which by their character fulfilled what is intimated by the Greek word *apokalypsis*, which means unveiling of truth which would otherwise be concealed. Although apocalyptic works abound outside the Bible, relatively few are found in Scripture. In the New Testament only the book of Revelation can be classified as apocalyptic; but in the Old Testament, Ezekiel and Zechariah may be so classified in addition to Daniel.

Ralph Alexander has provided an accurate and comprehensive definition of apocalyptic literature in his study of this literary genre. He defines apocalyptic literature as follows: "Apocalyptic literature is symbolic visionary prophetic literature, composed during oppressive conditions, consisting of visions whose events are recorded exactly as they were seen by the author and explained through a divine interpreter, and whose theological content is primarily eschatological."[5] Alexander goes on to define the limits of apocalyptic literature, "On the basis of this definition, a corpus of apocalyptic literature was determined. The biblical and extrabiblical apocalyptic passages are shown to include the Apocalypse of the New Testament; Ezekiel 37:1-14, Ezekiel 40-48; Daniel's visions in chapters 2, 7, 8, and 10-12; Zechariah 1:7—6:8; I Enoch 90; II Esdras; II Baruch; and A Description of New Jerusalem."[6]

Apocalyptic books outside the Bible are included among the pseudepigrapha, many of which appeared about 250 B.C. and continued to be produced in the apostolic period and later. Many of these attempted to imitate the style of biblical apocalyptic books. Usually they developed the theme of deploring the contemporary situation but prophesying a glorious future of blessing for the saints and judgment on the wicked. The real author's name is normally not given in apocalyptic works outside the Bible. Apocalyptic works rightly included in the Old Testament may be sharply contrasted to the pseudepigrapha because of the more restrained character of their revelation, identification of the author, and their contribution to biblical truth as a whole.

Apocalyptic works classified as the pseudepigrapha include such titles as *Ascension of Isaiah; Assumption of Moses; Book of Enoch; Book of Jubilees; Greek Apocalypse of Baruch; Letters of Aristeas; III and IV Maccabees; Psalms of Solomon; Secrets of Enoch; Sibylline Oracles; Syriac Apocalypse of Baruch; Testament of the Twelve Patriarchs; Apocalypses of Adam, Elijah,* and *Zephaniah;* and *Testament of Abram, Isaac, and Jacob.*

Although higher criticism, often opposed to supernatural revelation in symbolic form, tends to deprecate apocalyptic books in the Bible and equate them with the sometimes incoherent and extreme symbolism of the pseudepigrapha,[7] there is really no justification for this. Even a casual reader can detect the difference in quality between scriptural and non-scriptural apocalyptic works. Frequently, the apocalypses of scriptural writings is attended by divine interpretation which provides the key to understanding the revelation intended. The fact that a book is apocalyptic does not necessarily mean that its revelation is obscure or uncertain, and conservative scholarship has recognized the legitimacy of apocalyptic revelation as a genuine means of divine communication. If close attention is given to the contextual interpretive revelation, apocalyptic books can yield solid results to the patient exegete.

LANGUAGES

An unusual feature of the book of Daniel is the fact that the central portion (2:4—7:28) is written in biblical Aramaic also called Chaldee (AV, "Syriack"). A similar use of Aramaic is found in Ezra 4:8—6:18; 7:12-26; Jer 10:11; and the two words of the compound name *Jegar-Sahadutha* in Genesis 31:47.[8] The use of the Aramaic, which was the lingua franca of the period, was related to the fact that the material concerned the Gentile world rather than Israel directly. The fact that there are similar portions elsewhere in the Bible should make clear that there is nothing unusual or questionable about the Aramaic section in Daniel. As pointed out by Brownlee,[9] the shifts from Hebrew to Aramaic and back again in Daniel are found in the scrolls of Daniel at Qumran, supporting the legitimacy of this feature of the Massoretic text commonly used in English translations.

The argument that the Aramaic of Daniel was western and not used in Babylon, as popularized by S. R. Driver,[10] now has been clearly shown to be erroneous by later archeological evidence. As Martin observes, relative to Driver's contention, "When he [Driver] wrote, the only material available was too late to be relevant. Subsequently, R. D. Wilson, making use of earlier materials that had come to light, was able to show that the distinction between Eastern and Western Aramaic did not exist in pre-Christian times. This has since been amply confirmed by H. H. Schaeder."[11]

As Gleason L. Archer expresses the Aramaic problem, "The Jews apparently took no exception to the Aramaic sections in the book of Ezra, most of which consists in copies of correspondence carried on in Aramaic between the local governments of Palestine and the Persian imperial court from approximately 520 to 460 B.C. If Ezra can be accepted as an authentic document from the middle of the fifth century, when so many of its chapters were largely composed in Aramaic, it is hard to see why the six Aramaic chapters of Daniel must be dated two centuries later than that. It should be carefully observed that in the Babylon of the late sixth century, in which Daniel purportedly lived, the predominant language spoken by the heterogeneous population of this metropolis was Aramaic. It is therefore not surprising that an inhabitant of that city should have resorted to Aramaic in composing a portion of his memoirs."[12]

MAJOR DIVISIONS AND UNITY

The traditional division of the book of Daniel into two halves (1-6; 7-12) has usually been justified on the basis that the first six chapters are historical and the last six chapters are apocalyptic or predictive. There is much to commend this division which often also regards chapter 1 as introductory.

As indicated in the exposition of chapter 7, an alternative approach, recognizing the Aramaic section as being significant, divides the book into three major divisions: (1) Introduction, Daniel 1; (2) The Times of the Gentiles, presented in Aramaic, Daniel 2-7; (3) Israel in Relation to the Gentiles, in Hebrew, Daniel 8-12. This view is advanced by Robert Culver following Carl A. Auberlen.[13] Although this has not attracted the majority of conservative scholars, it has the advantage of distinguishing the program of God for the Gentiles and His program for Israel, with the break coming at the end of chapter 7. Robert Dick Wilson recognizes both principles of division.[14]

Although the principle of division may be debated, it is most significant that the great majority of interpreters, whether liberal or conservative, have agreed to the unity of the book. Some, beginning with Spinoza in the seventeenth century, had other views. Montgomery, for instance, offers a minority view, even among critics, that chapters 1-6 were written by an unknown writer in the third century B.C. and that chapters 7-12 were written in the Maccabean period, 168-165 B.C. It is significant that all who deny the unity of the book also deny its genuineness as a sixth century B.C. writing. Although the two halves of Daniel differ in character, there is obvious historical continuity which supports the unity of the book.[15] The same Daniel who is introduced in chapter 1 is mentioned three times in chapter 12. The evidence is overwhelmingly in favor of the unity of the book.

APOCRYPHAL ADDITIONS

In the Greek version of Daniel, several additions are made to the book, which are not found in the Hebrew or Aramaic text as we now have it Included are *The Prayer of Azarias, The Song of the Three Holy Children, Susanna,* and *Bel and the Dragon.*

The Prayer of Azarias and *The Song of the Three Holy Children* contain the prayer and praise of Daniel's three companions while in the fiery furnace in Daniel 3, with phrases from Psalm 148. *Susanna* is the story of a woman protected by Daniel, who obtains conviction of two judges guilty of attempting her seduction. These judges were executed according to Mosaic Law. *Bel and the Dragon* includes three stories in which Daniel destroys the image of Bel, kills the Dragon, and was fed by Habakkuk the prophet while living in the lions' den for six days, an amplified account of Daniel 6. These stories have been rejected from the Scriptures as not properly in the book of Daniel.[16]

GENUINENESS

The genuineness of Daniel as a sixth century B.C. writing by the prophet Daniel does not seem to have been questioned in the ancient world until the third century A.D. At that time, Porphyry, a pagan neo-Platonist, attacked the book, asserting that it was a second century B.C. forgery. Porphyry's fifteen books, *Against the Christians,* are known to us only through Jerome. Porphyry's attack immediately aroused a defense of Daniel on the part of the early fathers.

Jerome (A.D. 347-420) in his introduction to his *Commentary on Daniel* summarized the situation at that time in these words,

> Porphyry wrote his twelfth book against the prophecy of Daniel, (A) denying that it was composed by the person to whom it is ascribed in its title, but rather by some individual living in Judea at the time of Antiochus who was surnamed Epiphanes. He furthermore alleged that 'Daniel' did not foretell the future so much as he related the past, and

lastly, that whatever he spoke of up till the time of Antiochus contained authentic history, whereas anything he may have conjectured beyond that point was false, inasmuch as he would not have foreknown the future. Eusebius, Bishop of Caesarea, made a most able reply to these allegations in three volumes, that is, the eighteenth, nineteenth, and twentieth. Appollinarius did likewise in a single large book, namely his twenty-sixth. (B) Prior to these authors, Methodius made a partial reply.

". . . I wish to stress in my preface this fact, that none of the prophets has so clearly spoken concerning Christ as has this prophet Daniel. For not only did he assert that he would come, a prediction common to the other prophets as well, but also he set forth the very time at which he would come. Moreover he went through the various kings in order, stated the actual number of years involved, and announced beforehand the clearest signs of events to come. And because Porphyry saw that all these things had been fulfilled and could not deny that they had taken place, he overcame this evidence of historical accuracy by taking refuge in this evasion, contending that whatever is foretold concerning Antichrist at the end of the world was actually fulfilled in the reign of Antiochus Epiphanes, because of certain similarities to things which took place at his time. But this very attack testifies to Daniel's accuracy. For so striking was the reliability of what the prophet foretold, that he could not appear to unbelievers as a predictor of the future, but rather a narrator of things already past. And so wherever occasion arises in the course of explaining this volume, I shall attempt briefly to answer his malicious charge, and to controvert by simple explanation the philosophical skill, or rather the worldly malice, by which he strives to subvert the truth and by specious legerdemain to remove that which is so apparent to our eyes.[17]

This statement of Jerome may be taken as the attitude of the church consistently held until the rise of higher criticism in the seventeenth century. At that time, the suggestion of Porphyry began to be taken seriously and arguments were amassed in support of a second century date for Daniel. It should be noted at the outset (1) that the theory had an anti-Christian origination; (2) that no new facts had been determined to change the previous judgment of the church; (3) that the support of Porphyry by higher critics was a part of their overall approach to the Scriptures, which tended almost without exception to denial of traditional authorship, claimed that books frequently had several authors and went through many redactions, and—most important—included the almost universal denial by the higher critics of the traditional doctrine of biblical inerrancy and verbal, plenary inspiration. The attack on Daniel was part of an attack upon the entire Scriptures, using the historical-critical method.

The great volume of these objections, based for the most part on higher critical premises which in themselves are subject to question, involves so many details that an entire volume is necessary to answer them completely. At best, a summary of the problem and its solution can be considered here. Generally speaking, critical objections to particular texts have been treated in the exposition of Daniel where they occur in the text. A review, however, of major features of the critical attack on the genuineness of Daniel may be presented appropriately here.

Thomas S. Kepler has summarized critical objections under ten heads:

> There are, however, a number of factors which make it difficult for this Daniel living at the time of Nebuchadrezzar to be the author of Daniel: (1) About 200 B.C. the *Prophets* were added to the *Law* to compose the Jewish "Bible." Yet Daniel is not among the *Prophets*, being added to the *Sacred Writings* about A.D. 90, when the Jewish "Bible" was completed. (2) The book of Daniel is not mentioned in any Jewish literature until 140 B.C., when the Sibylline Oracles (3:397-400) refer to it. In Baruch 1:15—3:3 (written about 150 B.C.) there is a prayer similar to that in Daniel 9:4 ff. The book of Daniel is also alluded to in I Maccabees 2:59 ff. (written about 125 B.C.). Daniel is referred to 164 times in I Maccabees, the Sibylline Oracles, and Enoch (written about 95 B.C.). (3) Jesus Ben Sirach about 190 B.C., lists the great men of Jewish history (Ecclesiasticus 44:1—50:24); but among these names that of Daniel is missing. (4) Words borrowed from the Babylonian, Persian, and Greek languages appear in Daniel. (5) Jeremiah is mentioned as a prophet (9:2) and his writings are referred to. (6) In Jeremiah's time (also the period of Nebuchadrezzar) the Chaldeans are spoken of as a nation or people, referring to the Babylonians; but in the book of Daniel they are known as astrologers, magicians, diviners of truth. (7) The book of Daniel is written partly in Aramaic, a language popular among the Jews in the second century B.C., but not at the time of Nebuchadrezzar. (8) The author has an excellent view of history after the time of Alexander the Great, especially during the Maccabean struggles; but his history shows many inaccuracies during the Babylonian and Persian periods. (9) The theology regarding the resurrection of the dead and ideas about angels show that the author lived at a later time than that of Nebuchadrezzar. The same may be said in regard to his concern for diet, fasting, and ritualistic prayers. (10) The pattern and purpose of the book of Daniel as an apocalypse, which *reinterprets* history from the time of Nebuchadrezzar until the time of Judas Maccabeus and Antiochus IV, and written in 165 B.C., fits better into the scheme and purpose of Daniel than if the book were written in the period of Nebuchadrezzar, predicting history for the next 450 years.[18]

These critical objections, answered already in part and considered further in the exposition of the text of Daniel, may be grouped under six heads: (1) rejection of its canonicity; (2) rejection of detailed prophecy; (3) rejection of miracles; (4) textual problems; (5) problems of language; (6) alleged historical inaccuracies.

Rejection of canonicity. As previously explained under consideration of the place of Daniel in the Scriptures, the book is included in the Writings, the third section of the Old Testament, not in the prophetic section. Merrill Unger has defined the erroneous critical view of this as follows:

"Daniel's prophecy was placed among writings in the third section of the Hebrew canon and not among the prophets in the second division because it was not in existence when the canon of the prophets was closed, allegedly between 300-200 B.C."[19] As previously explained, Daniel was not included because his work was of a different character from that of the other prophets. Daniel was primarily a government official, and he was not commissioned to preach to the people and deliver an oral message from God as was, for instance, Isaiah or Jeremiah. It is questionable whether his writings were distributed in his lifetime. Further, the Writings were not so classified because they were late in date, inasmuch as they included such works as Job and 1 and 2 Chronicles, but the division was on the classification of the material in the volumes. Most important, the Writings were considered just as inspired and just as much the Word of God as the Law and the Prophets. This is brought out by the fact that Daniel is included in the Septuagint along with other inspired works, which would indicate that it was regarded as a genuine work of inspiration.

The denial that the book was in existence in the sixth century B.C. disregards the three citations referring to Daniel in Ezekiel (Eze 14:14, 20; 28:3), as well as all the evidence in the book of Daniel itself. Liberal critics tend to disregard the references to Daniel in Ezekiel. James Montgomery, for instance, states, "There is then no reference to our Daniel as an historic person in the Heb. O.T. . . . ."[20] Montgomery holds that Ezekiel's reference is to another character, whom he describes as "the name of an evidently traditional saint."[21]

The "traditional saint" mentioned by Montgomery refers to a "Daniel" who apparently lived about 1400 B.C. In 1930, several years after Montgomery wrote his commentary, archeologists digging at ancient Ugarit (modern Ras Shamra) found some clay tablets detailing a legend of a Canaanite by name of Aqhat who was the father of a man called Daniel. In the tablet Daniel is portrayed as being a friend of widows and orphans, and as a man who was unusually wise and righteous in his judgments. This is the one who Montgomery asserts is referred to in Ezekiel 14:14, 20 as a worthy ancient character on the same plane as Noah and Job. Daniel, the son of Aqhat, however, was a Baal worshiper who prayed to Baal and partook of food in the house of Baal. He is pictured as worshiping his ancestral gods and offering oblations to idols. He was also guilty of cursing his enemies and living without a real hope in God.[22] It is hard to imagine that Ezekiel, writing by inspiration, would hold up such a character as an example of a godly man. Such a judgment is hardly in keeping with the facts.[23]

If the Ezekiel references were insufficient, certainly the clear attestation of Christ to the genuineness of Daniel in Matthew 24:15 should be admitted as valid. As Boutflower expresses it,

> Now, what is the witness of Christ respecting this Book of Daniel, for it is evident from His position as a teacher, His tastes, and the time at which He lived, that He must know the truth of the matter; whilst from His lofty morality we are sure that He will tell us the truth, the whole truth, and nothing but the truth? How does Christ treat this Book, of which the critics form so low an estimate, regarding it as a religious romance with a pseudonymous title, and its prophetic portion as a Jewish apocalypse, a *vaticinium post eventum?* The answer is that this is the Book which Christ specially delights to honour. To Him its title is no pseudonym, but the name of a real person, "Daniel the prophet"— "the prophet" in the sense of one inspired of God to foretell the future, "what shall come to pass hereafter." Our Saviour in His own great Advent prophecy—Matt. xxiv.—uttered on the eve of His death, quotes this Book of Daniel no less than three times [Matt. 24:15, 21; cp. Dan. 12:1; Matt. 24:30; cp. Dan 7:13].[24]

The recent discoveries at Qumran have given impetus to the trend to reconsider late dating of such books as the Psalms and 1 and 2 Chronicles. Brownlee on the basis of recent discoveries indicates that the Maccabean authorship of the Psalms can no longer be held. He states, "If this is true, it would seem that we should abandon the idea of any of the canonical Psalms being of Maccabean date."[25] Myers gives ample evidence that the Maccabean dating of 1 and 2 Chronicles (after 333 B.C.) is no longer tenable since the publication of the Elephantine materials. He concludes that 1 and 2 Chronicles now must be considered written in the Persian period (538-333 B.C.).[26]

This trend toward recognition of earlier authorship of these portions of the Old Testament point also to the inconsistency of maintaining a late date for Daniel. If, on the basis of the scrolls recently discovered, Psalms and Chronicles can no longer be held to be Maccabean, then Daniel, on the same kind of evidence, also demands recognition as a production of the Persian period and earlier. Raymond K. Harrison has come to this conclusion when he states, "While, at the time of writing, the Daniel manuscripts from Qumran have yet to be published and evaluated, it appears presumptuous, even in the light of present knowledge, for scholars to abandon the Maccabean dating of certain allegedly late Psalms and yet maintain it with undiminished fervor in the case of Daniel when the grounds for such modification are the same."[27] Harrison points out that the Qumran manuscripts of Daniel are all copies; and if the Qumran sect was actually Maccabean in origin itself, it would necessarily imply that the original copy of Daniel must have been at least a half century earlier, which would place it before the time of the alleged Maccabean authorship of Daniel. The principles adopted by critics in evaluating other manuscripts and assigning them to a much earlier period than had been formerly accepted, if applied to Daniel, would make impossible the liberal critical position that Daniel is a second century B.C. work. Strangely, liberal critics have been slow to publish and comment upon the Qumran fragments of Daniel which seem to indicate a pre-Maccabean authorship. The facts as they are now before the investigator tend to destroy the arguments of the liberals for a late date for Daniel. The evidence against the canonicity of Daniel is without support. Besides, it is highly questionable whether the Jews living in the Maccabean period would have accepted Daniel if it had not had a previous history of canonicity.

Rejection of detailed prophecy. In the original objection of Porphyry to Daniel, the premise was taken that prophecy is impossible. This, of course, is based on a rejection of theism in general, a denial of the doctrine of supernatural revelation as is ordinarily assumed in the Scriptures by conservative scholars, and a disregard of the omniscience of God which includes foreknowledge of all future events. The defense of the possibility of prophecy should be unnecessary in treating the Scriptures inasmuch as it is related to the total apology for the Christian faith.

A more particular attack, however, is made on the book of Daniel on the ground that it is apocalyptic and therefore unworthy of serious study as prophecy. That there are many spurious apocalyptic works both in the Old Testament period and in the Christian era can be readily granted. The existence of the spurious is not a valid argument against the possibility of genuine apocalyptic revelation anymore than a counterfeit dollar bill is proof that there is no genuine dollar bill. If Daniel were the only apocalyptic work in the entire Scriptures, the argument could be taken more seriously; but the other apocalyptic sections of the Old Testament and the crowning prophetic work of the New Testament, the book of Revelation, have usually been considered adequate evidence that the apocalyptic method is sometimes used by God to reveal prophetic truth.

Further, it should be observed in the book of Daniel that the apocalyptic is not left to human interpretation, but along with the revelation is given divine interpretation which delivers the biblical apocalyptic from the vague, obscure, and subjective interpretations often necessary in spurious works. Actually, the problem in Daniel is not that the apocalyptic sections are obscure, but critics object to the clear prophetic truth which is therein presented.

The argument sometimes advanced, that apocalyptic writings had not yet begun in Daniel's time in the sixth century B.C., is of course answered by the contemporary work of Ezekiel and the essential weakness of such an argument from silence. Actually, apocalyptic writings extended over a long period. Conservative scholarship, accordingly, while admitting the apocalyptic character of the book of Daniel, rejects this as a valid ground for questioning the sixth century authorship and therefore the genuineness of the book.

Rejection of miracles. If the book of Daniel is to be considered spurious on the ground that it presents miracles, it would follow that most of the Scriptures would also be eliminated as valid inspired writings. The objection to miracles reveals the essentially naturalistic point of view of some of the critics. Daniel's miracles are no more unusual than some of those attributed to Christ in the gospels or to Moses and Aaron in the Pentateuch. Aside from the supernatural as related to revelation in the Bible, the deliverance of Daniel's three companions in Daniel 3 and of Daniel himself in Daniel 6 is no more unusual than Christ passing through the mob that was threatening to throw Him over a cliff (Lk 4:29-30) or Peter's deliverance from prison (Ac 12:5-11). In the biblical context, the rejection of a book because of miraculous incidents must be judged invalid.

Textual problems. Critics have raised textual problems almost without number in relation to the book of Daniel; but they have also contradicted each other, testifying to the subjective character of these criticisms. Critics have especially concentrated on the Aramaic portions, alleging many redactions and various degrees of tampering with the text; but there is wide divergence in their findings. The idea that Daniel himself may have originally written this section in either Hebrew or Babylonian and then changed it to the lingua franca of the time is not necessarily a reflection upon the inspiration of the final form which now appears in the book of Daniel.

Robert Dick Wilson, probably the outstanding authority on ancient languages of the Middle East, summarized his findings in these words,

> We claim, however, that the composite Aram. of Dnl agrees in almost every particular of orthography, etymology and syntax, with the Aram. of the North Sem inscriptions of the 9th, 8th and 7th cents. BC and of the Egyp papyri of the 5th cent. BC, and that the vocabulary of Dnl has an admixture of Heb, Bab and Pers words similar to that of the papyri of the 5th cent. BC; whereas, it differs in composition from the Aram. of the Nabateans, which is devoid of Pers, Heb, and Bab words, and is full of Arabisms, and also from that of the Palmyrenes, which is full of Gr words, while having but one or two Pers words, and no Heb or Bab.[28]

Wilson finds the textual problems are no different from that of other books whose genuineness has not been assailed. While problems of text continue in the book of Daniel as in many other books in the Old Testament, these problems in themselves are not sufficiently supported by factual evidence to justify disbelief in the present text of Daniel. As in many other arguments against Daniel, the presuppositions of the higher critics which lead to these arguments are in themselves suspect; and the widespread disagreement among the critics themselves as to the nature and extent of the textual problem tends to support the conclusion that they are invalid.

Problems of language. Critics have objected to the presence of various Greek and Persian words in the book of Daniel as if this proved a late date. As brought out in the exposition of Daniel 3 where a number of these Persian and Greek words are found, in the light of recent archeological discoveries this objection is no longer valid. It has now been proved that one hundred years before Daniel Greek mercenaries served in the Assyrian armies under the command of Esarhaddon (683 B.C.) as well as in the Babylonian army of Nebuchadnezzar.[29] As Robert Dick Wilson has noted, if Daniel had been written in the second century, there would have been far more Greek words rather than the few that occur.[30] Yamauchi has also demonstrated that the critical objections to Greek words in Daniel are without foundation.[31]

The use of Persian words is certainly not strange in view of the fact that Daniel himself lived in the early years of the Persian empire and served as one of its principal officials. He naturally would use contemporary Persian description of various officials in chapter 3 in an effort to update the understanding of these offices for those living after the Persian conquest of Babylon in 539 B.C. It must be concluded that objections to the book of Daniel as a sixth century writing on the basis of Greek and Persian words is without reasonable scholarly support and increasingly becomes an untenable position in the light of archeological evidence.

Alleged historical inaccuracies. These supposed inaccuracies of the book of Daniel have been treated in the exposition where it has been demonstrated that there is no factual manuscript discovery which reasonably can be construed as questioning the historical accuracy of Daniel's statements. On the other hand, it would be most unusual for a writer in the second century B.C. to have had the intimate knowledge of Babylonian history presented in the book of Daniel in view of the probability that the texts and other materials now in our possession may not have been available at that time.

Adequate answers to critical objections to the dating involved in Daniel 1:1 are treated in the exposition of the verse.

The difficulty of identifying Belshazzar (chap. 5), the source of much critical objection to the accuracy of Daniel on the ground that his name did not occur in ancient literature, has been remedied by precise information provided in the *Nabonidus Chronicle*.

While questions may continue to be raised concerning the identity of

Darius the Mede (also considered in the exposition) the argument on the part of the critics is entirely from silence. Nothing in history has been found to contradict the conclusion that Darius is either another term for Cyrus himself or, preferably, an appointee of Cyrus who was of Median race and therefore called "the Mede." As there are several plausible solutions to the identity of Darius the Mede, there is no legitimate ground for the objections to Daniel's statements because of lack of support in ancient literature. Obviously, there are hundreds of facts in the Bible of historical nature which cannot be completely supported, and the Bible itself must be taken as a legitimate ancient manuscript whose testimony should stand until well-established facts raise questions.

On the basis of the critical idea that Daniel was written in the second century B.C., it is alleged that the "prophecies" relative to the Medo-Persian Empire and the Grecian Empire are often inaccurate. Particularly the claim is made that Daniel teaches a separate Median kingdom as preceding the Persian kingdom, which is historically inaccurate. The problem here is that the critics in the first place are seemingly willfully twisting Daniel's statement to teach what he does not teach, namely, a separate Median empire. Second, the alleged discrepancy between the prophecy and its fulfillment is in the minds of the critics. Conservative scholars have no difficulty in finding accurate historical fulfillment of genuine prophecies made by Daniel in the sixth century B.C. Here the critics are guilty of circular argument, based on a false premise which leads to questionable conclusions. The larger problem of the interpretation of Daniel's prophecy does not in itself invalidate the genuineness of the book unless it can be demonstrated that the prophecy itself is inaccurate. Up to the present, the critics have not been able to prove this.

Taken as a whole, the major objections of critics against the book of Daniel, as well as many minor questions commonly raised, are of the same kind as those hurled against Scripture as a whole and against the doctrine of supernatural revelation. Often the objections are products of the critics' own theory in which they criticize Daniel for not corresponding to their idea of second century authorship. Prominent in the situation is the argument from silence in which they assume that Daniel is guilty of error until proved otherwise.

The broad historical questions raised in the study of Daniel have been answered by Robert Dick Wilson, who has demonstrated that the critics have not made an adequate case for their theories or their conclusions.[32] Wilson shows that our problem is not with facts, as no facts have been discovered which contradict Daniel, but with theories too often supported by circular argument. To date, the critical arguments have not been confirmed by fact and must be accepted by faith. For the conservative expositor, it is far more preferable to accept the book of Daniel by faith in view of its confirmation by Christ Himself in Matthew 24:15.

Problems of interpretation in the book of Daniel have naturally been considered in the exposition of the text. If the premise be granted that the book of Daniel is genuine Scripture and that detailed prediction of the future as in Daniel may be admitted as genuine, the problems of interpretation are then reduced to determining what the text actually says.

The interpretation of apocalyptic literature such as the visions of Daniel requires special skills and close attention to hermeneutics as it applies to such revelation. Alexander, for instance, in his illuminating study of this problem, offers twenty-three rules to be used in the interpretation of Old Testament apocalyptic literature.[33] In general, however, the meaning of the text can be ascertained, especially with the help of fulfillment in history which is now available to the expositor.

Historical records have been kind to Daniel in providing such adequate proofs of the fulfillment of his prophecy as to induce the critics to want to place its writing after the event. As pointed out in the exposition, the book of Daniel supports the interpretation that Daniel is presenting truth relative to the four great world empires beginning with Babylon, with the fourth empire definitely prophetic even from a second century point of view. The interpretation of chapter 2 is confirmed by chapter 7, which has special revelation concerning the fourth empire in its yet future stage, and by the considerable detail added in chapter 8 on the Medo-Persian and Grecian Empires. Most, if not all, of chapter 8 was fulfilled in history in the five hundred years from the death of Daniel to the formal beginning of the Roman Empire in 27 B.C.

The concentrated prophecy of Daniel 11:36—12:13 is properly regarded as a detailed discussion of "the time of the end," the period immediately preceding the second advent of Christ. Chapter 9:24-27, giving the broad view of Israel's history, may be considered fulfilled from the viewpoint of the twentieth century with the exception of Daniel 9:27, another prophecy of the role of Israel in the years immediately preceding the second advent.

Taken as a whole, the interpretation of Daniel provides a broad outline of the program of God for the Gentiles from Daniel to the second coming of Christ and the program for Israel for the same period with Daniel 9:24 beginning in Nehemiah's time. The support of these interpretations as opposed to contrary views has been presented in the exposition.

THEOLOGY

In its broad revelation, the book of Daniel provides the same view of God that appears elsewhere in the Old Testament, namely, a God who is sovereign, loving, omnipotent, omniscient, righteous, and merciful. He is the God of Israel, but He is also the God of the Gentiles. Both of these theses are amply sustained in the content of the book.

Although Daniel does not concern himself primarily with Messianic prophecy, the first coming of Christ is anticipated in Daniel 9:26, including His death on the cross and the later destruction of Jerusalem. The second advent of Christ is given more particular revelation in chapters 7 and 12.

The doctrine of angels is prominent in the book of Daniel with Gabriel and Michael named and active in the events of the book. In this, Daniel is an advance on the Old Testament doctrine, but the liberal criticism that Daniel borrowed from Babylonian and Persian sources is unjustified and is not supported by the text.[34]

In his doctrine of man, Daniel fully bears witness to the depravity of man, to God's righteous judgment upon him, and the possibility of mercy and grace, as illustrated in chapter 4 in the conversion of Nebuchadnezzar.

Daniel's clear testimony to the subject of resurrection in chapter 12 has been contradicted by critics as being out of keeping with his times, as being borrowed from pagan sources, and as being unnoticed by the Minor Prophets who followed him. All of these allegations are without adequate foundation. The doctrine of resurrection is brought out clearly in Job 19:25-26 as normally interpreted. The resurrection of Israel is mentioned in Isaiah 26:19. Ezekiel's vision of the valley of dry bones (chap. 37), while referring to the restoration of Israel nationally, requires the individual resurrection of Israel to accomplish its purpose. Also embedded in the Old Testament are references to the Book of Life or the Book of Remembrance which is related to resurrection as early as Exodus 32:32-33. The Old Testament doctrine of Messiah carries with it a doctrine of resurrection; and this theme begins, of course, in Genesis 3:15. On the other hand apocryphal books rarely mention the resurrection of both the righteous and the wicked; Archer finds mention only in the Book of the Twelve Patriarchs. Further, as Archer points out, the doctrine of the last judgment which implies resurrection is a frequent theme of prophecy, including minor prophets such as Zephaniah, Haggai, Zechariah, and Malachi, as well as in many of the Psalms. Accordingly, the objection of Montgomery and other critics that Daniel's doctrine of resurrection was unsuited for sixth century B.C., was borrowed from pagan sources, or was

unnoticed by the Minor Prophets who wrote after Daniel, is completely
without adequate support and is contradicted by the facts of Scripture.*[35]
There is no good reason why God could not reveal these truths to Daniel
in the sixth century B.C. Of interest is Daniel's faith that he would be
resurrected "at the end of the days," that is, at the second advent of Christ
(Dan 12:13).

Daniel's contribution to eschatology is evident with his main theme
being the course of history and Israel's relation to it, culminating in the
second advent of Christ. On the whole, Daniel makes a tremendous contribution to theology in keeping with the general revelation of Scripture,
but constituting a distinct advance in Old Testament revelation.

CONCLUSION

In many respects, the book of Daniel is the most comprehensive prophetic revelation of the Old Testament, giving the only total view of world
history from Babylon to the second advent of Christ and interrelating
Gentile history and prophecy with that which concerns Israel. Daniel
provides the key to the overall interpretation of prophecy, is a major element in premillennialism, and is essential to the interpretation of the book
of Revelation. Its revelation of the sovereignty and power of God has
brought assurance to Jew and Gentile alike that God will fulfill His
sovereign purposes in time and eternity.

*R. D. Wilson shows that the Egyptians believed in resurrection more than 3000
years before Daniel and that Babylonians also commonly believed in a doctrine of
resurrection (Wilson, *Studies,* pp. 124-27).

1

EARLY LIFE OF DANIEL IN BABYLON

THE FIRST CHAPTER OF DANIEL is a beautifully written, moving story of the early days of Daniel and his companions in Babylon. In brief and condensed form, it records the historical setting for the entire book. Moreover, it sets the tone as essentially the history of Daniel and his experiences in contrast to the prophetic approach of the other major prophets, who were divine spokesmen to Israel. In spite of being properly classified as a prophet, Daniel was in the main a governmental servant and a faithful historian of God's dealings with him. Although shorter than prophetical books like Isaiah, Jeremiah, and Ezekiel, the book of Daniel is the most comprehensive and sweeping revelation recorded by any prophet of the Old Testament. The introductory chapter explains how Daniel was called, prepared, matured, and blessed of God. With the possible exceptions of Moses and Solomon, Daniel was the most learned man in the Old Testament and most thoroughly trained for his important role in history and literature.

THE CAPTIVITY OF JUDAH

1:1-2 In the third year of the reign of Jehoiakim king of Judah came Nebuchadnezzar king of Babylon unto Jerusalem, and besieged it. And the Lord gave Jehoiakim king of Judah into his hand, with part of the vessels of the house of God: which he carried into the land of Shinar to the house of his god; and he brought the vessels into the treasure house of his god.

The opening verses of Daniel succinctly give the historical setting which includes the first siege and capture of Jerusalem by the Babylonians. According to Daniel, this occurred "in the third year of the reign of Jehoiakim king of Judah," or approximately 605 B.C. Parallel accounts are found in 2 Kings 24:1-2 and 2 Chronicles 36:5-7. The capture of Jerusalem and the first deportation of the Jews from Jerusalem to Babylon, including Daniel and his companions, were the fulfillment of many warnings from the prophets of Israel's coming disaster because of the nation's sins against God. Israel had forsaken the law and ignored God's covenant (Is 24:1-6). They had ignored the Sabbath day and the sabbatic year

29

(Jer 34:12-22). The seventy years of the captivity were, in effect, God claiming the Sabbath, which Israel had violated, in order to give the land rest.

Israel had also gone into idolatry (1 Ki 11:5; 12:28; 16:31; 18:19; 2 Ki 21:3-5; 2 Ch 28:2-3), and they had been solemnly warned of God's coming judgment upon them because of their idolatry (Jer 7:24—8:3; 44:20-23). Because of their sin, the people of Israel, who had given themselves to idolatry, were carried off captive to Babylon, a center of idolatry and one of the most wicked cities in the ancient world. It is significant that after the Babylonian captivity, idolatry never again became a major temptation to Israel.

In keeping with their violation of the Law and their departure from the true worship of God, Israel had lapsed into terrible moral apostasy. Of this, all the prophets spoke again and again. Isaiah's opening message is typical of this theme song of the prophets: They were a "sinful nation, a people laden with iniquity, a seed of evildoers, children that are corrupters: they have forsaken the LORD, they have provoked the Holy One of Israel unto anger, they are gone away backward. . . . Ye will revolt more and more: the whole head is sick, and the whole heart faint. From the sole of the foot even unto the head there is no soundness in it; but wounds, and bruises, and putrifying sores: they have not been closed, neither bound up, neither mollified with ointment" (Is 1:4-6). Here again, the ironic judgment of God is that Israel, because of sin, was being carried off captive to wicked Babylon. The first capture of Jerusalem and the first captives were the beginning of the end for Jerusalem, which had been made magnificent by David and Solomon. When the Word of God is ignored and violated, divine judgment sooner or later is inevitable. The spiritual lessons embodied in the cold fact of the captivity may well be pondered by the church today, too often having a form of godliness but without knowing the power of it. Worldly saints do not capture the world but become instead the world's captives.

According to Daniel 1:1, the crucial siege and capture of Jerusalem by Nebuchadnezzar king of Babylon came "in the third year of the reign of Jehoiakim king of Judah." Critics have lost no time pointing out an apparent conflict between this and the statement of Jeremiah that the first year of Nebuchadnezzar king of Babylon was in the fourth year of Jehoiakim (Jer 25:1). Montgomery, for instance, rejects the historicity of this datum.[1] This supposed chronological error is used as the first in a series of alleged proofs that Daniel is a spurious book written by one actually unfamiliar with the events of the captivity. There are, however, several good and satisfying explanations.

The simplest and most obvious explanation is that Daniel is here using

Babylonian reckoning. It was customary for the Babylonians to consider the first year of a king's reign as the year of accession and to call the next year the first year. Keil and others brush this aside as having no precedent in Scripture.[2] Keil is, however, quite out of date with contemporary scholarship on this point. Jack Finegan, for instance, has demonstrated that the phrase *the first year of Nebuchadnezzar* in Jeremiah actually means "the accession year of Nebuchadnezzar"[3] of the Babylonian reckoning. Tadmor was among the first to support this solution, and the point may now be considered as well established.[4]

What Keil ignores is that Daniel is a most unusual case because he of all the prophets was the only one thoroughly instructed in Babylonian culture and point of view. Having spent most of his life in Babylon, it is only natural that Daniel should use a Babylonian form of chronology. By contrast, Jeremiah would use Israel's form of reckoning which included a part of the year as the first year of Jehoiakim's reign. This simple explanation is both satisfying and adequate to explain the supposed discrepancy. However, there are other explanations.

Leupold, for instance, in consideration of the additional reference in 2 Kings 24:1 where Jehoiakim is said to submit to Nebuchadnezzar for three years, offers another interpretation. In a word, it is the assumption that there was an earlier raid on Jerusalem, not recorded elsewhere in the Bible, which is indicated in Daniel 1:1. Key to the chronology of events in this crucial period in Israel's history was the battle at Carchemish in May-June 605 B.C., a date well established by D. J. Wiseman.[5] There Nebuchadnezzar met Pharaoh Necho and destroyed the Egyptian army; this occurred "in the fourth year of Jehoiakim" (Jer 46:2). Leupold holds that the invasion of Daniel 1:1 took place prior to this battle, instead of immediately afterward. He points out that the usual assumption that Nebuchadnezzar could not have bypassed Carchemish to conquer Jerusalem first, on the theory that Carchemish was a stronghold which he could not ignore, is not actually supported by the facts, as there is no evidence that the Egyptian armies were in any strength at Carchemish until just before the battle that resulted in the showdown. In this case, the capture of Daniel would be a year earlier or about 606 B.C.[6]

In the present state of biblical chronology, however, this is too early. Both Finegan[7] and Thiele,[8] present-day authorities on biblical chronology, accept the assumption that the accession-year system of dating was in use in Judah from Jehoash to Hoshea. Thiele resolves the discrepancy by assuming that Daniel used the old calendar year in Judah which began in the fall in the month Tishri (Sept.-Oct.) and that Jeremiah used the Babylonian calendar which began in the spring in the month Nisan (March-April). According to the Babylonian Chronicle, "Nebuchadnezzar conquered the whole area of the Hatti country," an area that includes all of Syria and the territory south to the borders of Egypt, in the late spring or early summer of 605. This would be Jehoiakim's fourth year according to the Nisan reckoning and the third year according to the Tishri calendar.

Still a third view, also mentioned by Leupold,[9] offers the suggestion that the word *came* in Daniel 1:1 actually means "set out" rather than "arrived" and cites the following passages for similar usage (Gen 45:17; Num 32:6; 2 Ki 5:5; Jon 1:3). Keil, following Hengstenberg and others, also supports this explanation.[10] This argument, which hangs on the translation "set out" (for the Hebrew *bo'*), is weak, however, as the examples cited are indecisive. In verse 2, the same word is used in the normal meaning of "came."

Both of Leupold's explanations given as alternates are far less satisfactory than the method of harmonization offered by Finegan and Thiele. The probability is that Wiseman is right, that Daniel was carried off captive shortly after the capture of Jerusalem in the summer of 605 B.C. In any case, the evidence makes quite untenable the charge that the chronological information of Daniel is inaccurate. Rather, it is entirely in keeping with information available outside the Bible and supports the view that Daniel is a genuine book.

According to Daniel, Nebuchadnezzar, described as "king of Babylon," besieged Jerusalem successfully. If this occurred before the battle of Carchemish, Nebuchadnezzar was not as yet king. The proleptic use of such a title is so common (e.g. in the statement "King David as a boy was a shepherd") that this does not cause a serious problem. Daniel does record, however, the fact that Jehoiakim was subdued and that "part of the vessels of the house of God" were "carried into the land of Shinar to the house of his god." "Shinar" is a term used for Babylon with the nuance of a place hostile to faith. It is associated with Nimrod (Gen 10:10), became the locale of the Tower of Babel (Gen 11:2), and is the place to which wickedness is banished (Zec 5:11).

The expression *he carried* is best taken as referring only to the vessels and not to the deportation of captives. Critics, again, have found fault with this as an inaccuracy because nowhere else is it expressly said that Daniel and his companions were carried away at this time. The obvious answer is that mention of carrying off captives is unnecessary in the light of the context of the following verses, where it is discussed in detail. There was no need to mention it twice. Bringing the vessels to the house of Nebuchadnezzar's god Marduk[11] was a natural religious gesture, which would attribute the victory of the Babylonians over Israel to Babylonian deities. Later other vessels were added to the collection (2 Ch 36:18), and they all appeared on the fateful night of Belshazzar's feast in Daniel 5. Jehoiakim himself was not deported, later died, and was succeeded by his son Jehoiachin. Jehoiakim, although harrassed by bands of soldiers sent against him, was not successfully besieged (2 Ki 24:1-2).

JEWISH YOUTHS SELECTED FOR TRAINING

1:3-7 And the king spake unto Ashpenaz the master of his eunuchs, that he should bring certain of the children of Israel, and of the king's seed, and of the princes; Children in whom was no blemish, but well favoured, and skilful in all wisdom, and cunning in knowledge, and understanding science, and such as had ability in them to stand in the king's palace, and whom they might teach the learning and the tongue of the Chaldeans. And the king appointed them a daily provision of the king's meat, and of the wine which he drank: so nourishing them three years, that at the end thereof they might stand before the king. Now among these were of the children of Judah, Daniel, Hananiah, Mishael, and Azariah: Unto whom the prince of the eunuchs gave names: for he gave unto Daniel the name of Belteshazzar; and to Hananiah, of Shadrach; and to Mishael, of Meshach; and to Azariah, of Abed-nego.

In explanation of how Daniel and his companions found the way to Babylon, Daniel records that the king "spake unto Ashpenaz," better translated "told" or "commanded," to bring some of the children of Israel to Babylon for training to be servants of the king. The name *Ashpenaz,* according to Siegfried H. Horn, "appears in the Aramaic incantation texts from Nippur as *'SPNZ*, and is probably attested in the Cuneiform records as *Ashpazanda.*" Horn goes on to identify him as, "the chief of King Nebuchadnezzar's eunuchs (Dan. 1:3)."[12] The significance of the name *Ashpenaz* has been much debated, but it seems best to agree with Young that "its etymology is uncertain."[13]

It is probable that by *eunuchs* reference is made to important servants of the king, such as Potiphar (Gen 37:36), who was married. It is not stated that the Jewish youths were made actual eunuchs as Josephus assumes.[14] Isaiah had predicted this years before (Is 39:7), and Young supports the broader meaning of *eunuch* by the Targum rendering of the Isaiah passage which uses the word *nobles* for *eunuchs*.[15] However, because the word *saris* means both "court officer" and "castrate," scholars are divided on the question of whether both meanings are intended. Montgomery states, "It is not necessary to draw the conclusion that the youths were made eunuchs, as Jos. hints: 'he made some of them eunuchs,' nor to combine the ref. after Theodt., with the alleged fulfillment of Is 39:7."[16] Charles writes in commenting on the description in Daniel 1:4, *no blemish,* "The perfection here asserted is physical, as in Lev. xxi.17. Such perfection could not belong to eunuchs."[17] All agree, however, that *saris*, translated "eunuch" in Isaiah 56:3, refers to a castrate. Ultimately the choice is left to the interpreter, although, as indicated above, some favor the thought of "court officer."

Those selected for royal service are described as being "the children of Israel, and of the king's seed, and of the princes." The reference to the children of Israel does not mean that they were selected out of the Northern Kingdom which already had been carried off into captivity, but rather that the children selected were indeed Israelites, that is, descendants of Jacob. The stipulation, however, was that they should be of the king's seed, literally "of the seed of the kingdom," that is, of the royal family or of "the princes"—the nobility of Israel.

The Hebrew for *the princes* is a Persian word, *partemim*, which is cited as another proof for a late date of Daniel. However, inasmuch as Daniel lived in his latter years under Persian government as a high official, there is nothing strange about an occasional Persian word. As a matter of fact, it is not even clear that the word is strictly Persian, as its origin is uncertain.*

In selecting these youths for education in the king's court in Babylon, Nebuchadnezzar was accomplishing several objectives. Those carried away captive could well serve as hostages to help keep the royal family of the kingdom of Judah in line. Their presence in the king's court also would be a pleasant reminder to the Babylonian king of his conquest and success in battle. Further, their careful training and preparation to be his servants might serve Nebuchadnezzar well in later administration of Jewish affairs.

The specifications for those selected are carefully itemized in verse 4. They were to have no physical blemish and were to be "well favoured," that is, "good ones in appearance." They were to be superior intellectually, that is, "skilful in all wisdom"; and their previous education, such as was afforded royal children or children of the nobility, was a factor. Their capacity to have understanding in "science" should not be taken in the modern sense, but rather as pertaining to their skill in all areas of learning of their day. In a word, their total physical, personal, and intellectual capacities as well as their cultural background were factors in the choice. Their training, however, was to separate them from their previous Jewish culture and environment and teach them "the learning and the tongue of the Chaldeans."

The reference to Chaldeans may be to the Chaldean people as a whole or to a special class of learned men, as in Daniel 2:2, i.e., those designated as *kasdîm*. The use of the same word for the nation as a whole and for a special class of learned men is confusing, but not necessarily unusual.

---

*In his discussion, Leupold observes correctly, "Critics should use uncertain terms with proper caution" (Leupold, p. 59).

The meaning here may include both: the general learning of the Chaldeans and specifically the learning of wise men, such as astrologers. It is most significant that the learning of the Chaldeans was of no help to Daniel and his companions when it came to the supreme test of interpreting Nebuchadnezzar's dream. Their age at the time of their training is not specified, but they were probably in their early teens.

Although an education such as this did not in itself violate the religious scruples of Jewish youths, their environment and circumstances soon presented some real challenges. Among these was the fact that they had a daily provision of food and wine from the king's table. Ancient literature contains many references to this practice. A. Leo Oppenheim lists deliveries of oil for the sustenance of dependents of the royal household in ancient literature and includes specific mention of food for the sons of the king of Judah in a tablet dating from the tenth to the thirty-fifth year of Nebuchadnezzar II.[18] Such food was "appointed," or "assigned, in the sense of numerical distribution."[19]

The expression *a daily provision* in the Hebrew is literally "a portion of the day in its day." The word for "meat" (Heb. *pathbagh*), according to Leupold, "is a Persian loan word from the *Sanscrit pratibagha.*"[20] Although it is debatable whether the word specifically means "delicacies," as Young considers that it means "assignment,"[21] the implication is certainly there that the royal food was lavish and properly called "rich food" (as in the RSV).[22]

The bountiful provision of the king was intended to give them ample food supplies to enable them to pursue their education for a three-year period. The expression *so nourish them three years* literally refers to training such as would be given a child. The goal was to bring them to intellectual maturity to "stand before the king," equivalent to becoming his servant and thereby taking a place of responsibility.

In verse 6, Daniel and his three companions—Hananiah, Mishael and Azariah—are mentioned as being children of Judah included among the captives. These only of the captives are to figure in the narrative following, and no other names are given. The corrupting influences of Babylon were probably too much for the others, and they were useless in God's hands.

The name of Daniel is a familiar one in the Bible and is used of at least three other characters besides the prophet Daniel (1 Ch 3:1, a son of David; Ezra 8:2, a son of Ithamar; and in Neh 10:6, a priest). Conservative scholars, however, find a reference to the prophet Daniel in Ezekiel 14:14, 20; and Ezekiel 28:3. As pointed out in the Introduction, critics usually dispute the identification of Ezekiel's mention of Daniel as the same person as the author of the book as this would argue against their

contention that the book of Daniel is a second century B.C. forgery. As
noted previously, however, it would be most significant and natural for
Ezekiel, a captive, to mention one of his own people who, though also a
captive, had risen to a place of power second only to the king. Jewish
captives would not only regard Daniel as their hero, but as a godly example. The contention of critics that Ezekiel is referring to a mythological
character mentioned in the Ras Shamra Text (dated 1500-1200 B.C.) is,
as Young states, "extremely questionable."[23]

The change in the name of Daniel and his three companions focuses
attention upon the meaning of both their Hebrew and Babylonian names.

Scholars are generally agreed that Daniel's name means "God is judge"
or "my judge is God" or "God has judged." Hananiah, whose name also
appears elsewhere in the Bible, referring to other individuals (1 Ch 25:23;
2 Ch 26:11; Jer 36:12; etc.) is interpreted as meaning "Jehovah is gracious" or "Jehovah has been gracious." Mishael (Ex 6:22; Neh 8:4) may
be understood to mean "who is He that is God?"[24] or "who is what God
is?"[25] Azariah may be interpreted, "The Lord helps"[26] or "Jehovah hath
helped." All of the Hebrew names of Daniel's companions appear again
in other books of the Old Testament in reference to others by the same
name. Significantly, all of their Hebrew names indicate their relationship
to the God of Israel, and in the customs of the time, connote devout
parents. This perhaps explains why these, in contrast to the other young
men, are found true to God: they had godly homes in their earlier years.
Even in the days of Israel's apostasy, there were those who corresponded
to Elijah's seven thousand in Israel who did not bow the knee to Baal.

All four of the young men, however, are given new names as was customary when an individual entered a new situation (cf. Gen 17:5; 41:45;
2 Sa 12:24-25; 2 Ki 23:34; 24:17; Est 2:7).[27] The heathen names given to
Daniel and his companions are not as easily interpreted as their Hebrew
names, but probably they were given in a gesture to credit to the heathen
gods of Babylon the victory over Israel and to further divorce these young
men from their Hebrew background. Daniel is given the name of Belteshazzar, identical to Belshazzar and meaning "protect his life,"[28] or
preferably "May Bel protect his life" (see Dan 4:8).[29] Bel was a god of
Babylon (cf. Baal, the chief god of the Canaanites).

Hananiah was given the name of Shadrach. Leupold interprets this as
being a reference to the compound of *Sudur,* meaning "command," and
Aku, the moon-god. Hence the name would mean "command of Aku."[30]
Young considers the name a perversion of Marduk, a principal god of
Babylon.

Mishael is given the name of Meshach. Leupold considers this to be a
contraction of *Mi-sha-aku* meaning, "who is what Aku (the moon-god)

is?" Montgomery holds that the first part of Mishael means "salvation," following Schrader and Torrey but rejecting an alternate translation "who is what god is?" followed by most modern commentaries.[31] Montgomery is probably right, although Young does not feel the identification of this name is sufficient to give a definition.[32]

Azariah is given the name of Abed-nego which probably means "servant of Nebo" with *Nebo* corrupted to *nego*. Keil does not venture an opinion on the meaning of Shadrach or Meshach, but agrees with the interpretation of Abed-nego.[33] Nebo was considered the son of the Babylonian god Bel.

Daniel, in his later writing, generally prefers his own Hebrew name, but frequently uses the Babylonian names of his companions. The fact that the Hebrew youths were given heathen names, however, does not indicate that they departed from the Hebrew faith any more than in the case of Joseph (Gen 41:45).

DANIEL'S PURPOSE NOT TO DEFILE HIMSELF

1:8-10 But Daniel purposed in his heart that he would not defile himself with the portion of the king's meat, nor with the wine which he drank: therefore he requested of the prince of the eunuchs that he might not defile himself. Now God had brought Daniel into favour and tender love with the prince of the eunuchs. And the prince of the eunuchs said unto Daniel, I fear my lord the king, who hath appointed your meat and your drink: for why should he see your faces worse liking than the children which are of your sort? then shall ye make me endanger my head to the king.

Daniel and his companions were confronted with the problem of compromise in the matter of eating food provided by the king. No doubt, the provision for them of the king's food was intended to be generous and indicated the favor of the king. Daniel, however, "purposed in his heart" or literally, "laid upon his heart" not to defile himself (cf. Is 42:25; 47:7; 57:1, 11; Mal 2:2). The problem was twofold. First, the food provided did not meet the requirements of the Mosaic law in that it was not prepared according to regulations and may have included meat from forbidden animals. Second, there was no complete prohibition in the matter of drinking wine in the Law; but here the problem was that the wine, as well as the meat, had been dedicated to idols as was customary in Babylon. To partake thereof would be to recognize the idols as deities. A close parallel to Daniel's purpose not to defile himself is found in the book of Tobit (1:10-11, RSV) which refers to the exiles of the northern tribes: "When I was carried away captive to Nineveh, all my brethren and my relatives ate the food of the Gentiles: but I kept myself from eating it, because I remembered God with all my heart." A similar reference is found in 1 Maccabees (1:62-63, RSV), "But many in Israel stood firm and were resolved in their hearts not to eat unclean food. They chose to die rather than to be defiled by food or to profane the holy covenant; and they did die."*

The problem of whether Daniel and his companions should eat the food provided by the king was a supreme test of their fidelity to the law and probably served the practical purpose of separating Daniel and his three companions from the other captives who apparently could compromise in this matter. His decision also demonstrates Daniel's understanding that God had brought Israel into captivity because of their failure to observe the law. Daniel's handling of this problem sets the spiritual tone for the entire book.

Keil summarizes the problem in these words:

> The command of the king, that the young men should be fed with the food and wine from the king's table, was to Daniel and his friends a test of their fidelity to the Lord and to His law, like that to which Joseph was subjected in Egypt, corresponding to the circumstances in which he was placed, of his fidelity to God (Gen. xxxix. 7 f.). The partaking of the food brought to them from the king's table was to them contaminating, because forbidden by Law; not so much because the food was not prepared according to the Levitical ordinance, or perhaps consisted of the flesh of animals which to the Israelites were unclean, for in this case the youths were not under the necessity of refraining from the wine, but the reason of their rejection of it was that the heathen at their feasts offered up in sacrifice to their gods, a part of the food and the drink, and thus consecrated their meals by a religious rite; whereby not only he who participated in such a meal participated in the worship of idols, but the meat and the wine as a whole were the meat and the wine of an idol sacrifice, partaking of which, according to the saying of the apostle (1 Cor. x. 20 f.), is the same as sacrificing to devils. Their abstaining from such food and drink betray no rigorism going beyond the Mosaic law, a tendency which first showed itself in the time of the Maccabees . . . . Daniel's resolution to refrain from such unclean food flowed, therefore, from fidelity to the law, and from steadfastness to the faith that 'man lives not by bread only, but by every word that proceedeth out of the mouth of the Lord" (Deut. viii. 3).[34]

Daniel's handling of this difficult situation reflects his good judgment and common sense. Instead of inviting punishment by rebellion, he courteously requests of the prince of the eunuchs that he might be excused from eating food which would defile his conscience (1 Co 10:31). Although critics attempt to equate this abstinence with fanaticism and thereby link it to the Maccabean Period,[35] there is no excuse for such a

---

*Cf. Judith 12:1-4; Book of Jubilees 22:16; and the interesting account in Josephus, *Life* 3 (14), where we hear of certain Jewish priests in Rome who avoided defilement with Gentile food by living solely on figs and nuts (cf. Montgomery, p. 130).

charge since Daniel handles the situation well. Leupold points out that Daniel did not object to the heathen names given to them nor to their education which involved the learning of the heathen, including their religious view.* This was not a direct conflict with the Jewish law. Here Daniel is exercising a proper conscience in matters that were of real importance.

When Daniel brought his request to the prince of the eunuchs, we are told that God had brought Daniel into favor and compassion with him. The King James Version implies that this predated his request. It is more probable that it occurred at the time the request was given, as brought out by the literal rendering of the Hebrew, "God gave Daniel favour" and so forth. As Young puts it, "The sequence of ideas is historical."[36] The word "favour" (Heb. *hesed*) means kindness or good will. The translation "tender love" (Heb. *rahamim*) is a plural intended to denote deep sympathy. It is clear that God intervened on Daniel's part in preparing the way for his request.

The prince of eunuchs, however, was not speaking idly when he replied to Daniel, "I fear my lord the king," for indeed it was not an overstatement that, if he did not fulfill his role well, he might lose his head. Life was cheap in Babylon and subject to the whims of the king. The prince, therefore, did not want to be caught changing the king's orders in regard to the diet of the captives. If later they showed any ill effects and inquiry was made, he would have been held responsible. The expression "worse liking" (i.e., worse looking, poor in comparison) does not imply any dangerous illness but only difference of appearance, such as paleness or being thinner than his companions. Although the prince could have peremptorily denied Daniel's request, Ashpenaz attempted to explain the problem. This opened the door for a counterproposal.

DANIEL'S REQUEST FOR A TEN-DAY TEST

1:11-14 Then said Daniel to Melzar, whom the prince of the eunuchs had set over Daniel, Hananiah, Mishael, and Azariah, Prove thy servants, I beseech thee, ten days; and let them give us pulse to eat, and water to drink. Then let our countenances be looked upon before thee, and the countenance of the children that eat of the portion of the king's meat: and as thou seest, deal with thy servants. So he consented to them in this matter, and proved them ten days.

Daniel's next step was to appeal to the steward who had immediate charge of Daniel and his companions for a ten-day test. Montgomery observes, "Dan. then appeals privately to a lower official, the 'warden,' as the Heb. word means, who was charged with the care of the youths and their diet. . . . Tradition has rightly distinguished between this official and the

*Leupold credits Kliefoth as expressing this concept (Leupold, p. 66).

Chief Eunuch."[37] The King James Version indicates this request is made to Melzar (Heb. *Hamelṣar*). The probability is that this is not a proper name and simply means "the steward" or the chief attendant.[38] The Septuagint changes the text here to indicate that Daniel had actually spoken to "Abiezdri who had been appointed chief eunuch over Daniel." Critics, such as Charles, have used this as a basis for questioning the text of Daniel with the idea that Daniel would not speak to the steward but would rather continue his conversation with the prince of eunuchs. Young, after Calvin, refutes this idea, however, and holds that Daniel's action is perfectly natural and in keeping with the situation.[39] Having been refused permission for a permanent change in diet, Daniel naturally took the next course of attempting a brief trial. As Montgomery says, "An underling might grant the boon without fear of discovery."[40] The chief steward, not being in as close or responsible a position as the prince of eunuchs in relation to the king, could afford to take a chance.

The proposal was to give a ten-day trial, a reasonable length of time to test a diet and yet one that would not entail too much risk of incurring the wrath of the king. The request to eat "pulse" or vegetables included a broad category of food. Young agrees with Driver that this did not limit the diet to peas and beans but to food that grows out of the ground, i.e., "the sown things."[41] Calvin may be right that Daniel had a special revelation from God in seeking this permission and for this reason the youth made the proposal that at the end of the ten days their countenance (or appearance) should be examined and judgment rendered accordingly.[42] The steward granted their request, and the test was begun.

DANIEL'S REQUEST GRANTED

1:15-16 And at the end of ten days their countenances appeared fairer and fatter in flesh than all the children which did eat the portion of the king's meat. Thus Melzar took away the portion of their meat, and the wine that they should drink; and gave them pulse.

At the conclusion of the test, Daniel and his companions not only were better in appearance but also were fatter in flesh than those who had continued to eat the king's food. Although God's blessing was on them, it is not necessary to imagine any supernatural act of God here. The food they were eating was actually better for them. On the basis of the test their request was granted, and their vegetable diet continued.

GOD'S BLESSING ON DANIEL AND HIS COMPANIONS

1:17-21 As for these four children, God gave them knowledge and skill in all learning and wisdom: and Daniel had understanding in all visions and dreams. Now at the end of the days that the king had said he should bring them in, then the prince of the eunuchs brought them in before Nebuchadnezzar. And the king communed with them; and among them all was found none like Daniel, Hananiah, Mishael, and Azariah: therefore stood they before the king. And in all matters of wisdom and understanding, that the king enquired of them, he found them ten times better than all the magicians and astrologers that were in all his realm. And Daniel continued even unto the first year of king Cyrus.

The closing section of Daniel 1 is a summary of the three years of hard study and the result of God's blessing upon the four faithful young men. The word *children* is better translated "youths." By the time they completed their education, they were probably nearly twenty years of age. In addition to their natural intellectual ability and their evident careful application to their studies, God added His grace. The article precedes the name of God, and by this is meant that He is the true God. By knowledge and skill (or intelligence) is indicated that they not only had a thorough acquaintance with the learning of the Chaldeans, but that they had insight into its true meaning (James 1:5). Calvin is probably wrong that they were kept from study of the religious superstitions and magic which characterized the Chaldeans.[43] In order to be fully competent to meet the issues of their future life, they would need a thorough understanding of the religious practices of their day. Here the grace of God operated, however, in giving them understanding so they could distinguish between the true and the false. They not only had knowledge but discernment.

The expression "in all learning and wisdom" has reference to literature and the wisdom to understand it. As Keil puts it, Daniel "needed to be deeply versed in the Chaldean wisdom, as formerly Moses was in the wisdom of Egypt (Acts vii. 22), so as to be able to put to shame the wisdom of this world by the hidden wisdom of God."[44]

Although all four youths shared in an intelligent understanding of the literature of the Chaldeans and were able to separate wisely the true from the false, only Daniel had understanding "in all visions and dreams." This was not a foolish boast but an actual fact necessary to understand Daniel's role as a prophet in the chapters which followed. In this, Daniel differed from his companions as a true prophet. His ability to discern and interpret visions and dreams primarily had in view the interpretation of the dreams and visions of others. However, this did not include the ability to know Nebuchadnezzar's dream in chapter 2, which Daniel received only after earnest prayer; and it did not necessarily as yet give Daniel the capacity to have visions and dreams himself as he did in chapter 7 and following.

Daniel's capacity included distinguishing a true dream from one that had no revelatory meaning and also the power to interpret it correctly.

41

God's hand was already on Daniel even as a young man much as it was on Samuel centuries before. Although critics like Montgomery and others deprecate the significance and the importance of the prophetic gift in Daniel on the assumption of a second century date for the book, it becomes quite clear as the book progresses that though Daniel differed somewhat from the major prophets, his contribution is just as important and in fact, more extensive than that of any other book of the Old Testament.* To no other was the broad expanse of both Gentile and Hebrew future history revealed in the same precision.

In verse 18 the conclusion of their period of preparation is marked by a personal interview before Nebuchadnezzar, and they were brought into his presence by the prince of eunuchs himself. The expression *at the end of the days* means at the end of the three-year period. At this time, apparently all of the young men in training were tested by the king.

Under Nebuchadnezzar's searching questions, Daniel and his three companions, named with their Hebrew names, were found "ten times better than all the magicians and astrologers that were in all his realm." By this is meant that they had high intelligence and keen discernment in the matters which they had studied. The statement that they were "ten times better," literally, "ten hands," at first glance sounds extravagant but signifies that they were outstandingly different. Even this praise, however, is mentioned in such a matter of fact way and so evidently due to the grace of God that Daniel is delivered from the charge of boasting. Their straightforward character and honesty, as well as the deep insight of these young men into the real meaning of their studies, must have stood in sharp contrast to the wise men of the king's court, who often were more sly and cunning than wise. Nebuchadnezzar, himself an extraordinarily intelligent man as manifested in his great exploits, was quick to respond to these bright young minds.

Chapter 1 concludes with the simple statement that Daniel continued unto the first year of king Cyrus. Critics have seized upon this as another inaccuracy because, according to Daniel 10:1, the revelation was given to Daniel in the third year of Cyrus. The large discussion that this has provoked is much ado about nothing. Obviously to Daniel, the important point was that his ministry spanned the entire Babylonian empire, and he was still alive when Cyrus came on the scene. The passage does not

---

*Montgomery states, "Dan.'s specialty in visions and dreams does not belong to the highest category of revelation, that of prophecy; the Prophets had long since passed away, 1 Mac. 4:46, and the highest business of the Jewish sage was the interpretation of their oracles" (Montgomery, p. 132). Montgomery rejects, of course, a sixth century b.c. date for Daniel, well before the last of the prophets. For refutation, see Young, pp. 49-50.

say nor necessarily imply that Daniel did not continue after the first year of Cyrus—which, as a matter of fact, he did.

The attempts to dislodge both verses 20 and 21 as illustrated in the comments of Charles, who wants to put them at the end of the second chapter, have been satisfactorily answered by Young.[45] Charles argues, "If the king had found the Jewish youths *ten times wiser than all the sages of Babylon* he would naturally have consulted them before the wise men of Babylon, and not have waited till, in ii.16, they volunteered their help."[46] This is, however, an arbitrary change in the text. If the events of chapter 2 follow chronologically at the end of chapter 1, they had demonstrated only proficiency in study, not ability to interpret dreams as in chapter 2. There is no indication in chapter 1 that they were immediately given the rank of chief wise men. Therefore, they were not called to interpret the dream of chapter 2. A similar situation is found in chapter 5, where Daniel, even with his record of interpreting dreams and visions, is not called in until others have failed. Critics are too eager to change the text of Scripture to suit their interpretations.

As is pointed out in the discussion of Daniel 2:1, it is entirely possible that the vision of Daniel 2 and the interpretation of the dream occurred during the third year of Daniel's training, *before* the formal presentation of the four youths to the king. This would take away all objections concerning the statement of Daniel 1:20, as it would make Daniel's graduation after the events of Daniel 2. That the book of Daniel is not written in strict chronological order is evident from the placing of chapters 5 and 6 before chapters 7 and 8, out of chronological order. In any case, there is no justification for arbitrary criticism of Daniel's record.

The narrative as it stands is beautifully complete—an eloquent testimony to the power and grace of God in a dark hour of Israel's history when the faithfulness of Daniel and his companions shines all the brighter because it is in a context of Israel's captivity and apostasy. In every age, God is looking for those whom He can use. Here were four young men whose testimony has been a source of strength to every saint in temptation. Certainly Daniel would not have been recognized as a prophet of God and the channel of divine revelation if he had not been a man of prayer and of uncompromising moral character, whom God could honor fittingly. Daniel and his companions represent the godly remnant of Israel which preserved the testimony of God even in dark hours of apostasy and divine judgment. The noble example of these young men will serve to encourage Israel in their great trials in the time of the end.

2

NEBUCHADNEZZAR'S VISION OF THE GREAT IMAGE

BEGINNING WITH THE SECOND CHAPTER of Daniel, the grand outline of the program of God for the period of Gentile supremacy and chastisement of Israel is presented for the first time. Tregelles, in his introduction to chapter 2 of Daniel, observes, "The book of Daniel is that part of Scripture which especially treats of the power of the world during the time of its committal into the hands of the Gentiles, whilst the ancient people of God, the children of Israel, are under chastisement on account of their sin."[1]

What is true of the book in general is especially true of chapter 2. Nowhere else in Scripture, except in Daniel 7, is a more comprehensive picture given of world history as it stretched from the time of Daniel, 600 years before Christ, to the consummation at the second advent of Christ. It is most remarkable that Daniel was not only given this broad revelation of the course of what Christ called "the times of the Gentiles" (Lk 21:24), but also the chronological prophecy of Israel's history stretching from the rebuilding of Jerusalem to the second advent of Christ. These two major foci of the book of Daniel justify the general description of the book as world history in outline with special reference to the nation of Israel.

Interpretations of the book of Daniel, and especially chapter 2, divide into two broad categories. Higher critics who label the book of Daniel a second century forgery challenge the prophetic meaning of chapter 2 at every turn and assert that the writer is merely recording history. If they are right, an exposition of this chapter becomes a meaningless interpretation of a curious but unimportant document.

On the other hand, reverent scholars have consistently defended the authenticity of this book as a genuine portion of the Word of God written by Daniel in the sixth century B.C. Only if this second view is adopted, which assigns to Daniel the role of a genuine prophet and regards the book as inspired Scripture, can a sensible explanation be given of the broad prophecies which this chapter details.

Among those who regard this chapter as genuine Scripture, there is a further subdivision into two classes: (1) those who interpret the vision from the amillennial or postmillennial point of view; (2) those who interpret the vision from a premillennial perspective. The difference here resolves itself largely in differing views of how the image is destroyed, and how the revelation relates to the present age and the two advents of Christ. Few chapters of the Bible are more determinative in establishing both principle and content of prophecy than this chapter; and its study, accordingly, is crucial to any system of prophetic interpretation.

NEBUCHADNEZZAR DREAMS DREAMS

2:1   And in the second year of the reign of Nebuchadnezzar Nebuchadnezzar dreamed dreams, wherewith his spirit was troubled, and his sleep brake from him.

The important event of Nebuchadnezzar's dream and its interpretation is introduced by the statement that the dream occurred "in the second year of the reign of Nebuchadnezzar." The question immediately arises how this relates to the three years of the training of Daniel and his companions described in chapter 1. This time indication, standing first in the sentence for emphasis, is connected to the previous chapter by *and* or "now" (the conjunction *waw*). This implies consecutive information but not necessarily chronological succession.

Although critics have assailed this reference to Nebuchadnezzar's second year as an inaccuracy, the explanation is relatively simple. Nebuchadnezzar had carried off Daniel and his companions immediately after his victory over the Egyptians at Carchemish, which probably took place May-June, 605 B.C.[2] Wiseman states, "The effects of the Babylonian victory were immediate and far-reaching. 'At that time,' recorded the chronicler, 'Nebuchadrezzar conquered the whole area of Hatti,' the geographical term Hatti including, at this period, the whole of Syria and Palestine."[3]

According to Wiseman, "The effect on Judah was that King Jehoiakim, a vassal of Necho, submitted voluntarily to Nebuchadrezzar, and some Jews, including the prophet Daniel, were taken as captives for hostages to Babylon."[4] This was June-August 605 B.C. Daniel and his companions, therefore, entered their training at Babylon soon thereafter, probably after Nebuchadnezzar had been made king, September 7, 605 B.C. at the death of his father, Nabopolassar. In view of this sequence of events, Leupold concludes that "the phrase 'in the second year' is both harmless and unassailable."[5] It was actually the third year in modern reckoning. Leupold continues, "The Babylonian manner of reckoning a king's reign did not regard the unexpired portion of the last year of the deceased monarch as the first year of the new king, but reserved that designation for the first full year of the new monarch's rule. Since the kings did not, as a rule, die

at the close of the last year of their reign, there were usually months intervening between reigns, which would allow just enough latitude to make
the initial phrase of our chapter entirely proper."[6] In other words, the first
year of Nebuchadnezzar's reign was not counted, and this gives a plausible explanation of why the dream could occur in the second year and
yet conceivably follow the three school years of Daniel's training. Edward
Young, after Driver, supports the idea that the three years of Daniel's
training were not necessarily three full years by illustrations from Hebrew
usage.[7]

The chronology of the period, following Wiseman, Thiele, and Finegan,[8]
seems to require the following order of events.

> May-June, 605 B.C.: Babylonian victory over the Egyptians at Car-
> chemish
>
> June-August, 605 B.C.: Fall of Jerusalem to Nebuchadnezzar, and
> Daniel and companions taken captive
>
> September 7, 605 B.C.: Nebuchadnezzar, the general of the army,
> made king over Babylon after the death of his father, Nabopo-
> lassar
>
> September 7, 605 B.C. to Nisan (March-April) 604 B.C.: Year of ac-
> cession of Nebuchadnezzar as king, and first year of Daniel's
> training
>
> Nisan (March-April) 604 B.C. to Nisan (March-April) 603 B.C.: First
> year of the reign of Nebuchadnezzar, second year of training of
> Daniel
>
> Nisan (March-April) 603 B.C. to Nisan (March-April) 602 B.C.: Sec-
> ond year of the reign of Nebuchadnezzar, third year of training
> of Daniel, also the year of Nebuchadnezzar's dream

The arguments of Montgomery[9] and others that the datum of Daniel
1:20–2:1 is hopelessly contradictory were based on an obvious prejudice
against the historicity of Daniel. These objections are satisfactorily answered by scholars such as Robert Dick Wilson, who show there is no
evidence of a positive nature which contradicts Daniel's statement here or
elsewhere.[10]

The important event which took place is simply expressed in the statement that "Nebuchadnezzar dreamed dreams." As *dreams* is plural, it
implies that he had several dreams which were of such character that he
was troubled by their significance and unable to sleep. The Hebrew for
"dreamed dreams" can be understood to be the pluperfect, i.e., "had
dreamed dreams."[11] This would imply that the dream took place some-
where in the sequence of events of chapter 1 but is only now being detailed. Hence, it allows for the conclusion that the dream was interpreted
before Daniel's graduation at the end of his three years of training. Commentators generally have been so occupied with the plural of *dreams*
that the verb has been neglected.

The Hebrew for *troubled* indicates a deep disturbance inducing apprehension. Nebuchadnezzar seems to have sensed that this was more than an ordinary dream and was a response to his questioning concerning the future, mentioned later by Daniel in 2:29. The result was that "his sleep brake from him." Literally, because of the passive form of the verb, Leupold translates it "was done for,"[12] or as Montgomery translates it, "sleep broke from him."[13]

Geoffrey R. King, in an extended comment on this, observes, "As is so often the case, the cares of the day became also the cares of the night. Now Nebuchadnezzar did a thing which no believer in God should ever dream of doing: Nebuchadnezzar took his problems to bed with him."[14] However, Nebuchadnezzar was no Christian; and after all, the circumstances and the dream were providentially induced by God Himself. On other occasions in Scripture, dreams have been used by God to give revelation to a Gentile ruler as in the cases of Abimelech (Gen 20:3) and of Pharaoh (Gen 41:1-8), which is an interesting parallel to Nebuchadnezzar's experience. Sleeplessness also has its purpose in divine providence as in the case of Ahasuerus in Esther 6 which started the chain of events leading to Haman's execution and Israel's deliverance. Nebuchadnezzar's experience was obviously ordered by God.

ALL THE WISE MEN SUMMONED

2:2-3 Then the king commanded to call the magicians, and the astrologers, and the sorcerers, and the Chaldeans, for to shew the king his dreams. So they came and stood before the king. And the king said unto them, I have dreamed a dream, and my spirit was troubled to know the dream.

Because of the king's agitation, he apparently immediately summoned all four classifications of wise men here described as "the magicians, and the astrologers, and the sorcerers, and the Chaldeans." The designation, *wise men,* which does not occur in verse 2, is found in verse 27. Numerous similar listings occur throughout Daniel (1:20; 2:10, 27; 4:7; 5:7, 11, 15). Wise men, apparently a general description of all of them, are referred to frequently alone (2:12, 13, 14, 18, 24, 48; 4:6, 18; 5:7, 8) and the *Chaldeans* are mentioned elsewhere also (1:4; 2:4; 3:8; 5:11). *Magicians* is the translation of a Hebrew word with a root meaning of stylus or a pen, according to Leupold, and hence could refer to a scholar rather than a magician in the ordinary sense.[15] *Astrologers* is also translated "enchanters," referring to the power of necromancy or communications with the dead according to Leupold[16] but is understood as "astrologers," by Young.[17] This translation suggests the study of the stars to predict the future. Young, however, does not specifically define *astrologer*. *Sorcerers* are those who practice sorcery or incantations. The most significant term, however, is *the Chaldeans*. This is usually interpreted as a reference to a group of astrologers. But the name itself designates a people who lived in Southern Babylonia (cf. Gen 11:28) and who eventually conquered the Assyrians when Nabopolassar, father of Nebuchadnezzar, was their king. It would be only natural for the conquerors to assert themselves at the level of wise men, and there is no justification for seizing on this reference to Chaldeans as an inaccuracy.[18] The obvious purpose of the recital of all four classes of wise men is that the king hoped, through their various contributions, to be able to interpret his dream.

With the wise men before him, the king announces that he has dreamed a dream, using the singular of *dream* indicating that only one of his many dreams was really significant prophetically.

REVELATION OF THE DREAM AND ITS INTERPRETATION DEMANDED BY THE KING

2:4-6 Then spake the Chaldeans to the king in Syriack [Aramaic], O king, live for ever: tell thy servants the dream, and we will show the interpretation. The king answered and said to the Chaldeans, The thing is gone from me: if ye will not make known unto me the dream, with the interpretation thereof, ye shall be cut in pieces, and your houses shall be made a dunghill. But if ye shew the dream, and the interpretation thereof, ye shall receive of me gifts and rewards and great honour: therefore shew me the dream, and the interpretation thereof.

The Chaldeans, acting as spokesmen for the group, then address the king. The phrase "in Aramaic" introduces the extended section written in Aramaic instead of Hebrew, beginning with verse 4 and continuing through chapter 7. Much discussion has arisen concerning this simple statement.[19] The obvious reason for this reference is that, from this point on, Daniel uses Aramaic, which although similar to the Hebrew also differs from it. Although some critics, such as Driver,° question whether Aramaic was spoken at the time of the sixth century B.C. in Babylon, it seems reasonable to assume that it was a language familiar to Daniel and was the language commonly used by the Jews in Babylon instead of Hebrew. It is not necessary to deduce from this that it was the formal court language, but there is no real evidence that the Chaldeans did not use Aramaic in addressing the king. The Aramaic section of Daniel deals with prophecy of primary interest to the Gentiles and to Daniel's day.

°S. R. Driver states dogmatically, "The author, it seems, must mean to indicate that in his opinion Aramaic was used at the court for communications of an official nature. That, however, does not explain why the use of Aramaic continues to the end of ch. vii.; and it is besides quite certain that Aramaic, such as that of the Book of Daniel, was *not* spoken in Babylon" (Driver, p. 19). Driver takes for granted a second century date for Daniel.

In the light of recent scholarship, the dogmatic dismissal of the Aramaic of Daniel is no longer tenable. As K. A. Kitchen has written, "This subject has been closely studied by two or three generations of modern scholars—S. R. Driver, R. D. Wilson, G. R. Driver, W. Baumgartner, H. H. Rowley, J. A. Montgomery, H. H. Schaeder, F. Rosenthal, and various others. Nevertheless, there is today ample scope for reassessment. The inscriptional material for Old and Imperial Aramaic and later phases of the language is constantly growing."[20]

Kitchen goes on to state, concerning the "entire word-stock of Biblical Aramaic" which is largely Daniel, that "nine-tenths of the vocabulary is attested in texts of the fifth century B.C. or earlier."[21] Most of the findings have been fifth century, as there is a scarcity of sixth century B.C. texts; but, if Daniel's Aramaic was used in the fifth century, it in all probability was also used in the sixth century B.C. The conclusion is quite clear that Driver and company argued from a priori assumption that Daniel is a second century forgery and on the lack of available materials. Materials are now coming to light, however, and contradict his point of view. Driver's position is no longer tenable if recent discoveries be admitted.

The Chaldeans, eager to please the king, address him with typical elaborate oriental courtesy, "O king, live for ever" (cf. 1 Ki 1:31; Neh 2:3; Dan 3:9; 5:10; 6:21). They declare with confidence that, if the king would tell them the dream, they would give the interpretation.

In reply to the Chaldeans, the king said, "The thing is gone from me." This translation (KJV) has been challenged by many expositors. All agree that the translation is difficult because the word used, *azda*, occurs only here and in verse 8. Franz Rosenthal translates the word, "publicly known, known as decided."[22] In the Greek translation of the Old Testament (LXX), this word with slight alterations is considered to be a verb form meaning "is gone from me," that is, the dream had been forgotten. The verb could, however, also mean "gone forth" in the sense of "I have decreed." Such expositors as Keil,[23] Leupold,[24] and Young[25] agree that the king actually had not forgotten the dream. Young translates the word as meaning "sure" or "certain," a definition supported by the Syriac and based on the assumption that the word is of Persian origin.[26] Hence the translation would be, "The thing is certain with me," or "fully determined."

The debate as to whether the king actually had forgotten his dream cannot, at the present state of investigation, be determined finally. In favor of the idea that the king had forgotten the dream would be the argument that he, anxious to know its interpretation, would certainly have divulged it to the wise men to see what they had to offer by way of interpretation. This would be in keeping with the translation "The thing is gone from me," which is still a possibility.

There are, however, a number of reasons why the king might have been induced to make this extreme demand of his counselors in order to test their ability to have real contact with the gods and divulge secrets. The king was a young man who had been extraordinarily successful in his military conquests. He undoubtedly had developed a great deal of confidence in himself. It is entirely possible that the wise men were much older than the king, having served Nebuchadnezzar's father. It would be understandable that the king might have previously been somewhat frustrated by these older counselors and may have had a real desire to be rid of them in favor of younger men whom he had chosen himself. Nebuchadnezzar might well have doubted their honesty, sincerity, and capability, and may even have wondered whether they were loyal to him. He may also have questioned some of their superstitious practices.

In his combined frustration with his counselors and his irritation stemming from the uncertainty of the meaning of the dream, it is entirely possible that Nebuchadnezzar should have suddenly hardened in his attitude toward his wise men and demanded that they should not only interpret the dream but also state the dream itself. Such a capricious action on the part of a monarch is in keeping with his character and position. It may have been a snap decision arising from the emotion of the moment, or it may have been the result of frustration with these men over a long period. It is significant that the younger wise men, such as Daniel and his companions, were not present.

To reinforce his demand for both the dream and its interpretation, Nebuchadnezzar declares that the wise men "shall be cut in pieces" and their houses "made a dunghill." This was not an idle threat but was in keeping with the cruelty which could be expected from a despot such as Nebuchadnezzar. It was all too common for victims to be executed by being dismembered, and whether their houses were literally made a dunghill or simply a "ruin" as Young and Montgomery favor[27] did not really matter. Driver states, "The violence and peremptoriness of the threatened punishment is in accordance with what might be expected at the hands of an Eastern despot; the Assyrians and Persians, especially, were notorious for the barbarity of their punishments."[28]

If, however, the wise men were able to respond to the king's request, they were promised "gifts and rewards and great honour." It was customary, when monarchs were pleased with their servants, to lavish upon them expensive gifts and great honor, a custom to which the Bible bears consistent testimony, as in the case of Joseph, Mordecai, and Daniel himself. "Rewards" is the translation of a Persian word, a singular rather than plural, and has the idea of a "present."[29] To receive these, they had only to tell the king the dream and its meaning. Obviously, the wise men were confronted with a supreme test of their superhuman claims. If they had genuine supernatural ability to interpret a dream, they should also have the power to reveal its content.

THE DEMAND OF THE KING REPEATED

2:7-9 They answered again and said, Let the king tell his servants the dream, and we will show the interpretation of it. The king answered and said, I know of certainty that ye would gain the time, because ye see the thing is gone from me. But if ye will not make known unto me the dream, there is but one decree for you: for ye have prepared lying and corrupt words to speak before me, till the time be changed: therefore tell me the dream, and I shall know that ye can show me the interpretation thereof.

Confronted with the king's ultimatum, the wise men repeated their request to be told the dream and again affirmed their ability to interpret it. It would seem that if the king had actually forgotten the dream, the wise men would have attempted some sort of an answer. The fact that they did not tends to support the idea that the king was willfully withholding information about the dream. Even if the king was hazy as to the details of the dream and could not recall it enough to provide a basis of interpretation, he probably would have been able to recognize complete fabrication on the part of the wise men. In any case, they did not attempt such a subterfuge.

The king, however, cuts them off abruptly, stating that he is sure that they are simply trying to gain time. The phrase "of certainty" stands first in the sentence for emphasis. He accuses the wise men of attempting to "gain the time," literally, "to buy" time, "because ye see the thing is gone from me." This last phrase is a duplicate of the statement in verse 5 with the same problem of interpretation and could be translated "because ye see the thing is certain with me," or "determined by me." Nebuchadnezzar's accusation implies that he did remember the main facts of the dream sufficiently to detect any invented interpretation which the wise men might offer.

Keil commenting on this states,

That the king had not forgotten his dream, and that there remained only some oppressive recollection that he had dreamed, is made clear from ver. 9, where the king says to the Chaldeans, "if ye cannot declare to me the dream, ye have taken in hand to utter deceitful words before me; therefore tell me the dream, that I may know that ye will give to me also the interpretation." According to this, Nebuchadnezzar wished to hear the dream from the wise men that he might thus have a guarantee for the correctness of the interpretation which they might give. He could not thus have spoken to them if he had wholly forgotten the dream, and had only a dark apprehension remaining in his mind that he had dreamed. In this case, he would neither have offered a great reward for the announcement of the dream, nor have threatened severe punishment, or even death, for failure in announcing it. For then he would have given the Chaldeans the opportunity, at the cost of truth, of declaring any dream with an interpretation. But as threatening and promise on the part of the king in that case would have been unwise, so also in the sight of the wise men, their helplessness in complying with the demand of the king would have been incomprehensible. If the king had truly forgotten the dream, they had no reason to be afraid of their lives if they had given some self-conceived dream with an interpretation of it; for in that case, he could not have accused them of falseness and deceit, and punished them on that account. If, on the contrary, he still knew the dream which so troubled him, and the contents of which he desired to hear from the Chaldeans, so that he might put them to the proof whether he might trust in their interpretation, then neither his demand nor the severity of his proceeding was irrational.[30]

It seems clear from the entire context that Nebuchadnezzar was not willing to accept any easy interpretation of his dream but wanted proof that his wise men had divine sources of information beyond the ordinary. He also sensed that they were attempting to gain time, hoping that his ugly mood would change. He wanted them to know that he had made up his mind.

FINAL PLEA OF THE WISE MEN DENIED

2:10-13 The Chaldeans answered before the king, and said, There is not a man upon the earth that can shew the king's matter: therefore there is no king, lord, nor ruler, that asked such things at any magician, or astrologer, or Chaldean. And it is a rare thing that the king requireth, and there is none other that can show it before the king, except the gods, whose dwelling is not with flesh. For this cause the king was angry and very furious, and commanded to destroy all the wise men of Babylon. And the decree went forth that the wise men should be slain; and they sought Daniel and his fellows to be slain.

Although the Chaldeans had confidently claimed to be able to interpret the dream, they were baffled by the demand to tell the dream itself. With as much courtesy as they could summon, they attempted to communicate to Nebuchadnezzar that his demand was unreasonable and that "no king, lord, nor ruler" would expect such a revelation from his wise men. The phrase "before the king" delicately expresses their consciousness that they were standing in the presence of an absolute ruler. They confess that the king's demand is beyond any human knowledge, even such as they might possess. With an attempt at subtle flattery, they refer to him as king, lord, and ruler, which could be translated by combining the three terms as "great and powerful ruler," as Young suggests.[31] The thought is that such a great and powerful ruler as Nebuchadnezzar would be too great a man to expect such knowledge of his servants. That which the king demands is "rare" or "difficult" and is a matter which only the gods could reveal. The expression "whose dwelling is not with flesh" may distinguish gods who are above human connection and those who might appear in human form, but the probable meaning is that only god and not men could reveal a secret like the dream. This very statement, reflecting the bankruptcy of human wisdom, sets the stage for Daniel's divine revelation.

The humility of the wise men and their protestation were of no avail. It apparently only confirmed the king's suspicion that they were incompetent and incapable of really helping him. It only made him more angry, the word "furious" coming from a root similar to that from which came the Hebrew word for the wrath of Pharaoh (Gen 40:2; 41:10).[32] Accordingly, the decree is issued "to destroy all the wise men of Babylon." By "wise men" he included not only the four classes that were before him but all others such as Daniel and his companions. Although Babylon could refer to the entire empire, it is probable that the decree was limited to the city of Babylon (2:49; 3:1).

It is not entirely clear from verse 13 whether the executioners killed the wise men right where they were when found or whether they were being collected for a public execution. The latter is probably the case as subsequent scripture reveals that Daniel has the time to ask questions. Montgomery writes, "It was not to be a Sicilian Vespers but a formal execution under the proper officials and in the appointed place, hence the first purpose of the officials was to assemble the condemned."[33]

The fact that Daniel and his companions were included among the wise men has given rise to the false accusation that he had become a part of the heathen religious system of Babylon. There is no support whatever for this in Scripture. His training in chapter 1 did not make him a priest but merely a counselor of the king. But as such, he was included in the broad category of wise men.

DANIEL'S REQUEST FOR TIME TO SEEK INTERPRETATION OF THE DREAM

2:14-16 Then Daniel answered with counsel and wisdom to Arioch the captain of the king's guard, which was gone forth to slay the wise men of Babylon: He answered and said to Arioch the king's captain, Why is the decree so hasty from the king? Then Arioch made the thing known to Daniel. Then Daniel went in, and desired of the king that he would give him time, and that he would shew the king the interpretation.

When Daniel is informed of the decree of the king, it is stated "Then Daniel answered with counsel and wisdom to Arioch the captain of the king's guard." Although the wise men previously could hardly be accused of discourtesy, there seems to be an additional dignity and calmness in Daniel's approach to the problem. As Keil expresses it, "Through Daniel's judicious interview with Arioch, the further execution of the royal edict was interrupted."[34]

Arioch, as the captain of the king's guard, had the duty also of serving as chief executioner, although he personally may not have had the responsibility of killing the wise men. Accustomed as he was to the cruelty of his day, Arioch apparently did not question the king's decree. When Daniel, however, asked the question, "Why is the decree so hasty from the king?" a discussion followed in which Daniel is apprised of the total situation. That Arioch would take time to explain this to one already condemned to death speaks well both of Daniel's approach and of Arioch's regard for him. That Daniel refers to the decree as "hasty" or "severe" has been held by some to contradict his prudence. Obviously, however, a decree to execute wise men who have not had an opportunity to speak to the king was indeed harsh and severe, and occasioned Arioch's explanation.

In verse 16, only the briefest summary is offered of what actually transpired. Undoubtedly, Daniel expressed to Arioch the possibility that he could interpret the dream and secured Arioch's co-operation in going before the king. It would hardly have been suitable, especially with the king in the mood he was in, for Daniel to go in to the king unannounced without proper procedure. Possibly, the king by this time had cooled down a bit. In any event, Daniel was given his audience in which he asked for time and promised to show the king the interpretation. In contrast to the other wise men who were so filled with terror that they had no plans and had already been cut off from any additional time, Daniel, who had not been a part of the king's frustration with his older counselors, was granted his request. It is possible that Daniel's calm assurance that his God was able to help him somehow impressed the king that here was honesty and integrity quite in contrast to his fawning, older counselors.

Daniel and His Companions Pray for Wisdom

2:17-18 Then Daniel went to his house, and made the thing known to Hananiah, Mishael, and Azariah, his companions: That they would desire mercies of the God of heaven concerning this secret; that Daniel and his fellows should not perish with the rest of the wise men of Babylon.

Daniel lost no time in going to his own house and informing his three companions. His purpose was an obvious one, that they might join him in prayer that God would reveal the secret. As they shared in the danger, so they could share also in the intercession. They were to seek "mercies of the God of heaven," or "compassion" sometimes used of the mercy or compassion of men (Dan 1:9; Zec 7:9), or more commonly of the mercies of God (Neh 9:28; Is 63:7, 15; Dan 9:9, etc.).[35] The mercies or compassions of God are in contrast to the decree of Nebuchadnezzar of death for the wise men without mercy.

The reference to "the God of heaven" or literally "of the heavens" is an obvious contrast to the religious superstitions of the Babylonians who worshiped the starry heaven. Daniel's God was the God of the heavens, not heaven itself. Abraham first used this term in Genesis 24:7, and it is found frequently later in the Bible (Ezra 1:2; 6:10; 7:12, 21; Neh 1:5; 2:4; Ps 136:26). Although these four godly young men were in great extremity, one can almost visualize them on their knees before God, fully believing that their God was able to meet their need. Instead of being in a panic, they prayed. For this supreme hour of crisis they were well prepared, as their faith had been tested previously (see chap. 1). The result could be expected: "The effectual fervent prayer of a righteous man availeth much" (Ja 5:16). They obviously were motivated by the desire to save their lives. That they would be willing to die if necessary is revealed in chapter 3. Their petition was to the effect that they would not be included in the decree of death which extended to all the wise men of Babylon. Verse 18 does not necessarily imply that the other wise men had already perished, although this is a possibility. The probability is that Daniel's ultimate deliverance also extended to the other wise men.

DANIEL'S PRAYER ANSWERED

2:19-23 Then was the secret revealed unto Daniel in a night vision. Then Daniel blessed the God of heaven. Daniel answered and said, Blessed be the name of God for ever and ever: for wisdom and might are his: and he changeth the times and the seasons: he removeth kings, and setteth up kings: he giveth wisdom unto the wise, and knowledge to them that know understanding: he revealeth the deep and secret things: he knoweth what is in the darkness, and the light dwelleth with him. I thank thee, and praise thee, O thou God of my fathers, who hast given me wisdom and might, and hast made known unto me now what we desired of thee: for thou hast now made known unto us the king's matter.

Deliverance came to Daniel and his companions in the form of a night vision. This apparently was not a dream but a supernatural revelation given to Daniel in his waking hours. Possibly both he and his companions prayed on into the night, and the vision came when Daniel was awake. The nature of the revelation required both a vision and its interpretation as the image was a visual concept. Hence a vision was more proper than a dream, although frequently God revealed secrets to prophets in dreams as well as visions. There is no foundation for the critical claim that this was a low form of divine revelation. Modern criticism tends to regard a dream as a lower form of revelation than a vision and hence depreciates

Nebuchadnezzar's dream. The reasoning is that a dream is a natural event, whereas a vision is a supernatural experience and therefore a better medium for revelation. Montgomery writes, for instance, in commenting on the vision of Daniel, "It comes by night, as again in c. 7, but in a 'vision,' not in a dream, the lower means of communication to the Pagan."[36] Attempting to classify the value of revelation on its medium is beside the point. The only question is whether the revelation is from God, and its importance stems from its author rather than the means of revelation.

Most significant is Daniel's immediate response in a hymn of praise as he blessed the God of heaven who had answered his prayers. The hymn not only reveals the devout thankfulness of Daniel but also the depth and comprehension of his faith. The first phrase of his psalm, "Blessed be the name of God for ever and ever," reflects, as does the entire psalm, Daniel's acquaintance with hymns of praise found in the Psalms and other Scriptures of the Old Testament. In praising "the name of God" Daniel is speaking of God in His revealed character. W. H. Griffith Thomas writes, "The *name* stands in Holy Scripture for the nature or revealed character of God, and not a mere label or title. It is found very frequently in the Old Testament as synonymous with God Himself in relation to man. . . . In the New Testament the same usage is perfectly clear."[37]

Griffith Thomas cites as illustrations of usage Proverbs 18:10; Psalm 74:10; 118:10; Matthew 28:19; John 1:12; 2:23; 3:18; 5:43; 10:25; 17:6, 26; Philippians 2:10. Montgomery adds this comment, "The saint praises the Name of God, *i.e.*, God in his self-revelation, for his omniscience and omnipotence, attributes revealed in human history, v. 21. His power is exhibited in his providence over 'times and seasons,' Moff. [Moffatt], 'epochs and eras,' and in his sovereign determination of all political changes. In this expression lies a challenge to the fatalism of the Bab. astral religion, a feature which in its influence long survived in the Graeco-Roman world."[38]

A parallel to this hymn can be found in Psalm 113:1-2, as well as in Psalm 103:1-2. To God, Daniel attributes wisdom and might, as in Job 12:12-13, 16-22, and God's might is mentioned frequently as in I Chronicles 29:11-12. Daniel's God also "changes the times and the seasons," an evidence of sovereign power (cf. Dan 7:25). David the psalmist declared, "My times are in thy hand" (Ps 31:15). Here again Daniel is contrasting his God to the deities of Babylon who supposedly set the times and seasons by the movements of the sun, moon, and stars. Daniel's God could change this.

Daniel's faith also contemplated a God greater than the king's, and who could, therefore, remove a king or set up a king. This was not Babylonian fatalism but a sovereign God who acts as a person with infinite power. Such a God is also able to give wisdom to those who are wise and knowledge to those able to receive it. The wise men of Babylon were not so wise, for they were not the recipients of divine wisdom. To those wise enough to trust in the God of Daniel, however, and who had sufficient insight to see through the superstitions of Babylonian religions, there was the possibility of divine understanding. God's power over kings is hailed in Job 12:18 and Psalm 75:6-7, and His divine wisdom is a frequent theme of Scripture. From the same God, Solomon had sought an understanding heart (1 Ki 3:9-10); and the Scriptures record that "God gave Solomon wisdom and understanding exceeding much, and largeness of heart, even as the sand that is on the sea shore" (1 Ki 4:29). Such was also to be Daniel's experience.

In Daniel's ascription of greatness to God, he emphasizes that God not only has knowledge and wisdom but power to do what He wills. Daniel's God is in control of history and hence can reveal the future as in the king's dream. This description of God can be contrasted to Daniel 7:25 where the little horn, the future world ruler, shall "think to change times and laws," that is, take the place of God who "changeth the times and the seasons" (Dan 2:21). Daniel later comments on man's complete dependence upon God for wisdom in Daniel 2:30.

God's capacity to reveal secrets is mentioned specifically in verse 22. This again is attested by other Scriptures such as Job 12:22 (cf. 1 Co 2:10). The darkness does not hide anything from God, as David wrote in Psalm 139:12. Although knowing what is in darkness, God characteristically dwells in light. In Psalm 36:9 it is declared, "In thy light shall we see light," that is, God's light is presented as the light by which men see. In the gospel of John, the Logos, Christ, is identified as the light of the world (Jn 1:9; 3:19; 8:12; 9:5; 12:46).

Having attributed to God these infinite qualities of wisdom, power, sovereignty, and knowledge, Daniel directly expresses his thanks to God for His revelation to him of the secret. Although no mention is made of his deliverance from death, obviously this is included. Although Daniel does not have the infinite wisdom and power of God, he has that which is derived by divine impartation, wisdom and might—wisdom and ability to interpret the dream.

The expression *God of my fathers* is a common one in the Old Testament, here *Elohim* being used for God, rather than *Jehovah* (Gen 31:42 also uses Elohim, the common name for God rather than Jehovah, the peculiar name of the God of Israel). As Leupold notes, the reference to "my Fathers" indicates that Daniel "is having an experience of God's mercy which is analogous to that to which the fathers of old give testi-

mony on the pages of the sacred story."[39] Significant also is the fact that
thee stands first in verse 23 for emphasis, "Thee I thank," and with a desire
to place God first. Again, this is in contrast to the Babylonian deities
whom Daniel knows to be frauds. Notice should be made of the pronouns,
namely, that while the revelation was given to Daniel as an individual, it
was what "we [plural] desired," and through Daniel the king's secret was
"made known unto us," that is, Daniel's companions. Daniel does not attribute to his own prayers any special efficacy.

DANIEL REPORTS REVELATION OF THE SECRET

2:24-28 Therefore Daniel went in unto Arioch, whom the king had
ordained to destroy the wise men of Babylon: he went and said thus unto
him; Destroy not the wise men of Babylon: bring me in before the king,
and I will show unto the king the interpretation. Then Arioch brought
in Daniel before the king in haste, and said thus unto him, I have found
a man of the captives of Judah, that will make known unto the king the
interpretation. The king answered and said to Daniel, whose name was
Belteshazzar, Art thou able to make known unto me the dream which I
have seen, and the interpretation thereof? Daniel answered in the presence of the king, and said, The secret which the king hath demanded
cannot the wise men, the astrologers, the magicians, the soothsayers,
show unto the king; but there is a God in heaven that revealeth secrets,
and maketh known to the king Nebuchadnezzar what shall be in the
latter days. Thy dream, and the visions of thy head upon thy bed, are
these.

Daniel, now fully in command of the situation, reports to Arioch not to
destroy the wise men of Babylon. This is another confirmation of the fact
that the decree had not been executed and the wise men were only in
process of being rounded up. In support of his request Daniel declares,
"I will show unto the king the interpretation." The poise of Daniel, in
feeling free to tell Arioch not to carry out the command of the king, reveals
that Daniel fully understood that God's hand was upon him and that he
would probably be richly rewarded by the king for the information he
was able to give.

Arioch also at once saw the importance of what had happened and,
using his office to introduce Daniel to the king, attempted to get as much
credit as he could under the circumstances for discovering a man who
could reveal the secret. His statement is obviously designed to help him
participate in the reward, "I have found a man of the captives of Judah,
that will make known unto the king the interpretation." It is understandable that Arioch would not give God the credit for the interpretation but
rather "a man of the captives of Judah." The introduction of Daniel also
served to disassociate him from the wise men who had previously incurred
the king's wrath. Although there is no mention of Daniel's previous audi-

ence with the king which probably at the time had only the king's briefest attention, now the eager king immediately addresses Daniel, "Art thou able to make known unto me the dream which I have seen, and the interpretation thereof?" The form of the sentence makes the knowledge of the dream the prominent part of the question. Daniel's Babylonian name, Belteshazzar, is understandably inserted here as a means of proper identification.

Daniel's answer is a masterpiece of setting the matter in its proper light and giving God the glory. Although the temptation to imagine supernatural powers as resident in him was possibly present, Daniel immediately declares that what has been revealed to him was a secret which no wise men of Babylonia could have discovered, "The secret which the king hath demanded cannot the wise men, the astrologers, the magicians, the soothsayers, shew unto the king" (cf. Gen 41:16). The repetition of all classes of the wise men is an indication that no branch of Babylonian religious superstition could possibly have met the king's need. In describing the wise men, a new word is used to describe "the astrologers" with reference to the idea that astrologers consider various parts of the heavens as having particular significance or power. By using this particular word, Daniel is preparing the way to introduce his God as the God of the whole heavens.[40] In stating that the wise men could not be expected to reveal the secret, Daniel is, in effect, defending them somewhat from the king's wrath while at the same time affirming their impotence.

Having disposed of any possible solution of the problem on the part of the wise men, Daniel now seizes the opportunity to glorify his own God and, at the same time, disavows that the interpretation of the dream stems from any innate powers which he might have. Daniel declares, "but there is a God in heaven that revealeth secrets, and maketh known to the king Nebuchadnezzar what shall be in the latter days." This implies that the God of Daniel is far superior to the god of the Babylonians and that He is the God who is able to reveal secrets as well as know them.

Of particular interest to all expositors is the expression, "in the latter days." Driver is quoted by Montgomery as limiting this expression to the perspective of the alleged spurious Daniel of the second century.[41] Driver states, "[. . . *in the latter days*] lit. *in the end (closing-part) of the days.* An expression which occurs fourteen times in the O. T., and which always denotes the *closing period* of the future so far as it falls within the range of view of the writer using it. The sense expressed by it is thus relative, not absolute, varying with the context."[42]

This would, in effect, regard it as stopping short of the coming of the Messiah in the New Testament. Driver, however, goes on, "Elsewhere it is used of the ideal, or Messianic age, conceived as following at the close of the existing order of things: Hos. iii. 5; Is. ii. 2 (Mic. iv. 1); Jer. xlviii. 47, xlix. 39; comp. xxiii. 20 (xxx. 24). Here, as the sequel shews, it is similarly the period of the establishment of the Divine Kingdom which is principally denoted by it (vv. 34, 35; 44, 45); but the closing years of the fourth kingdom (vv. 40-43) may also well be included in it."[43] Leupold objects to any implied limitation on the Messianic content and writes, "But to stop short at this point and to deny Messianic import to the passage as such is misleading. Though the content must determine how much of the future is involved, a careful evaluation of all the passages involved shows that from the first instance of the use of the phrase (Gen. 49:1) onward the Messianic future is regularly involved. In this passage the Messianic element will be seen to be prominent."[44] Conservative scholars usually regard this expression as including the Messianic age in general, with some considering it especially the end of the period.

The Aramaic phrase which is translated "in the latter days" or "in the latter part of the days" is almost a transliteration of a Hebrew expression which is common in the Old Testament. Daniel is unquestionably using this Aramaic expression in the same sense as its Hebrew counterpart; and, accordingly, its definition should be based on Hebrew usage. The expression is found as early as Genesis 49:1 where Jacob predicts the future of his sons. The term is employed by Balaam in Numbers 24:14 and Moses in Deuteronomy 4:30; 31:29 in connection with the future of Israel. An examination of these prophecies indicates that the latter days include much that is now history. But with reference to the consummation in Messianic times, Jeremiah uses the expression a number of times to refer to the climax of the age relating to the second coming of Jesus Christ (Jer 23:20; 30:24; 48:47; 49:39). Ezekiel identifies the times of the invasion of Gog and Magog as "in the latter days" (38:16). The expression is also found in the minor prophets (Ho 3:5; Mic 4:1) in reference to the Messianic age.

On the basis of scriptural usage, it is clear that "the latter days" is an extended period of time regarded as the consummation of the prophetic foreview involved in each instance. Accordingly, Robert Culver's definition is accurate that the expression "refers to the future of God's dealings with mankind as to be consummated and concluded historically in the times of the Messiah."[45] He goes on to point out that the expression always has in view the ultimate establishment of the Messianic kingdom on earth, even though "the latter days" include an event now history, such as the division of Israel in the promised land. On the basis of scriptural usage in the Old Testament, it can be concluded that the expression is larger than that of Messianic times specifically, but that it always includes this element in its consummation.

In the New Testament there is allusion to the Old Testament concept in Acts 2:17-21 (cf. Joel 2:28-32), but elsewhere reference to "the last days" (Jn 6:39, 40, 44, 54; 7:37; 11:24; 12:48; Acts 2:17; 2 Ti 3:1; Heb 1:2; Ja 5:3; 2 Pe 3:3) and "last time" (1 Pe 1:5, 20; 1 Jn 2:18; Jude 18) must be interpreted contextually and is not always the same concept as "the latter days" (cf. Jn 7:37). The latter days for Israel are not precisely the same as the last days for the church, as the Old Testament characteristically spans the present age without including it in consideration.

Taking both the Old and New Testament uses together, it is clear that the latter days for Israel begin as early as the division of the land to the twelve tribes (Gen 49:1) and include the first and the second advent of Christ. The last days for the church culminate at the rapture and resurrection of the church, and are not related to the time of the end for Israel. Culver is going beyond the New Testament revelation when he writes: "Interpretation of 'the latter days' must allow it to include not only the first advent and the second advent with the coming of Messiah's future kingdom, but also the age intervening between the advents in which we now live. We are now, and have been since Jesus came, in the latter days.[46] Daniel actually does not deal with the age between the two advents except for the time of the end, and the New Testament does not clearly use it of the present church age. Culver, however, properly concludes that "the time of the end" as found in Daniel 11:35 is not identical to "the latter days."

In the context of Daniel 2, "the latter days" include all the visions which Nebuchadnezzar received and stretches from 600 B.C. to the second coming of Christ to the earth. It is used in a similar way in Daniel 10:14, including the extensive revelation concerning the remainder of the kingdom of Medo-Persia, many details concerning Alexander's empire as in chapter 11, and the consummation called "the time of the end" in Daniel 11:36-45. These prophecies served to give added detail not included in the revelation to Nebuchadnezzar. Having stated the general purpose, Daniel now is able to unfold what will occur "in the latter days," namely, the majestic procession of the four great world empires, and its destruction and replacement by the fifth empire, the kingdom from heaven. Nebuchadnezzar's dream and the visions he had in the dream can now be unfolded.

THE PURPOSE OF THE DREAM

2:29-30 As for thee, O king, thy thoughts came into thy mind upon thy bed, what should come to pass hereafter: and he that revealeth secrets maketh known to thee what shall come to pass. But as for me, this secret is not revealed to me for any wisdom that I have more than any living, but for their sakes that shall make known the interpretation to the king, and that thou mightest know the thoughts of thy heart.

Nebuchadnezzar had had a meteoric rise to power as one of the great conquerors and monarchs of the ancient world. He had begun his brilliant career even while his father was still alive, but after his father's death, he had quickly consolidated his gains and established himself as absolute ruler over the Babylonian empire. All of Southwest Asia was in his power, and there was no rival worthy of consideration at the time. Under these circumstances, it was only natural that Nebuchadnezzar should wonder what was going to come next. His meditation on this subject should not be confused with the dream which followed, but rather it was the preparation for it in the providence of God.

In this context Nebuchadnezzar had his dream; and God, referred to here by Daniel as "he that revealeth secrets" (in effect a new title for God), had used the dream as a vehicle to reveal the answer to Nebuchadnezzar's question. As Nebuchadnezzar was a remarkable man, so was the dream a remarkable revelation. While Daniel still has the attention of the king eager to learn the secret of his dream, he presses home the fact that the dream was a means of divine revelation in which God had signally honored the Babylonian monarch.

Before proceeding to the dream, however, Daniel once more emphasizes the fact that the secret had not come to him from any natural or accrued wisdom, but because God in His providence had selected Nebuchadnezzar as the recipient of the dream and Daniel as its interpreter that Nebuchadnezzar and others should receive this revelation. The expression "for their sakes that shall make known the interpretation to the king" is better translated as a passive, i.e., "that the interpretation may be made known to the king." The construction is actually impersonal.[47] Daniel now is able to proceed to the dream itself.

THE DREAM REVEALED

2:31-35 Thou, O king, sawest, and behold a great image. This great image, whose brightness was excellent, stood before thee; and the form thereof was terrible. This image's head was of fine gold, his breast and his arms of silver, his belly and his thighs of brass, His legs of iron, his feet part of iron and part of clay. Thou sawest till that a stone was cut out without hands, which smote the image upon his feet that were of iron and clay, and brake them to pieces. Then was the iron, the clay, the brass, the silver, and the gold, broken to pieces together, and became like the chaff of the summer threshingfloors; and the wind carried them away, that no place was found for them: and the stone that smote the image became a great mountain, and filled the whole earth.

Daniel first declares the king saw "a great image." This must have been immediately most fascinating to the king as it was evident to him, if he remembered the dream at all, that Daniel was on the right track. By *image* is not meant an idol as Hitzig holds[48] but a statue corresponding to human form. It was "great " in the sense of being immense or large in form, and by its very size the statue must have been overwhelming in its implication of power. Even Nebuchadnezzar, the absolute ruler, recognized this as something greater than himself.

In addition to the great size of the statue, it was remarkable for its brilliant appearance. It apparently reflected light, indicated by *brightness* which is described as "excellent," or unusual in its brilliance. The image apparently was not seen at a distance but as standing very close to Nebuchadnezzar, "stood before thee." The total effect of the image was "terrible" or "terrifying." Nebuchadnezzar, fearless man that he was, cringed before this unusual spectacle.

Having revealed the impression that the image had made on Nebuchadnezzar, Daniel quickly proceeds to describe the metallic character of the image, namely, its head of gold, its breast and arms of silver, its abdomen and thighs of brass (i.e., bronze or copper), the legs of iron, and the feet part of iron and part of clay or pottery. There is an apparent symbolism in the major metals and the form of the image. As Keil observes, quoting Kliefoth, "Only the first part, the head, constitutes in itself a united whole."[49] The silver is divided into the arms and breast. The brass apparently extends from the abdomen into the upper legs or thighs. The legs, of course, also constitute a division which ends in the toes of the feet with further subdivision.

The preciousness of the metal deteriorates from the top or gold to the clay of the feet, and there is a corresponding lower specific gravity; that is, the gold is much heavier than the silver, the silver than the brass, the brass than the iron, and the clay in the feet is the lightest material of all. The approximate specific gravity of gold is 19, silver 11, brass 8.5, and iron 7.8. The gold head has twice the weight of similar amounts of the other metals. The weight of brass varies according to the amount of tin or zinc which is added to the copper. While the materials decrease in weight, they increase in hardness with the notable exception of the clay in the feet. The image is obviously top heavy and weak in its feet.*

As Daniel reveals, the king in his dream saw the stone described as "cut out without hands" smite the image at its feet, the weakest place in the image, with the result that the feet are broken. Then in rapid succession the disintegration of the entire image follows, and it breaks into small

---

*Charles, with insufficient warrant, thinks that the order of mention, "iron, clay, brass" in verse 35 is wrong and should be "clay, iron, brass" as in verse 33, in reverse order. As Charles admits, the KJV rendering is supported by the LXX and the Vulgate, and in any case no rigid order is observed in the passage as a whole, as illustrated in another order in verse 45, where "clay" comes after "brass" (R. H. Charles, *The Book of Daniel*, pp. 24-25).

pieces corresponding to the chaff of a summer threshingfloor. Then a wind blows away the chaff until the pieces of the image totally disappear. The stone which destroyed the image grows into a great mountain and fills the whole earth.

The stone which is cut out without hands is stated later in Daniel 2:45 to be cut out of a mountain. There is no evidence, however, that the stone rolls downhill as Leupold infers.[50] In the absence of an express statement, it is possible that the stone flies through the air as a missile. In any event, it smites the image with terrific force.

Daniel's description is a masterpiece of concise and yet complete narration. As Leupold says, "There is not a superfluous word in Daniel's entire description and account."[51] Nebuchadnezzar is so fascinated by the obvious accuracy of the revelation to Daniel that he does not interpose a word. This permits Daniel to proceed immediately to the interpretation.

THE INTERPRETATION: BABYLON THE HEAD OF GOLD

2:36-38 This is the dream; and we will tell the interpretation thereof before the king. Thou, O king, art a king of kings: for the God of heaven hath given thee a kingdom, power, and strength, and glory. And wheresoever the children of men dwell, the beasts of the field and the fowls of the heaven hath he given into thine hand, and hath made thee ruler over them all. Thou art this head of gold.

Daniel now makes a clear transition from the dream itself to its interpretation. Considerable attention has been focused by commentators on the "we." Did Daniel mean by "we" God and himself, or his three companions who had joined with him in prayer as Leupold suggests,[52] following Keil,[53] or is it merely an editorial plural which Young states is "employed with a certain humility, for the message was not Dan.'s own."[54] Of the various interpretations, the editorial plural, which would denote more humility than "I" seems to be the best explanation.

Nebuchadnezzar is addressed as "king of kings," which position of power Daniel assigns as a gift from "the God of heaven"; and therefore his kingdom is one of power, strength, and glory. Critics have seized upon this as not a suitable reference to the king of Babylon. Young points out that there is not sufficient evidence to support such a criticism, especially in view of the fact that the inscription of the Persian king Ariyaramna (610-580 B.C.) is called "king of kings."[55] Although there is no clear evidence how such a king as Nebuchadnezzar would be addressed by his subject, there is no contrary evidence that such a title would not be fitting. As a matter of fact, it was quite accurate, for Nebuchadnezzar was actually a supreme monarch who was above all the kings of his generation. Interestingly, Ezekiel gives exactly the same title to Nebuchadnezzar in Ezekiel 26:7.

More significant than Daniel's description of supreme authority to Nebuchadnezzar is his fearless declaration that Nebuchadnezzar owes all his power to the God of heaven who has revealed this secret to Daniel. How different this is from the subservient respect given by the other wise men. Here is a voice of truth which even Nebuchadnezzar must receive with submission.

Daniel, however, does not deprecate the role of Nebuchadnezzar and goes on in verse 38 to describe his universal rule over "the children of men, the beasts of the field, and the fowls of the heaven." He summarizes it: God "hath made thee ruler over them all. Thou art this head of gold." Some have regarded this as hyperbole in that Nebuchadnezzar actually did not control the entire earth's surface and the men, beasts, and fowls of the entire earth. What is obviously meant, however, is that he is in supreme authority insofar as any man could be.

Heaton, following the suggestion of Bentzen, considers the reference to Nebuchadnezzar's authority over both men and nature to be a reflection of the Babylonian New Year Festival. Heaton states, "The sweeping terms in which his sovereignty over men and all living creatures is described in vv. 37 f. may well reflect elements of the Babylonian New Year festival, when the reigning king was annually enthroned as the earthly representative of the god and the Epic of Creation was recited. . . . Nebuchadnezzar's dominion over the beasts of the field and the fowls of the heaven recalls the God-given status of man as it is depicted in Gen. 1.26, which is itself closely related to the Babylonian Epic of Creation."[56] At one fixed element in the ceremonies, they recited the Epic of Creation in honor of the creator god, Marduk, whose representative the king was supposed to be. This and other references in the book of Daniel suggest that Daniel is the author, for the writer had a good knowledge of Babylonian and related mythologies stemming from his three years of study and other intimate contact with Babylonian life.

The identification of the head of gold with Nebuchadnezzar is a reference to the empire as personified in its ruler. As Young points out, critics have had a field day in attempting to explain this expression, but there is no solid reason for not taking it in its simplest sense, that is, that the reference is to the king as the symbol of the empire.[57]

THE INTERPRETATION: THE SECOND AND THIRD KINGDOM TO FOLLOW

2:39 And after thee shall arise another kingdom inferior to thee, and another third kingdom of brass, which shall bear rule over all the earth.

Daniel mentions only in the briefest way the second and the third kingdoms represented by the upper and lower parts of the body. Brief as is the reference, critics have lost no time in taking exception to the normal interpretation that Daniel has in view here of Medo-Persia and Greece, empires which he later identifies by name (5:28; 8:20-21; 11:2). The statement that the second kingdom is "inferior" means inferior in quality but not necessarily in every respect.

Persia actually had more territory than ancient Babylon, and the Greek Empire was greater than the Persian. The Roman Empire was greatest of all in extent. To infer, however, from the larger geographic area of succeeding kingdoms that they were not "inferior" is to misread both the meaning of the dream and Daniel's comment upon it. Daniel did not say that the head was larger in size than the body; but the nature of the metal, gold, was more precious than that of silver or brass, which were obviously inferior metals. History certainly confirms that the Medo-Persian Empire, and the empire of Alexander which followed, lacked the central authority and fine organization which characterized the Babylonian Empire. The image and Daniel's comment upon it is most accurate. Daniel himself seems to imply that the inferiority of the succeeding empires does not prevent them from wide geographic control, for he specifically states that the "third kingdom" will "bear rule over all the earth."

The descending scale of value of the four metals suggests the degeneration of the human race through the ages, as implied in Genesis 4. Classical writers, such as Hesiod (*Works and Days*, 109-201), and Ovid (*Metamorphoses* I, 89-150), conceive of history in this way. This concept contradicts the evolutionist's interpretation of human history. Instead of man beginning in the dust and consummating in fine gold, God reveals man in the times of the Gentiles to begin with fine gold and end in dust.

The descending value of the metals, however, permits their ascending strength, which suggests increased military might during the times of the Gentiles, leading to the final world conflict of Revelation 16 and 19 to which Daniel refers (11:36-45).

The attempt to divide the second and third kingdom as if the second kingdom is that of the Medes and the third kingdom that of the Persians followed by the fourth empire identified as Greece, which Farrar supports so enthusiastically,[58] is obviously motivated by the desire to reduce the prophetic element to a minimum. Even a spurious Daniel living in the second century, according to these critics, could not have predicted accurately a future Roman Empire, but he could have reported on the Babylonian, Median, and Grecian empires.

Critics do not take into consideration that Rome already had taken the western Mediterranean and subdued Greece and parts of western Asia. While they might be expected to claim that a writer in the second century B.C. might have guessed that Rome was the fourth empire, they are unwilling to admit that even a spurious Daniel writing in the second century could refer to the Roman Empire, for it is obvious that apart from prophetic insight he could not have predicted the extent of the empire and its fall in the way Daniel prophesies. They prefer to hold that the four empires are Babylon, the Medes, the Persians, and the Grecian Empires, and that all of what Daniel "predicted" was actually already history by the Maccabean period. As Leupold points out, Robert Dick Wilson in his discussions on the Medo-Persian kings has refuted the concept that the Medes and Persians are the second and third empires.[59]

In substantiating the identification of the four empires normally accepted by conservative scholars, R. D. Wilson points out that the supposed "confusion" in the mind of Daniel regarding his facts (presumably supporting the theory of a second century B.C. Daniel) is in the mind of the critics, not in the book of Daniel.* In brief, Wilson points out that the critics do not have sufficient evidence to support their objections to the data supplied by Daniel. Most of their problems assume Daniel must be wrong. A similar objection to the account of the fall of Babylon as recorded by Daniel has the same answer. The objections are on the basis of unproved assumptions on the part of critics. Remaining problems arise from insufficient records, not from express contradictions.

Wilson discusses many minor criticisms where critics have attacked the accuracy of Daniel. Frequently it arises from erroneous interpretation, such as criticism of Daniel's description of the four-winged and four-headed beast of Daniel 7:6 as not being an accurate picture of Persia. Conservative scholars do not refer it to Persia but to Greece where it fits the facts of history precisely. The alleged confusion of Xerxes and Darius Hystaspis arises from the same faulty identification of the third beast with Persia.[60] The basic difficulty is that the critics cannot admit that the fourth kingdom is Rome without attributing genuine prophecy even to a second-century B.C. Daniel. As Wilson patiently points out again and again, the main problem is not with Daniel but with the critics' interpretation of Daniel. Many problems disappear when the correct evaluation of Daniel as prophecy rather than pseudo-prophecy is recognized. The revelation of chapter 2 does not give sufficient detail to identify the kingdoms completely; but when this revelation is coupled with that of chapters 7-8, the identification becomes clear and unmistakable.

*Wilson comments, "When one asserts that the author of Daniel has 'confused' events or persons, it is not enough for him to affirm that the author was thus confused. This confusion is a matter of evidence. With all due deference to the *opinion* of other scholars, I am firmly convinced that no man to-day has sufficient evidence to prove that the author of Daniel was confused. There are no records to substantiate the assertions of confusion" (Wilson, p. 128). Wilson then deals with the major criticisms of the critics. The most important of these concerns Darius the Mede (Dan 5:31). For further discussion of this problem see the introduction of chapter 6.

Daniel does not make any comment on the symbolic meaning of the breast which would contain the heart or of the lower part of the body containing the abdomen. It is probably reading too much into the Scriptures to infer from this that Cyrus, the Persian, was a noble man with some compassion for Israel and to conclude, according to oriental custom, that this is supported by the fact that the abdomen is considered the seat of affection. More important and significant is the fact that the third empire ends with the upper part of the legs, or the thighs, indicating that the third empire would *territorially* embrace both East and West. This will be quite significant in analysis of the next world empire, unnamed in Daniel, but obviously Rome.

INTERPRETATION: THE FOURTH EMPIRE, ROME

2:40-45 And the fourth kingdom shall be strong as iron: forasmuch as iron breaketh in pieces and subdueth all things: and as iron that breaketh all these, shall it break in pieces and bruise. And whereas thou sawest the feet and toes, part of potters' clay, and part of iron, the kingdom shall be divided; but there shall be in it of the strength of the iron, forasmuch as thou sawest the iron mixed with miry clay. And as the toes of the feet were part of iron, and part of clay, so the kingdom shall be partly strong, and partly broken. And whereas thou sawest iron mixed with miry clay, they shall mingle themselves with the seed of men: but they shall not cleave one to another, even as iron is not mixed with clay. And in the days of these kings shall the God of heaven set up a kingdom, which shall never be destroyed: and the kingdom shall not be left to other people, but it shall break in pieces and consume all these kingdoms, and it shall stand for ever. Forasmuch as thou sawest that the stone was cut out of the mountain without hands, and that it brake in pieces the iron, the brass, the clay, the silver, and the gold; the great God hath made known to the king what shall come to pass hereafter: and the dream is certain, and the interpretation thereof sure.

The fourth kingdom in Nebuchadnezzar's dream represented by the legs and feet of the image is obviously the most important. Daniel gives more attention to this fourth kingdom than to the preceding kingdoms put together. Because various schools of prophetic interpretation have differed more on the fourth kingdom than on the three preceding kingdoms, it is necessary to give particular attention to what Daniel actually says.

The first aspect of interpretation of the fourth kingdom stresses the strength of the iron legs and their power to break in pieces and subdue all that opposes. This, of course, was precisely what characterized ancient Rome. As Leupold states it, "The Roman legions were noted for their ability to crush all resistance with an iron heel. There is apparently little that is constructive in the program of this empire in spite of Roman law and Roman roads and civilization because the destructive work out-weighed all else, for we have the double verb 'crush and demolish ["break in pieces and bruise," AV].' "⁶¹

The description of Rome is so apt in verse 40 that most conservative commentaries agree that it represents the Roman Empire. Critics who accept the late date for Daniel and who proceed on the principle that prophecy of the future in detail is impossible offer a discordant note, as previously indicated, and identify the four kingdoms as Babylon, Media, Persia, and the Alexandrian kingdom. By this means they escape the admission that even a second century date for Daniel would involve considerable prophecy of the future. Those who acknowledge Daniel as a sixth century writing by the prophet Daniel, having already accepted the concept of the validity of predictive prophecy, have no real difficulty in accepting the fourth kingdom as that of Rome. Even with this agreement, however, there is serious disagreement on the identification of the feet of the image and the destruction of the whole by the stone cut out without hands.

Because of difference even among orthodox commentaries on the meaning of the feet of the image, it is all the more significant that Daniel gives special attention to this, and in fact, says as much about the feet of the image as he does about the whole image above the feet.

Daniel dwells at length upon the fact that the feet and the toes are part of potters' clay and part of iron. On the basis of this, Daniel observes, "The kingdom shall be divided." There has been much discussion on the meaning of the word *divided*. Young feels that this is simply a reference to composite material.⁶² Here it seems that too much is being made of too little. What Daniel implies is simply that the material which forms the feet portion of the image is not all one kind but is composed of iron and pottery, which do not adhere well one to the other. This is what Daniel himself brings out in subsequent explanation.

The presence of the iron in the feet, however, is an element of strength as Daniel states, "but there shall be in it of the strength of the iron." The clay is obviously not still in its soft state but has been hardened into tile as Montgomery holds.⁶³ Montgomery comments on *clay*, as follows: "The one stumbling-block in the description of this fine work of artifice is the word translated 'clay.' The word (*ḥasap*) which appears with phonetic modifications in all Sem. stocks exc. Heb., invariably means a formed pottery object, whether a complete vessel or its fragments, *i.e.*, potsherds. And so the ancient VSS universally render the word."⁶⁴

Montgomery goes on to explain that an entirely different word is used for raw clay. On the use of the tile in Babylon, he continues, "There is no question about the use of tile work in ancient Babylonian architecture;

we have the terracotta reliefs in Greek art, the tiling of Saracenic art, while the tile-covered towers of modern Persia are witness to this ancient mode of construction."[65] The intrusion of tile in an essentially metal construction, while perhaps decorative, has the symbolic meaning of weakness. Keil expresses it, "As the iron denotes the firmness of the kingdom, so the clay denotes its brittleness. The mixing of iron with clay represents the attempt to bind the two distinct and separate materials into one combined whole as fruitless, and altogether in vain."[66] This weakness extends to both feet of the image; and, accordingly, the division indicating that the kingdom was divided is not only reflected in the division of the two legs and feet but in the further subdivisions of the feet into toes, where the weakness of the iron and clay mixture becomes more evident.

This is brought out in verse 42 where the toes expressly are said to be part of iron and part of clay which Daniel interprets as indicating that the kingdom is partly strong, because of the presence of iron, and partly breakable, because of the brittleness of the pottery. Daniel's description of the image and the dream has been quite sparing of words and is a masterpiece of condensation. In describing the feet, however, he goes over the same point several times to the extent that critics have called this redundant. Montgomery, for instance, states, "As in v. 40, so here is an unnecessary repetition of phrases, and to a greater extent. . . . Jahn and Lohr have noticed this insipid repetitiousness. . . . With these critics the writer agrees as to v. 42."[67] This is hardly fair to Daniel, as any repetition in this passage is obviously for greater understanding and emphasis.

A clear interpretation of the meaning of iron and clay, apart from the inherent weakness, is not given except as indicated in verse 43. Here the statement is made that the mingling of the two materials means that "they shall mingle themselves with the seed of men: but they shall not cleave one to another, even as iron is not mixed with clay." Because this description is not entirely clear, it has given commentators a good deal of latitude in using their imagination. As Keil points out, "The mixing of themselves with the seed of men (ver. 43), most interpreters refer to the marriage politics of the princes." Keil refutes the many explanations arising from this principle of intermarriage.[68]

Another common interpretation of the meaning of the mixture of clay and iron is that it refers to diverse forms of government, such as democracy as opposed to dictatorship. H. A. Ironside, for instance, defines it as "speaking of an attempted union between imperialism and democracy."[69]

A. C. Gaebelein has a similar interpretation, "But what does the clay represent? Clay is of the earth. It stands for that which does not belong to the great statue at all, a foreign ingredient brought in. The metals represent monarchies, but the clay stands for democratic rule, the rule by the people."[70]

In view of the fact that the text actually does not tell us, probably the safest procedure is to follow the argument of Keil and gain the interpretation from the meaning of the metals in the three preceding kingdoms. Keil accordingly writes, "As, in the three preceding kingdoms, gold, silver, and brass represent the material of these kingdoms, *i.e.* their peoples and their culture, so also in the fourth kingdom iron and clay represent the material of the kingdoms arising out of the division of this kingdom, *i.e.* the national elements out of which they are constituted, and which will and must mingle together in them."[71] While intermarriage may form an element of it, it is not necessarily the main idea. Keil concludes, "The figure of mixing by seed is derived from the sowing of the field with mingled seed, and denotes all the means employed by the rulers to combine the different nationalities, among which the *connubium* [intermarriage] is only spoken of as the most important and successful means."[72] The final form of the kingdom will include diverse elements whether this refers to race, political idealism, or sectional interests; and this will prevent the final form of the kingdom from having a real unity. This is, of course, borne out by the fact that the world empire at the end of the age breaks up into a gigantic civil war in which forces from the south, east, and north contend with the ruler of the Mediterranean for supremacy, as Daniel himself portrays in Daniel 11:36-45.

An important aspect of the fourth kingdom which is portrayed in the two legs is often overlooked by expositors, partly because of difficulty of fitting it into history precisely and partly because some do not feel that this aspect has a particular meaning. Because of the problem some have questioned whether the fourth empire is really Rome after all. The dilemma of the interpreter is illustrated in the comment of Geoffrey R. King, who claims the first three kingdoms or empires "proved by history"[73] but finds it difficult to trace this proof of the fourth empire. King writes,

> This is where I find I have to join issue with the commonly accepted interpretation. I have heard it said more than once or twice that the two legs of the image represent the Roman Empire, because in A.D. 364 the Roman Empire split into two. There was the Eastern Empire, with its capital at Constantinople and the Western Empire, with its capital at Rome. *Two* legs, you see. All right. But wait a minute! To begin with, the division occurs before you get to the iron! The two legs begin under the copper, unless this image was a freak. Nebuchadnezzar knew nothing about our modern sculptury, futuristic and grotesque, where a man's legs may begin and end anywhere! But this was a plain, straightforward, honest-to-goodness figure with his feet in the right place! So you see, you cannot do anything with these two legs. After all it is a man and a

man cannot help having two legs anymore than he can help having two arms. Why don't they make something of the two arms of silver? I don't think there is any significance in the two legs at all. And, of course, if you want to make two parts of the Roman Empire to be represented by the two legs, you are in difficulty because the Western Empire only lasted for a few hundred years, but the Eastern Empire lasted until 1453. You have to make this image stand on one leg for most of the time!"[74]

King goes on to question the interpretation that the feet portion of the image is the revived Roman Empire of the future and concludes, "But now, having come to study it carefully, I wash my hands of the whole of it."[75] King then identifies the foot stage of the image as being Muslim governments we know today and identifies the Antichrist as a Muslim.[76]

Robert Culver offers still another approach to this difficult problem of interpretation by holding that the image as a whole indicates *"a continuous succession," "a progressive division,"* and *"a progressive deterioration"* of Gentile sovereignty.[77] Culver sees growing division in the image beginning with the head of gold or a single ruler, then the dualism of the Medo-Persian Empire, then the fourfold division of Alexander's Empire, then the leg stage of the image ending in further division into ten toes.[78] While Culver's analysis has much to commend itself, as far as the image is concerned, it does not reflect the fourfold division of Alexander's kingdom. Instead, the last portion of the third empire is the upper portion of the two legs, fulfilled in history by the eventual emergence of Syria and Egypt as the two main components of the Alexandrian period (although Macedonia at times was also powerful). Actually there is no indication of diversity of sovereignty apart from the two arms and the two legs until the feet stage is reached.

Probably the best solution to the problem is the familiar teaching that Daniel's prophecy actually passes over the present age, the period between the first and second coming of Christ or, more specifically, the period between Pentecost and the rapture of the church. There is nothing unusual about such a solution, as Old Testament prophecies often lump together predictions concerning the first and second coming of Christ without regard for the millennia that lay between (Lk 4:17-19; cf. Is 61:1-2).

This interpretation depends first of all upon the evidence leading to the conclusion that the ten-toe stage of the image has not been fulfilled in history and is still prophetic. The familiar attempts in many commentaries to find a ten-toe stage of the image in the fifth and sixth centuries A.D. do not correspond to the actual facts of history and do not fulfill the ten-toe stage. According to Daniel's prophecy, the ten-toe stage is simultaneous, that is, the kingdoms existed side by side and were destroyed by one sudden catastrophic blow. Nothing like this has yet occurred in history.

If the leg stage of the image has been fulfilled in history, it obviously does not correspond to the period of more than a thousand years stretching from the time of Christ to when the Roman Empire finally gasped its last. As King has rightly pointed out, during most of this period it would have had to stand upon one leg.

The solution, therefore, is a simple and yet effective means of understanding this image. The upper part of the legs represented the twofold stage of the last period of the Alexandrian Empire, which especially concerned the Jews, namely, Syria and Egypt. This was two-legged because it embraced two continents, or two major geographic areas, the East and the West. The Roman Empire continued this twofold division and extended its sway over the entire Mediterranean area as well as western Asia.

In ordinary history Egypt was usually grouped with Syria as belonging to the East because of the long relationship politically and commercially which tied Egypt to western Asia. By contrast Macedonia in Europe was considered the West. From the divine viewpoint and especially the prophetic outlook which is symbolized in the image of Daniel, both Egypt on the continent of Africa as well as the European nations, including Macedonia, could well be considered the Western division, which eventually expanded to include the whole Mediterranean area west of Asia. The image portrays the divine viewpoint, which anticipated the rise of the Roman Empire and its geographic inclusion of the East and the West. This was recognized ultimately in the political division of the East and West by Emperor Valentinian I in A.D. 364. Although Daniel does not deal with the interadvent age as such, it still is true that at the time of the first advent of Christ Rome already was geographically spread over the East and the West. Prophetically it indicates that at the time of the end Rome again will involve both the East and the West.

The meaning of the two legs, therefore, is geographic rather than a matter of nationalities. A comparison of the extension of the various empires will reveal that the Babylonian Empire and the Medo-Persian Empire extended principally over western Asia, although Egypt was also conquered. In the Alexandrian Empire, the Western division began to take real form and power was divided between Syria and Egypt. The Roman Empire embraced a much wider territory in which the Western division became fully as strong as the Eastern, and this seems to be portrayed by the two legs.

This political and geographic situation continued to the time of Christ; and if Daniel's vision ended here only to pick up the situation again at the end of the age, it would be understandable that the two legs would be seen as equal. The feet portion of the image representing the final stage will also include on an equal basis the Eastern and Western areas once possessed by ancient Rome. In view of the fact that there is nothing whatever in the image of Daniel to portray events from the time of Christ to the present time, if the feet stage be considered future, this interpretation makes sense out of a symbol which must at least in its major elements correspond to the facts of history.

The crux of the interpretation of the entire symbolic vision is found in the prediction of a kingdom which the God of heaven will set up. According to verse 44, this is a kingdom which will never be destroyed, will never be left to other people, shall destroy and break in pieces the preceding kingdom, and will stand forever. There is general agreement among all classes of expositors that the kingdom which shall not be destroyed is indeed the kingdom of God. Having agreed on this important point, however, expositors are widely divided concerning the nature of the kingdom, the nature of the destruction of the preceding empires, and the time element which is provided.

In general, expositors may be divided into premillennial and amillennial interpretation, with the postmillennial view being included as a variation of amillennialism. According to both amillenarians and some postmillenarians, the kingdom of God which is here mentioned is that which was introduced by Christ at His first coming. This, of course, presupposes the destruction of the image by the church in succeeding centuries. This view is confidently offered as if it were supported by history. Leupold, for instance, while conceding that there were many factors in the destruction of Rome, states, "All students of history are ready to grant that the Christian Church was able to salvage out of the wreckage of the Roman Empire all elements that were worth conserving. But it is just as true that the Christian Church broke the power of pagan Rome. The disintegrating and corrupt empire crumbled through decay from within as well as through the impact of the sound morals and the healthy life of Christianity that condemned lascivious Rome. . . . Christianity was in a sense God's judgment upon sinful Rome."[79]

The principal difficulty is that as a matter of fact Christianity was not the decisive force that broke the Roman Empire. The main reason was its internal decay and the political conditions which surrounded it. Further, the decay of the Roman Empire extended for more than a thousand years after the first coming of Christ. In other words, the time factor was greater than the period from Nebuchadnezzar to Christ. To have such a long period of time described in the symbolism of a stone striking the feet of the image and the chaff being swept away by wind simply does not correspond to the facts of history. In view of the very accurate portrayal of preceding history by the image, it is a reasonable and natural conclusion that the feet stage of the image including destruction by the stone is still future and unfulfilled. There is certainly no evidence, nineteen hundred years after Christ, that the kingdom of God has conquered the entire world.

Not only is there no scriptural evidence whatever that the first coming of Christ caused the downfall of Gentile world power which is still very much with us today, but express prophecies relating to the second advent of Christ picture just such a devastating defeat of Gentile power. Revelation 19:11-21, which all agree is a picture of the second coming of Christ, is expressly the time when Jesus Christ assumes command as King of kings and Lord of lords. It is declared that at that time "He should smite the nations: and he shall rule them with a rod of iron" (Rev 19:15). If it were not necessary to make Daniel's image conform somehow to the amillennial and postmillennial concept of the gradual conquering of the world by the gospel, no one would ever have dreamed that the smiting by the stone of Nebuchadnezzar's dream described a long process now more than nineteen hundred years underway and still far from completion.

Young states extensively some of his objections to considering the destruction of the image as being fulfilled at the second coming of Christ. He objects that this interpretation "makes too much of the symbolism."[80] He objects that Daniel 2 does not state that there are ten toes on the image although he admits that Daniel 7:24-27 speaks of ten kings as being the last stage of Gentile power. He further holds that the image is smitten on the feet, not on the toes.[81] Such minor criticisms, of course, are irrelevant to the main question, because the feet and the toes are obviously all part of the same period. The fact is that his interpretation does not give any reasonable explanation of the catastrophic character of the stone smiting the image.

The only rule on which prophetic interpretation can be judged is whether the interpretation corresponds to the fulfillment. Nothing is more evident after nineteen hundred years of Christianity than that the stone, if it reflects the church or the spiritual kingdom which Christ formed at His first coming, is not in any sense of the term occupying the center of the stage in which Gentile power has been destroyed. As a matter of fact, in the twentieth century the church has been an ebbing tide in the affairs of the world; and there has been no progress whatever in the church's gaining control of the world politically. If the image represents the political power of the Gentiles, it is very much still standing.

Accordingly, the interpretation is much preferred that the expression "in the days of these kings" refers to the kings who rule during the last generation of Gentile power. While it is true that this is not specifically related to the toes of the image, in the nature of the case the destruction will come for the last generation of rulers. Inasmuch as other passages speak specifically of ten kings in the end times (Dan 7:24; Rev 17:12), it is not unreasonable to hold that this is a reference to the final state of the kingdom and the final rulers.

The description of the stone as being cut out "of the mountain without hands" has sometimes been referred to Mount Zion specifically, but it is better to consider this as a symbolic picture of political sovereignty. The stone is part and parcel of the sovereignty of God of which it is an effective expression. The symbolism clearly makes this originate in God rather than in men. The effect is that the fifth kingdom, the kingdom of God, replaces completely all vestiges of the preceding kingdoms, which prophecy can only be fulfilled in any literal sense by a reign of Christ over the earth. The fact is that the amillennial interpretation, attempting to find fulfillment of the destruction of the image in history, does not provide a reasonable explanation of this passage. Only the premillennial position, which assigns this event as coinciding with the second advent of Christ, gives literal fulfillment to the symbolism involved in the destruction of the image.

In concluding his interpretation, Daniel reaffirms the absolute certainty of the fulfillment of the dream, stating again that its interpretation comes from God, that the dream is certain, and the interpretation thereof sure. Taken as a whole, it assures the ultimate rule of God over the earth to be fulfilled, not only in the millennial kingdom but in the continued display of the sovereignty of God in the new heaven and the new earth.

Nebuchadnezzar Worships and Promotes Daniel

2:46-49 Then the king Nebuchadnezzar fell upon his face, and worshipped Daniel, and commanded that they should offer an oblation and sweet odours unto him. The king answered unto Daniel, and said, Of a truth it is, that your God is a God of gods, and a Lord of kings, and a revealer of secrets, seeing thou couldest reveal this secret. Then the king made Daniel a great man, and gave him many great gifts, and made him ruler over the whole province of Babylon, and chief of the governors over all the wise men of Babylon. Then Daniel requested of the king, and he set Shadrach, Meshach, and Abed-nego, over the affairs of the province of Babylon: but Daniel sat in the gate of the king.

Nebuchadnezzar, overwhelmed by the tremendous significance of the image and the demonstration that Daniel's God was greater than any god whom he worshiped, fell upon his face and worshiped Daniel, commanding an oblation and sweet odors be offered to him. Critics have lost no time criticizing Daniel for accepting this as equating him with deity. It is quite clear, however, from the resulting conversation of the king with Daniel, that Nebuchadnezzar merely regarded Daniel as a worthy priest or representative of his God and was honoring him in this category. This is brought out in the king's statement to Daniel, "Of a truth it is, that your God is a God of gods, and a Lord of kings, and a revealer of secrets, seeing thou couldest reveal this secret." In other words, even the king understood that Daniel was the ambassador and representative of God but not deity himself. It is probably for this reason that Daniel permitted the king to do what he did. In any case, it hardly would have been proper for Daniel under these circumstances to have interrupted the king with a protest.

An interesting parallel is found in Josephus, recording the instance where Alexander the Great bowed before the high priest of the Jews. When Parmenion, one of his generals, asked him why, when ordinarily all men would prostrate themselves before Alexander the Great, he had prostrated himself before the high priest of the Jews, Alexander replied, "It was not before him that I prostrated myself, but the God of whom he has the honour to be high priest."[82] In view of the previous statements of Daniel repeated several times and Nebuchadnezzar's own statement of verse 47, the record leaves no doubt that Daniel was not claiming deity or any of the powers of deity. It is clear that Nebuchadnezzar did not worship Daniel again.

In the process of offering worship to Daniel's God, Nebuchadnezzar actually pays a great tribute to the God of Daniel. It is most significant that he does not even mention his own gods which had failed to produce a suitable revelation, except in the statement that Daniel's God is "a God of gods," that is, Daniel's God is supreme over any other gods commonly worshiped in a polytheistic system. Although Nebuchadnezzar was short of true faith in Daniel's God at this point in his life, the evidence that Daniel's God could reveal a secret and may indeed have been the author of his dream impressed Nebuchadnezzar with the fact that no other god could be greater.

In keeping with the king's desire to honor Daniel and also according to his promise, Daniel is now exalted and immediately becomes a great man. Many valuable gifts are given to him, and he is installed in the exalted position of ruler over the whole province of Babylon as well as chief of the governors over the wise men. Although critics reprobate this position as objectionable for a Jew, no doubt Daniel found a way to avoid involvement in the usual practices of divination, heathen rites, and other things that might normally fall to this office. As Young points out, however, if Daniel had lived in the second century during a period of strict legalism among the Jews, it would be doubtful that Daniel would have been pictured as receiving such honors from a heathen king.[83]

Having been thus signally honored by the king, Daniel, in fairness to his three companions who had joined him in prayer that the secret might be revealed, requested that they too might have a position of power and influence in the province of Babylon. Apparently, although Daniel had great authority, it did not include appointing such officials without the king's permission. Granting Daniel's request, the king appointed Shadrach, Meshach, and Abed-nego to positions of trust in the government of the province of Babylon. Daniel himself apparently had a position of honor "in the gate of the king," by which is meant that he served in the court itself. Thus Daniel, the obscure Jewish captive who could have been lost to history like many others if he had compromised in chapter 1, is now exalted to a place of great honor and power. Like Joseph in Egypt, he was destined to play an important part in the subsequent history of his generation.

3

THE GOLDEN IMAGE OF
NEBUCHADNEZZAR

THE ACCOUNT OF THE GOLDEN IMAGE which was erected on the plain of
Dura records Nebuchadnezzar's reaction to the revelation of chapter 2
in which he was symbolized by the head of gold. The astounding courage
and deliverance of Daniel's companions, who refused to worship the
image, has inspired the people of God in similar times of trial. The chapter as a whole, however, is often regarded as merely providing historical
insight into the characteristics of this period. Works devoted to study of
the prophecies of Daniel often omit consideration of chapter 3 entirely
as do S. P. Tregelles[1] and Robert D. Culver.[2] Others, such as Geoffrey R.
King, interpret the chapter as not only history but parable and prophecy.[3]
The introduction of the golden image of Nebuchadnezzar in chapter 3
immediately following Nebuchadnezzar's dream of the great image
depicting Gentile times, even if its parabolic implications are ignored,
obviously is intended to convey not only spiritual truth in general, but
characteristics of the times of the Gentiles. Its study, accordingly, not
only provides spiritual insights but contributes to the overall presentation
of prophecy in Daniel.

THE IMAGE OF GOLD

3:1-7 Nebuchadnezzar the king made an image of gold, whose height
was threescore cubits, and the breadth thereof six cubits: he set it up in
the plain of Dura, in the province of Babylon. Then Nebuchadnezzar the
king sent to gather together the princes, the governors, and the captains,
the judges, the treasurers, the counsellors, the sheriffs, and all the rulers
of the provinces, to come to the dedication of the image which Nebuchadnezzar the king had set up. Then the princes, the governors, and
captains, the judges, the treasurers, the counsellors, the sheriffs, and all
the rulers of the provinces, were gathered together unto the dedication
of the image that Nebuchadnezzar the king had set up; and they stood
before the image that Nebuchadnezzar had set up. Then an herald cried
aloud, To you it is commanded, O people, nations, and languages, that
at what time ye hear the sound of the cornet, flute, harp, sackbut,
psaltery, dulcimer, and all kinds of musick, ye fall down and worship

the golden image that Nebuchadnezzar the king hath set up: And whoso falleth not down and worshippeth shall the same hour be cast into the midst of a burning fiery furnace. Therefore at that time, when all the people heard the sound of the cornet, flute, harp, sackbut, psaltery, and all kinds of musick, all the people, the nations, and the languages, fell down and worshipped the golden image that Nebuchadnezzar the king had set up.

The erection of the golden image by Nebuchadnezzar is clearly subsequent to the events of chapter 2 since Daniel 3:12, referring to the appointment of Daniel's companions over the affairs of the province of Babylon, and Daniel 3:30 imply that the event was subsequent to Daniel 2:49. The exact date of the erection of the image, however, is debated. The Septuagint and Theodotion connect the event with the destruction of Jerusalem, which, according to 2 Kings 25:8-10 and Jeremiah 52:12, places this event in the nineteenth year of Nebuchadnezzar. There is no certainty, however, that there is a relationship between the destruction of Jerusalem and the erection of the image, although the general narrative and the fact that Daniel apparently is away would imply considerable passage of time. It may well be, however, that twenty years elapsed between chapter 2 and chapter 3.[4]

The image of gold is described as being sixty cubits (90 ft.) high and six cubits (9 ft.) broad, a very impressive sight erected in the plain of Dura. The Hebrew word for *image* implies, as Leupold says, "An image in the very broadest sense," probably in human form although the proportions are far too narrow for a normal figure.[5] Scripture does not solve this problem, but most commentators agree that images of this kind in antiquity frequently varied from ordinary human proportions. The image may have been on a pedestal with only the upper part of the image resembling human form. The obvious intent was to impress by the size of the image rather than by its particular features. Leupold cites numerous ancient images such as that of Zeus in a temple at Babylon; the golden images on the top of the Belus temple, one of which was forty cubits high; and the Colossus at Rhodes which was seventy cubits high.[6] While an image of this size was unusual, it was by no means unique; and there is no reason to question the historical accuracy of its dimensions.

Although Nebuchadnezzar had tremendous wealth and could conceivably have erected this image of solid gold, it is probable that it was made of wood overlaid with gold as was customary. Montgomery observes, "Its construction of gold has also given rise to extensive argument, with charge of absurdity on one side, *e. g.*, JDMich [J. D. Michaelis], with defence based on the fabulous riches of the East on the other. But Herodotus' statements about the golden idols in Babylon afford sufficient background. (*Cf.* Pliny's account of an all-gold image of Anaitis, which was looted by

Antony, *Hist. nat.*, xxxiii, 24.) The gold consisted in overlaid plates, for which we possess not only abundant Classical evidence . . . but also that of the Bible."[7] The "golden altar" (Ex 39:38) was actually wood overlaid with gold (Ex 37:25-26). Idols overlaid with gold are mentioned in Isaiah 40:19 and Isaiah 41:7. Jeremiah describes the same process (Jer 10:3-9). The appearance of the image, however, was much the same as if it were solid gold.

The use of the golden metal for the image may have been derived from Nebuchadnezzar's previous experience with the image of chapter 2 where Daniel informed him that he, Nebuchadnezzar, was the head of gold. Although Nebuchadnezzar did not do this intentionally, the dimensions of six cubits wide and sixty cubits high introduces the number six which is prominent in the Bible as the number of man (cf. Rev 13:18). The intended significance of the image from Nebuchadnezzar's point of view is, however, debatable. It may have been in honor of the god of Babylon, either Bel or Marduk, but in this case it would have been natural to mention the name of the god. Nebuchadnezzar may have regarded the image as representing himself as the embodiment of divine power, and the worship of the image would then be a recognition of his personal power. In view of his pride as dealt with in chapter 4, this becomes a plausible explanation.

The image was set up "in the plain of Dura, in the province of Babylon." The expression *Dura*, as Leupold states, "is a rather common name in Mesopotamia, being a name that is applicable to any place which is enclosed by a wall," and a number of locations bear this title as Keil points out.[8] Both Keil and Young mention two possible locations which seem to be eliminated by being too far from Babylon. As Young states, "The name Dura has occurred in classical sources; Polybius 5:48, Amm. Mar. 23:5, 8; 24:1, 5 mention a Dura at the mouth of the Chaboras where it empties into the Euphrates, but this can hardly be reckoned as being in the province of Babylon, and another Dura is mentioned as being beyond the Tigris not far from Appollonia, Polybius 5:52 and Amm. Mar. 25:6, 9. This also would be too distant."[9]

The consensus of conservative scholarship is that the most probable location is a mound located six miles southeast of Babylon consisting of a large square of brick construction which would have ideally served as a base for such an image as Nebuchadnezzar erected. Montgomery earlier had come to the same conclusion based on the findings of Oppert.[*] Its proximity to Babylon would make it convenient and yet its location in a

---

[*]Montgomery cites Oppert, *Expédition scientifique en Mésopotamie*, 1:238 ff., expressing the belief "that a massive square of brick construction found *in situ*, 14 metres square by 6 high, is the pedestal of Neb.'s image" (Montgomery, p. 197).

valley plain would make its height impressive. The fact that a specific name is given to the location, which implies an intimate knowledge of Babylon in the sixth century B.C., as Young points out, "is in reality an evidence of genuineness in that it seems to presuppose some knowledge of Babylonian geography."[10]

The image having been erected, Nebuchadnezzar, according to the Scripture record, gathered the principal officials of his empire for its dedication. As there are parallels in similar situations in the ancient world, such as Sargon's feast upon the completion of a palace erected at Dur Sharrukin,[11] scholars, both liberal and conservative, have agreed that this ceremony is in keeping with the times. Such a display of officials was on the one hand a gratifying demonstration of the power of Nebuchadnezzar's empire and on the other hand was significant as recognizing the deities who in their thinking were responsible for their victories. The worship of the image was intended to be an expression of political solidarity and loyalty to Nebuchadnezzar rather than an intended act of religious persecution. It was in effect a saluting of the flag, although, because of the interrelationship of religious with national loyalties, it may also have had religious connotation.

The list of the officials gathered for the event has occasioned comment because some of them are Persian rather than Babylonian terms. The speculation as to why Persian terms should be used is much ado about nothing. It would be natural for Daniel, who may have written or at least edited this passage after the Persian government had come to power, to bring the various offices up-to-date by using current expressions. The fact that Daniel was so familiar with these offices is another evidence that he lived in the sixth century B.C. The official titles used in Daniel 3:2-3 help to date the book in the sixth century and refute the second century date given by the critics. The Septuagint versions (Old Greek and Theodotion)[12] are hopelessly inexact and are merely guesswork in their rendering of *'drgzr*, "counsellor"; *gdbr*, "treasurer"; *dtbr*, "law-officer"; *t(y)pt*, "magistrate, police chief." Kitchen points out,

> If the first important Greek translation of Daniel was made some time within *c.* 100 BC-AD 100, roughly speaking, and the translator could not (or took no trouble to) reproduce the proper meanings of these terms, then one conclusion imposes itself: their meaning was already lost and forgotten or, at least, drastically changed long before he set to work. Now if Daniel (in particular, the Aramaic chapters 2-7) was wholly a product of *c.* 165 BC, then a century or so in a continuous tradition is surely embarrassingly inadequate as a sufficient interval for that loss (or change) of meaning to occur, by Near Eastern standards. Therefore, it is desirable on *this* ground to seek the original of such verses (and hence of the narratives of which they are an integral part) much earlier than

this date, preferably within memory of the Persian rule—i. e. *c.* 539 (max.) to *c.* 280 BC (allowing about fifty years' lapse from the fall of Persia to Macedon).[13]

The exact functions of each office are not given, but seven classes of officials are designated. The official titles and their modern meanings are as follows:

KJV	ARAMAIC (singular form)	MEANING
princes	*'āhashdarpan*	satrap
governors	*s^egan*	prefect
captains	*pehâ*	governor
judges	*'ădargāzar*	counsellor
treasurers	*g^edābar*	treasurer
counsellors	*d^etābar*	law official, judge
sheriffs	*tiptāy*	magistrate

Keil probably gives the best explanation of the various terms. The *princes* are administrators, guardians or watchers, and the chief representatives of the king, corresponding to the Greek expression satrap. The *governors* were commanders or military chiefs. The *captains* seemed to refer to presidents or governors of civil government. The *judges* were counsellors of the government or chief arbitrators. The *treasurers* were superintendents of the public treasury. The *counsellors* were lawyers or guardians of the law. The *sheriffs* were judges in a stricter sense of the term, that is, magistrates who gave a just sentence. The *rulers* were lesser officials who were governors of the provinces subordinate to the chief governor.[14] The list of officers stated in verse 2 is repeated in verse 3 and some of them are repeated in verse 27. They had been summoned by messengers sent by Nebuchadnezzar to participate in this important event.

According to verse 3, they were assembled before the image awaiting the call to universal worship signalled by the cry of the herald. The word for *herald* (*kārôz*), because it closely resembles the Greek word *kērux*, introduces the interesting problem of Greek words in Daniel. Several of the instruments listed in verse 5 also seem to be of Greek origin. This has been claimed as confirmation that Daniel wrote during the period of Greek dominance of Western Asia.

Archer and others have challenged whether these words are actually Greek words, pointing out that *karoz* (*herald*, classified as a Greek word by Brown, Driver, and Briggs *Lexicon*, has in recent works like Koehler-Baumgartner's *Hebrew Lexicon* been traced to the old Persian *khrausa*, meaning "caller."[15]

Conservative biblical scholarship has fully answered the objection of critics which would tend to reflect upon the accuracy and historicity of

the book of Daniel.[16] Robert Dick Wilson, for instance, has pointed out
that the argument actually boomerangs as, if Daniel was written in a
Greek period, there would be many more Greek words than the few that
occur here and there.[17] The fact is that there is nothing strange about
some amount of Greek influence in Babylonian culture in view of the
contacts between them and the Greeks. Greek traders were common in
Egypt and western Asia from the seventh century B.C. onward.[18] The
Greek mercenaries, who served as soldiers for various countries, are found
more than one hundred years before Daniel, as for instance in the Assyrian
army of Esarhaddon (682 B.C.) and even in the Babylonian army of
Nebuchadnezzar.[19] Not only did the Greeks affect the Semitic world but
also influences of Assyria and Babylonia appear in the Greek language as
well.[20]

Recent studies on the musical instruments mentioned in Daniel 3 conducted by T. C. Mitchell and R. Joyce have given support to the authenticity of these instruments in the sixth century B.C.[21] Further studies by
Yamauchi support the conclusion that Greek words in Daniel are not to
be unexpected and in fact refer to the interchange of cultures in the
ancient world.[22]

Not much help is given by attempting to find synonyms for these instruments as actually we do not have any information as to their precise
character. T. C. Mitchell and R. Joyce provide a table for all six instruments with their corresponding translations in nine different translations.
Actually, none of the alternate terms improve much on that which is
provided in Daniel 3:5 and repeated in verses 7, 10, and 15. These instruments probably provided as full an orchestra as could be arranged
in Babylon.

The cornet was obviously a horn instrument, the word coming originally
from the horn of a beast which was sometimes used to make a musical
instrument. The flute was probably made of reeds with a sound similar
to a fife. The harp was some sort of a stringed instrument. The sackbut
may have been a triangular board to which strings were attached. The
psaltery, sometimes also considered a harp, was another stringed instrument with twenty strings. The dulcimer is a wind instrument. To these
were added other instruments described as "all kinds of music."[23]

At the sound of the music, all those gathered were to "fall down and
worship the golden image," that is, they were to fall prostrate to the
ground and do homage. This has been taken by some to prove that the
image was a deity or idol. But Keil and others are probably correct that
they were simply recognizing a symbol of the power of the empire which
included recognition of heathen gods but was not the specific object of
their homage.[24] As Keil puts it, "A refusal to yield homage to the gods of

the kingdom, they regarded as an act of hostility against the kingdom and its monarch, while every one might at the same time honour his own national god. This acknowledgment, that the gods of the kingdom were the more powerful, every heathen could grant; and thus, Nebuchadnezzar demanded nothing in a religious point of view which every one of his subjects could not yield. To him, therefore, the refusal of the Jews could not but appear as opposition to the greatness of his kingdom."[25] There is, therefore, no direct parallel between this and the persecution of Antiochus Epiphanes which liberals cite as the background for this story in Daniel. Antiochus was attempting to destroy the Jewish religion, but this was not Nebuchadnezzar's objective. A fair analysis of the situation in Daniel 3 is that the issue was more political than religious, but it was obnoxious religiously to Daniel's three companions.

The herald made plain that anyone who did not obey the command to fall down and worship would be cast immediately into the burning fiery furnace. Montgomery suggests that the furnace "must have been similar to our common lime-kiln, with a perpendicular shaft from the top and an opening at the bottom for extracting the fused lime; *cf.* illustration of such an Oriental *tannur* or *ṭâbûn* in Benzinger, *Hebr. Archäologie*, 65, and Haupt's description, AJSL 23, 245. Häv. notes Chardin's remarks on the existence of similar ovens in Persia for execution of criminals (*Voyage en Perse*, ed. Langles, 6, c. 18, end, p. 303)."[26] This would explain both the way in which the victims were put into the furnace and the circumstances which permitted the king to see what was happening inside the furnace.[27]

The expression *the same hour* has in it the thought of "immediately" but cannot be pushed to the extent of concluding that the furnace was already burning. The threat of being executed by being burned alive was sufficient to cause the entire group to fall down and worship when the music sounded. Apparently, the only exceptions were the three companions of Daniel. It is useless to speculate how this related to Daniel himself. Either Daniel considered this a political act which did not violate his conscience, or Daniel did not worship and his high office prevented his enemies from accusing him, or more probably, Daniel for some reason was absent. The stage was now set for the trial of the three faithful Jews.

DANIEL'S COMPANIONS ACCUSED BY THE CHALDEANS

3:8-12 Wherefore at that time certain Chaldeans came near, and accused the Jews. They spake and said to the king Nebuchadnezzar, O king, live for ever. Thou, O king, hast made a decree, that every man that shall hear the sound of the cornet, flute, harp, sackbut, psaltery, and dulcimer, and all kinds of musick, shall fall down and worship the golden image: And whoso falleth not down and worshippeth, that he should be cast into the midst of a burning fiery furnace. There are certain Jews whom thou hast set over the affairs of the province of Babylon, Shadrach, Meshach, and Abed-nego; these men, O king, have not regarded thee: they serve not thy gods, nor worship the golden image which thou hast set up.

Although the historic account previously given by Daniel does not include that Shadrach, Meshach, and Abed-nego had not bowed down to the golden image, the Chaldeans, who were the court astrologers, approach the king and bring their accusation. Undoubtedly there was resentment against these Jews who had been placed by Nebuchadnezzar in charge of the province of Babylon because they were of another race and of a captive people. It was quite clear to the Chaldeans also that the Jews did not worship the gods of Babylon and were actually a foreign element in the government. They saw in the fact that the Jews had not worshiped the image an occasion to bring accusation against them. The expression *accused* is a translation of an Aramaic expression common to Semitic languages which literally means, "they ate their pieces," hence, to devour piecemeal. This connotes slander or malicious accusation which devours the accused piece by piece.

The Chaldeans approached the king with the customary courtesies addressing Nebuchadnezzar, "O king, live for ever." They remind the king of the details of his decree and the penalty for disobedience. With the stage thus set for the accusation, the Chaldeans make three charges against Shadrach, Meshach, and Abed-nego. First, they show no regard for the king. Second, they do not serve the gods of the king. Third, they do not worship the golden image which Nebuchadnezzar had set up.

The form of the accusation is almost a rebuke to the king himself. It is clear that the Chaldeans had deep-seated resentment against the Jews and felt the king had made a serious mistake in trusting these foreigners with such high offices. They remind the king that these men are Jews, different in race and culture from the Babylonians. The king had set them over the affairs of the province of Babylon, the most important province in the empire and the key to political security for the entire realm. The personal loyalty of such officers should be beyond question; but, as the Chaldeans point out, Shadrach, Meshach, and Abed-nego had not shown any regard for the king himself.

The second accusation that they do not serve Nebuchadnezzar's gods is more than merely a religious difference. The whole concept of political loyalty, of which the worship of the image was an expression, is bound up in the idea that Nebuchadnezzar's gods have favored him and given him victory. To challenge Nebuchadnezzar's gods, therefore, is to challenge Nebuchadnezzar himself and to raise a question as to the political integrity of the three men accused. As proof of their suspicions, they charge Daniel's three companions with not worshiping the golden image. The arguments were calculated to arouse the anger of Nebuchadnezzar and to bring about the downfall of these three men with the possibility that the Chaldeans themselves might be given greater authority in political affairs.

DANIEL'S COMPANIONS REFUSE TO WORSHIP THE IMAGE

3:13-18 Then Nebuchadnezzar in his rage and fury commanded to bring Shadrach, Meshach, and Abed-nego. Then they brought these men before the king. Nebuchadnezzar spake and said unto them, Is it true, O Shadrach, Meshach, and Abed-nego, do not ye serve my gods, nor worship the golden image which I have set up? Now if ye be ready that at what time ye hear the sound of the cornet, flute, harp, sackbut, psaltery, and dulcimer, and all kinds of musick, ye fall down and worship the image which I have made; well: but if ye worship not, ye shall be cast the same hour into the midst of a burning fiery furnace; and who is that God that shall deliver you out of my hands? Shadrach, Meshach, and Abed-nego, answered and said to the king, O Nebuchadnezzar, we are not careful to answer thee in this matter. If it be so, our God whom we serve is able to deliver us from the burning fiery furnace, and he will deliver us out of thine hand, O king. But if not, be it known unto thee, O king, that we will not serve thy gods, nor worship the golden image which thou hast set up.

The argument and accusation of the Chaldeans had a telling effect upon Nebuchadnezzar, who regarded the disobedience of Shadrach, Meshach, and Abed-nego not only a threat to his political security but also a personal affront. However, in view of the fact that they probably had held their offices for some years and had evidently been efficient in the conduct of their duties, Nebuchadnezzar in spite of his anger gave them a second chance which lesser men might not have been offered. Highly enraged, he commanded to bring the men before him. He asked them two questions: first, "Do not ye serve my gods?" and second, "Do not ye . . . worship the golden image which I have set up?" The fact that he distinguished between serving his gods and worshiping the image, though they are interrelated, seems to confirm the idea that the worship is primarily political, although the fact that they do not worship his gods is a condemning circumstance. He gives them the opportunity to obey the command to worship, restating in full the description of the music and the obligation to fall down and worship. He makes clear the alternative that they "shall be cast the same hour into the midst of a burning fiery furnace." The repetition of the entire edict no doubt was done with a flourish; and, although he was probably well aware of the jealousy of the Chaldeans and took this into account, he makes it clear that there is no alternative but to worship the image.

87

The question Nebuchadnezzar asked in verse 14, translated "Is it true" in the King James Version and Revised Standard Version, is translated "Is it of purpose?" in the American Standard Version. Scholars differ on the proper reading here and resulting translation, but Montgomery and Rosenthal support the King James Version translation, "Is it true."[28]

It is an amazing fact that Nebuchadnezzar adds the challenging question, "Who is that God that shall deliver you out of my hands?" He is quite conscious of the demonstration of the superiority of the God of the Hebrews over Babylonian gods in interpreting his dream in chapter 2, but he cannot bring himself to believe that the God of the Jews would be able in these circumstances to deliver these three men from his hand. The fact is that Nebuchadnezzar feels supreme in his power and does not expect any god to interfere. Rabshakeh made the same arrogant and blasphemous claim when threatening King Hezekiah (Is 36:13-20)—the claim to the possession of a human power so great that there is no divine power to which the victim can turn for help.

The reply of Shadrach, Meshach, and Abed-nego to the king might ordinarily call for a long discourse explaining why they could not worship the image. They seem to recognize, however, that all this would be of no avail and that the issue is clearly whether their God is able to deliver them or not. Accordingly, they confront the king with their confidence in God to such an extent that they say, "we are not careful to answer thee in this matter." Such an answer by itself might be considered arrogant and disrespectful to the king; but coupled with the explanation, it is clear that they feel their case is not in their hands anyway. The Aramaic word *hashhin* translated "careful," may be considered a technical word for "need." Hence, the statement may be translated, "there is no need for us to answer thee in this matter."[29] A further difficulty is occasioned by the expression *O Nebuchadnezzar* which in the Massoretic is in the vocative. Young translates the entire sentence as omitting whatever formal address they made with the record here simply saying that they "said to the king Nebuchadnezzar, we have no need with respect to this matter to make defense before thee."[30] Montgomery holds that no discourtesy was intended, "The discourteous vocative of the Mass. pointing was not only impossible in etiquette but also in the spirit of the writer."[31]

Although the full salutation to Nebuchadnezzar seems to have been omitted, Daniel gives the gist of their reply and in so doing answered the question raised by the king in verse 14 when he asked, "Is it true?" Actually there was no doubt about what they had done, but their purpose in not conforming was in question. Was it really true that their purpose in nonconformity was to dishonor the gods of Babylon and to disobey Nebuchadnezzar. Their explanation leaves no question as to the answer.

They state positively that their God is able to deliver them from a fiery furnace. The article should be omitted before "burning fiery furnace" in verse 17, with the resultant meaning that He could deliver them from any fiery furnace, not just the one immediately at hand. They not only affirm that their God is able but that He will deliver them.

The three men, however, also face the alternative that God might not deliver them. The expression, "But if not," should be understood as referring to the deliverance not to the ability of God. They take into consideration that sometimes it is not in the purpose of God to deliver faithful ones from martyrdom. Even if God does not deliver them, however, this will not change their decision in which they refuse to worship the gods of Babylon as well as the golden image. Leupold aptly says, "The quiet, modest, yet withal very positive attitude of faith that these three men display is one of the noblest examples in the Scriptures of faith fully resigned to the will of God. These men ask for no miracle; they expect none. Theirs is the faith that says: 'Though He slay me, yet will I trust in Him,' Job 13:15."[32]

DANIEL'S COMPANIONS CAST INTO THE FURNACE

3:19-23   Then was Nebuchadnezzar full of fury, and the form of his visage was changed against Shadrach, Meshach, and Abed-nego: therefore he spake, and commanded that they should heat the furnace one seven times more than it was wont to be heated. And he commanded the most mighty men that were in his army to bind Shadrach, Meshach, and Abed-nego, and to cast them into the burning fiery furnace. Then these men were bound in their coats, their hosen, and their hats, and their other garments, and were cast into the midst of the burning fiery furnace. Therefore because the king's commandment was urgent, and the furnace exceeding hot, the flame of the fire slew those men that took up Shadrach, Meshach, and Abed-nego. And these three men, Shadrach, Meshach, and Abed-nego, fell down bound into the midst of the burning fiery furnace.

The answer of the three men to Nebuchadnezzar left no doubt as to their determined purpose not to serve the gods of Babylon and worship the image. After all, this was forbidden in Exodus 20:4-6. Nebuchadnezzar takes their determination not only as proof of the full accusation made by the Chaldeans but also as evidence of disloyalty to him personally. His anger knows no bounds as stated in the expression "full of fury" or "filled with anger." He is as angry as he possibly could be under any circumstance, his face is distorted, his pride has been severely punctured, and he gives the foolish order to heat the furnace seven times hotter than usual, as if this would increase the torment. Actually, a slow fire would have been far more torture as Geoffrey King puts it, "And then he lost his temper! That is always the mark of a little man. His furnace was hot, but he himself got hotter! And when a man gets full of fury, he gets full of folly. There is no fool on earth like a man who has lost his temper. And Nebuchadnezzar did a stupid thing. He ought to have cooled the furnace seven times *less* if he had wanted to hurt them; but instead of that in his fury he heated it seven times *more*."[33]

Instead of giving Shadrach, Meshach, and Abed-nego another opportunity to refuse to bow before the image as Nebuchadnezzar had originally proposed, he now immediately commands their execution. The strongest men in the army are selected, who bind Shadrach, Meshach, and Abed-nego as a preliminary to casting them in the burning fiery furnace. The Scriptures relate that they are bound in their coats, hose, and hats as well as other garments. Normally criminals are stripped before execution; but in view of the form of the execution and the haste of the whole operation, there was no particular point in stripping off their clothes. This later becomes a further testimony to the delivering power of God.

While the men were prepared for execution, the furnace is heated until it is extremely hot. This would not necessarily take very long, but it must have added a high note of tension to the entire situation as the multitude waited probably in dead silence. When the furnace reached its proper heat, the king demanded immediate execution of his orders. In casting the three men into the furnace, the strong men who did it were killed by the flame which reached out to take their lives. As the decree had indicated that they should be thrown into the midst of the furnace, so it was executed.

The Septuagint inserts the "Prayer of Azariah" and the "Song of the Three Youths" with some additional explanation. Conservative scholarship is agreed that this is not part of the scriptural text, although it is possible that these men, godly as they were, might have expressed prayer in a similar way if time permitted. Verse 23 of the text has also been challenged by Charles who claims it is an interpolation and needless duplication of verse 21, and that part of the passage has been lost.[34] Actually the narrative reads very well as it is, and the objections are without proper ground. Even in ordinary narrative important facts are sometimes repeated more than once. Nebuchadnezzar had now accomplished his purpose, his decree had been fulfilled, and he could leave to the furnace the task of consuming these men who had challenged his authority and his gods.

The Miraculous Deliverance from the Furnace

3:24-27 Then Nebuchadnezzar the king was astonied, and rose up in haste, and spake, and said unto his counsellors, Did not we cast three men bound into the midst of the fire? They answered and said unto the king, True, O king. He answered and said, Lo, I see four men loose, walking in the midst of the fire, and they have no hurt; and the form of the fourth is like the Son of God. Then Nebuchadnezzar came near to the mouth of the burning fiery furnace, and spake, and said, Shadrach, Meshach, and Abed-nego, ye servants of the most high God, come forth, and come hither. Then Shadrach, Meshach, and Abed-nego, came forth of the midst of the fire. And the princes, governors, and captains, and the king's counsellors, being gathered together, saw these men, upon whose bodies the fire had no power, nor was an hair of their head singed, neither were their coats changed, nor the smell of fire had passed on them.

Nebuchadnezzar apparently was seated in such a way as to be able to observe the interior of the furnace from a safe distance. What he saw, however, brought him to complete astonishment. He could not believe his eyes and in his excitement stood up and asked his counsellors whether the three men had not been cast bound into the midst of the fire. The occasion of his question was what he saw. Instead of three men, he saw four; instead of being bound, they were free; instead of writhing in anguish in the flames, they were walking about in the fire and making no attempt to come out; further, it was quite apparent that they were not hurt; most astounding of all, he had the impression that "the form of the fourth is like the Son of God." It is probable that, at these pronouncements, Nebuchadnezzar's counsellors also rose to look into the furnace; and led by Nebuchadnezzar, they came as close as they could to see the miraculous deliverance.

Most contemporary scholars translate the phrase *the Son of God,* as "a son of the gods." While it is entirely possible that the fourth person in the fiery furnace was indeed the Son of God, it would be doubtful whether Nebuchadnezzar would comprehend this, unless he had prophetic insight. The Aramaic form *elahin* is plural and whenever used in the Aramaic section of Daniel seems to be a plural in number, as the singular is used when the true God is meant. The textual problem of Daniel 6:20 where Darius refers to the true God is decided in favor of the singular by Kittel[35] rather than the plural. On the basis of this consistent use, the translation "a son of the gods" is preferable and in keeping with Nebuchadnezzar's comprehension at this point in his experience. The presence of a fourth person in the furnace nevertheless added to Nebuchadnezzar's astonishment at the miracle he was witnessing.

Addressing the three faithful men in the fiery furnace, Nebuchadnezzar said, "Shadrach, Meshach, and Abed-nego, ye servants of the most high God, come forth, and come hither." It was immediately apparent to Nebuchadnezzar, as well as the others who watched, that the God of

Shadrach, Meshach, and Abed-nego was greater than the gods of Babylon. In using the expression "the most high God," Nebuchadnezzar was not disavowing his own deities but merely recognizing on the basis of the tremendous miracle which had been performed that the God of Israel was higher, hence "the most high God."

At the command of Nebuchadnezzar, Shadrach, Meshach, and Abed-nego, who could not obey the king in the matter of worshiping the image, do not hesitate to fulfill his command in this instance. The assembled multitude led by the king's most important officials acted as witnesses of the delivering power of God. Although obviously all the great throng could not get close enough to see precisely what had happened, Scripture records that "the princes, governors, and captains, and the king's counsellors" witnessed the event. There could be little question that a mighty miracle had been performed. The hair of the three Hebrews had not been singed, their garments in which they had been bound had not changed, and not even the smell of fire was retained. Leupold translates *coats* as "shoes" which would be most remarkable as they had walked on the hot ashes.[36] The fire had damaged their garments in no way; only the ropes which bound them, the symbols of Nebuchadnezzar's unbelief and wrath, were destroyed in the flames.

Just as the reign of Nebuchadnezzar is symbolic of the entire period of the times of the Gentiles, so the deliverance of Daniel's three companions is typical of the deliverance of Israel during the period of Gentile domination. Particularly at the end of the Gentile period Israel will be in fiery affliction, but as Isaiah prophesied, "But now thus saith the Lord that created thee, O Jacob, and he that formed thee, O Israel, Fear not: for I have redeemed thee, I have called thee by thy name; thou art mine. When thou passest through the waters, I will be with thee; and through the rivers, they shall not overflow thee: when thou walkest through the fire, thou shalt not be burned; neither shall the flame kindle upon thee" (Is 43:1-2).

The Decree of Nebuchadnezzar

3:28-30 Then Nebuchadnezzar spake, and said, Blessed be the God of Shadrach, Meshach, and Abed-nego, who hath sent his angel, and delivered his servants that trusted in him, and have changed the king's word, and yielded their bodies, that they might not serve nor worship any god, except their own God. Therefore I make a decree, That every people, nation, and language, which speak any thing amiss against the God of Shadrach, Meshach, and Abed-nego, shall be cut in pieces, and their houses shall be made a dunghill: because there is no other God that can deliver after this sort. Then the king promoted Shadrach, Meshach, and Abed-nego, in the province of Babylon.

Just as Nebuchadnezzar had acknowledged Daniel's God at the conclusion of chapter 2, so here Nebuchadnezzar admitting the power of the God of Shadrach, Meshach, and Abed-nego issues a decree in oriental style commemorating the event. First, he recognizes the delivering power of their God "who hath sent his angel, and delivered his servants that trusted in him." That the heathen gods used messengers to accomplish their purpose was generally believed, and Nebuchadnezzar analyzes the event in this way. Although there is no clear proof that the fourth person in the furnace with Shadrach, Meshach, and Abed-nego was actually deity or an angel—as all we have is Nebuchadnezzar's conclusion on the basis of what he saw—it may well be that the protector of Shadrach, Meshach, and Abed-nego was Christ Himself appearing in the form of an angel. The expression *the Son of God* (3:25) is a translation of the Aramaic *bar 'elāhin*, which means "a divine being." Nebuchadnezzar interprets this in verse 28 as a *mal'ak*, meaning, "an angel." The alternative that God sent a mighty angel to protect them is, of course, also plausible and in keeping with other Scripture.

Nebuchadnezzar not only recognizes the God of Shadrach, Meshach, and Abed-nego but now belatedly commends them for their trust in God even though it resulted in changing his word. He recognizes the superior obligation of the men not to worship any deity except their own. This was a remarkable admission for a king in Nebuchadnezzar's situation.

Having given this preamble, Nebuchadnezzar now makes his decree. In it, he does not deprecate his own gods but recognizes the fact of the power of the God of Shadrach, Meshach, and Abed-nego. He calls upon all the people in his realm not to say anything amiss concerning this God at the threat of being cut to pieces and their houses made a dunghill. That the king has the power to do this was obvious to everyone. The basis of his decree is the simple statement, "because there is no other God that can deliver after this sort." It is clear at this point that though Nebuchadnezzar is greatly impressed, he has not yet been brought to the place where he is willing to put his trust in the God of Israel.

The chain of events which had brought about this miracle also consolidated the position of Shadrach, Meshach, and Abed-nego as principal officials in the province of Babylon. Whatever their former rank and authority, they are now promoted. Although probably in the same office, they were relieved of any opposition and had the special favor of the king in what they did.

As pointed out in an extended discussion by Leupold, the nature of this trial and persecution was quite different from that of Antiochus Epiphanes in the second century B.C.; and scholars who attempt to draw parallels to support the idea of a pseudo-Daniel writing the book of Daniel in the second century have no real basis in fact. Nebuchadnezzar at least respected the God of Israel, something which was quite untrue in the case of Antiochus Epiphanes.[37] As recorded in the Word of God, it is characteristic of Gentile times that there will be tensions between obedience to God and obedience to men. This will reach its peak in the future great tribulation when once again the tension between obeying an earthly ruler and obeying God will result in many martyrs.

Taken as a whole, chapter 3 is a thrilling account of young men who remained true to God under severe trial. The common excuses for moral and spiritual compromise, especially the blaming of contemporary influences, are contradicted by the faithfulness of these men. In spite of separation from parents and of the corrupting influences of Babylonian religion, political pressure, and immorality, they did not waver in their hour of testing. Critics are probably right that Daniel intended this chapter to remind Israel of the evils of idolatry and the necessity of obeying God rather than men. But the main thrust of the passage is not an invented moral story which actually never happened, as critics infer, but rather a display of a God who is faithful to His people even in captivity and is ever ready to deliver those who put their trust in Him. The contrast of the God of Israel to the idols of Babylon is a reminder that the god of this world, behind Gentile dominion, is doomed to judgment at the hands of the sovereign God. This is illustrated in the fall of Babylon and of the succeeding empires of Medo-Persia, Greece, and Rome. The downfall of these nations is a foreshadowing of the end of the times of the Gentiles when the Lion of the tribe of Judah returns to reign.

Chapter 3, the first of four chapters dealing with individuals, is an obvious preparation for chapter 4, which relates Nebuchadnezzar's conversion. In the deliverance of the three faithful companions of Daniel, Nebuchadnezzar is confronted by the superior power of God which can nullify Nebuchadnezzar's commandment to execute the three men. This is a preparation for the lesson he was to learn in chapter 4 that all of his power was delegated by God and could be withdrawn at His will. In this chapter we see for the last time Daniel's three companions, and no further reference is made to their subsequent experiences.

4

NEBUCHADNEZZAR'S PRIDE AND PUNISHMENT

THIS CHAPTER which occupies such a large portion of the book of Daniel is more than a profound story of how God can bring a proud man low. Undoubtedly, it is the climax of Nebuchadnezzar's spiritual biography which began with his recognition of the excellence of Daniel and his companions, continued with the interpretation of the dream of the image in chapter 2, and was advanced further by his experience with Daniel's three companions.

In the background of this account is the obvious concern of Daniel the prophet for the man whom he had served for so many years. Daniel, a man of prayer, undoubtedly prayed for Nebuchadnezzar and eagerly sought some evidence of God's working in his heart. While the experience of Nebuchadnezzar in chapter 4 was not what Daniel had anticipated, the outcome must have approximated Daniel's fondest hope. Although some like Leupold, after Calvin, "doubt whether the king's experience led to his conversion,"[1] it may well be that this chapter brings Nebuchadnezzar to the place where he puts his trust in the God of Daniel. Even merely as a lesson in the spiritual progress of a man in the hands of God, this chapter is a literary gem.

In the light of Daniel's revelation of the broad scope of Gentile power beginning in chapter 2, Nebuchadnezzar's experience seems to take on the larger meaning of the humbling of Gentile power by God and the bringing of the world into submission to Himself. In the light of other passages in the Bible speaking prophetically of Babylon and its ultimate overthrow, of which Isaiah 13 and 14 may be taken as an example, it becomes clear that the contest between God and Nebuchadnezzar is a broad illustration of God's dealings with the entire human race and especially the Gentile world in its creaturely pride and failure to recognize the sovereignty of God. The theme of the chapter, as given by Daniel himself in the interpretation of the king's dream, is God's dealings with Nebuchadnezzar "till thou know that the most High ruleth in the kingdom of men, and giveth it to whomsoever he will" (Dan 4:25). Not only is the sovereignty of God demonstrated, but the bankruptcy of Babylonian wisdom forms another motif. It is obviously by design that this chapter precedes the downfall of Babylon itself which follows in chapter 5. To push this to the extreme of making it a particular application to Antiochus Epiphanes in the effort to support a late date of Daniel is, however, without justification. There is nothing whatever to link this passage to the second century B.C. In fact, it is far more applicable to that fateful night in October 539 B.C. when Babylon fell as recorded in Daniel 5.

The content of the chapter is in the form of a decree recording his dream, Daniel's interpretation, and Nebuchadnezzar's subsequent experience. Whether written by Nebuchadnezzar himself, or more probably by one of his scribes at his dictation, or possibly by Daniel himself at the king's direction, the inclusion of it here in Daniel is by divine inspiration. Although critics have imagined a series of incredible objections to accepting this chapter as authentic and reasonably accurate, the narrative actually reads very sensibly and the objections seem trivial and unsupported.*[2]

Those who reject chapter 4 of Daniel without exception assume that the account is not inspired of the Holy Spirit, that an experience like Nebuchadnezzar's is essentially incredible, and that it is a myth rather than an authentic historical record. Such objections obviously assume that higher criticism is right in declaring Daniel a forgery of the second century B.C. This conclusion is now subject to question not only because of the fallacious reasoning which supports it, but because it is now challenged by the documentary evidence in the Qumran text of Daniel, which on the basis of the critics' own criteria would require Daniel to be much older than the second century B.C. (see Introduction). Conservative scholarship has united in declaring this chapter a genuine portion of the Word of God, equally inspired with other sections of Daniel.

INTRODUCTION OF NEBUCHADNEZZAR'S PROCLAMATION

4:1-3 Nebuchadnezzar the king, unto all people, nations, and languages, that dwell in all the earth; Peace be multiplied unto you. I thought it good to shew the signs and wonders that the high God hath wrought toward me. How great are his signs! and how mighty are his wonders! his kingdom is an everlasting kingdom, and his dominion is from generation to generation.

Although it is clear that the opening verses are an introduction to the decree of Nebuchadnezzar, various versions differ in their versification, with the Massoretic beginning the decree at the close of chapter 3. The

*For the relation of the Qumran document designated the "Prayer of Nabonidus," see later discussion on Daniel 4:28-33.

Septuagint rendering of chapter 4 also differs considerably from the Hebrew-Aramaic text, used for the King James Version translation. Charles summarizes the differences in these words,

> In the Massoretic text, which is followed by Theodotion, the Vulgate, and the Peshitto, the entire narrative *is given in the form of an edict or letter of Nebuchadnezzar to all his subjects*. It begins with a greeting to 'all the peoples, nations, and languages that dwell in all the earth,' and proceeds to state the king's desire to make known to them the signs and wonders that the Most High had wrought upon him (1-3). He then recounts a dream which troubled him, and tells how he summoned the magicians, Chaldeans, and soothsayers to make known its interpretation.[3]

Charles then contrasts this with the Septuagint,

> Turning now to the LXX we observe first of all that there is nothing in it corresponding to the first three verses in the Massoretic, which transform the next thirty-four verses into an edict. The chapter begins simply, in the LXX, with the words: 'And in the eighteenth year of his reign Nebuchadnezzar said: I Nebuchadnezzar was at rest in mine house': *then follows in the same narrative form the next thirty-three verses. At their close comes the edict* as a result of the king's spiritual and psychical experiences, in which are embodied very many of the phrases in iv.1-3. A close study of the texts and versions has forced me to the conclusion that the older order of the text is preserved in the LXX and not in the Aramaic. The complete evidence for this conclusion will be found in my larger Commentary.[4]

Although liberal critics generally unite in a low view of this chapter, not only assigning it to a pseudo-Daniel of the second century but finding the text itself suspect, there is insufficient evidence in favor of the Greek translation of the Septuagint. Even Montgomery, who does not regard this as authentic Scripture, rejects the view that the Septuagint is the older text than the present Aramaic text, although he considers the Aramaic also a revision of an earlier text.[5] There is actually little justification for all these variations of unbelief. The chapter on the face of it is credible, albeit a record of supernatural revelation. Generally, those who accept the sixth century date for Daniel also accept this chapter more or less as it is.

The first verse of chapter 4 is the natural form for such a decree, beginning with the name of the sender, the people to whom it is sent, and a general greeting. That it should be sent "unto all people, nations, and languages, that dwell in all the earth" is not out of keeping with the extensive character of Nebuchadnezzar's empire, although he was well aware of the fact that all of the earth's geography was not under his power. It is similar to the extensive decree of Daniel 3:29 which is addressed to "every people, nation, and language." Montgomery is obviously prejudiced in his judgment, "As an edict the document is historically absurd; it has no similar in the history of royal conversions nor in ancient imperial edicts."[6] The folly of this kind of objection is evident in that if Montgomery had found one example in any other literature his criticism would become invalid, but he feels perfectly free to ignore the parallels in chapter 3 and chapter 6 of Daniel. In this case, as is so often true, the critics argue from alleged silence in the records, although admittedly we possess only fragments of ancient literature. This chapter is no more difficult to believe than any other unusual divine revelation.

Although the benediction, "Peace be multiplied unto you," is strikingly similar to some of Paul's greetings in his epistles, it was a common form of expression in the ancient world. A greeting very much like 4:1 is found in Daniel 6:25 where Darius wrote a similar decree with almost the same wording. It is possible that Daniel himself affected the form even if he did not write it as in both places he is in a position of high authority, and the edicts in both cases may have been issued under his particular direction. The decree in any case actually begins with the word *peace* as that which preceded it was the address.

Nebuchadnezzar then sets the stage for the presentation of his experience by declaring that it was his judgment that the amazing signs and wonders wrought in his life by "the high God" were of such unusual significance that he should share them with his entire realm. The expression *signs and wonders* is a familiar idiom of Scripture occurring, as Leupold notes, in many passages (Deu 6:22; 7:19; 13:1, 2; 26:8; Neh 9:10; Is 8:18, etc.). Because it is so biblical, it has led to questions by higher critics; but actually there is a great deal of similarity between Babylonian psalms and biblical psalms, and there is nothing technical about this phrase.[7] The expression "the high God" is another evidence that Nebuchadnezzar regards the God of Israel as exalted; but it is not in itself proof that he is a monotheist, trusting only in the true God.

Nebuchadnezzar's exclamation of the greatness of God and His signs and wonders is quite accurate and in keeping with his experience. The signs wrought in his life were indeed great, and God's wonders were indeed mighty. His conclusion that the kingdom is an everlasting kingdom extending from generation to generation is a logical one based on his experience and reveals God in a true light (cf. Ps 145:13).

Wise Men Unable to Interpret Dream

4:4-7 I Nebuchadnezzar was at rest in mine house, and flourishing in my palace: I saw a dream which made me afraid, and the thoughts upon my bed and the visions of my head troubled me. Therefore made I a decree to bring in all the wise men of Babylon before me, that they might make known unto me the interpretation of the dream. Then came in the magicians, the astrologers, the Chaldeans, and the soothsayers: and I told the dream before them; but they did not make known unto me the interpretation thereof.

Nebuchadnezzar's account of his experience describes his secure and flourishing situation in his palace prior to the dream. In his early reign he was active in military conquest. Now his vast domains had been made secure, and Nebuchadnezzar was fulfilling his heart's desire by making Babylon one of the most fabulous cities of the ancient world. He was already enjoying his beautiful palace; and at the time of the dream itself he was in bed in his house as indicated in verses 5 and 10. In describing himself as "flourishing in my palace" he used a word meaning "to be green" such as the growth of green leaves on a tree, an evident anticipation of the dream which followed. In this context of security and prosperity surrounded by the monuments of his wealth and power, Nebuchadnezzar had a dream which made him afraid. The sequence in verse 5 that he "saw a dream" and had "thoughts upon my bed" as well as "visions of my head" seems to imply that the dream came first, and then upon awakening from the dream which was also a vision his thoughts troubled him. The expression *made me afraid* is actually much stronger in the original and indicates extreme terror or fright.

As he contemplated the meaning of his experience, he issued a decree to bring all the wise men of Babylon before him to make known its interpretation. As illustrated in chapter 2 this was a standard procedure, and the wise men of Babylon were supposed to be able to interpret mystical experiences. Upon being told the dream, the wise men, described here in their various categories, as also in Daniel 2:2, did not make known to the king the interpretation. It seems that they not only did not make known the interpretation but were unable to do so, as Leupold translates this expression, "but they could not make known to me the interpretation."[8] Even though the dream was adverse and might present a problem in telling Nebuchadnezzar, they probably would have made some attempt to explain it to him, if they had understood it.

DANIEL TOLD THE KING'S DREAM

4:8-18 But at the last Daniel came in before me, whose name was Belteshazzar, according to the name of my god, and in whom is the spirit of the holy gods: and before him I told the dream, saying, O Belteshazzar, master of the magicians, because I know that the spirit of the holy gods is in thee, and no secret troubleth thee, tell me the visions of my dream that I have seen, and the interpretation thereof. Thus were the visions of mine head in my bed; I saw, and behold a tree in the midst of the earth, and the height thereof was great. The tree grew, and was strong, and the height thereof reached unto heaven, and the sight thereof to the end of all the earth: the leaves thereof were fair, and the fruit thereof much, and in it was meat for all: the beasts of the field had shadow under it, and the fowls of the heaven dwelt in the boughs thereof, and all flesh was fed of it. I saw in the visions of my head upon my bed, and, behold, a watcher and an holy one came down from heaven; he cried aloud, and said thus, Hew down the tree, and cut off his branches, shake off his leaves, and scatter his fruit: let the beasts get away from under it, and the fowls from his branches: nevertheless leave the stump of his roots in the earth, even with a band of iron and brass, in the tender grass of the field; and let it be wet with the dew of heaven, and let his portion be with the beasts in the grass of the earth: let his heart be changed from man's, and let a beast's heart be given unto him; and let seven times pass over him. This matter is by the decree of the watchers, and the demand by the word of the holy ones: to the intent that the living may know that the most High ruleth in the kingdom of men, and giveth it to whomsoever he will, and setteth up over it the basest of men. This dream I king Nebuchadnezzar have seen. Now thou, O Belteshazzar, declare the interpretation thereof, forasmuch as all the wise men of my kingdom are not able to make known unto me the interpretation: but thou art able; for the spirit of the holy gods is in thee.

For some unexplained reason Daniel was not with the other wise men when the king told his dream. Coming in late, he was immediately addressed personally by Nebuchadnezzar in attempt to have his dream interpreted. Questions have been raised why verse 8 not only calls him Daniel but adds the expression "whose name was Belteshazzar." In view of the fact that this is part of a record where Daniel is prominent, why the double name?

The answer, however, is quite simple. This decree was going throughout the kingdom where most people would know Daniel by his Babylonian name, Belteshazzar. The king, in recognition of the fact that Daniel's God is the interpreter of his dream, calls Daniel by his Hebrew name, the last syllable of which refers to Elohim, the God of Israel. Nebuchadnezzar explains that his name Belteshazzar was given "according to the name of my god," that is, the god Bel. The double name is not unnatural in view of the context and the explanation.

Of Daniel it is said "in whom is the spirit of the holy gods." It is debatable whether *gods* is singular or plural, as it could be translated either way. Young, with a wealth of evidence from Montgomery, considers it a singular noun and thus a recognition by the king "that the God of Dan. was different from his own gods."[9] This distinction is borne out by the adjective "holy" (4:8, 18; 5:11). The philological evidence supports the singular, although Leupold agrees with Driver that the noun and its adjective are plural and a reflection of the king's polytheism.[10] Driver notes, "The same expression occurs in the Phoenician inscription of Eshmunazar, king of Sidon (3–4 cent. B.C.), lines 9 and 22."[11] The word *holy*, according

100

to Young, refers to gods who are divine, rather than specifically having moral purity.[12] The ultimate judgment of the expression depends on how well Nebuchadnezzar comprehended the nature of Daniel's God. He obviously had high respect for the God of Daniel and may have had a true faith in the God of Israel. Nebuchadnezzar, having justified his singling out Daniel of all the wise men, now records in his decree his conversation with Daniel which includes a restatement of his dream.

Daniel, addressed by his heathen name, is further described as the "master of the magicians." This was intended by Nebuchadnezzar to be a compliment in recognition of the genius of Daniel. Having already spoken of his intimate contact with God and the indwelling of the Spirit of God in him, he refers to Daniel's thorough knowledge of the whole field of Babylonian astrology and religion. Leupold suggests that *magicians* should be translated "scholars" to give the true meaning and avoid the implication of mere magic.[13]

Nebuchadnezzar, on the basis of his previous experience, restates that the Spirit of God is in Daniel and that secrets do not trouble him, that is, he is able to declare their meaning. Of interest is the statement concerning the prince of Tyrus, "Behold, thou art wiser than Daniel; there is no secret that they can hide from thee" (Eze 28:3). This statement, which the critics work hard to explain, as it confirms a sixth century Daniel, also supports the idea that Daniel's fame had spread far and wide. By the expression, "tell me the visions of my dream," Nebuchadnezzar obviously meant that Daniel should interpret the dream which the king was now to relate. Verses 10-12 have been regarded as in poetic form if some alteration of the text were permitted, and verses 14-17 are considered free verse also, but with no metrical evenness.[14] Most conservatives ignore this as requiring too much alteration of the text to conform to the poetic pattern. The ideas are poetic, if the form is not.

In his vision, Nebuchadnezzar saw a tree apparently standing somewhat by itself and dominating the view because of its great height. Porteous notes that Bentzen "refers to a building inscription of Nebuchadnezzar in which Babylon is compared to a spreading tree."[15] The use of trees in the Bible for symbolic purposes as well as in extrascriptural narratives is found frequently (cf. 2 Ki 14:9; Ps 1:3; 37:35; 52:8; 92:12; Eze 17). An obvious parallel to Nebuchadnezzar's dream is recorded in Ezekiel 31, where the Assyrian as well as the Egyptian Pharaoh are compared to a cedar of Lebanon. Young states, "Among the commentators Haevernick particularly has illustrated the fondness with which the Orientals depicted the rise and fall of human power by means of the symbol of a tree."[16] In extrabiblical literature, there is the account of Astyages the Mede who had a dream in which a vine grew out of the womb of

Mandane his daughter and subsequently covered all Asia. Herodotus interpreted this as referring to Cyrus. Another famous illustration is that of Xerxes, who in a dream was crowned with a branch of an olive tree which extended over the world. According to Haevernick, there are similar allusions in Arabic and Turkish sources.[17] Nebuchadnezzar probably anticipated that the tree represented himself, and this added to his concern.

As Nebuchadnezzar described his dream, the tree was pictured as growing, becoming very strong and very high until it was visible all over the earth, obviously exceeding the possibilities of any ordinary tree. Abundant foliage characterized the tree, and it bore much fruit so that it provided for both beast and fowl and "all flesh fed of it." This obviously included all beasts and fowls. Whether or not it was intended to apply literally to men is open to question, but symbolically it included mankind as under the rule of Nebuchadnezzar.

As Nebuchadnezzar observed the scene, an actor appears in the form of "a watcher and an holy one" who is described as coming "down from heaven." This expression has generated a great deal of comment, especially by liberal critics who consider this a vestige of polytheism. Even Keil says, "The conception . . . is not biblical, but Babylonian heathen."[18] In the religion of the Babylonians, it was customary to recognize "council deities" who were charged with the special task of watching over the world. The question raised on this passage is whether Nebuchadnezzar uses this heathen concept.

In his detailed note on the subject of watchers, Montgomery refers to the considerable role played by the "watchers" in the intertestamental literature and to a possible occurrence in the Zadokite fragment. He quotes Meinhold as drawing attention in this connection to "the eyes of the Cherubs," in Ezekiel 1:18, and " 'the seven, which are the eyes of the LORD, which run to and fro through the whole earth,' Zech. 4:10," and goes on to trace the still closer parallel with " 'the Watchers' " (*shōmᵉrîm*) and " 'the Remembrancers of the LORD' " (*hammazkirîm 'eth-Yahweh*) of Isaiah 62:6.[19]

In the light of the full revelation of the Word of God, the most natural conclusion is that this person described as "a watcher and an holy one" is an angel sent from God even though the word *angel* is not used. That angels are watchers, or better translated "vigilant, making a sleepless watch," is not foreign to the concept of angels in Scripture. The expressions "watchers" and "the holy ones" are mentioned in verse 17 by the messenger himself. Nebuchadnezzar seems to use the term in its heathen connotation as he understood it. He probably would not have understood what was meant by using the term *angel* in this connection, although he used *angel* himself in 3:28. The extended discussion of Keil on this point does not clarify the issue too much but probably says all that can be said, even though his conclusions are not entirely satisfactory.[20]

The heavenly messenger cries aloud, literally cries "with might." To the unnamed listeners, he calls for the tree to be cut down, its branches cut off, its leaves to be shaken off, and its fruit to be scattered. The beasts under it and the fowls in its branches were instructed to get away. The record does not say that the command is carried out, but this is implied.

Special instructions, however, are given regarding the stump; and these indicate that the tree will be revived later. The stump is to be bound with a band of iron and brass. The purpose of this is not clear unless in some way it helps preserve it. However, in real life, such a band would not prevent the stump from rotting; and it is probable here that it is symbolic of the madness which would afflict Nebuchadnezzar and hold him symbolically, if not in reality, in chains. The stump is to be surrounded by the tender grass of the field, to be wet with the dew of heaven, and to have its portion with the beasts of the earth. It seems evident that the description goes beyond the symbol of a stump to the actual fulfillment in Nebuchadnezzar's experience. This becomes more clear in verse 16 where the person in view is given a beast's heart instead of a man's heart. This, of course, has no relationship to the characteristics of the stump. The prophecy is concluded with the expression, "let seven times pass over him." This may refer to seven years or merely to a long period of time. Probably the most common interpretation is to consider it seven years as in the Septuagint. It is certain that the period is specific and not more than seven years.

The messenger then concludes that his decree proceeds from "the watchers" and from "the holy ones." The purpose is that people living in the world may recognize the true God described as "the most High" and acknowledge Him as the true ruler of men, who has the power to place "the basest of men" over earthly kingdoms. That God can set up in a position of power the lowliest of men is a common truth of Scripture (see 1 Sa 2:7-8; Job 5:11; Ps 113:7-8; Lk 1:52; and the story of Joseph). This statement is a direct confrontation of Nebuchadnezzar's pride in his own attainments and power.

The major problem of verse 17 is the reference to the watchers and the holy ones who seem to originate the decree. If these are understood as agencies of God, who actually is the source, the problem is alleviated. The verse itself calls our attention to the fact that God as "the most High" is the ultimate sovereign and certainly does not imply that the messengers are in any sense independent of God. The problems created by this text, therefore, are greatly overdrawn by those who see this in conflict with the scriptural doctrine of God.

In concluding his statement concerning the dream, Nebuchadnezzar appeals to Daniel to provide the interpretation. He explains to Daniel that the wise men of Babylon were not able to do this, but he expresses confidence in Daniel, "for the spirit of the holy gods is in thee" (cf. 4:8). The stage is now set for Daniel's interpretation.

DANIEL INTERPRETS THE DREAM

4:19-27 Then Daniel, whose name was Belteshazzar, was astonied for one hour, and his thoughts troubled him. The king spake, and said, Belteshazzar, let not the dream, or the interpretation thereof, trouble thee. Belteshazzar answered and said, My lord, the dream be to them that hate thee, and the interpretation thereof to thine enemies. The tree that thou sawest, which grew, and was strong, whose height reached unto the heaven, and the sight thereof to all the earth; whose leaves were fair, and the fruit thereof much, and in it was meat for all; under which the beasts of the field dwelt, and upon whose branches the fowls of the heaven had their habitation: it is thou, O king, that art grown and become strong: for thy greatness is grown, and reacheth unto heaven, and thy dominion to the end of the earth. And whereas the king saw a watcher and an holy one coming down from heaven, and saying, Hew the tree down, and destroy it; yet leave the stump of the roots thereof in the earth, even with a band of iron and brass, in the tender grass of the field; and let it be wet with the dew of heaven, and let his portion be with the beasts of the field, till seven times pass over him; this is the interpretation, O king, and this is the decree of the most High, which is come upon my lord the king: That they shall drive thee from men, and thy dwelling shall be with the beasts of the field, and they shall make thee to eat grass as oxen, and they shall wet thee with the dew of heaven, and seven times shall pass over thee, till thou know that the most High ruleth in the kingdom of men, and giveth it to whomsoever he will. And whereas they commanded to leave the stump of the tree roots; thy kingdom shall be sure unto thee, after that thou shalt have known that the heavens do rule. Wherefore, O king, let my counsel be acceptable unto thee, and break off thy sins by righteousness, and thine iniquities by showing mercy to the poor; if it may be a lengthening of thy tranquillity.

Keil summarizes the situation facing Daniel with these words, "As Daniel at once understood the interpretation of the dream, he was for a moment so astonished that he could not speak for terror at the thoughts which moved his soul. This amazement seized him because he wished well to the king, and yet he must now announce to him a weighty judgment from God."[21] No doubt, Daniel was not only troubled by the content of the dream but by the need to tell Nebuchadnezzar the interpretation in an appropriate way.

Verse 19 introduces both names of Daniel again, the Hebrew name in recognition that he is acting as a servant of the God of Israel and his Babylonian name by which he was known officially. Daniel's consternation at the interpretation of the dream is indicated in that he "was astonied for one hour," to be understood as being in a state of perplexity for a period of time. An accurate translation would be "was stricken dumb for a while" (ASV), or "was perplexed for a moment."[22] The Revised Standard Version translation, "for a long time," is probably inaccurate. Probably a full sixty minutes would have been too long for him to have remained silent in these circumstances.

Nebuchadnezzar comes to his rescue in this situation and urges him not to let the dream trouble him. The comment reflects his respect for Daniel as a person as well as an interpreter of the dream, and indirectly this is an assurance that Daniel himself need not fear the king regardless of what he reveals.

With this encouragement, Daniel replies with typical oriental courtesy that the dream be to them that hate Nebuchadnezzar and the interpretation to his enemies. Leupold believes that there is an ethical objection to Daniel's sinking to mere flattery in this case and avoiding the real import of the dream. He interprets the statement as meaning that the dream would please the king's enemies.[23] It would seem more natural, however, to have the expression refer to Daniel's wishes in the matter. It is hard to see how the expression in any sense would be flattery. Daniel had a high regard for Nebuchadnezzar and undoubtedly wished the interpretation of the dream could be otherwise than it was.

Having begun his interpretation, he now describes Nebuchadnezzar's dream in detail, restating what the king had already told him. With the facts of the dream before him, he then proceeds to the interpretation in verse 22. Daniel immediately identifies the tree as representing Nebuchadnezzar. Just like the tree in the dream, the king had grown and become strong, had grown great and reached unto heaven with his dominion to the end of the earth. After recapitulating the announced destruction of the tree and the other details which the king already had recited, Daniel proceeds to the detailed interpretation in verse 24. It is significant that he mentions here, "this is the decree of the most High," which is Daniel's interpretation of the expression in verse 17 "the decree of the watchers, and the demand by the word of the holy ones." Although Nebuchadnezzar's description did not immediately specify divine agency, it is clear that this is the interpretation according to Daniel in verse 24.

The meaning of the tree being cut down and the attendant circumstances is then defined. Nebuchadnezzar is to be driven from ordinary association with men and will dwell with the beasts of the field. In this condition he will eat grass as the ox and suffer the dew of heaven until he understands that God gives to men the power to rule as He wills. The interpretation of the stump with its bands of iron and brass is that Nebuchadnezzar will retain control of his kingdom and that it will be restored to him after he comes back to his senses. To have had his mind restored without the kingdom would have been a hollow victory. In spite of his pride, Nebuchadnezzar was to know the graciousness of God to him.

The expression, *that the heavens do rule,* is of particular interest for it is the only time in the Old Testament where the word *heaven* is substituted for God. This usage became prominent in later literature as in 1 Maccabees and in the New Testament in Matthew where the term *kingdom of heaven* is similar to *kingdom of God.* Daniel, in using the expression *the heavens do rule,* is not accepting the Babylonian deification of heavenly bodies, as he makes clear in 4:25 that "the most High" is a person. He is probably only contrasting divine or heavenly rule to earthly rule such as Nebuchadnezzar exercised, with the implication that Nebuchadnezzar's sovereignty was much less than that of "the heavens."

With the interpretation of the dream now clearly presented to Nebuchadnezzar, Daniel, as a prophet of God, gives a word of solemn exhortation to the king. With utmost courtesy, he urges the king to replace his sins with righteousness and his iniquities with showing mercy to the poor, if perchance God would lengthen the period of his tranquillity. Nebuchadnezzar undoubtedly had been morally wicked and cruel to those whom he ruled. His concern had been to build a magnificent city as a monument to his name rather than to alleviating the suffering of the poor. All of this was quite clear to Daniel as it was to God, and the exhortation is faithfully reproduced in this decree going to Nebuchadnezzar's entire realm.

This passage has created some controversy because of a mistranslation in the Vulgate which reads in translation, "Cancel thy sins by deeds of charity and thine iniquities by deeds of kindness to the poor." This, of course, is not what is recorded in the book of Daniel. Nebuchadnezzar is not promised forgiveness on the ground of good works or alms to the poor; but rather the issue is that, if he is a wise and benevolent king, he would alleviate the necessity of God's intervening with immediate judgment because of Nebuchadnezzar's pride.[24]

THE DREAM FULFILLED

4:28-33 All this came upon the king Nebuchadnezzar. At the end of twelve months he walked in the palace of the kingdom of Babylon. The king spake, and said, Is not this great Babylon, that I have built for the house of the kingdom by the might of my power, and for the honour of my majesty? While the word was in the king's mouth, there fell a voice from heaven, saying, O king Nebuchadnezzar, to thee it is spoken; The kingdom is departed from thee. And they shall drive thee from men, and thy dwelling shall be with the beasts of the field: they shall make thee to eat grass as oxen, and seven times shall pass over thee, until thou know that the most High ruleth in the kingdom of men, and giveth it to whomsoever he will. The same hour was the thing fulfilled upon Nebuchadnezzar: and he was driven from men, and did eat grass as oxen, and his body was wet with the dew of heaven, till his hairs were grown like eagles' feathers, and his nails like birds' claws.

Although fulfillment of the dream was not immediate, the decree sums it up concisely, "All this came upon king Nebuchadnezzar." Twelve months later as he walked in the palace in Babylon, one of his crowning architectural triumphs, and looked out upon the great city of Babylon, his pride reached a new peak as he asked the question "Is not this great Babylon, that I have built for the house of the kingdom by the might of my power, and for the honour of my majesty?" From the flat roof of the palace, he undoubtedly had a great perspective. This statement contradicts any notion of some critics that he was not actually in Babylon at that time. Everything points to the contrary. What he surveyed was indeed impressive. There are frequent mentions of the great buildings of Babylon in ancient literature.*

Montgomery finds this description of Nebuchadnezzar precisely fitting the historical context: "The setting of the scene and the king's self-complaisance in his glorious Babylon are strikingly true to history. Every student of Babylonia recalls these proud words in reading Neb.'s own records of his creation of the new Babylon; for instance (Grotefend Cylinder, *KB* iii, 2, p. 39): 'Then built I the palace the seat of my royalty (*ékallu mûšâb šarrûtia*), the bond of the race of men, the dwelling of joy and rejoicing'; and (East India House Inscr., vii, 34, *KB ib.*, p. 25): 'In Babylon, my dear city, which I love was the palace, the house of wonder of the people, the bond of the land, the brilliant place, the abode of majesty in Babylon.' The very language of the story is reminiscent of the Akkadian. The glory of Babylon, 'that great city' (Rev. 18), remained long to conjure the imagination of *raconteurs*. For the city's grandeur as revealed to the eye of the archaeologist we may refer to R. Koldewey, *Das wieder erstehende Babylon*, 1913 (Eng. tr. *Excavations at Babylon*, 1915), with its revelation of Neb.'s palace, the temples, etc."[25]

The building of Babylon was one of Nebuchadnezzar's principal occupations. Inscriptions for about fifty building projects have been found,

---

*Keil mentions the statements of Berosus in Josephi *Ant.* x. 11, 1, and *con. Ap.* i. 19, and of Abydenus in Eusebii *praepar. evang.* ix. 41, and *Chron.* i. p. 59; also the delineation of these buildings in Duncker's *Gesch. des Alterth.* i. p. 854 ff. (Keil, p. 159). See also the excellent description by Charles Boutflower, *In and Around the Book of Daniel*, pp. 66-67.

usually made of brick and sometimes of stone. Among the wonders of Nebuchadnezzar's creation were the gardens of Semiramis, the famous "hanging gardens" regarded as one of the Seven Wonders of the World. The gardens were planted on top of a building and served both to beautify and to keep the building cool from the heat of summer. They probably were in view of Nebuchadnezzar's palace. Although his palaces which he constructed were all in Babylon, there were numerous temples built in other cities. The city of Babylon itself, however, was regarded as the symbol of his power and majesty; and he spared no expense or effort to make it the most beautiful city of the world. If the construction of a great city, magnificent in size, architecture, parks, and armaments, was a proper basis for pride, Nebuchadnezzar was justified. What he had forgotten was that none of this would be possible apart from God's sovereign will.

No sooner were the words expressing his pride out of his mouth than he heard a voice from heaven, "O king Nebuchadnezzar, to thee it is spoken; The kingdom is departed from thee." The voice goes on to state how Nebuchadnezzar will be driven from men and fulfill the prophecy of living the life of a beast until the proper time had been fulfilled and he was willing to recognize the most high God. His transition from sanity to insanity was immediate, and so was the reaction as he was driven from the palace to begin his period of trial. Added in verse 33 is that which had not been previously mentioned—that his hair would grow like the feathers of an eagle, completely neglected and matted, and his nails would grow like birds' claws. How quickly God can reduce a man at the acme of power and majesty to the level of a beast. The brilliant mind of Nebuchadnezzar, like the kingdom which he ruled, was his only by the sovereign will of God.

Scripture draws a veil over most of the details of Nebuchadnezzar's period of trial. It is probable that Nebuchadnezzar was kept in the palace gardens away from abuse by common people.[26] Although given no care, he was protected; and in his absence his counsellors, possibly led by Daniel himself, continued to operate the kingdom efficiently. Although Scripture does not tell us, it is reasonable to assume that Daniel himself had much to do with the kind treatment and protection of Nebuchadnezzar. He, no doubt, informed the counsellors of what the outcome of the dream would be and that Nebuchadnezzar would return to sanity. In this, God must have inclined the hearts of Nebuchadnezzar's counsellors to cooperate, quite in contrast to what is often the case in ancient governments when at the slightest sign of weakness rulers were cruelly murdered. Nebuchadnezzar seems to have been highly respected as a brilliant king by those who worked with him, and this helped set the stage for his recovery.

Although his insanity was supernaturally imposed, it is not to be regarded as much different in its result from what might be expected if it had been produced by natural causes. The form of insanity in which men think of themselves as beasts and imitate the behavior of a beast is not without precedent. Keil designates the malady as *insania zoanthropica.*[*][27]

Young in his treatment of this designates the disease as Boanthropy, i.e., he thought himself to be an ox, and cites Pusey as having collected considerable data on the subject. A person in this stage of insanity in his inner consciousness remains somewhat unchanged, but his outer behavior is irrational. Young states, "Pusey adduces the remarkable case of Pere Surin, who believed himself to be possessed, yet maintained communion with God. It is true to fact, then, that Neb., although under the influence of this strange malady, could lift up his eyes unto heaven."[28] In any case, the malady supernaturally imposed by God was supernaturally relieved at the proper time.

Raymond Harrison recites a personal experience with a modern case similar to that of Nebuchadnezzar, which he observed in a British mental institution in 1946. Harrison writes,

> A great many doctors spend an entire, busy professional career without once encountering an instance of the kind of monomania described in the book of Daniel. The present writer, therefore, considers himself particularly fortunate to have actually observed a clinical case of boanthropy in a British mental institution in 1946. The patient was in his early 20's, who reportedly had been hospitalized for about five years. His symptoms were well-developed on admission, and diagnosis was immediate and conclusive. He was of average height and weight with good physique, and was in excellent bodily health. His mental symptoms included pronounced anti-social tendencies, and because of this he spent the entire day from dawn to dusk outdoors, in the grounds of the institution . . . . His daily routine consisted of wandering around the magnificent lawns with which the otherwise dingy hospital situation was graced, and it was his custom to pluck up and eat handfuls of the grass as he went along. On observation he was seen to discriminate carefully between grass and weeds, and on inquiry from the attendant the writer was told the diet of this patient consisted exclusively of grass from hospital lawns. He never ate institutional food with the other inmates, and his only drink was water. . . . The writer was able to examine him cursorily, and the only physical abnormality noted consisted of a lengthening of the hair and a coarse, thickened condition of the finger-nails. Without institutional care, the patient would have manifested precisely the same physical conditions as those mentioned in Daniel 4:33. . . . From the

---

[*]Keil notes that historical documents on this form of madness have been collected by Trusen in his *Sitten, Gebr. u. Krank. der alten Hebräer*, p. 205 f., 2d ed., and by Friedreich in *Zur Bibel*, i. p. 308 f. (Keil, p. 160).

foregoing it seems evident that the author of the fourth chapter of Daniel was describing accurately an attestable, if rather rare, mental affliction.[29]

The experience of Nebuchadnezzar has been compared by liberal critics to the "Prayer of Nabonidus," in Cave IV Document of the Qumran literature. The prayer is introduced as, "The words of the prayer which Nabonidus, King of Assyria and Babylon, the great king, prayed. . . ." The prayer describes Nabonidus as being afflicted with a "dread disease by the decree of the Most High God," which required his segregation at the Arabian oasis of Teima for a period of seven years. An unnamed Jewish seer is said to have advised Nabonidus to repent and give glory to God instead of the idols he formerly worshiped. Because of the parallelism between this account and that of Nebuchadnezzar, liberal scholars who consider the book of Daniel as written in the second century have concluded that the account of Nabonidus is the original account, and that what we have in Daniel 4 is a tradition about it which substituted the name of Nebuchadnezzar for that of Nabonidus. As Frank M. Cross has expressed it,

> There is every reason to believe that the new document [the Prayer of Nabonidus] preserves a more primitive form of the tale [Daniel 4]. It is well known that Nabonidus gave over the regency of his realm to his son Belshazzar in order to spend long periods of time in Teima; while Nebuchadnezzar, to judge from extrabiblical data, did not give up his throne. Moreover, in the following legend of Belshazzar's feast, the substitution of Nebuchadnezzar for Nabonidus as the father of Belshazzar (Dan. 5:2) is most suggestive. Evidently in an older stage of tradition, the cycle included the stories of Nebuchadnezzar (cf. Dan. 1-3), Nabonidus (Dan. 4), and Belshazzar (Dan. 5).[30]

Conservative scholars, who recognize the genuineness of the book of Daniel as a sixth century B.C. writing, see no conflict in accepting both Daniel 4 as it is written and the "Prayer of Nabonidus" as having some elements of truth, although apocryphal. In fact, as the discussion of Daniel 5 brings out, the fact that Nabonidus lived at Teima for extended periods, well attested in tradition, gives a plausible explanation as to why Belshazzar was in charge in Babylon in Daniel 5. It is not necessary to impugn the record of Daniel in order to recognize the uninspired story relating to Nabonidus.

Nebuchadnezzar's Restoration

4:34-37 And at the end of the days I Nebuchadnezzar lifted up mine eyes unto heaven, and mine understanding returned unto me, and I blessed the most High, and I praised and honoured him that liveth for ever, whose dominion is an everlasting dominion, and his kingdom is from generation to generation: And all the inhabitants of the earth are

reputed as nothing: and he doeth according to his will in the army of
heaven, and among the inhabitants of the earth: and none can stay his
hand, or say unto him, What doest thou? At the same time my reason
returned unto me; and for the glory of my kingdom, mine honour and
brightness returned unto me; and my counsellors and my lords sought
unto me; and I was established in my kingdom, and excellent majesty
was added unto me. Now I Nebuchadnezzar praise and extol and
honour the King of heaven, all whose works are truth, and his ways
judgment: and those that walk in pride he is able to abase.

Although the previous narrative had been couched in the third person,
Nebuchadnezzar now returns to first person narrative. He records how
he lifted up his eyes to heaven and his understanding returned. Whether
this was simultaneous or causal is not stated, but looking to the heavens
possibly was the first step in his recognition of the God of heaven and
gaining sane perspective on the total situation. Nebuchadnezzar's immediate reaction was to express praise to God, whom he recognizes as
"the most High." What effect this had on his belief in other deities is not
stated, but it at least opens the door to the possibility that Nebuchadnezzar had placed true faith in the God of Israel.

In praising and honoring God, he attributes to Him the quality of living
forever, of having an everlasting dominion, and of directing a kingdom
which is from generation to generation. These qualities of eternity and
sovereignty are far greater than those attributed to Babylonian deities.
Because of His sovereignty, God can consider all the inhabitants of the
earth as nothing. He is able to do as He wills whether in heaven or in
earth, and no one can stay his hand or ask, "What doest thou?" Even as
these words of praise were uttered to God, his reason returned to him.
No doubt his counsellors had maintained some sort of a watch upon him,
and upon the sudden change the report was given. They immediately
sought his return to his former position of honor. Apparently the transition was almost immediate, and Nebuchadnezzar was once more established in his kingdom. It is in this role that he is able to issue the decree
and make the public confession that is involved.

Nebuchadnezzar concludes with praise and worship for the "King of
heaven," whom he describes in conclusion, "all whose works are truth,
and his ways judgment: and those that walk in pride he is able to abase."
Nebuchadnezzar's experience brings the obvious spiritual lesson that
even the greatest of earthly sovereigns is completely subject to the sovereign power of God. Montgomery summarizes the chapter concisely,
"Neb. holds his fief from Him who is King in heaven and in the kingdom
of man."[31]

The debate as to whether Nebuchadnezzar was actually saved in a
spiritual sense remains unsettled. Such worthies as Calvin, Hengstenberg,

Pusey, and Keil believe the evidence is insufficient.[32] As Young and others point out, however, there is considerable evidence of Nebuchadnezzar's spiritual progress of which chapter 4 is the climax (cf. 2:47; 3:28; 4:34-35). There can be little question that he acknowledges Daniel's God as the omnipotent eternal sovereign of the universe (4:34, 35, 37). His issuance of a decree somewhat humiliating to his pride and an abject recognition of the power of God whom he identifies as "King of heaven" (4:37) would give us some basis for believing that Nebuchadnezzar had a true conversion. Inasmuch as in all ages some men are saved without gaining completely the perspective of faith or being entirely correct in the content of their beliefs, it is entirely possible that Nebuchadnezzar will be numbered among the saints.

In chapter 4 Nebuchadnezzar reaches a new spiritual perspicacity. Prior to his experience of insanity, his confessions were those of a pagan whose polytheism permitted the addition of new gods, as illustrated in Daniel 2:47 and 3:28-29. Now Nebuchadnezzar apparently worships the King of heaven only. For this reason, his autobiography is truly remarkable and reflects the fruitfulness of Daniel's influence upon him and probably of Daniel's daily prayers for him. Certainly God is no respecter of persons and can save the high and mighty in this world as well as the lowly.

5

BELSHAZZAR'S FEAST AND THE FALL
OF BABYLON

ALMOST SEVENTY YEARS HAVE PASSED since the events of chapter 1 of
Daniel. Nebuchadnezzar himself had died in 562 B.C. Daniel does not
record his immediate successors, and extrabiblical literature is somewhat
confused. A plausible account of Berosus, in his third book, found in a
fragment preserved by Josephus summarizes the history between Nebuchadnezzar's death in 562 B.C. and the fall of Babylon 539 B.C.

According to Berosus, Nebuchadnezzar died after a reign of 43 years
and was followed by his son Evil-Merodach. Because his rule was arbitrary
and licentious, he was assassinated by Neriglisar after he had reigned
only two years. The next four years Neriglisar occupied the throne. At his
death his son Laborosoarchod, who was only a child, reigned for nine
months until a conspiracy resulted in his being beaten to death. The conspirators appointed Nabonidus, one of their number, who reigned for
seventeen years before being defeated by Cyrus the Persian. Nabonidus
fleeing Babylon went to Borsippa but was forced to surrender to Cyrus.
Nabonidus was allowed to live in Carmania until the time of his death,
but he was not allowed to come to Babylonia.°

°The actual text of Berosus is as follows: "After beginning the wall of which I have
spoken, Nabuchodonosor fell sick and died, after a reign of forty-three years, and the
realm passed to his son Evilmaraduch. This prince, whose government was arbitrary
and licentious, fell a victim to a plot, being assassinated by his sister's husband,
Neriglisar, after a reign of two years. On his death Neriglisar, his murderer, succeeded
to the throne and reigned four years. His son, Laborosoardoch, a mere boy, occupied
it for nine months, when, owing to the depraved disposition which he showed, a conspiracy was formed against him, and he was beaten to death by his friends. After his
murder the conspirators held a meeting, and by common consent conferred the kingdom upon Nabonnedus, a Babylonian and one of their gang. In his reign the walls of
Babylon abutting on the river were magnificently built with baked brick and bitumen.
In the seventeenth year of his reign Cyrus advanced from Persia with a large army,
and, after subjugating the rest of the kingdom, marched upon Babylonia. Apprised
of his coming, Nabonnedus led his army to meet him, fought and was defeated, where-
upon he fled with a few followers and shut himself up in the town of Borsippa. Cyrus
took Babylon, and after giving orders to raze the outer walls of the city, because it
presented a very redoubtable and formidable appearance, proceeded to Borsippa to
besiege Nabonnedus. The latter surrendering, without waiting for investment, was
humanely treated by Cyrus, who dismissed him from Babylonia, but gave him Carmania for his residence. There Nabonnedus spent the remainder of his life, and there
he died" Flavius Josephus, "Against Apion," in *Josephus* I:221-25. For discussion of
Josephus' account, see Keil, pp. 164-71.

The account of Berosus preserved by Josephus is supported by other evidence such as the short fragment of Abydenus preserved by Eusebius.[1]

Until the discovery of the Nabonidus Cylinder, no mention of Belshazzar, whom Daniel declares to be king of Babylon, had been found in extrabiblical literature. Critics of the authenticity and historicity of Daniel accordingly were free to question whether any such person as Belshazzar existed. Since the publication of Raymond Dougherty's scholarly research .on Nabonidus and Belshazzar, based on the Nabonidus Cylinder and other sources, there is no ground for questioning the general historicity of Belshazzar; and only the details of the scriptural account unverified by extrabiblical sources can be challenged by the critics.[2] Montgomery states that the story is "unhistorical" but "nevertheless contains indubitable reminiscences of actual history."[3]

On the other hand, such a careful scholar as Edward J. Young states, "The identity of Belshazzar has long caused difficulty to commentators. Some have denied his historicity. . . . The king's name, however, has now appeared upon the cuneiform documents, so that there can be no question as to his historicity. This is the first point at which this ch. exhibits its remarkable accuracy."*[4] The controversy over Belshazzar, because of the extensive investigation and great variety of findings, has become one of the most complicated problems in the entire book, but the problem itself is comparatively simple. Was Belshazzar actually king of Babylon and was he murdered on the night that Babylon was conquered?

A solution of the problem has depended largely on the premises of the scholars dealing with it. Those critical of the authenticity and accuracy of Daniel, especially those zealous to prove second-century authorship, proceed on the premise that Daniel must be in error until he is proved otherwise. Here the discussion is lost in a maze of conflicting facts in extrabiblical literature concerning which the critics themselves are not agreed. Although such ancient records are notoriously inaccurate and at best are fragmentary, the argument of the critics was that Belshazzar never existed because his name did not appear in any of the ancient records. This omission, however, was later remedied, as mentioned above, by the discovery of the name of Bel-shar-usur (Belshazzar) on cylinders

*According to J. A. Brinkman, "Probably the first recorded mention of Belshazzar, Prince of Babylonia under Nabonnedus" is in a cuneiform text 135 in a collection at the Archaeological Museum in Florence published in 1958-60 by Professor Karl Oberhuber of the University of Innsbruck. The text is definitely from the sixth century B.C. This text indicates that a person known as Bel-sarra-usur was a *res sarri*, an officer of the king, under Neriglissar who came to the throne in 560 B.C., as had been earlier pointed out in a text YBC 3765:2 published by R. P. Dougherty in 1929 in *Nabonidus and Belshazzar*, pp. 67-68. This, no doubt, prepared the way for the co-regency under Nabonidus which probably began 553 B.C., supporting Daniel 5. (Cf. J. A. Brinkman, "Neo-Babylonian Texts in the Archaeological Museum at Florence," *Journal of Near Eastern Studies* 25:202-9.)

in which he is called the son of Nabonidus. Critics, having to recede from their former position that no such person existed, have since centered their attack on the fact that the word *king* does not occur in connection with Belshazzar on any extant Babylonian records.[5] The establishment of Nabonidus as the father of Belshazzar, or at least his stepfather, nullifies most of the critical objections, although Rowley in an extensive discussion maintains stoutly that to call Belshazzar a king "must still be pronounced a grave historical error."[6]

Since Rowley, however, even liberal scholars have tended to accept the explanation that Belshazzar acted as a regent under his father, Nabonidus. Norman Porteous, for instance, writes, "On the other hand it is known that Belshazzar was a historical person, the son of the last Babylonian king Nabonidus, who acted as regent of Babylon for several years before its fall, while his father was absent at the oasis of Teima in Arabia."[7] This would begin Belshazzar's regency about 553 B.C., when Nabonidus went to Teima. Not only the record in Daniel but also the external evidence is now sufficient to support the conclusion that Belshazzar's coregency is almost beyond question. This is another illustration of how critical objections based on lack of external evidence are frequently overthrown when the evidence is uncovered.*

Additional evidence that Nabonidus was away from Babylon on the night of Daniel 5 is given in the fragment from Berosus, previously cited, which indicates that Nabonidus had left Babylon only to be vanquished in battle and flee to Borsippa. This would involve the premise that Nabonidus, although usually living at Teima, had returned to Babylon for a visit just prior to the siege of Babylon, had gone out to battle before Babylon was actually surrounded, and then was defeated, thereby permitting the Persians to besiege Babylon itself. Under these circumstances, Belshazzar would indeed be king of Babylon in the absence of his father. Problems of his relationship will be considered at the proper place in the exposition, including the possibility that Belshazzar's mother was a daughter of Nebuchadnezzar and thus in the royal line, whereas Nabonidus was not. There are actually so many plausible possibilities in Daniel's account, supported by the evidence cited, that the storm of objections can hardly be taken seriously.[8]

---

*The new evidence confirming the theory that Nabonidus was absent is found in the statement in the "Prayer of Nabonidus" that Nabonidus was at the oasis of Teima in Arabia at this time. See J. T. Milik, " 'Priere de Nabonide' et autres ecrits d'un cycle de Daniel," *Revue Biblique* 63:407-15. Although it is possible to question the historicity of portions of the "Prayer of Nabonidus," as it is undoubtedly apocryphal, the consensus of both liberal and conservative scholarship seems to take the account as repeating in the main a true story. Cf. Norman Porteous, *Daniel: A Commentary*, p. 76.

BELSHAZZAR'S FEAST IN HONOR OF THE GODS OF BABYLON

5:1-4 Belshazzar the king made a great feast to a thousand of his lords, and drank wine before the thousand. Belshazzar, whiles he tasted the wine, commanded to bring the golden and silver vessels which his father Nebuchadnezzar had taken out of the temple which was in Jerusalem; that the king, and his princes, his wives, and his concubines, might drink therein. Then they brought the golden vessels that were taken out of the temple of the house of God which was at Jerusalem; and the king, and his princes, his wives, and his concubines, drank in them. They drank wine, and praised the gods of gold, and of silver, of brass, of iron, of wood, and of stone.

About seventy years had elapsed since the capture of Jerusalem recorded in Daniel 1. In the interpretation of the image in chapter 2, Daniel had predicted to Nebuchadnezzar, "After thee shall arise another kingdom inferior to thee" (Dan 2:39). Now, in chapter 5, this prophecy is about to be fulfilled. Nebuchadnezzar's humiliating experience in chapter 4 had been followed by his death in 562 B.C. Approximately twenty-three years elapsed between chapter 4 and chapter 5. In this period, a number of monarchs had succeeded Nebuchadnezzar. According to Berosus, Nebuchadnezzar was succeeded by his son, Evil-Merodach, also known as Amel-Marduk, who was killed in 560 B.C. He was followed by Neriglissar, also spelled Nergal-shar-usur, a son-in-law of Nebuchadnezzar who died in 556 B.C. of natural causes. He was succeeded by Laborosoarchad, also known as Labashi-Marduk, a grandson of Nebuchadnezzar, who was assassinated after less than a year. Nabonidus assumed the throne in 556 B.C. and reigned until 539 B.C. when conquered by the Medes. Belshazzar is best identified as his son, whose mother was either a wife or a daughter of Nebuchadnezzar and thereby strengthened the claim of Nabonidus to the throne. This explains why Belshazzar in the lineal descent from Nebuchadnezzar was honored as a coruler under Nabonidus. Although there are alternative explanations and some dates vary, this succession of kings and identification of characters seems to have reasonable justification. Most expositors disagree with Keil, who identifies Belshazzar with Evil-Merodach, preferring the identification of a son of Nabonidus, based on later evidence not available to Keil.[9] The identifications of Leupold are more satisfactory.[10]

In the quarter of a century which elapsed between chapter 4 and chapter 5, the further revelations given to Daniel in chapters 7 and 8 occurred. Chapter 7 was revealed to Daniel "in the first year of Belshazzar, king of Babylon" (Dan 7:1) and the vision of the ram and he-goat in chapter 8 occurred "in the third year of the reign of King Belshazzar" (Dan 8:1). The information embodied in these two visions, insofar as Daniel understood it, therefore was known to Daniel before the event of chapter 5 which chronologically came after chapters 7 and 8. If Belshazzar began his reign in 553 B.C., when Nabonidus went to Teima, the visions of chapters 7 and 8 actually occurred about twelve years before the events of chapter 5.

Verse 1 of chapter 5 introduces the fact that Belshazzar as king of Babylon had made a great feast to which a thousand of his lords had been invited with their wives. That such a large feast should be held by a monarch like Belshazzar is not at all strange. Leupold cites the ancient historian Ktesias to the effect that Persian monarchs frequently were known to dine daily with 15,000 people.*[11] M. E. L. Mallowan mentions the great feast that Ashusnasirpal II gave to 69,574 guests when he dedicated his new capital city of Calah (Nimrud) in 879 B.C.[12]

Although the size of the banquet is not amazing, the situation was most unusual. If the setting can be reconstructed, Nabonidus previously had gone forth from Babylon to fight the Medes and the Persians and had already been captured. The whole surrounding territory of the city of Babylon and the related provinces already had been conquered. Only Babylon with its massive walls and fortifications remained intact. Possibly to reassert their faith in their Babylonian gods and to bolster their own courage, this feast in the form of a festival had been ordered. The storehouses of Babylon were still abundant with food and wine, and there is evidence that there was plenty of both at this feast. The expression "drunk wine before the thousand" indicates that Belshazzar was probably on a platform at a higher level than other guests and led them in drinking toasts to their deities. Under the stimulus of wine, the thought occurred to Belshazzar to bring in the gold and silver vessels taken from the temple in Jerusalem by Nebuchadnezzar almost seventy years before. The implication in the clause "whiles he tasted the wine" is that Belshazzar in his right mind probably would not have committed this sacrilegious act.

Drinking bouts such as characterized Babylon were also common among other peoples, such as the Persians. Athenaeus quotes Heracleides of Cumae, the author of *Persian History*, in describing in detail the custom of drinking to excess after dinner.[13] The luxury of both the drinking and the eating is also illustrated in Athenaeus in describing dinners among the Persians of high station as follows: "For one thousand animals are slaughtered daily for the king; these comprise horses, camels, oxen, asses, deer, and most of the smaller animals; many birds also are consumed, including Arabian ostriches—and the creature is large—geese, and cocks."[14]

Much has been made of the reference of Belshazzar's relationship to Nebuchadnezzar, who is described as "his father" in verse 2; and even

---

*Montgomery mentions a marriage feast of Alexander with 10,000 guests (Montgomery, p. 250).

Keil is influenced by this to consider Belshazzar a literal son of Nebuchadnezzar.[15] This is not entirely impossible, of course, for as Leupold shows,[16] Nabonidus could have married a widow of Nebuchadnezzar who had a son by Nebuchadnezzar who then could be adopted by Nabonidus by way of strengthening his own hold upon the throne. As Nabonidus assumed the throne in 556 B.C., only six years after the death of Nebuchadnezzar, and Belshazzar was probably at least a teenager when Nebuchadnezzar died—if he was old enough to be coregent with Nabonidus in 553 B.C.— it is possible that he was a genuine son of Nebuchadnezzar and that his mother, after Nebuchadnezzar's death, was married to Nabonidus. This, however, is conjecture; and probably it is more natural to consider Belshazzar a son of Nabonidus himself.

Although the precise identity of Belshazzar may continue to be debated, available facts support accepting Daniel's designation of Belshazzar as king. The reference to *father* may be construed as "grandfather." As Pusey states, "Neither in Hebrew, nor in Chaldee, is there any word for 'grandfather,' 'grandson.' Forefathers are called 'fathers' or 'fathers' fathers.' But a single grandfather, or forefather, is never called 'father's father' but always 'father' only."[17]

The sacred vessels taken from Jerusalem had apparently been kept in storage without sacrilegious use from Nebuchadnezzar's day until the occasion of this feast. Now these holy vessels are distributed among the crowd and used as vessels from which to drink wine. Verse 2 cites that "the king, and his princes, his wives, and his concubines" drink from them; and this fact is restated in the actual act in verse 3 where only the golden vessels are mentioned. The Revised Standard Version, following the Vulgate, adds in verse 3 "and silver vessels." This act of sacrilege was an intentioned religious gesture in praise of the gods of Babylon mentioned in descending order of importance as "gods of gold, and of silver, of brass, of iron, of wood, and of stone." That Belshazzar well knew the blasphemous character of his act is evident from Daniel 5:13, 22. He knew Daniel and knew the history of Nebuchadnezzar's experience with God's chastening. Some have found, in the six materials mentioned, a typical reference to "the number of the world amenable to judgment because of its hostility to God."[18] In the original, the gods of gold and silver are separated by the conjunction "and," not true of the listing of the gods of brass, iron, wood, and stone, as if there were two classes of deities. This distinction is supported by Keil.[19]

Their pride in their deities may have been bolstered by the magnificence of the city of Babylon itself, interpreted as an evidence of the power of their gods. Herodotus gives a glowing account of Babylon as a monument to the genius of Nebuchadnezzar and undoubtedly a source of much pride to all the Babylonians. According to Herodotus, Babylon was about fourteen miles square, with great outer walls 87 feet thick and 350 feet high, with a hundred great bronze gates in the walls. A system of inner and outer walls with a water moat between the walls made the city very secure. So broad and strong were the walls that chariots four abreast could parade around its top. Herodotus pictures hundreds of towers at appropriate intervals reaching another 100 feet into the air above the top of the wall.[20]

Modern interpreters view Herodotus' figures as greatly exaggerated, with the real dimensions only about one-fourth of what Herodotus claimed. The outer wall seems to have been only seventeen miles in circumference, instead of about fifty-six as Herodotus claimed, with much fewer towers and gates; and probably even the towers were not more than 100 feet tall. While the dimensions may be questioned, the magnificence of the city was not seriously exaggerated.[21]

The great Euphrates River flowed through the middle of the city in a general north-south direction and was bordered by walls on each side to protect the city from attack from the river. Within these walls were beautiful avenues, parks, and palaces. Many of the streets were lined with buildings three and four stories high. Among these buildings were the Temple of Bel, an eight-story structure, and the magnificent palace of the king, actually a complex of buildings, which have now been excavated. A great bridge spanned the Euphrates River, connecting the eastern section and the western or new section of the city. The bridge was later supplemented by a tunnel mentioned by Diodorus. The famed "hanging gardens" of Babylon were large enough to support trees.

Although Babylon has been only partially excavated with but a small part of the original city recovered, the system of mounds which mark the city today more or less indicate its boundaries. Archeological research is complicated by a change in the course of the Euphrates River and a higher water level, but more than 10,000 inscribed texts have been discovered.

In many respects, Babylon was the most fabulous city of the ancient world both for the beauty of its architecture and for the safety of its huge walls and fortifications. It was hard for the Babylonians to believe that even the Medes and the Persians who had surrounded their beloved city could possibly breach the fortifications or exhaust their supplies which were intended to be ample for a siege of many years. Their confidence in their gods was bolstered by their confidence in their city.

THE HANDWRITING ON THE WALL

5:5-9 In the same hour came forth fingers of a man's hand, and wrote over against the candlestick upon the plaister of the wall of the king's palace: and the king saw the part of the hand that wrote. Then the king's countenance was changed, and his thoughts troubled him, so that the joints of his loins were loosed, and his knees smote one against another. The king cried aloud to bring in the astrologers, the Chaldeans, and the soothsayers. And the king spake, and said to the wise men of Babylon, Whosoever shall read this writing, and shew me the interpretation thereof, shall be clothed with scarlet, and have a chain of gold about his neck, and shall be the third ruler in the kingdom. Then came in all the king's wise men; but they could not read the writing, nor make known to the king the interpretation thereof. Then was king Belshazzar greatly troubled, and his countenance was changed in him, and his lords were astonied.

While the feast was in progress with its drinking of wine and shouting of praises to the gods of Babylon, suddenly there appeared the fingers of a man's hand which wrote on the plastered wall of the palace. With only the fingers of the hand visible and producing writing upon the wall, the spectacle immediately attracted attention.

In the ruins of Nebuchadnezzar's palace archeologists have uncovered a large throne room 56 feet wide and 173 feet long which probably was the scene of this banquet. Midway in the long wall opposite the entrance there was a niche in front of which the king may well have been seated. Interestingly, the wall behind the niche was covered with white plaster as described by Daniel, which would make an excellent background for such a writing.[22]

If the scene can be reconstructed, it is probable that the banquet was illuminated by torches which not only produced smoke but fitful light that would only partially illuminate the great hall. As the writing according to Daniel was written "over against the candlestick upon the plaister of the wall of the king's palace," it may have appeared in an area of greater illumination than the rest of the room and thus also have attracted more attention.

The effect upon the king and his associates was immediate. According to Daniel, his countenance changed, that is, changed color and became pale. His thin courage, bolstered by wine drunk from vessels which Nebuchadnezzar had plundered and were seemingly a symbol of the power of the gods of Babylon, now deserted him. He was instead filled with terror to the point that "the joints of his loins were loosed, and his knees smote one against another." In his excitement, he no longer could sit down but hardly had the strength to stand. Probably before the babble of conversation in the banquet room had subsided, the king began to cry aloud "to bring in the astrologers, the Chaldeans, and the soothsayers." Only three classes of wise men are mentioned, but it is doubtful whether any class was intentionally omitted as verse 8 refers to "all the king's wise men." The astrologers were actually the magicians; the Chaldeans were a broad class of scholars and learned men in the lore of the Babylonians; and the soothsayers corresponded more closely to the modern concept of astrologers, although they may have also practiced sorcery. It is possible in the decline of the Babylonian Empire that the number of the wise men was far more limited at this point in history than it was under Nebuchadnezzar's reign. In any event, there is no proof for the suggestion discussed by Keil that the classification of wise men mentioned purposely excluded Daniel. As Keil points out, the king was ready to listen to anyone who could interpret the writing.[23]

As soon as a suitable number of the wise men had assembled, the king addressed them offering the reward that, if one of them could read the writing and show the interpretation, he would be clothed with scarlet and have a chain of gold about his neck and become third ruler in the kingdom. To be clothed in scarlet and to wear a chain of gold about the neck were special tokens of the king's favor and certainly would have been coveted by any of the wise men.

Much speculation has arisen concerning the expression that he offered them the position of being "the third ruler in the kingdom." There is some question as to whether the Aramaic indicates specifically "the third ruler." The ordinal numeral would be *t^elîtāy* (as in Dan 2:39) whereas the Aramaic here is actually *talti*. Scholars are not agreed as to the precise meaning of this term, but the suggestion is made that it may be a title for an office of honor which did not necessarily correspond precisely to the meaning of the word. As Keil expresses it, "It is not quite certain what the princely situation is which was promised to the interpreter of the writing. . . . That it is not the *ordinale* of the number third, is, since Havernick, now generally acknowledged."[24] However, recent scholarship has tended to confirm the translation "the third ruler." Franz Rosenthal, for instance, confidently translates the term "one-third (ruler), triumvir."[25]

In spite of the problem in the word, it is probable that the offer of honor was that of being the third ruler. Belshazzar under Nabonidus was considered the second ruler, and the position of a third ruler would be the highest that he could offer. Belshazzar was evidently in no mood to bargain but was terrified and desperately desired to know the meaning of the writing.

The large reward that was offered, however, was to no avail, for the wise men who assembled could not read the writing nor interpret it. This implies a twofold difficulty. Some have claimed that the text does not plainly indicate the language. Charles, for instance, suggests that the writing was in unfamiliar ideograms.[26] This, however, is mere conjecture.

The probability is that the writing was in Aramaic and therefore not entirely unknown to the wise men.

In any case Daniel read the writing as Aramaic, and the suggestion of puns in the language (see later discussion) depends upon the Aramaic. The difficulty of the wise men in reading the writing may have been that it was written in Aramaic script without the vowels being supplied; but if written in cuneiform, the vowels would have been included. Daniel does not explain the difficulty in reading the writing on the wall, but the problem apparently was not that it was a strange language but rather what the words signified prophetically. For further discussion, see exposition of Daniel 5:25-27.

The inability of the wise men to decipher the writing only increased the concern of Belshazzar. Perhaps the full force of his wickedness in using the vessels taken from the temple in Jerusalem had begun to dawn upon him, or the fears suppressed concerning the presence of the armies which surrounded Babylon may have now emerged. His concern was shared by the entire assembly.

Belshazzar's predicament is another illustration of the insecurity and powerlessness of the rulers of this world when confronted by the power and wisdom of God. How God holds in derision the rulers of the world who take counsel against Him (Ps 2:1-4)! Like Nebuchadnezzar before him, Belshazzar was soon to experience divine judgment but without the happy ending.

Daniel Suggested as the Interpreter

5:10-12 Now the queen by reason of the words of the king and his lords came into the banquet house: and the queen spake and said, O king live for ever: let not thy thoughts trouble thee, nor let thy countenance be changed. There is a man in thy kingdom, in whom is the spirit of the holy gods; and in the days of thy father light and understanding and wisdom, like the wisdom of the gods, was found in him; whom the king Nebuchadnezzar thy father, the king, I say, thy father, made master of the magicians, astrologers, Chaldeans, and soothsayers; Forasmuch as an excellent spirit, and knowledge, and understanding, interpreting of dreams, and shewing of hard sentences, and dissolving of doubts, were found in the same Daniel, whom the king named Belteshazzar: now let Daniel be called, and he will show the interpretation.

The crisis produced by the inability of the wise men to interpret the handwriting on the wall is met by the entrance of one described as "the queen." Much speculation surrounds the identity of this person as it is related to the larger question of Belshazzar's lineage. Keil and Leupold both consider her to be a wife of Nebuchadnezzar and the mother of Belshazzar.[27] As the wives of the lords and the king himself had earlier been declared to be at the banquet (v. 3) one who had the role of "queen" would most probably be Belshazzar's mother. She had not attended the banquet. This would be understandable if she was elderly and the widow of Nebuchadnezzar. If she were the wife of Nabonidus who was in captivity she probably would not have desired to come alone. Hearing the unusual clamor at the banquet and learning of the distress of her son, because of her position she was able to enter the banquet hall freely and speak to the king. Her address is courteous, "O king, live for ever," but directly to the point. Like a mother, she told her son in effect to pull himself together because there must be some solution to his problem. As one holding her position was normally highly regarded and treated with respect, she could speak out in a way that no other could do. Honoring of parents was characteristic of the Israelites (Ex 20:12; 1 Ki 2:13-20; 2 Ki 24:12-15). The same was true in the Gentile world, and the dowager queen was able to enter the banquet hall without an invitation.

Montgomery, opposing the idea that the queen is Belshazzar's wife, comments, "Also the lady's masterful appearance on the scene betokens rather the queen-mother than the consort."[28] Jeffery, likewise, writes, ". . . she speaks to him of his father in a way that suggests a mother speaking to a son rather than a wife to a husband."[29]

The solution to the problem which the queen suggested was that they invite Daniel the prophet, who had been discovered as a man of wisdom by Nebuchadnezzar, to interpret the writing. The queen uses the very words which presumably she had heard Nebuchadnezzar express (Dan 4:8, 9, 18). According to the queen, Daniel had "the spirit of the holy gods." In the time of Nebuchadnezzar, to whom she refers as "thy father," Daniel had been found to have the wisdom of gods and possessing "light," that is, enlightenment, "understanding" or insight, and in general wisdom comparable to the wisdom of the gods. So great was his genius that Nebuchadnezzar had made him "master" or chief of his wise men, which in itself was a remarkable position for one who was not a Chaldean; and this honor placed upon him testified to the confidence of Nebuchadnezzar in Daniel's abilities. The reference to Nebuchadnezzar as the father of Belshazzar, as previously indicated, should probably be either grandfather or great-grandfather as the same term would be used for any of these designations. It does imply, however, that Belshazzar was in descent from Nebuchadnezzar.

Daniel's excellent qualities manifested themselves in "an excellent spirit," unusual knowledge and understanding, and the ability to interpret dreams, difficult sentences, and "dissolving of doubts," that is, solutions to problems. The word for *doubts* (*qit*e*rîn*) is actually *knots, joints, difficult problems*. Daniel had not been assembled with the other wise men because he probably was in semiretirement and was no longer chief of the wise men. The queen urged, however, that now he be brought in to solve the present problem.

DANIEL CALLED BEFORE THE KING

5:13-16 Then was Daniel brought in before the king. And the king spake and said unto Daniel, Art thou that Daniel, which art of the children of the captivity of Judah, whom the king my father brought out of Jewry? I have even heard of thee, that the spirit of the gods is in thee, and that light and understanding and excellent wisdom is found in thee. And now the wise men, the astrologers, have been brought in before me, that they should read this writing, and make known unto me the interpretation thereof: but they could not show the interpretation of the thing: And I have heard of thee, that thou canst make interpretations, and dissolve doubts: now if thou canst read the writing, and make known to me the interpretation thereof, thou shalt be clothed with scarlet, and have a chain of gold about thy neck, and shalt be the third ruler in the kingdom.

When Daniel was brought before the king, he addressed a natural question to reassure himself of the identity of Daniel. It seems clear that Belshazzar knew something of Daniel, for his form of address in verse 13 goes beyond the information supplied by his mother. He knew for instance that Daniel was of the captivity of Judah and that he was one of the captives which Nebuchadnezzar had brought out of Jerusalem. It may well be that because of awareness of his ancestry and religious convictions that Daniel had been demoted by Belshazzar himself. Now Belshazzar was all too eager to have the gifts of this man exercised to interpret the writing. Belshazzar goes on in verse 14 to repeat what his mother had said concerning Daniel's wisdom.

Belshazzar informs Daniel of the inability of all the wise men either to read or to interpret the writing. Belshazzar then offers Daniel the same promise he made to the others of being clothed with scarlet and having a chain of gold and the privilege of being "the third ruler in the kingdom," that is, the triumvir. As in the previous instances in Daniel 2 and 4, the wisdom of the world is demonstrated to be totally unable to solve its major problems and to understand either the present or the future. Daniel as the prophet of God is the channel through which divine revelation would come, and Belshazzar in his extremity was willing to listen.

Too often the world, like Belshazzar, is not willing to seek the wisdom of God until its own bankruptcy becomes evident. Then help is sought too late, as in the case of Belshazzar, and the cumulative sin and unbelief which precipitated the crisis in the first place becomes the occasion of downfall.

The situation before Belshazzar had all the elements of a great drama. Here was Daniel, an old man well in his eighties, with the marks of godly living evident in his bearing—in sharp contrast to the wine-flushed faces of the crowd. In the midst of this atmosphere of consternation, apprehension, and fear, Daniel's countenance alone reflected the deep peace of God founded on confidence in God and His divine revelation.

DANIEL'S REBUKE OF BELSHAZZAR

5:17-23   Then Daniel answered and said before the king, Let thy gifts be to thyself, and give thy rewards to another; yet I will read the writing unto the king, and make known to him the interpretation. O thou king, the most high God gave Nebuchadnezzar thy father a kingdom, and majesty, and glory, and honour: And for the majesty that he gave him, all people, nations, and languages, trembled and feared before him: whom he would he slew; and whom he would he kept alive; and whom he would he set up; and whom he would he put down. But when his heart was lifted up, and his mind hardened in pride, he was deposed from his kingly throne, and they took his glory from him: And he was driven from the sons of men; and his heart was made like the beasts, and his dwelling was with the wild asses: they fed him with grass like oxen, and his body was wet with the dew of heaven; till he knew that the most high God ruled in the kingdom of men, and that he appointeth over it whomsoever he will. And thou his son, O Belshazzar, hast not humbled thine heart, though thou knewest all this: But hast lifted up thyself against the Lord of heaven; and they have brought the vessels of his house before thee, and thou, and thy lords, thy wives, and thy concubines, have drunk wine in them; and thou hast praised the gods of silver, and gold, of brass, iron, wood, and stone, which see not, nor hear, nor know: and the God in whose hand thy breath is, and whose are all thy ways, hast thou not glorified:

Daniel's reply to the king is properly called a sermon, and as King says, "What a great sermon it is!"[30] Daniel begins by disavowing any interest in the gifts or rewards which the king offered. This was not prompted by disrespect nor by the evident fact that they would be short-lived. What Daniel is saying is that he will give an unprejudiced interpretation with no attempt to seek favor from the king. He promises both to read and to make known the interpretation.

In addressing the king, Daniel does not begin with a formal salutation as he does for instance in connection with Darius in Daniel 6:21 where he says, "O king, live for ever." No doubt Daniel holds Belshazzar in contempt for his desecration of the sacred vessels. However, the narration here must be considered in the form of a condensation; and probably Daniel addressed the king in a formal way. A parallel is found in Daniel 2:27, where Daniel addresses Nebuchadnezzar without formal greeting, and in Daniel 4:19, where Daniel replies to Nebuchadnezzar simply with the expression, "My lord." This was hardly a time in any case for Daniel to greet Belshazzar with such an expression as he gave to Darius, "O king, live for ever," when as a matter of fact, Belshazzar's hours were numbered. Instead, in verse 18 he recognizes him as king but then immediately delivers his prophetic message of condemnation.

Daniel first reminds Belshazzar that God gave Nebuchadnezzar his great kingdom and the honor that went with it. Daniel describes graphically in verse 19 how Nebuchadnezzar was feared and had absolute authority of life and death over his people and, accordingly, was an absolute sovereign. As Young points out, however, the very character of this absolute authority delegated to Nebuchadnezzar by God also made Nebuchadnezzar responsible.[31] This is demonstrated and supported by Nebuchadnezzar's experience of insanity in Daniel 4 when, as Daniel expresses it, "he was deposed from his kingly throne, and they took his glory from him." Daniel then itemizes in detail the characteristics of Nebuchadnezzar's insanity, how he lived with the wild beasts, ate grass like the ox, and was wet with the dew of heaven. All of this proved that God was greater than Nebuchadnezzar and held him responsible for his authority. Only when Nebuchadnezzar was properly humbled did God restore him to his glory and kingdom.

These facts are pertinent to Belshazzar's situation as they were well known by everyone as Daniel expresses it in verse 22, "And thou his son, O Belshazzar, hast not humbled thine heart, though thou knewest all this." The contrast between the supreme power of Nebuchadnezzar and the very limited power of Belshazzar is also evident. Belshazzar was not even the first ruler in the kingdom and was humiliated by the fact that Babylon was besieged and had already lost its power over the provinces surrounding the city.

Belshazzar's situation and his knowledge of Nebuchadnezzar's humbling made all the more blasphemous his taking of the vessels captured in Jerusalem from the house of the Lord and using them to drink wine in praising the gods of Babylon. With what eloquent scorn Daniel declares that Belshazzar, his lords, wives and concubines had drunk wine from these sacred vessels and had "praised gods of silver, and gold, of brass, iron, wood, and stone, which see not, nor hear, nor know: and the God in whose hand thy breath is, and whose are all thy ways, hast thou not glorified."*

Although the Scriptures do not state so expressly, it is probable that the message of Daniel to the king was heard by the entire company. It would have been quite improper for the entire company to keep on talking, especially in these dramatic circumstances, when Daniel was reporting to the king. They would naturally want to hear what he had to say. One

*There is a remarkably close parallel to the language of 5:23 in the "Prayer of Nabonidus" found in Qumran Cave IV. See J. T. Milik, pp. 407-15.

can well imagine the tense moment as these ringing words reached every ear in the vast hall in the deathlike silence that greeted Daniel's prophetic utterance. Here was a man who did not fear man and feared only God. Daniel spoke in measured tones the condemnation of that which was blasphemous in the sight of the holy God. There was, however, nothing insolent or discourteous in Daniel's address to the king; and the charges were stated in a factual and objective way. In any case, the king was in no position to dispute with Daniel, even though Daniel's words brought even greater fear and apprehension to his heart.

DANIEL'S INTERPRETATION OF THE WRITING

5:24-28 Then was the part of the hand sent from him; and this writing was written. And this is the writing that was written, MENE, MENE, TEKEL, UPHARSIN. This is the interpretation of the thing: MENE; God hath numbered thy kingdom, and finished it. TEKEL; Thou art weighed in the balances, and art found wanting. PERES; Thy kingdom is divided, and given to the Medes and Persians.

In beginning his explanation of the handwriting on the wall, Daniel first of all reads the writing; and for the first time, the words are introduced into the text of this chapter. Transliterated into English, they are given as "MENE, MENE, TEKEL, UPHARSIN." There has been almost endless critical discussion as to what the meaning of this inscription is, and the interpretation is complicated by a number of factors.*[32] In the book of Daniel the words are given in Aramaic, but some have questioned this.[33] If it was written in Aramaic script, however, only the consonants may have appeared. If in cuneiform, the vowels would be included. While in ordinary discourse the lack of vowels could normally be supplied rather easily, in a cryptic statement such as this the addition of vowels is a problem. The inscription on the wall may have appeared like this, "MN' MN' TQL UPRSN." The order of the letters in the Aramaic, of course, would be the reverse of this, that is, from right to left.

Young suggests, after some of the rabbis, that the characters may have been written vertically,[34] and in that case in the Aramaic order they would have appeared as follows:

P T M M
R Q N N
S L ' '

If, in addition to the complications of the Aramaic, a language which was known, some unfamiliar form of their characters was used, it would in-

---

*In the end, even the critics accept either the interpretation of Daniel (*mene,* "numbered"; *tekel,* "weighed"; *peres,* "divided"); or the reading, " a maneh, a maneh, a shekel, and a half-maneh," see exposition.

deed have required divine revelation to give a suitable explanation and interpretation, and may account for the difficulty in reading the writing.

Because of the variety of words that could be identified merely by the consonants, another suggestion has been made. MENE could be considered equivalent to the maneh of Ezekiel 45:12; Ezra 2:69. TEQEL could be considered as representing the Hebrew shekel. PERES could be read as PERAS, or a half-maneh, although this identification is questionable. Under this interpretation, the writing would read, "A maneh, a maneh, a shekel, and a half-maneh." Having arrived at this conclusion, however, it still remains to be determined what it means. Young in his discussion on this point gives J. Dymeley Prince[*] the credit for the suggestion that the maneh refers to Nebuchadnezzar, the shekel (of much less value) to Belshazzar, and the half-minas refers to the Medes and the Persians.[35] Daniel's explanation, however, is far more cogent and reasonable, and does not give any indication that the words mean other than he indicates.

The word MENE means "numbered," and Daniel interprets this in verse 26 as indicating "God hath numbered thy kingdom, and finished it." It is in keeping with the idea that man's days are numbered, and the repetition of the word twice is probably for emphasis. Like the other words, it is a passive participle.

TEQEL means "weighed," with the thought that Belshazzar has been put into the balances and found wanting, that is, short of true weight.

PERES means "divided," and is merely another form for UPHARSIN as in verse 25 having the *u*, which is equivalent to the English *and*, with PHARSIN being the plural of PERES. Leupold suggests that PHARSIN could be understood by changing the vowels to be "Persians"[36] and might have a double meaning as indicated by Daniel's explanation "given to the Medes and Persians." A pun may be intended on this third word. Having been interpreted to mean "divided," it is also understood as a reference to the Aramaic word for *Persian*, thereby hinting a Persian victory over Babylon.

The interpretation of Daniel is clear and much more satisfactory than the alternatives offered by some expositors. Belshazzar is made to under-

---

[*]Since Prince, who wrote his commentary in 1899, many others have followed the suggestion of Clermont-Ganneau (*Journal Asiatique*) 1886, that the inscription contained a string of weight names. E. G. Kraeling ("The Handwriting on the Wall," *Journal of Biblical Literature* 63 [1944]: 11-18) assuming that five kings are in view—i.e., *mene* is given twice and the *upharsin* equals two half-minas—suggests that the five kings following Nebuchadnezzar were intended, viz., Evil-Merodach, Neriglissar, Labashi-Marduk, Nabonidus and Belshazzar. D. N. Freedman ("Prayer of Nabonidus," *Bulletin of the American Schools of Oriental Research* 145 [1957]: 32) identifies the three kings as Nebuchadnezzar, Nabonidus and Belshazzar. Freedman cites H. Louis Ginsberg (*Studies in Daniel*, pp. 24-26) as holding that only three kings are referred to, viz., Nebuchadnezzar, Evil-Merodach and Belshazzar.

stand that Babylon will be given to the Medes and the Persians. Even while Daniel was interpreting the writing on the wall, the prophecy was being fulfilled as the Medes and the Persians poured into the city.

DANIEL'S REWARD AND THE PROPHECY FULFILLED

5:29-31 Then commanded Belshazzar, and they clothed Daniel with scarlet, and put a chain of gold about his neck, and made a proclamation concerning him, that he should be the third ruler in the kingdom. In that night was Belshazzar the king of the Chaldeans slain. And Darius the Median took the kingdom, being about threescore and two years old.

The drama of the writing on the wall and its interpretation is now brought to its fulfillment as Belshazzar keeps his promise. Daniel is clothed with scarlet, a chain of gold put about his neck, and a proclamation issued that he should be the third ruler in the kingdom. All of these honors, however, were short-lived and useless, as Daniel well knew, and typical of the honors of this world. In its rise to power the Babylonian Empire had conquered Jerusalem, taken its inhabitants into captivity, looted its beautiful temple, and completely destroyed the city. Yet this empire was to have as its last official act the honoring of one of these captives who by divine revelation predicted not only the downfall of Babylon but the course of the times of the Gentiles until the Son of man should come from heaven. Man may have the first word, but God will have the last word.

Herodotus gives an interesting account of the circumstances surrounding the capture of Babylon:

"Cyrus . . . then advanced against Babylon. But the Babylonians, having taken the field, awaited his coming; and when he had advanced near the city, the Babylonians gave battle, and, being defeated, were shut up in the city. But as they had been long aware of the restless spirit of Cyrus, and saw that he attacked all nations alike, they had laid up provisions for many years, and therefore were under no apprehensions about a siege. On the other hand, Cyrus found himself in difficulty, since much time had elapsed, and his affairs were not at all advanced. Whether, therefore, someone else made the suggestion to him in his perplexity, or whether he himself devised the plan, he had recourse to the following stratagem. Having stationed the bulk of his army near the passage of the river where it enters Babylon, and again having stationed another division beyond the city, where the river makes its exit, he gave order to his forces to enter the city as soon as they should see the stream fordable. Having stationed his forces and given these directions, he himself marched away with the ineffective part of his army; and having come to the lake, Cyrus did the same with respect to the river and the lake as the queen of the Babylonians had done; for having diverted the river, by means of a canal, into the lake, which was before a swamp, he made the ancient channel fordable by the sinking of the river. When this took place, the

Persians who were appointed to that purpose close to the stream of the river, which had now subsided to about the middle of a man's thigh, entered Babylon by this passage. If, however, the Babylonians had been aware of it beforehand, or had known what Cyrus was about, they would not have suffered the Persians to enter the city, but would have utterly destroyed them; for, having shut all the little gates that lead to the river, and mounting the walls that extend along the banks of the river, they would have caught them as in a net; whereas the Persians came upon them by surprise. It is related by the people who inhabited this city, that, by reason of its great extent, when they who were at the extremities were taken, those of the Babylonians who inhabited the centre knew nothing of the capture (for it happened to be a festival); but they were dancing at the time, and enjoying themselves, till they received certain information of the truth. And thus Babylon was taken for the first time."[37]

Keil discusses at length both Herodotus' account and that of Xenophon in his *Cyropaedia*, which is similar, and summarizes the arguments of Kranichfeld discounting these records. Discoveries since Keil tend to support Herodotus and Xenophon, although not accounting for Darius the Mede. The battle probably took place much as Herodotus records it.[38]

Prophecy anticipating the fall of Babylon is found in both Isaiah and Jeremiah, written many years before. Isaiah and Jeremiah had prophesied that Babylon would fall to the Medes on just such a night of revelry as Daniel records (Is 13:17-22; 21:1-10; Jer 51:33-58). Some of these prophecies may have their ultimate fulfillment in the future (Rev 17-18). More specifically of the invasion of the Medes, Isaiah writes, "Go up, O Elam: besiege, O Media" (Is 21:2), and continues, after describing their dismay, "My heart panted, fearfulness affrighted me: the night of my pleasure hath he turned into fear unto me. Prepare the table, watch in the watchtower, eat, drink: arise, ye princes, and anoint the shield" (Is 21:4-5). Finally, the tidings come, "Babylon is fallen, is fallen; and all the graven images of her gods he hath broken unto the ground" (Is 21:9). Jeremiah is explicit, "And I will make drunk her princes, and her wise men, her captains, and her rulers, and her mighty men: and they shall sleep a perpetual sleep, and not wake, saith the King, whose name is the LORD of hosts. Thus saith the LORD of hosts; The broad walls of Babylon shall be utterly broken, and her high gates shall be burned with fire" (Jer 51:57-58).

The account of Cyrus, himself, of the fall of Babylon has now been recovered in an inscription on a clay barrel:

Marduk, the great lord, a protector of his people/worshipers, beheld with pleasure his (i.e., Cyrus') good deeds and his upright mind (lit.: heart) (and therefore) ordered him to march against his city Babylon. . . . He made him set out on the road to Babylon . . . going at his side like a real friend. His widespread troops—their number, like that of the water of a river, could not be established—strolled along, their weapons packed away. Without any battle, he made him enter his town Babylon, . . . sparing Babylon . . . any calamity. He delivered into his (i. e., Cyrus') hands Nabonidus, the king who did not worship him (i.e., Marduk).[39]

Daniel himself records with graphic simplicity the fulfillment of his prophecy in the words, "In that night was Belshazzar the king of the Chaldeans slain." The concluding verse of the chapter in English versification records how Darius the Median became ruler of Babylon at the age of 62 years. The identity of this conqueror, unknown outside the Bible by this name, has touched off endless controversy and discussion which will be considered in the next chapter.

The long chapter devoted to this incident which brought the Babylonian Empire to its close is undoubtedly recorded in the Word of God not only for its historic fulfillment of the prophecies relative to the Babylonian Empire but also as an illustration of divine dealing with a wicked world. The downfall of Babylon is in type the downfall of the unbelieving world. In many respects, modern civilization is much like ancient Babylon, resplendent with its monuments of architectural triumph, as secure as human hands and ingenuity could make it, and yet defenseless against the judgment of God at the proper hour. Contemporary civilization is similar to ancient Babylon in that it has much to foster human pride but little to provide human security. Much as Babylon fell on that sixteenth day of Tishri (Oc. 11 or 12) 539 B.C., as indicated in the Nabonidus Chronicle,[40] so the world will be overtaken by disaster when the day of the Lord comes (1 Th 5:1-3). The disaster of the world, however, does not overtake the child of God; Daniel survives the purge and emerges triumphant as one of the presidents of the new kingdom in chapter 6.

6

DANIEL IN THE LIONS' DEN

THE ACCOUNT OF DANIEL being cast into the lions' den is one of the most familiar stories of the Old Testament. The fact that such an event should be given the same amount of space in Scripture as the panoramic view of world history recorded in chapter 7 leads to the conclusion that, from God's viewpoint, this was an important event not only to Daniel but to all students of Scripture.

From the standpoint of biblical scholarship, however, more attention has been directed to Darius the Mede, the king of Babylon at this time, than to the events of the chapter itself. The reason for this is that much of the critical unbelief in relation to the book of Daniel is based on what is claimed to be a palpable historical error, for it is claimed that history allows no room for such a person by this name. The alleged error is another important argument used to prove a second-century date for Daniel at which the true facts of four hundred years before would be obscure. The problem has attracted scholars who continue to write entire books discussing the questions involved.

H. H. Rowley, who has written one of the most important scholarly studies on this question, begins his work by saying, "The references to Darius the Mede in the book of Daniel have long been recognized as providing the most serious historical problem in the book."[1] The problem to which he refers is that the book of Daniel states that Darius the Mede, at the age of 62, received the kingdom after the death of Belshazzar (Dan 5:31) and was "the son of Ahasuerus, of the seed of the Medes, which was made king over the realm of the Chaldeans" (Dan 9:1). In chapter 6 we learn that Darius organized "the whole kingdom," setting up one hundred and twenty princes and three presidents of which Daniel was the first. The Septuagint translates Daniel 6:28 to read that after the death of Darius, Cyrus the Persian king took control, implying a Median kingdom under Darius which was followed by a Persian kingdom under Cyrus. Sources outside the Bible, however, clearly indicate that this is not the case.

As D. J. Wiseman has itemized, basing his findings on the *Nabonidus Chronicle*, the actual events went something like this.[2] Babylon was conquered by Ugbaru, the governor of Gutium, who led the army of

Cyrus and entered the city of Babylon on the night of Belshazzar's feast. Nabonidus, who was Belshazzar's father, had fled Babylon the day before only to be captured and later die in exile. When Babylon fell to Ugbaru on October 11, 539 B.C., Cyrus himself had remained with other troops at Opis, and not until eighteen days later, October 29, 539 B.C., did he actually arrive in Babylon. A man by the name of Gubaru was appointed by Cyrus to rule in Babylon. Eight days after the arrival of Cyrus, Ugbaru died. If this precise history of the events following the fall of Babylon is correct, it is obvious that there is no room for Darius the Mede to reign over Babylon. Although there are several explanations, three predominate.

First, the book of Daniel is here historically in error, and the writer has confused Darius the Mede with some other important personage. One of the most important advocates of this explanation is H. H. Rowley, who successively discards identification of Darius the Mede with Astyages, the last of the Median kings;[3] Cyaxares, the son of Astyages;[4] Gobryas, another form of the name Gubaru, or Ugbaru, who led the forces conquering Babylon;[5] and Cambyses, a son of Cyrus.[6] Rowley offers rather thorough proof that none of these suggestions are valid and supports the conclusion that there is no reliable evidence that a person named Darius the Mede ever lived, as only Daniel mentions him. Rowley suggests that this ruler was so designated by the author of Daniel because of confusion with Darius the son of Hystaspes, who is associated with a later fall of Babylon in 520 B.C. In a word, Rowley believes that Daniel's book is not reliable historically in its reference to Darius the Mede. This would also support the theory that Daniel the prophet of the sixth century B.C. could not have written the book as he would have had accurate information.

Two explanations have been offered by conservative scholars. Both recognize Darius the Mede as an actual historical character who fulfilled the role assigned him in Daniel 6.

One of these explanations, which is quite popular, is that Darius the Mede is the same as Gubaru, the governor appointed over Babylon by Cyrus. This view is strongly supported by Robert Dick Wilson[7] and a host of others such as Friedrich Delitzsch, C. H. H. Wright, Joseph D. Wilson, and W. F. Albright.[8] John C. Whitcomb, Jr. has attempted to revive this view and answer Rowley.[9] Whitcomb distinguishes Gubaru from Ugbaru, both of whom are called Gobryas in some translations of the *Nabonidus Chronical*. Whitcomb holds that Ugbaru, identified previously as the governor of Gutium in the *Nabonidus Chronical*, led the army of Cyrus into Babylon and died less than a month later. Gubaru, however, is identified by Whitcomb as Darius the Mede, a king of Babylon under the authority of Cyrus. Although sources outside the Bible do not call Gubaru a Median or king of Babylon, nor do they give his age, there is no real contradiction between the secular records and that which Daniel states of Darius the Mede.

The third view, held by the conservative scholar, D. J. Wiseman, has simplicity in its favor. It claims that Darius the Mede is another name of Cyrus the Persian. This is based upon a translation of Daniel 6:28 which the Aramaic permits to read "Daniel prospered in the reign of Darius, even the reign of Cyrus the Persian."[10] The fact that monarchs had more than one name is common in ancient literature, and Wiseman's view offers another conservative explanation of this problem in Daniel.

All who discuss the question of Darius the Mede must necessarily found their arguments on a relative scarcity of factual material. Critics frequently appeal to silence as an argument in their favor, as if the absence of a fact from our fragmentary records is a conclusive point. Most Bible-believing Christians feel that, until there is overwhelming evidence to the contrary, the Scripture record itself should be given more consideration than the fragmentary records outside the Bible or, specifically, than the lack of record. K. A. Kitchen has summarized the inconclusive nature of this negative evidence, demonstrating that it does not support the sweeping conclusion that Daniel is in error.[11] It must be emphasized that there is no established fact which contradicts a person by the name of Darius the Mede reigning over Babylon if Darius is an alternate name for a known ruler.

DANIEL EXALTED BY DARIUS

6:1-3 It pleased Darius to set over the kingdom an hundred and twenty princes, which should be over the whole kingdom; and over these three presidents; of whom Daniel was first: that the princes might give accounts unto them, and the king should have no damage. Then this Daniel was preferred above the presidents and princes, because an excellent spirit was in him; and the king thought to set him over the whole realm.

With the successful conquest of Babylon and the surrounding territory, it now is appropriate for the new kingdom to organize, both from the standpoint of law and order and from the benefit of taxation which this would allow. In such an organization, it would not be unsuitable to use qualified men who had served previously in the Babylonian kingdom. The conquerors did what they could to set up a friendly relationship with the people in their power; and although Belshazzar was slain, his father, Nabonidus, lived for some years afterward. Even some of the gods of Babylon were honored by the conquerors.°

°Wiseman states that the temple ritual was restored when agreement for the surrender of Babylon was reached (*Ancient Orient and O.T.,* p. 10).

The organization of the new kingdom is detailed in the opening verses of chapter 6. One hundred and twenty princes or "satraps" were appointed. Some have held that this figure is inaccurate. Montgomery, for instance, says, "The *120 satraps* (AV 'princes') is an exaggeration, or at least an inaccuracy. Her[odotus], iii, 89, records that Darius created 20 satrapies, and that king's inscriptions give their numbers successively as 21, 23, 29."[12] Montgomery goes on, however, to admit that there were 127 provinces according to Esther 1:1 but still insists that Daniel is inaccurate. Montgomery also objects to the "three presidents" as being without parallel.[13] The fact is that the appointment of 120 officials to rule such a vast territory and of three presidents to rule over them was not at all unreasonable. Whether or not there were precisely 120 subdivisions of his territory is not indicated, but the need for this number of officials is obvious.

The point of introducing these facts in Daniel's narrative is to give the setting for Daniel's place of honor. Daniel himself was named one of the three presidents who would coordinate the work of the 120 princes. Of them, it was required to give financial accounts and protect the king's interest. In such a function, an honest and capable administrator familiar with the territory and problems of taxation would undoubtedly be of immeasurable benefit to Darius. For this reason, Daniel, according to verse 3, was preferred above the others and had such "an excellent spirit" that the king thought to put all of the princes under him. All of this makes a great deal of sense and actually sets the stage for the supreme test of Daniel which followed.

THE PLOT AGAINST DANIEL

6:4-5 Then the presidents and princes sought to find occasion against Daniel concerning the kingdom; but they could find none occasion nor fault; forasmuch as he was faithful, neither was there any error or fault found in him. Then said these men, We shall not find any occasion against this Daniel, except we find it against him concerning the law of his God.

The excellent services and integrity of Daniel soon became a barrier to the ambitions of the princes and presidents with whom he was associated. Daniel's integrity made impossible any corruption, and his favor with Darius aroused the jealousy of his fellow officials. It was only natural under these circumstances that these men, most of them probably much younger than Daniel and anxious to get ahead, should try to find some means of disposing of Daniel. Daniel's faithfulness was such that they could not put their finger on any error or fault in the execution of his office. Some other method must be found if Daniel was to be eliminated. The men themselves came to the conclusion that the only way they could trip up Daniel was to provide a conflict between official regulations and Daniel's conscience and observance of the law of God. Scriptures do not reveal all the machinations which went on behind Daniel's back, but apparently there were numerous conferences and finally a plot was formed.

THE CONSPIRATORS SECURE A BAN ON PRAYER

6:6-9 Then these presidents and princes assembled together to the king, and said thus unto him, King Darius, live for ever. All the presidents of the kingdom, the governors, and the princes, the counsellors, and the captains, have consulted together to establish a royal statute, and to make a firm decree, that whosoever shall ask a petition of any God or man for thirty days, save of thee, O king, he shall be cast into the den of lions. Now, O king, establish the decree, and sign the writing, that it be not changed, according to the law of the Medes and Persians, which altereth not. Wherefore king Darius signed the writing and the decree.

The conspirators, having conceived of a plan, lost no time in putting it into effect. In a major appearance before the king, they presented their request. Verse 6 seems to indicate that they all were there, which was a most unusual occasion. Their spokesman, after properly addressing King Darius, represented to him that all the presidents and other officials whom they named in verse 7 had agreed on their petition. Some object to this account as being most improbable, if not impossible, but stranger things have happened. Montgomery notes, "Their ostensibly honorific plea that the king sign a decree that none should make request of god or man except of the king for thirty days appears to many commentators as absurd, and probably for this reason [the LXX] omits the item."[14] But even Montgomery adds, "But these stories are generally reasonable; the terms of the request may be meant as a satiric hyperbole, *cf.* Jon. 3:8, where the Ninevite king orders both man and beast to put on sackcloth. Behr.'s [Behrmann] position is an entirely sensible one that the implication of the story means a petition of religion (not with Bev. [Bevan] any kind of request), and that this one king was to be regarded for the time being as the only representative of Deity."[15]

Their petition to the king was to the effect that a decree should be issued that no one could present a petition to any god or man for thirty days except to the king. The penalty for disobedience would be that they would be cast into the den of lions. Under the psychological impact of these officials assembling in such force and presenting such an unusual petition designed to honor Darius and recognize in him divine powers, Darius signed the writing and the decree; and it became a law which could not be changed. The book of Esther (1:19; 8:8) and Diodorus Siculus (XVII. 30) also establish the fact that Medo-Persian law stipulated that a royal edict could not be revoked. The verb translated "sign" (*rshm*) in verses 8, 9, and 10 can be understood to mean "to draw, to draw up, to inscribe, to write," and hence "to draft," which would be more comprehensive than merely signing.[16]

As Young and others have pointed out, there is nothing unusual in ascribing to Persian kings worship such as would be afforded the pagan gods. Young observes, "The action of Darius was both foolish and wicked. What led him to yield to the request of the ministers can only be conjectured, but probably he was greatly influenced by the claim of deity which many of the Persian kings made."[17] Stuart justifies this situation in these words, "*Parsism* did not indeed require men to regard the king as a god in his own proper nature, but to pay him supreme homage as the *representative* of Ormusd. Such being the state of the case, it is easy to see that the account of Darius' behavior, when he was importuned by his courtiers and nobles, wears no special marks of improbability."[18] The probability is that Darius regarded this act as a pledge of loyalty to himself and a token of their desire to respect his authority to the utmost.

DANIEL'S FAITHFULNESS IN TESTING

6:10-11 Now when Daniel knew that the writing was signed, he went into his house; and his windows being open in his chamber toward Jerusalem, he kneeled upon his knees three times a day, and prayed, and gave thanks before his God, as he did aforetime. Then these men assembled, and found Daniel praying and making supplication before his God.

The remarkable faithfulness of Daniel in the face of this decree was similar to that of his three companions in chapter 3 as they faced the fiery furnace. According to the record, although he knew that the writing was signed and that discovery and execution were inevitable, he nevertheless went to his house where his windows were opened in the direction of Jerusalem, which still lay in ruins. The punctuation of the Revised Standard Version of verse 10 is preferable to the American Standard Version and follows the accentuation of the Massoretic text. It carries the implication that his windows were customarily open toward Jerusalem—"he went to his house where he had windows in his upper chamber open toward Jerusalem."

Then he knelt in keeping with his schedule of coming to God three times a day in prayer and thanksgiving. Daniel in his prayer life followed the inspired instructions of Jeremiah addressed to the elders, priests, prophets, and all the people of the captivity (Jer 29:1). Jeremiah had assured them, "Then shall ye call upon me, and ye shall go and pray unto me, and I will hearken unto you. And ye shall seek me, and find me, when ye shall search for me with all your heart" (Jer 29:12). According to Daniel 9:2, the book of Jeremiah was in Daniel's hands. The custom of praying toward the temple in Jerusalem was adopted by Solomon (cf. 2 Ch 6:34-39) and continued until the new instruction given by Christ to the Samaritan woman in John 4:20-24. Prayer thrice daily is mentioned in a Psalm of David (Ps 55:16-17). While Daniel's consistency of life and testimony has been evident throughout the book of Daniel, here we learn the inner secret. In spite of the pressures of being a busy executive with many demands upon his time, Daniel had retired to his house three times a day to offer his prayers for the peace of Jerusalem as well as for his personal needs. This was not the act of a person courting martyrdom but the continuation of a faithful ministry in prayer which had characterized his long life. The scripture observes that he did this as he had done before.

Of special interest are the details relating to his prayer life. The opening of the windows to Jerusalem was symbolic of his hope that someday the children of Israel would be able to return to this city of God. Later in chapter 9, Daniel's effective prayers were the prelude for the return under Zerubbabel. His posture in prayer is also indicative of his dependence upon God as a suppliant. The fact that he did this three times a day, not simply morning and evening or once a day, is also most enlightening. No doubt the thought also had crossed Daniel's mind concerning having his windows open. Why could not he pray in secret and thus avoid breaking the king's decree? To Daniel apparently this was subterfuge, and he did not swerve whatever from his usual customs in prayer.

Of great significance is the fact that even his enemies anticipated that this would be Daniel's response. Quite confidently, they assembled to witness his prayers and to have a basis for charging Daniel before the king. By prearrangement, they gathered in a place where they could observe and hear him, according to verse 11. What a testimony Daniel had that even his enemies knew he would be faithful to God although it would cost him his life.

DANIEL ACCUSED BEFORE DARIUS

6:12-15 Then they came near, and spake before the king concerning the king's decree; Hast thou not signed a decree, that every man that shall ask a petition of any God or man within thirty days, save of thee, O king, shall be cast into the den of lions? The king answered and said, The thing is true, according to the law of the Medes and Persians, which altereth not. Then answered they and said before the king, That Daniel, which is of the children of the captivity of Judah, regardeth not thee, O king, nor the decree that thou has signed, but maketh his petition three times a day. Then the king, when he heard these words, was sore dis-

pleased with himself, and set his heart on Daniel to deliver him: and he
laboured till the going down of the sun to deliver him. Then these men
assembled unto the king, and said unto the king, Know, O king, that the
law of the Medes and Persians is, That no decree nor statute which the
king establisheth may be changed.

The conspirators, with the evidence that Daniel had violated the decree,
now crowded once again into the king's courtroom. The punctuation and
translation of verse 12, "concerning the king's decree," is better than the
Revised Standard Version rendering, "concerning the interdict, 'O king!'"
The Revised Standard Version is based on the theory that the king had
to be addressed at the beginning of the sentence. Probably what is recorded in Scripture is, in any case, an abbreviated summary of the conversation. *God* in the King James Version should probably be rendered
"god," that is, any deity. They began by asking the question whether the
decree had been signed. The king assured them that it had been officially
executed, and "according to the law of the Medes and Persians, which
altereth not" the decree was the law of the land. With this assurance,
they then proceeded to accuse Daniel, introducing him not as a president
in an honored position, but as "of the children of the captivity of Judah."
They accuse Daniel of disregarding the king and his decree, and doing so
three times a day as he offered prayer to his God.

Their confidence in making this accusation was probably bolstered by
the justification for the decree in the first place. No doubt the Scriptures
do not record all the conversation between King Darius and the officials
who had asked for the decree. It is probable that they had justified the
decree as a means by which all the peoples in the kingdom would be
forced to recognize Darius as their ruler and present their petitions to
their deities in Darius' name. There was little in this that would be offensive to a pagan who worshiped many gods, and it could have been a
useful device to ascertain any in the kingdom who were still in a state of
rebellion against the king.

Now that the trap was sprung on Daniel, however, the king immediately
saw through the decree. Instead of being angry with Daniel as Nebuchadnezzar had been with Daniel's companions in chapter 3, the king
realized that he himself had made a mistake and attempted in every legal
way to find a loophole by which Daniel could be delivered. His labors,
however, were in vain. The officials once again assembling before the
king at the evening of the day reminded the king that the law could not
be changed according to their customs and beliefs. As the representative
of the gods, the king, having decreed, would have to execute the decree.
There was no way out but to issue the command that Daniel should be
cast into the lions' den.

Daniel Cast into the Lions' Den

6:16-17 Then the king commanded, and they brought Daniel, and
cast him into the den of lions. Now the king spake and said unto Daniel,
Thy God whom thou servest continually, he will deliver thee. And a stone
was brought, and laid upon the mouth of the den; and the king sealed it
with his own signet, and with the signet of his lords; that the purpose
might not be changed concerning Daniel.

In keeping with the decree which he had signed, Darius then issued
the formal command to cast Daniel into the lions' den. Prior to its execution, however, it is most remarkable that the king said to Daniel, "Thy
God whom thou servest continually, he will deliver thee." This may be
translated, "Thy God whom thou servest continually, he must deliver
thee." This is more accurate than the Revised Standard Version rendering,
"May your God . . . deliver you." The idea is that the king is saying,
"I have tried to save you but have failed. Now your God *must* save you."°
Observable in this assurance of Darius is the deep impression that Daniel's
personal piety and faithfulness to God had made upon the king and that
this impression had brought about Darius' own conviction that Daniel's
God would come to his rescue in Daniel's extremity.

The decree, however, is executed. Daniel is cast into the den of lions
and a stone is brought upon the mouth of the den sealed with the king's
signet as a token of execution and fulfillment of the decree. No human
hand could interfere, not even that of Darius himself.

Keil gives an interesting account of a lions' den such as has been found
in more modern times. Keil observes, "We have no account by the ancients of the construction of lions' dens. Ge. Höst, in his work on *Fez and
Morocco*, p. 77, describes the lions' dens as they have been found in
Morocco. According to his account, they consist of a large square cavern
under the earth, having a partition-wall in the middle of it, which is furnished with a door, which the keeper can open and close from above.
By throwing in food, they can entice the lions from one chamber into the
other, and then, having shut the door, they enter the vacant space for the
purpose of cleaning it. The cavern is open above, its mouth being surrounded by a wall of a yard and a half high, over which one can look
down into the den. This description agrees perfectly with that which is
here given in the text regarding the lions' den."[19] Keil goes on to explain
that there was a door in the wall surrounding the cavern through which

°The concept of "must deliver" is derived from the imperfect tense which in the
Aramaic may be used in a way identical to the use of the imperfect in Hebrew to
denote obligation (for the Hebrew usage, see P. P. Jouon, *Grammaire de L' Hebreu
Biblique*, p. 305). The tense is imperfect, not jussive as the RSV translators have
construed it, because when the form is imperfect the suffix is preceded by -(i)nn, as
it is here, whereas in the jussive imperative the suffix is attached directly to the verb
(see Rosenthal, pp. 54-55).

both the keepers and the lions could enter except when the stone was in place. This accounts for the fact that Darius was able to converse freely with Daniel before the stone was removed from the door.

THE KING'S LAMENT FOR DANIEL

6:18-20 Then the king went to his palace, and passed the night fasting: neither were instruments of musick brought before him: and his sleep went from him. Then the king arose very early in the morning, and went in haste unto the den of lions. And when he came to the den, he cried with a lamentable voice unto Daniel: and the king spake and said to Daniel, O Daniel, servant of the living God, is thy God, whom thou servest continually, able to deliver thee from the lions?

Quite in contrast to Nebuchadnezzar who showed no compassion for Daniel's three companions when they were cast into the fiery furnace, Darius manifests unusual concern. Although he was accustomed to brutality and execution of criminals and ordinarily did not give the matter a second thought, in this case there was something about Daniel that had involved the king emotionally. While the king had stated to Daniel in verse 16, "Thy God whom thou servest continually, he will deliver thee," it is quite clear that he did not have any real faith in Daniel's deliverance but only a remote superstition perhaps arising out of stories which had come to him of the escape of Daniel's companions earlier in Babylonian history as well as of other phenomenal deliverances of the people of Israel. In keeping with his grief for Daniel, the Scriptures record that the king fasted, did not have the usual entertainment of music, and was unable to sleep. The expression *instruments of music* is in doubt because the meaning of the word is uncertain. Rosenthal suggests as a translation the word *table*,[20] supported by the Arabian translation and Rashi (commentary). The meaning would be tables on which to serve food. In the present state of knowledge, the Revised Standard Version rendering "no diversions," although indefinite, is the best that can be done. In any case it was most unusual for the king to spend a night in this fashion. Probably never before in his entire life had the king had such an experience.

As the day was dawning and in the dim light of early morning, the king went in haste unto the den of lions. Probably being unable to see because of the early morning light and the shadows of the lions' den, the king called out to Daniel. The form of address is also most remarkable. He describes Daniel as the "servant of the living God" and raises the question once again, "is thy God, whom thou servest continually, able to deliver thee from the lions?" That the king thought that there was a possibility of it is substantiated by the fact that he came to the den of lions early

---

*Rosenthal comments, "other traditional guesses consider the word a pl. fem.: concubines, food, musical instruments, perfume" (*Grammar*, p. 81).

in the morning and called Daniel. That he had little actual faith, however, is shown in the "lamentable voice" in which he called Daniel. The
Aramaic for "lamentable" is *ʿăṣîb,* meaning "sad," hence the Revised
Standard Version reads "tone of anguish." He feared that there would be
nothing but silence and the growl of the lions in response to his call.

DANIEL'S DELIVERANCE

6:21-23 Then said Daniel unto the king, O king, live for ever. My
God hath sent his angel, and hath shut the lions' mouths, that they have
not hurt me: forasmuch as before him innocency was found in me; and
also before thee, O king, have I done no hurt. Then was the king exceeding glad for him, and commanded that they should take Daniel up
out of the den. So Daniel was taken up out of the den, and no manner
of hurt was found upon him, because he believed in his God.

In response to the king's inquiry and to his astounded ears, the calm
voice of Daniel arose from the lions' den with the usual courteous greeting, "O king, live for ever." Most people in Daniel's predicament would
have immediately cried out for deliverance from the lions. But Daniel,
after his greeting, informs the king that the lions' mouths have been shut
by an angel sent by God so that the lions were not able to hurt him.
Daniel attributes this not only to the power of God but to the fact that
Daniel was innocent of any crime either to God or to the king.

The Scriptures record that the king was overjoyed at the deliverance
of his favorite counselor and immediately gave order that Daniel should
be taken up out of the den of lions. Although the Scriptures are not explicit, it may be that by this is meant that Daniel was lifted by means of
ropes out of the den directly, without taking time to remove the stone
with the necessary prelude of enticing the lions to another part of the
cavern first so that they would not escape. To the unbelieving eyes of the
king and his servants, Daniel was found to have no hurt whatever because
of his faith in God (Heb 11:33). Just as the flames had not been able even
to bring the smell of fire upon Daniel's companions in chapter 3, the lions
were not permitted to touch the prophet of God.

DANIEL'S ENEMIES DESTROYED

6:24 And the king commanded, and they brought those men which
had accused Daniel, and they cast them into the den of lions, them, their
children, and their wives; and the lions had the mastery of them, and
brake all their bones in pieces or ever they came at the bottom of the den.

The sad end of Daniel's accusers is recorded as an act of divine justice
upon the enemies of the prophet of God. According to the Scriptures,
Daniel's accusers with their wives and children are cast into the lions' den
and immediately devoured by the lions. Such barbarity is common in the

ancient world, and not without parallel even in God's divine judgment upon the wicked as illustrated in the judgment of the Lord upon Dathan, Abiram, and Korah when they and their families were swallowed up in an earthquake (Num 16). The punishment meted out conforms to the injunction about the treatment of false witnesses in the law (Deu 19:16-21). This principle of *lex talionis* is also illustrated in the case of Haman (Est 7:9-10).

Some critics have pointed with ridicule to the impossibility of casting one hundred and twenty officials plus their wives and children into one lions' den. Montgomery, for instance, regards this "tragic denoue-ment" as "indeed absurd," as well as the entire story.[21] The Septuagint, apparently in an effort to counter this criticism, makes the victims only the two men who were presidents with Daniel, and, therefore, his prin-cipal accusers.[22] The Scriptures themselves do not say that all the princes and presidents were cast into the den of lions, but only those who accused Daniel, that is, the ringleaders. This served notice on the rest, if they had any further inclination to plot against Daniel, that they too might ex-perience the wrath of the king as well as the judgment of God. The ex-perience of the false accusers of Daniel is another illustration of God's faithfulness to the basic Abrahamic Covenant where God promised to bless them who blessed Abraham's seed and to curse him who curseth them (Gen 12:3).

THE DECREE OF DARIUS

6:25-28 Then king Darius wrote unto all people, nations, and lan-guages, that dwell in all the earth; Peace be multiplied unto you. I make a decree, That in every dominion of my kingdom men tremble and fear before the God of Daniel: for he is the living God, and stedfast for ever, and his kingdom that which shall not be destroyed, and his dominion shall be even unto the end. He delivereth and rescueth, and he worketh signs and wonders in heaven and in earth, who hath delivered Daniel from the power of the lions. So this Daniel prospered in the reign of Darius, and in the reign of Cyrus the Persian.

Much as Nebuchadnezzar had done in chapter 3 and again in chapter 4, Darius issued a decree to be sent throughout his entire domain calling on men everywhere to fear the God of Daniel. The inscription in which the decree is addressed to "all people, nations, and languages, that dwell in all the earth" is quite similar to Daniel 4:1. It may be in both instances that Daniel was the actual penman acting under command for the king, or it may be that the unknown penman is following the usual form of letter writing. In both cases, the king took for granted that the world was at his feet, and he used extravagant language including the entire world in his address. The expression "Peace be multiplied unto you" is identical to that found in Daniel 4:1, and almost reminds one of the letters of Paul in the New Testament.

The decree was short and to the point calling on men everywhere in the kingdom of Darius to "tremble and fear before the God of Daniel." Daniel's God is described as the living God, One who is steadfast, whose kingdom shall not be destroyed and whose dominion continues to the end. The Revised Standard Version rendering "enduring forever" is probably more explicit than "stedfast for ever." The point is that in a rapidly changing situation—that is, the Medo-Persians overcoming the Babylonians—God does not change. Again, this is remarkably similar to Daniel 4:3. In substantiation of this ascription of sovereignty and power, God is described as One who is able to deliver and rescue, who is able to work signs and wonders both in heaven and in earth, and who has confirmed this by delivering Daniel from the power of the lions. Verses 26-27 are in the form of a hymn in the original. Once again throughout the world of Daniel's day, the tidings were carried of the great God who is living, powerful, everlasting, and greater than the gods of the pagans.

The chapter closes with a brief historical note that Daniel continued to prosper in the reign of Darius and in the reign of Cyrus the Persian. Here again critics have attempted to claim an inaccuracy. The probable explanation is, as has been previously pointed out, that either Darius was a governor under Cyrus and later delivered the kingdom to him, possibly at his death, or that Darius and Cyrus were the same person with the word *and* understood as meaning "even."

Although the pointed claim of this chapter that God is able to accomplish miracles in delivering His servants from death is couched in such terms as to arouse the unbelief of those already predisposed to question the Scriptures, this chapter is a profound illustration of how God cares for His people. Although historical and to be accepted in its literal portrayal of an event, it is also parabolic like chapter 3 and is a foreshadowing of the ultimate deliverance of the people of Israel from their persecutors in the time of the great tribulation at the end of the times of the Gentiles. When the power of God is finally demonstrated at the second coming of Christ, the persecutors of Israel and the enemies of God will be judged and destroyed much like the enemies of Daniel. Like Daniel, however, the people of God in persecution must remain true regardless of the cost.

7

DANIEL'S VISION OF FUTURE WORLD HISTORY

IN THE INTERPRETATION of biblical prophecy, the seventh chapter of Daniel occupies a unique place. As interpreted by conservative expositors, the vision of Daniel provides the most comprehensive and detailed prophecy of future events to be found anywhere in the Old Testament. Although its interpretation has varied widely, conservative scholars generally are agreed, with few exceptions, that Daniel traces the course of four great world empires, namely, Babylon, Medo-Persia, Greece, and Rome, concluding in the climax of world history in the second coming of Jesus Christ and the inauguration of the eternal kingdom of God, represented as a fifth and final kingdom which is from heaven.[1]

Interpreted in this way, the chapter forms a major outline of future events to which additional details are given later in the book of Daniel and in the New Testament, especially in the Revelation. Such a panorama of future events is of great importance to the student of prophecy, as it provides a broad outline to which all other prophetic events may be related. Conservative interpreters are agreed that this is genuine prophecy, that it is futuristic, that is, related to future events from Daniel's point of view, and that its culmination is in the kingdom which Christ brings.

In the introduction to his discussion of "The Four World-kingdoms," Keil has well summarized the issues involved in chapter 7. He writes,

> There yet remains for our consideration the question, What are the historical world-kingdoms which are represented by Nebuchadnezzar's image (ch. ii.), and by Daniel's vision of four beasts rising up out of the sea? Almost all interpreters understand that these two visions are to be interpreted in the same way. "The four kingdoms or dynasties, which are symbolized (ch. ii.) by the different parts of the human image, from the head to the feet, are the same as those which were symbolized by the four great beasts rising up out of the sea."[2]

Keil continues, "These four kingdoms, according to the interpretation commonly received in the church, are the Babylonian, the Medo-Persian, the Macedo-Grecian, and the Roman. 'In this interpretation and opinion,' Luther observes, 'all the world are agreed, and history and fact abundantly establish it.' This opinion prevailed till about the end of the last century, for the contrary opinion of individual earlier interpreters had found no favour. But from that time, when faith in the supernatural origin and character of biblical prophecy was shaken by Deism and Rationalism, then as a consequence, with the rejection of the genuineness of the book of Daniel the reference of the fourth kingdom to the Roman world-monarchy was also denied."[3]

Conservative scholarship has solid reasons for interpreting the fourth kingdom as Roman as well as considering the second and third kingdoms as Medo-Persian and Grecian. As Keil has pointed out, supported by Luther, the prevailing opinion of orthodoxy has always held this position since the early church. Porphyry, the third century A.D. pagan antagonist of Christianity who invented the idea of a pseudo-Daniel writing the book of Daniel in the second century B.C., did not find Christian support until the rise of modern higher criticism. The whole attempt, therefore, to make the book of Daniel history instead of prophecy, written in the second century and fulfilled by that date, has been considered untenable by orthodoxy. With it, the view that the fourth kingdom is Greece and not Rome has been also rejected by conservative scholars as unsupported by the book of Daniel and contradicted by the New Testament as well as historic fulfillment.

Christ Himself in Matthew 24:15 predicted the abomination of desolation of Daniel 12:11 as future, not past. Prophecies of the book of Revelation written late in the first century also anticipate as future the fulfillment of parallel prophecies in Daniel. For example, Revelation 13 parallels the final stage of Daniel's fourth empire. This could not, therefore, refer to events fulfilled in the second century B.C. Daniel 9:26 prophesies that the Messiah will be cut off and the city of Jerusalem destroyed, events which occurred in the Roman period. The author of 2 Esdras, who lived near the close of the first century A.D., clearly identifies the fourth kingdom of Daniel's vision as the Roman Empire (2 Esd 12:11-12). To these arguments may be added the details of the second, third and fourth empires throughout the book of Daniel, which harmonize precisely with the Medo-Persian, Grecian, and Roman Empires. The alternate views of the critics can be held only if Daniel's prophecy be considered in factual error in several places as the details of the prophecies do not really coincide with the critics' theories. For these reasons, conservative scholars have held firmly to the traditional identification of the four empires in chapter 7 of Daniel as in chapter 2.

Daniel's Vision of Future World History

The conservative interpretation, however, has been confronted with a broadside of critical objection to the plausibility of such detailed prophecy of future events. In general, critical objections are based on the premise that the book of Daniel is a pious second-century forgery. Critics hold that the real author of Daniel lived in the time of the persecution of Antiochus Epiphanes (175-164 B.C.), and that from the viewpoint of the second century B.C. he looked backward over the preceding four centuries, organized history in a manner which was significant for him, and made this the basis for anticipating a climax to the Maccabean persecution then under way. Accordingly, the pseudo-Daniel considered Antiochus as symbolic of the wickedness of the powers of this world which the author believed were soon to be judged by God, who was to intervene and replace the rule of tyranny under Antiochus by that of the saints of the Most High. This interpretation, of course, requires interpretation of many statements in Daniel as less than factual and actually not scriptural prophecy at all. Their point of view as a whole is an expansion of the unbelief of Porphyry rather than a product of a reverent, believing study of the Scriptures.

Critics approach Daniel somewhat a priori, assuming that prediction of particular events in the future is incredible and, therefore, requiring a late date for the book of Daniel so that it is history rather than prophecy. This is often denied, however, by such scholarly writers as H. H. Rowley who states, "The conclusions we have reached have not been born of a priori disbelief in accurate prophecy, but of a posteriori demonstration that we have not accurate prophecy."[4] Nevertheless, it is quite plain, as the critical view is unfolded, that the content of Daniel itself is quite offensive to the critical mind and that broad statements are made that this or that fact in the book of Daniel is untrue either because of its nature or because there is no outside confirming evidence.

Although the multiplicity of variations in interpretation of the entire book of Daniel, and in particular chapter 7, is all too evident to any reader of the literature in the field, the critical view as defined by H. H. Rowley may be taken as representative.

According to the critics, the four empires of Daniel 2 and Daniel 7 are the empires of Babylon, Media, Persia, and Greece. Although their arguments embody many details, their theory has two major supports. First, they find evidence that the kingdom of Media is represented as being in existence in the book of Daniel by the mention of Darius the Mede (5:31; 6:1, 6, 9, 25, 28). Actually, there was no Median Empire in power at the time of the fall of Babylon in 539 B.C., as it had already been swallowed up by Persia by 550 B.C. Moreover, recent discoveries support the idea

147

that Cyrus the Persian ruler himself entered Babylon eighteen days after the fall of Babylon on the night of Belshazzar's feast.*⁵

The alleged error in relation to Darius the Mede, however, puts a teaching in the book of Daniel which actually is not there. The fact that Darius was a Median indicated his race, but it does not mean that the empire was Median. Chapter 6 of Daniel is very plain that the kingdom at that time over which Darius the Mede was reigning in Babylon was the kingdom of the "Medes and Persians" (vv. 8, 12, 15). In other words, the book of Daniel itself states clearly that this was a Medo-Persian empire, not a Median empire at this point. The error is in the critics' interpretation, not in what Daniel actually teaches.

The second critical argument is that the fourth empire is Greece—hence already history at the time the pseudo-Daniel wrote the book in the second century. This would require the second and third empires to be Media and Persia. The fact that Daniel's "prophecies" of these empires does not fit the facts of history is taken as error on the part of the pseudo-Daniel. The weakness of the critical approach here is unconsciously recognized in H. H. Rowley's discussion in which he puts most of his weight on the attempt to identify the fourth kingdom as Greece.† While few works can claim more scholarship and research than that of Rowley, the conservative interpreter of the book of Daniel finds that Rowley's interpretation tends to emphasize extrascriptural sources, magnify minor points of obscurity and often ignores the plain statements of the book of Daniel itself.

Montgomery adopts an interpretation even more extreme than Rowley. Montgomery not only attributes the book of Daniel to a second-century author but takes the position that the first six chapters of Daniel were written by a different author and at a different time from chapters 7 to 12. Montgomery states, "The criticism of the unity of the bk. began in the 17th cent. with the observation of the distinction of languages, the Aram. and Heb.; Spinoza discovered two documents, cc. 1-7 and 8-12, referring the latter to the undoubted authorship of Dan., and confessing ignorance as to the origin of the former."⁶ In order to support this, Montgomery holds that chapter 7 was originally written in Hebrew instead of Aramaic as we now have it.⁷ Montgomery confesses, however, "But a critical dis-

*For Daniel the prophet, living in the sixth century B.C., to make such a palpable error as to teach a Median empire is considered incredible by the critics. Therefore, they consider this another proof that the book of Daniel was written by a second century B.C. writer who was confused about the facts in general and about Darius the Mede in particular (for previous discussion on Darius the Mede, see chapter 6).
†In this attempt he uses a total of 67 pages, whereas he devotes only 21 pages to proving that Daniel taught that the second and third kingdoms are the Median and Persian kingdoms (Rowley, Darius the Mede and the Four World Empires, pp. 70-137).

tinction on the basis of diversity of language is now generally denied. The extreme positions taken respectively by the defenders and the impugners of the historicity of Dan. have induced the great majority of critics to assign the bk. as a whole to either the 6th or the 2d cent., with as a rule little or no discussion on the part of the comm. of the possibility of composite origin; indeed most ignore the problem."[8] Montgomery goes beyond the normal critical view of one pseudo-Daniel to the hypothesis that there were at least two pseudo-Daniels, both of whom were second century writers who may have used some earlier sources.

Montgomery credits his view as being first advanced by Sir Isaac Newton. Montgomery states, "The distinction between the Stories and the Visions was first made by Sir Isaac Newton: 'The bk. of Dan. is a collection of papers written at several times. The six last chapters contain Prophecies written at several times by Dan. himself; the six first are a collection of historical papers written by other authors'; and cc. 1. 5. 6 were written after his death."[9]

The final decision can only be made on which view offers the most plausible explanation of the text of Daniel. The inherent congruity of the conservative interpretation of Daniel 7 as opposed to the critical theories will be considered under the interpretation relating to each kingdom. If Daniel is genuine Scripture, of course, it tends to support the conservative interpretation. If Daniel is a forgery, as the critics assert, and its prophecy is actually history, the book of Daniel becomes quite meaningless for most Bible expositors. Rowley presents the hollow claim that the critical view "which has been adopted does not destroy faith but strengthens it, in that it provides a reasonable ground for it."[10] Actually Rowley is saying that the choice is between faith in error and faith in the "true view," that is, the critical interpretation.

DANIEL'S FIRST VISION: THE FOUR GREAT BEASTS

7:1-3 In the first year of Belshazzar king of Babylon Daniel had a dream and visions of his head upon his bed: then he wrote the dream, and told the sum of the matters. Daniel spake and said, I saw in my vision by night, and, behold, the four winds of the heaven strove upon the great sea. And four great beasts came up from the sea, diverse one from another.

In the opening verses of chapter 7, Daniel introduces his remarkable experience of having "a dream and visions of his head upon his bed" which occurred in the first year of Belshazzar king of Babylon. The year was probably 553 B.C., fourteen years before the fall of Babylon. Nabonidus, the actual king of Babylon beginning in 556 B.C., had appointed Belshazzar as his coregent in control of Babylonia itself while Nabonidus conducted military maneuvers in Arabia.[11] As Nebuchadnezzar himself had died in 562 B.C., nine years before Belshazzar began to reign, it is clear that the event of chapter 7 occurred chronologically between chapters 4 and 5 of Daniel.

In the mention of the specific time of the vision, Daniel is consciously and deliberately rooting the visions which he received as occurring in the historical background of the sixth century B.C. The vision of chapter 8 is dated in Belshazzar's third year. According to Daniel 9:1-2, Daniel discovered the prophecy of Jeremiah concerning the seventy years of captivity in the first year of Darius the Mede and, later in the same chapter, had a third vision. The fourth vision of Daniel in chapters 10-12 occurred in the third year of Cyrus (10:1). In chapter 11, there is mention of an earlier activity of the angel in strengthening Darius the Mede in his first year, another historical event related to the prophetic portion of Daniel. All of these are introduced so naturally and are so integral to the narrative that they support the sixth century date for the book of Daniel.

In the opening verse of chapter 7, Daniel speaks of his experience as a dream and a vision, apparently indicating that he had a vision in a dream. Here, for the first time in the book of Daniel, a vision is given directly to Daniel, and in verse 2, Daniel is quoted in the first person, reciting his experience of the dream and its interpretation.

A great deal of discussion has been devoted to the significance of the seventh chapter in relationship to the book as a whole. One point of view, held by conservative as well as liberal interpreters, is that the book of Daniel divides into two halves with the first six chapters providing a unit and the second six chapters providing a second unit. From the standpoint of world history, this has much to commend itself; for the vision of Daniel in chapter 7 is at once a summary of what has been revealed before, especially in the vision of Nebuchadnezzar in chapter 2, and the outline of world history with which the last half of Daniel is primarily concerned. In the first six chapters, generalities are revealed. In the last six chapters, specifics are given, such as the detailed end of the times of the Gentiles and the relationship of Israel to world history, with special reference to the time of great tribulation.

From a literary standpoint, there is good support for the obvious division of the book into the stories (1-6) and the visions (7-12). Chapter 7, moreover, contains in semipoetic form a more explicit version of the expectations disclosed in chapter 2. With the elucidation and prosaic details given in concluding chapters, the division of Daniel into two halves is the conclusion of the majority of conservative scholars.

Another point of view argued strongly by Robert Culver is that the book of Daniel divides into three major divisions: (1) introduction,

Daniel 1; (2) the times of the Gentiles, presented in Aramaic, the common language of the Gentiles at that time, Daniel 2-7; and (3) Israel in relation to the Gentiles, written in Hebrew, Daniel 8-12.[12] Culver's point of view, which he credits to Auberlen,[13] has much to commend itself and is especially theologically discerning because it distinguishes the two major programs of God in the Old Testament, namely, the program for the Gentiles and the program for Israel. In either point of view, however, chapter 7 is a high point in revelation in the book of Daniel; and, in some sense, the material before as well as the material which follows pivots upon the detailed revelation of this chapter.

Also to be noted in the introduction of chapter 7 is the sharp contrast between the vision given to Daniel and the vision given to Nebuchadnezzar in chapter 2. On the one hand, in chapter 2, a wicked and heathen king is used as a vehicle of divine revelation which pictures world history as an imposing image in the form of a man. In chapter 7, the vision is given through the godly prophet, Daniel, and world history is depicted as four horrible beasts, the last of which almost defies description. In chapter 2, Daniel is the interpreter. In chapter 7, an angel is the interpreter. Chapter 2 considers world history from man's viewpoint as a glorious and imposing spectacle. Chapter 7 views world history from God's standpoint in its immorality, brutality, and depravity. In detail of prophecy, chapter 7 far exceeds chapter 2 and is in some sense the commentary on the earlier revelation.

Critics have massed their severest criticism against the credibility of Daniel 7 and treated it almost contemptuously, but by so doing they only reveal the artificial criteria by which they judge divine revelation. Conservative scholars, on the other hand, have hailed chapter 7 as one of the great prophecies of the Bible and the key to the entire program of God from Babylon to the second coming of Christ. Critics have suggested that the original form of this chapter was Hebrew and later it was translated into Aramaic,[14] but there is really no justification or documentary support for this apart from a premise that Daniel itself is a forgery. From a literary standpoint, it is only natural that the Aramaic section of Daniel, dealing as it does with the Gentile world, should be in Aramaic, commonly used as the lingua franca of that time.

Beginning in verse 2, Daniel records what he calls "the sum of the matter" in verse 1, that is, the details of his vision which he declares he "saw" (see 7:7, 13; cf. "beheld," 7:4, 6, 9, 11, 21). The words *I saw* and *I beheld* are the same verb in the Aramaic (*ḥāzēh hăwêth*) and can be translated, "as I was looking." The verb *consider* in 7:8 is a different word. In the vision, four winds are seen striving on a great sea. Symbolically, the sea may represent the mass of humanity, or the nations of the world, as in Matthew 13:47 and Revelation 13:1 (cf. Is 8:6-8; Jer 46:7-8; 47:2; Rev 17:1, 15). The sea is identified with the earth in 7:17 and is clearly symbolic. The turbulence of the sea may well represent the strife of Gentile history (Is 17:12-13; 57:20; Jer 6:23).[15]

As Keil states, "The great sea is not the Mediterranean, . . . for such a geographical reference is foreign to the context. It is the ocean; and the storm on it represents the 'tumults of the people,' commotions among the nations of the world, . . . corresponding to the prophetic comparison found in Jer. xvii. 12, xlvi. 7 f. 'Since the beasts represent the forms of the world-power, the sea must represent that out of which they arise, the whole heathen world' (Hofmann)."[*16]

Keil continues, "The winds *of the heavens* represent the heavenly powers and forces by which God sets the nations of the world in motion."[17] Keil also finds that the number four has the symbolic meaning of representing people from all four corners of the earth, that is, all peoples and all regions.[18] The sea, however, is only a background to the vision which will follow; and Daniel records that out of the sea came four great beasts, each differing from the other.

Commentators such as Leupold[19] agree with Keil that the major elements of the introduction to the vision, namely, the four winds of heaven, the great sea, and the four great beasts indicate universality. It seems clear that the sea represents the nations and the four great beasts represent the four great world empires which are given subsequent revelation. If this is the case, what is the meaning of the four winds?

Although the Scriptures do not tell us, inasmuch as the wind striving with the world is a symbol of the sovereign power of God striving with men (Gen 6:3; Jn 3:8), the prophetic meaning may be the sovereign power of God in conflict with sinful man. God often used the wind as a means to attain His ends (Gen 8:1; Ex 10:13-19; 14:21; 15:10; Num 11:31; I Ki 18:45; 19:11). Compare Satan's use of wind in Job 1:19. Of more than 120 references in the Bible to wind (more than 90 in the O.T. and about 30 in the N.T.), well over half are related to events and ideas which reflect the sovereignty and power of God. In Daniel, wind is uniformly used to represent the sovereign power of God, which is the viewpoint of the book. The history of the Gentiles is the record of God striving with the nations and ultimately bringing them into subjection when Christ returns to reign (Ps 2).

---

*G. H. Lang argues at length that "the great sea" is the Mediterranean, citing a large number of Scripture references (Num 34:6-7; Jos 1:4; 9:1; 15:11-12; 15:47; 23:4; Eze 47:10, 15, 19, 20; 48:28). He concludes that the disturbance symbolized by the beast coming out of the sea prophesies that the origin of action would be the Mediterranean. This is, at least, a plausible interpretation (George Henry Lang, *The Histories and Prophecies of Daniel*, pp. 86-89).

THE FIRST BEAST: BABYLON

7:4 The first was like a lion, and had eagle's wings: I beheld till the wings thereof were plucked, and it was lifted up from the earth, and made stand upon the feet as a man, and a man's heart was given to it.

Daniel describes the first beast as being like a lion but having the wings of an eagle.[20] As Daniel beheld, or as Leupold puts it, "kept looking" that is, looking intently,[21] he saw the wings plucked from the beast, the beast lifted from the earth, made to stand upon his feet as a man, and given a man's heart, that is, a man's mind or nature. Interpreters of the book of Daniel, whether liberal or conservative, generally have agreed that chapter 7 is in some sense a recapitulation of chapter 2 and covers the same four empires. Likewise, there is agreement that the first empire represents the reign of Nebuchadnezzar or the Neo-Babylonian Empire. Concerning this identification, Rowley comments, "Of this there is little dispute. In Dn ii. 38 we read that Daniel specifically informed Nebuchadnezzar: 'Thou art the head of gold.' There is, therefore, no uncertainty that in this chapter, the first kingdom is either the reign of Nebuchadnezzar or the Neo-Babylonian empire which he represents. A few have adopted the former view, but most the latter."[22]

Rowley also finds that, apart from a few exceptions, scholars are agreed on the identification of the first kingdom of chapter 2 and chapter 7. One of the exceptions, according to Rowley, is Hitzig, who considered the first two empires of chapter 2 that of Nebuchadnezzar first, and Belshazzar second, but in chapter 7 identifies the first beast with Belshazzar.[23] Rowley also cites Eerdmans' view that the first beast of chapter 7 represents Egypt, and the viewpoint of Conring and Merx that the first beast represents the Median Empire. He goes on to say, "But apart from a few such rare exceptions, there is complete agreement that the Neo-Babylonian empire is again intended."[24] There is more unanimity on the identification of the first beast of chapter 7 than on any other point in this chapter.[25]

The elements of the revelation are most significant. The beast is compared to a lion with eagle's wings. The lion is a common representation of royal power. Solomon, for instance, had twelve lions on either side of the steps leading up to his throne (1 Ki 10:20; 2 Ch 9:19). Winged lions guarded the gates of the royal palaces of the Babylonians. The lion was indeed the king of the beasts. In like manner, the eagle was the king of the birds of the air. In Ezekiel 17:3, 7, a great eagle is used as a picture first of Babylon and then of Egypt.

In spite of the power indicated in the symbolism of the lion with eagle's wings, Daniel in his vision sees the wings plucked and the lion made to stand upon his feet as a man, with a man's heart given to it. This is most commonly interpreted as the symbolic representation of Nebuchadnezzar's experience in chapter 4 when he was humbled before God and made to realize that, even though he was a great ruler, he was only a man. His lion-like character, or royal power, was his only at God's pleasure. The symbolism is accurate and corresponds to the historical facts. As Leupold states, "This is undoubtedly an allusion to the experience of Nebuchadnezzar which is related in detail in chapter four. The incident signifies that, as nearly as it is possible for a beast to become like a man, so nearly did Babylon lose its beastlike nature."[26]

Although Daniel in this vision does not dwell on the fall of Babylon, described in detail in chapter 5, the decline of Babylon and the rise of the Medo-Persian Empire is implied. Other prophets spoke at length on the fall of Babylon. From the reference to the tower of Babel in Genesis 11, there is no biblical mention of Babylon until the major prophets, Isaiah, Jeremiah, and Ezekiel discuss Babylon's future. Isaiah describes the fall of Babylon as similar to that of Sodom and Gomorrah (Is 13:1-22), with particular mention of the Medes in Isaiah 13:17-19. A future destruction of Babylon at the second coming of Christ seems to be indicated in Isaiah 13:20-22 (cf. Rev 17). Another extended prophecy about Babylon is found in Isaiah 47.

Jeremiah who witnessed the capture of Jerusalem by the Babylonians refers to Babylon throughout his prophecy, of which the most important sections are Jeremiah 25:11-14; 29:10; 50:1–51:62. The last three long chapters of Jeremiah are devoted entirely to Babylon. Ezekiel, himself a captive, is occupied with Babylon (Eze 17:12-24), and predicts like Jeremiah Babylon's conquest of Egypt (Eze 29:18-20; 30:10-25; 32:1-32). Daniel, writing later, ties together these prophecies about Babylon.

THE SECOND BEAST: MEDO-PERSIA

7:5 And behold another beast, a second, like to a bear, and it raised up itself on one side, and it had three ribs in the mouth of it between the teeth of it: and they said thus unto it, Arise, devour much flesh.

The second beast of Daniel's vision is described as corresponding to a bear.[27] As Daniel observes, the bear raises itself on one side and Daniel notices three ribs in its mouth between its teeth. Daniel hears the instruction given to the bear to "Arise, devour much flesh."

In contrast to the unanimity of identifying the first beast with Babylon is the diversity of interpretation of the second beast. Critics such as Montgomery,[28] Rowley,[29] and R. H. Charles,[30] and practically all liberal higher critics, identify the second beast as the Median Empire. Rowley cites almost overwhelming support for this identification which, according to him, "is found in the Peshitta version of the book of Daniel, in Ephraem Syrus and in Cosmas Indicopleustes. It also stands in the anonymous commentator whose work is published in Mai's *Scriptorum Veterum Nova Collectio*."[31] Rowley notes that this long-forgotten theory was revived in the eighteenth century. Among its modern adherents he lists an imposing group of scholars, as follows: Eichhorn, deWette, Dereser, von Lengerke, Maurer, Bade, Hilgenfeld, Bleek, Westcott, Davidson, Kamphausen, Kranichfeld, Graf, Delitzsch, Kuenen, Reuss and Vatke, whom Rowley designates as the older scholars, and the more recent scholars, Schurer, Meinhold, Bevan, Behrmann, von Gall, Curtis, Buhl, Prince, Driver, Marti, Bertholet, Steuernagel, Andrews, Haller, Baumgartner, Montgomery, Charles, Willet, Obbink, and Eissfeldt.[32]

Although conservative scholars are outnumbered, it is significant that most scholars attributing accuracy to the book of Daniel regard the second kingdom as that of the Medo-Persians. Even Rowley admits that his view hangs upon the identification of the fourth empire as that of Greece which, as already has been stated, depends first on the conclusion that Daniel is a forgery, and second on the assumption that prophecy cannot be accurately given in detail concerning future events.

The identification of the second kingdom as the Medo-Persian Empire, which even Rowley recognizes as "the traditional identification," is ably supported by one of the greatest Old Testament scholars of modern times, Robert Dick Wilson. His entire work on *Studies in the Book of Daniel* methodically devastates the liberal point of view; and even though this work is brushed aside impatiently by Rowley, no one has actually answered Wilson's arguments.

Recent discoveries have proved beyond question that the second empire was in fact the Medo-Persian Empire. The Persian ruler Cyrus himself came to conquered Babylon in less than a month, and the myth of a separate Median empire at this time is not supported by the facts. The liberal position has to hold that the vision of the second beast is a false prophecy which does not correspond to the facts of history. If Daniel's revelation is truly from God, it must correspond precisely to what history itself records. In chapter 6 of Daniel, a combined kingdom of the Medes and Persians is mentioned repeatedly as in verses 8, 12, and 15. These references alone should shut the mouth of the critic who wants to attribute to Daniel a fallacious and unhistorical kingdom of the Medes. Daniel's record corresponds to history, whereas the critics' view does not.

If Daniel's revelation is true prophecy, what is the symbolism of the bear? Normally, this animal is not related to symbolism in the Old Testament. The meaning seems to be that the second empire will be powerful like a bear, ferocious (Is 13:17-18), but less majestic, less swift, and less glorious. The beast of Revelation 13 which gathers into its power the characteristics of all previous beasts is said to have feet as a bear (Rev 13:2).

The bear pictured apparently lying down is described as raising itself up on one side. Such an action, of course, is typical of an awkward animal like the bear. As Driver expresses it, "In the O. T. it is spoken of as being, next to the lion, the most formidable beast of prey known in Palestine (1 Sam. xvii. 34; Am. v. 19; cf. 2 Ki. ii. 24; Hos. xiii. 8); at the same time, it is inferior to the lion in strength and appearance, and is heavy and ungainly in its movements."[33] Why, however, does the beast raise itself on one side? Although the Scriptures do not answer directly, probably the best explanation is that it represented the one-sided union of the Persian and Median Empires. Persia at this time, although coming up last, was by far the greater and more powerful and had absorbed the Medes. This is represented also in chapter 8 by the two horns of the ram with the horn that comes up last being higher and greater. The ram with its unequal horns is identified as "The kings of Media and Persia" (Dan 8:20). This interpretation also helps to support the Medo-Persian character of the second empire and is true to the facts of history.

The bear is described as having three ribs in its mouth. Normally a bear lives mostly on fruits, vegetables, and roots, but will eat flesh when hungry and attack other animals and men. Scripture does not tell us the meaning of the three ribs, and many suggestions have been offered. Probably the best is that it refers to Media, Persia, and Babylon as representing the three major components of the Medo-Babylonian Empire. Jerome offered this suggestion.[34] An alternative view offered by Young is that it represents Babylon, Lydia, and Egypt.[35] Young's objection to Jerome's viewpoint is that it would make the bear devour itself.

The bear, however, is the symbol of government and military conquest and the ribs are the people subdued. The bear is instructed to continue its conquest and to "devour much flesh." This apparently refers to the additional conquests of the Medes and Persians in the years which followed the fall of Babylon. Young errs in making this command simply to devour the three ribs already in the mouth of the bear. It would seem clear that the flesh is not the same as the ribs but refers to further conquests. As Leupold expresses it, "The question arises whether the command, 'Arise, devour much flesh,' implies that the flesh on the ribs is to be eaten, or whether, after substantial conquests have been made, further conquests are to be attempted. The latter seems to be the more reasonable interpretation."[36] Among the nations yet to be conquered were Lydia and Egypt. Taken as a whole, the prophecy of the second beast accurately portrays the characteristics and history of the Medo-Persian Empire which, although beginning in Daniel's day, continued for over 200 years until the time of Alexander the Great, 336 B.C.

THE THIRD BEAST: GREECE

7:6 After this I beheld, and lo another, like a leopard, which had upon the back of it four wings of a fowl; the beast had also four heads; and dominion was given to it.

Daniel in describing the vision next depicts a third beast differing from either of the two preceding animals. The third is like a leopard, has four wings on its back, and has four heads. The third beast is commonly identified as the empire of Greece.[37] The only thing said about this beast is that dominion was given to it.

The expression "After this I beheld" has in it the implication of intense scrutiny. The leopard in contrast to the lion, the first beast, is less grand and majestic, but it is swifter and was much feared as an animal of prey in Old Testament times. The swiftness of the leopard made it the standard of comparison in Habakkuk 1:8 where the horses of the Chaldeans are described as swifter than leopards. Leopards characteristically would lie in wait for their prey (Jer 5:6; Ho 13:7) and then pounce upon their victims with great speed and agility. Young prefers the translation "panther" instead of leopard, to indicate a leopard of unusual size and power.[38]

The impression of great speed inherent in a leopard is further enhanced by the presence of four wings on its back. Although these wings are not declared to be the wings of an eagle as in the case of the first beast, their presence emphasizes the concept of speed. Of significance is the mention that there were precisely four wings in keeping with the four heads of the beast, whereas in the first beast the number of wings is implied to be only two, like an eagle.

The four heads obviously refer to intelligent direction of the beast and indicate, in contrast to the earlier beasts which had only one head, that the third empire would have four governmental divisions with corresponding heads.

In their zeal to promote the idea that the third empire is Persia, liberal critics bring up many petty objections to equating the third beast with Greece. On the face of it, however, the history of Greece under Alexander the Great corresponds precisely to what is here described.

With the swiftness of a leopard, Alexander the Great conquered most of the civilized world all the way from Macedonia to Africa and eastward to India. The lightning character of his conquests is without precedent in the ancient world, and this is fully in keeping with the image of speed embodied in the leopard itself and the four wings on its back.

It is a well established fact of history that Alexander had four principal successors. Calvin, after Jerome, considered these Ptolemy, Seleucus, Philip, and Antigonus.³⁹ Keil and most modern commentaries prefer to recognize the four kings who emerge about twenty-two years after the death of Alexander after the overthrow of Antigonus at the battle of Ipsus (301 B.C.). These four kings and their reigns were, according to Keil, Lysimachus, who held Thrace and Bithynia; Cassander, who held Macedonia and Greece; Seleucus, who controlled Syria, Babylonia, and territories as far east as India; and Ptolemy, who controlled Egypt, Palestine, and Arabia Petrea.⁴⁰

In spite of the aptness of the interpretation of verse 6 which would identify the leopard as the kingdom of Alexander and the four wings and four heads as its fourfold component parts which became evident after Alexander's death, other views have been offered. The conservative scholar, Young, although agreeing that the third empire is Greece, takes the four heads as representing the four corners of the earth; and, therefore, he denies that it refers to four Persian rulers (after Charles and Bevan) or to the four successors of Alexander (after Jerome and Calvin) or to the geographical divisions of Alexander's conquests, namely, Greece, Western Asia, Egypt and Persia. Young states, "Here the four heads, representing the four corners of the earth, symbolize ecumenicity of the kingdom."⁴¹ In view of the transparent fact that Alexander did have four generals who succeeded him and divided his empire into four divisions, neither more nor less, it would seem that the interpretation of the four wings and the four heads as referring to the divisions of the Grecian Empire with their rulers is the best interpretation. This would confirm the identification of the third beast as the Grecian Empire. As Leupold states, in regard to the critics' identification of the second and third kingdoms as Media and Persia, "We are more firmly convinced than ever that they [the four beasts] are Babylon, Persia, Greece, and Rome. The arguments advanced in support of Media as being the second in both series are not convincing."⁴²

The interpretation which takes the four horns as reference to the four subdivisions of Alexander's kingdom is quite superior to the interpretation of those who want to relate this to Persia in order to eliminate the prophetic element. The issue here, as so often in the book of Daniel, is whether Daniel can accurately foreshadow future events—in this instance, the fourfold division of the Grecian Empire several hundreds years before it occurred. The difficulty of the liberal critics in interpreting these prophecies is further evidence that they are operating on the wrong premises. The interpretation disputes of the first three empires, however, are relatively insignificant in comparison to the interpretative problems of the fourth world empire which was to extend to the end of human history as Daniel saw it and contains so many elements that by any stretch of the imagination cannot be conformed to history of the second century B.C. or earlier.

THE FOURTH BEAST: ROME

7:7-8   After this I saw in the night visions, and behold a fourth beast, dreadful and terrible, and strong exceedingly; and it had great iron teeth: it devoured and brake in pieces, and stamped the residue with the feet of it: and it was diverse from all the beasts that were before it; and it had ten horns. I considered the horns, and, behold, there came up among them another little horn, before whom there were three of the first horns plucked up by the roots: and, behold, in this horn were eyes like the eyes of man, and a mouth speaking great things.

The crucial issue in the interpretation of the entire book of Daniel, and especially of chapter 7, is the identification of the fourth beast. On this point, liberal critics generally insist that the fourth beast is Greece or the kingdom of Alexander the Great. Conservative scholars with few exceptions generally identify the fourth beast as Rome.

The dominion of Rome, beginning with the occupation of Sicily in 241 B.C. as a result of victory in the first Punic conflict, rapidly made the Mediterranean Sea a Roman lake by the beginning of the second century B.C. Spain was conquered first, and then Carthage at the battle of Zama in North Africa in 202 B.C. Beginning by subjugating the area north of Italy, Rome then moved east, conquering Macedonia, Greece, and Asia Minor. The Roman general Pompey swept into Jerusalem in 63 B.C. after destroying remnants of the Seleucid Empire (Syria). During following decades, Rome extended control to southern Britain, France, Belgium, Switzerland, and Germany west of the Rhine River. The Roman Empire continued to grow gradually for four centuries or more (reaching its height in A.D. 117), in contrast to the sudden rise of the other empires which preceded it. It likewise declined slowly, beginning in the third century. The decline became obvious in the fifth century A.D., with the Romans leaving Britain in A.D. 407 and suffering a sack of Rome in 410 by the Visigoths. It was not until A.D. 1453 that the last Roman or Byzantine ruler was killed in battle and Mohammed II conquered Constantinople. The question facing the exposition is whether Daniel is here describing the Roman empire, clearly the greatest of all empires of history. The interpreter of the book of Daniel is forced to make a decision as the evaluation of the supporting evidence, the theological implications, and the resulting prophetic program depend almost entirely on this question.[43]

On this issue the question of whether the book of Daniel is a genuine sixth-century writing or a second-century forgery is determinative. Row-

159

ley objects strenuously to the accusation that the liberal view—that the fourth kingdom is Greece—stems from prejudice, and he attempts to turn the argument against the conservative as unfairly accusing the liberal. Rowley quotes Charles H. H. Wright as follows, "Wright imports prejudice into the question by saying: 'the real objections of the modern school to the old "Roman" interpretation arise from a determination to get rid at all costs of the predictive element in prophecy, and to reduce the prophecies of the Scripture, Old and New, to the position of being only guesses of ancient seers, or *vaticinia post eventa.*' That the Greek view commanded so long and respectable an array of names among its supporters, prior to the establishment of the modern school, is a sufficient refutation of this unworthy remark. That since the establishment of the critical school, the Greek view has continued to be held by scholars of unimpeachable orthodoxy, is ample proof that the case for that view rests on a far more substantial basis than prejudice."[44]

It is probably fair to say that liberals are not conscious of their prejudice in this matter, but Rowley himself gives the matter away in his later discussion. After describing the bewildering variety of views, both in support of the Roman and of the Greek empire interpretations, Rowley states,

> Within the circle of those who hold the Greek view, therefore, there is wide divergence on this point, and while up to the time of Antiochus Epiphanes, their reading of history and of the visions run concurrently, and they may be considered together, the only form of the Greek view which is here claimed to fit the prophecies is that which locates the composition of these chapters, at any rate in the form in which they now stand before us, in the Maccabean Age. On this view, the author was a man who was moved of the spirit of God to encourage his fellows to resist the attack of Antiochus Epiphanes upon the religion and culture of his race, and who rightly perceives that the victory must lie with them, if they were to be loyal unto their God, but whose message was coloured with the Messianic hopes that were not to be fulfilled.[45]

In other words, Rowley himself says that the only sensible support for the Greek interpretation is that the book of Daniel is a second-century production.

In addition to making this major admission that identification of the fourth empire as Grecian depends on the thesis that the book of Daniel is a forgery of the second century, Rowley completely fails to support the Grecian empire interpretation by any consensus among its followers, and his discussion is a hopeless maze of alternating views which he either rejects or accepts often as mere matters of opinion.

While the diversity of interpretation is indeed confusing to any expositor of this portion of Scripture, if the book of Daniel is a sixth-century writing, and therefore genuine Scripture, it follows, even as Rowley indirectly admits, that the Roman view is more consistent than the Greek empire interpretation. This is especially true among those following premillennial interpretation. The Roman view is supported in the exegesis of the passage which follows, which endeavors to demonstrate that the prophecies of Daniel are best explained by identifying the fourth kingdom as the Roman Empire.

Daniel describes the fourth beast in verse 7 as a fascinating spectacle upon which he fixed his eyes. The fourth beast is described as "dreadful and terrible, and strong exceedingly." This description is supported by its great iron teeth which distinguished it from any known animal. As Daniel watched, the beast was observed to devour and break in pieces and stamp the residue of the preceding kingdoms. Daniel is explicit that the beast is quite different from any of the beasts which were before it.

The description of the beast to this point more obviously corresponds to the Roman Empire than that of the empire of Alexander the Great. Alexander conquered by the rapidity of his troop movements and seldom crushed the people whom he conquered. By contrast, the Roman empire was ruthless in its destruction of civilizations and peoples, killing captives by the thousands and selling them into slavery by the hundreds of thousands. This hardly is descriptive of either Alexander or the four divisions of his empire which followed. As Leupold states, referring to the iron teeth, "That must surely signify a singularly voracious, cruel, and even vindictive world power. Rome could never get enough of conquest. Rivals like Carthage just had to be broken: *Carthago delenda est.* Rome had no interest in raising the conquered nations to any high level of development. All her designs were imperial; let the nations be crushed and stamped underfoot."[46] The description of Daniel 7:7 clearly is more appropriate for the empire of Rome than for the Macedonian kingdom or any of its derived divisions.

Probably the most decisive argument in favor of interpreting the fourth empire as Roman is the fact, mentioned in earlier discussion, that the New Testament seems to follow this interpretation. Christ, in His reference to the "abomination of desolation" (Mt 24:15) clearly pictures the desecration of the temple, here prophesied as a future event. Even if Young is wrong in identifying this with the destruction of the temple in A.D. 70[47] and the view is followed that it represents a still future event signalling the start of the great tribulation, in either case, it is Roman not Grecian, as the Grecian view would require fulfillment in the second century B.C. The New Testament also seems to employ the symbolism of Daniel in the book of Revelation, presented as future even after the destruction of the temple.[48] These New Testament allusions to Daniel which require the fourth empire to be Roman (cf. also Dan 9:26) make unnecessary the tangled explanation of Rowley and others attempting to find an explanation of the ten horns or at least seven of them in the Seleucid kings.[49]

The interpretation identifying this as Rome immediately has a major problem in that there is no real correspondence to the Roman Empire historically in the phrase, "and it had ten horns." This and the succeeding matter has no correspondence either to the history of Greece or to the history of Rome. The interpretation of the vision later in the chapter only serves to emphasize this problem.

Interpreters of this chapter who agree that it is Roman divide three ways in their explanation of how this relates to the Roman Empire. Amillennial scholars like Young and Leupold tend to spiritualize both the number ten and the number three, and thus escape the necessity of finding any literal fulfillment. Both of them find literal fulfillment impossible because there are no ten kings reigning simultaneously in the Roman period.[50] Young, however, considers fulfillment in the Roman Empire in the past, and no further fulfillment is necessary.[51] Leupold finds ultimate fulfillment at the second coming of Christ, rather than in past history.[52] Premillennialists offer a third view, providing literal fulfillment: ten actual kingdoms will exist simultaneously in the future consummation.

In verse 8, as Daniel continued to gaze intently upon the vision, he saw another little horn emerging from the head of the beast, and in the process, uprooting three of the first horns, that is, three of the ten horns previously described. The little horn is described as having eyes like the eyes of a man and a mouth speaking great things.

If there were no commentary upon this passage and the interpreter was left to find its meaning simply on what the text states, it would be a reasonable conclusion that the little horn is a man, and that, therefore, the ten horns which precede were also men who were rulers in relationship to the fourth kingdom. The fact that the horn has eyes and a mouth identifies the human characteristics.

Commentators have been quick to note that in chapter 8 there is also a little horn which conservative expositors have identified with Antiochus Epiphanes. This has been taken as evidence that the little horn of Daniel 7 is also from the Grecian or Maccabean period in its latter stages. Further consideration is given to this in chapter 8. It must be observed, however, that the little horn of chapter 8 comes out of an entirely different context than the little horn of chapter 7. Although both horns are described as "little," the horn of chapter 7 is not said to grow like the horn in chapter 8, although in the end he becomes a greater power than the little horn of chapter 8. To assume that the two horns are one and the same because both are little horns is to decide a matter on assumed similarities without regard for the contradictions.

Archer, in an excellent discussion, states,

> There can be no question that the little horn in chapter 8 points to a ruler of the Greek empire, that is, Antiochus Epiphanes. The critics, therefore, assume that since the same term is used, the little horn in chapter 7 must refer to the same individual. This, however, can hardly be the case, since the four-winged leopard of chapter 7 clearly corresponds to the four-horned goat of chapter 8; that is, both represent the Greek empire which divided into four after Alexander's death. The only reasonable deduction to draw is that there are two little horns involved in the symbolic visions of Daniel. One of them emerged from the third empire, and the other is to emerge from the fourth.[53]

It is also true that the Aramaic word for horn in chapter 7 is different from the Hebrew word for horn in chapter 8. However, this may be accounted for on the basis of the difference in language and does not in itself determine the interpretation.

THE VISION OF THE ANCIENT OF DAYS

7:9-10 I beheld till the thrones were cast down, and the Ancient of days did sit, whose garment was white as snow, and the hair of his head like the pure wool: his throne was like the fiery flame, and his wheels as burning fire. A fiery stream issued and came forth from before him: thousand thousands ministered unto him, and ten thousand times ten thousand stood before him: the judgment was set, and the books were opened.

No system of biblical interpretation can claim to be adequate unless it provides a satisfactory interpretation of the conclusion of the vision. Three major facts stand out in verses 9-14. First, in verses 9 and 10, Daniel has a vision of heaven at the time of final judgment on the nations. Second, in verses 11 and 12, the little horn representing the last ruler of the times of the Gentiles is destroyed and with it his empire. Third, the fifth kingdom, the kingdom of the son of man who comes with the clouds of heaven is brought in, beginning the everlasting dominion of God. It is obvious that all three factors combine to make clear that this is a summary conclusion which is catastrophic in nature and introducing a radical change. The critical explanation of the fourth empire as belonging to Alexander has no reasonable explanation of any one of these three factors, let alone an explanation of all of them. If this is genuine prophecy, it belongs to a future consummation which was not realized by the Greek Empire nor by the Roman Empire as far as recorded history is concerned.

In verse 9, Daniel sees thrones in heaven on which the Ancient of days is seated. The expression in the King James Version that "the thrones were cast down," is better interpreted as "the thrones were placed." This is the establishment not the destruction of a throne in heaven. The scene as a whole corresponds to what John saw and recorded in Revelation 4-5. The Ancient of days seems to correspond to God the Father, as distinct from God the Son who is introduced in Daniel 7:13 as Son of man.

A. C. Gaebelein, basing his argument on John 5:22, declares, "The Ancient of Days is the Lord Jesus Christ," and finds confirmation in Revelation 1:12-14.[54] To support this, he divides chapter 7 into four separate visions instead of one vision as it is generally taken. However, if in the same chapter the Ancient of days is clearly God the Father in Daniel 7:13, it is futile to argue from other passages in the same chapter that the Ancient of days is Jesus Christ. The expression "Ancient of days" is used of God only in this chapter where the title is repeated in verse 13 and 22. His garments are said to be white as snow and His hair as pure wool. The emphasis is on purity rather than on age, although it also may imply that God is eternal.

The Ancient of days is described as sitting upon a throne, one of many, as indicated in the contrast between the plural early in verse 9 and the singular in the latter part of verse 9. Who sits on the thrones first mentioned is not indicated, but this may either refer to angelic authority or the Second and Third Persons of the Trinity may be intended. The major characteristic of the throne is that it is a burning flame (*like* is not in the original Aramaic), and the wheels of the throne, whatever their meaning, are also burning (cf. Eze 1:13-21). The glory of God, pictured as a fiery flame, is a common representation in Scripture. The fire is a symbol of judgment and is associated with theophanies in the Old Testament. In Psalm 97 it is revealed that "righteousness and judgment are the habitation ["foundation," RSV] of his throne" (v. 2), and "A fire goeth before him, and burneth up his enemies round about" (v. 3). In the glorified revelation of Jesus Christ a similar description of God is given, "His head and his hairs are white like wool, as white as snow; and his eyes were as a flame of fire; and his feet like unto fine brass, as if they burned in a furnace" (Rev 1:14-15; cf. Ex 3:2; Deu 4:24; 1 Ti 6:16; Heb 12:29). That Christ as the Son of man should have a similar glory to the Ancient of days is no contradiction, as their glory is the same even though their persons are distinguished in Daniel 7.

In this scene of blazing glory, innumerable saints and angels (cf. Deu 33:2) are pictured as ministering to God, in number ten thousand times ten thousand. In the glorious presence of God, the books are opened and the judgment is set. It is apparent that this is the hour of final decision as far as the nations of the world are concerned. Daniel does not enlarge on the concept of "the books." The implication is, however, from Revelation 20:12, that this is a record of the works of men (cf. Is 65:6 for record of evil deeds, and Mal 3:16 for remembrance of good deeds). As Leupold states it, "In them are written, not names, but *deeds* of men, a record of their ungodly acts, on the basis of which they will be judged."[55]

In Matthew 25:31-46, there is a corresponding judgment which chronologically may be considered to follow the one here pictured. In Daniel, the judgment is in heaven and relates to the little horn and the beast. In Matthew, the judgment follows the second coming of Christ pictured in Daniel 7:13-14 and extends the original judgment upon the beast to the entire world. Even without any emendation or explanation from other texts of the Bible, it is clear that this is at the end of the interadvent age and the end of the times of the Gentiles. It, therefore, demands a fulfillment which is yet future, and it is futile to attempt to find anything in history that provides a reasonable fulfillment of this passage.

The Destruction of the Beast

7:11-12 I beheld then because of the voice of the great words which' the horn spake: I beheld even till the beast was slain, and his body destroyed, and given to the burning flame. As concerning the rest of the beasts, they had their dominion taken away: yet their lives were prolonged for a season and time.

As Daniel kept looking intently upon the vision that was before him, the scene shifted once again to earth. Young, after Montgomery and Keil, holds that *because of* should be translated "from the time of."[56] Their point is that the vision of heaven immediately followed the arrogant words of the little horn. As the prophet listened to the great words uttered by the little horn of verse 8, he saw the beast destroyed and given to burning flame. This passage is another illustration of how quickly God can dispose of the mightiest of men, and how men in their wickedness are ultimately brought to divine judgment. Critics maintain that the beast here is the Seleucid power in general and the mouth is Antiochus Epiphanes, killed in battle in 164 B.C. But the kingdom of God from heaven did not follow the downfall of Antiochus. Although the Maccabean revolt was followed by the independent Jewish kingdom, and the Roman conquest was not until a century later in 63 B.C., the ultimate beneficiary of Antiochus was Rome. The destruction of the beast, however, does not fit the historic Roman Empire which took centuries to lose all its strength. This is a sudden act of divine judgment in which the major ruler is killed and his government destroyed. This passage is an obvious parallel to Revelation 19:20 where the beast and the false prophet are cast alive into the lake of fire burning with brimstone at the time of the second coming of Christ.

Verse 12 has been a stumbling block, especially to the liberal critics such as Rowley, who have great difficulty in understanding how the rest of the beasts have their lives prolonged even though their dominion is taken away. If the earlier beasts are empires which were succeeded by the fourth beast, how can they be prolonged after the fourth beast? As Rowley states it, "Further, we are told that when the fourth beast was destroyed, the other beasts were spared for a time, though denied any dominion. But how can it be maintained that at any time contemplated by the various forms of this interpretation Babylon, Medo-Persia, and Greece enjoyed a measured existence that was denied to Rome?"[57]

The point is that the destruction of the fourth beast here described refers to a time yet future in connection with the second advent of Christ. Montgomery suggests that the expression *a season and a time* are semantic equivalents (cf. Dan 2:21; Acts 1:7) and denote "a fixed fate."[58] What verse 12 is saying is that the Babylonian, Medo-Persian, and Grecian empires were to some extent continued in their successors; that is, Gentile power shifted as to rulership but continued more or less in the same pattern. By contrast, at the second coming of Christ the fourth beast is completely destroyed, and a totally different kingdom which is from heaven succeeds the fourth empire. The destruction of the first three beasts is not stated directly in this chapter. Evidently the first three continue to survive in another form in the kingdom which replaces them. Hence, "They had their dominion taken away: yet their lives were prolonged for a season and time." This is borne out by the image of chapter 2, as Driver states, "the entire image remains intact until the stone falls upon the feet (representing the fourth and last kingdom), when the whole of it breaks up together."[59]

When Medo-Persia followed Babylon, the dominion of Babylon was taken away, but in some sense the lives of the participants were prolonged. The same is true when Greece succeeded Medo-Persia and when Rome succeeded Greece. But the end of the fourth beast is to be dramatic, cataclysmic, and final. Both the rulers and the people involved are to be destroyed. This interpretation agrees with Revelation 19:19-20, which records the beast as destroyed and its ruler cast in the lake of fire at the second coming of Christ, and is confirmed by Matthew 25:31-46, the judgment of the nations at the return of Christ.

THE FIFTH KINGDOM OF THE SON OF MAN
FROM HEAVEN

7:13-14 I saw in the night visions, and, behold, one like the Son of man came with the clouds of heaven, and came to the Ancient of days, and they brought him near before him. And there was given him do-

166

minion, and glory, and a kingdom, that all people, nations, and languages, should serve him: his dominion is an everlasting dominion, which shall not pass away, and his kingdom that which shall not be destroyed.

The climax of the vision is now seen by Daniel. Again, it is heaven rather than earth that is in view. Verse 13 follows verse 10 chronologically. Verses 11-12 are explanatory and do not advance the narrative. Porteous correctly notes, "The interposition, however, of vv. 11 and 12 is necessary to express the author's meaning."[60] One described as "like the Son of man," in obvious contrast with the beasts and the little horn, comes before the throne of the Ancient of days, attended by the clouds of heaven. The phrase *they brought him near before him* can be better translated, "he was brought before him." The purpose of this heavenly presentation is indicated in verse 14 where the Son of man is given "dominion, and glory, and a kingdom." This kingdom would be a worldwide kingdom involving "all people, nations, and languages." In contrast to the preceding kingdoms, it would be an everlasting kingdom which shall not pass away and be destroyed. This kingdom is obviously the expression of divine sovereignty dealing dramatically with the human situation in a way which introduces the eternal state where God is manifestly supreme in His government of the universe.

Conservative scholars are agreed that the Son of man is a picture of the Lord Jesus Christ rather than an angelic agency. The description of Him as being worthy of ruling all nations is obviously in keeping with many passages in the Bible referring to the millennial rule of Jesus Christ, as for instance, Psalm 2:6-9 and Isaiah 11. Like the scene in Revelation 4-5, Christ is portrayed as a separate person from God the Father. The expression that He is attended by "clouds of heaven" implies His deity (1 Th 4:17). A parallel appears in Revelation 1:7, which states, "Behold, he cometh with clouds," in fulfillment of Acts 1 where in His ascension He was received by a cloud (Ac 1:9) and the angels say that he will "come in like manner as ye have seen him go into heaven" (Ac 1:11). Clouds in Scripture are frequently characteristic of revelation of deity (Ex 13:21-22; 19:9, 16; 1 Ki 8:10-11; Is 19:1; Jer 4:13; Eze 10:4; Mt 24:30; 26:64; Mk 13:26). The liberal scholar, Driver, interprets the clouds as meaning "superhuman majesty and state."[61]

Driver, however, objects to the phrase *the Son of man* which probably should be better translated "a son of man."[62] The Aramaic does not have the definite article. Driver does not like the concept that this is a formal title. He claims that it merely implies humanity.[63] Although there is some linguistic support for the concept that this is merely a human being in appearance, the frequent introduction of this term in the New Testament referring to Jesus Christ is the divine commentary on the phrase (cf. Mt

8:20; 9:6; 10:23; 11:19; 12:8, 32, 40; 13:37, 41; 16:13, 27, 28; 17:9, 12, 22, etc.)

Obviously, the expression *the Son of man* should be interpreted by the context. In verse 13, He is presented as being near the Ancient of days, and in verse 14 given dominion over all peoples and nations. This could not be an angel, nor could it be the body of saints, as it corresponds clearly to other Scriptures which predict that Christ will rule over all nations (Ps 72:11; Rev 19:15-16). Only Christ will come with clouds of heaven, and be the King of kings and Lord of lords over all nations throughout eternity. Inasmuch as all the nations which survive His purging judgment and come under His dominion are saints, it would be tautology to make the Son of man the personification of the saints. Keil states on this point,

> With all other interpreters, we must accordingly firmly maintain that he who appears with the clouds of heaven comes from heaven to earth and is a personal existence, and is brought before God, who judges the world, that he may receive dominion, majesty, and a kingdom. But in the words *"as a man"* it is not meant that he was only a man. He that comes with the clouds of heaven may, as Kranichfeld rightly observes, "be regarded, according to the current representations, as the God of Israel coming on the clouds, while yet he who appears takes the outward form of a man."[64]

Young observes that some expositors regard *the Son of man* as representing the people of Israel. Young states, "This view has been adopted by a long line of expositors of which M [Montgomery] is one of the latest representatives."[65] As Young goes on to point out, however, the earliest interpretation regarded this as Messianic and referring to Christ, and this interpretation is confirmed by the fact that Jesus Christ took the title Himself in the New Testament.*[66]

In the statements of verse 14, it should also be apparent that Daniel is given revelation in addition to what he could see visually in the vision. While the vision could portray the Son of man receiving authority, the purpose of this act would have to be revealed: that His domain would be over all people, and that His kingdom would be everlasting and not subject to destruction. At every point the kingdom from heaven is in contrast, superior, and a final answer to the preceding kingdoms of the four great world empires.

In the futuristic interpretation of the prophecy of Daniel beginning with the phrase "it had ten horns" in verse 7 and continuing through verse 14 as prophecy yet to be fulfilled, a question naturally arises why Daniel has not included in his prophetic scheme the events of the age between the first and second advents of Christ.

*The Jewish apocryphal Book of Enoch, which is earlier than Jude, attests that the term refers to an individual. See the excellent footnote in the Jerusalem Bible at Daniel 7:13 (p. 1437, O.T.) and Matthew 8:20 (p. 27, N.T.).

In the main, commentators have had three options: first, like the liberal scholars, they could deny literal fulfillment and even claim that Daniel was in error; second, they could find these prophecies symbolically fulfilled in church history—this has been the viewpoint in part of postmillennialism and amillennialism; third, they could find these prophecies to be distinctly future and not at all fulfilled by the first coming of Christ, the decline of the Roman Empire, or that which is historic. The third view, which is the futuristic interpretation, is the only one which provides the possibility of literal fulfillment of this prophecy.

Although it has been fondly projected and enthusiastically supported that the church is the fifth kingdom, that the coming of the Son of man is His first coming to the earth, and that the church is responsible for the decline of the Roman Empire, nothing is stranger to church history than this interpretation. It is questionable whether the Roman Empire had any serious opposition from the Christian church or that the growing power of the church contributed in a major way to its downfall. Edward Gibbon in his classic work on the Roman Empire enumerates "four principal causes of the ruin of Rome, which continued to operate in a period of more than a thousand years: I. The injuries of time and nature. II. The hostile attacks of the barbarians and Christians. III. The use and abuse of the materials. And, IV. The domestic quarrels of the Romans."[67] While undoubtedly the presence of the church in growing power in the declining Roman Empire was a factor in its history, and Gibbon includes, "the rise, establishment, and sects of Christianity"[68] in a detailed list of factors contributing to the decline and fall of the Roman Empire, it is quite clear to everyone that the church was not the major factor and in no ways can be identified as a sudden and catastrophic cause for the fall of the Roman Empire. Although the church dominated Europe during the Middle Ages, its power began to be disrupted by the Protestant Reformation at the very time that the Roman Empire was gasping its last in the fifteenth century. Although the power and influence of the Roman Catholic church is recognized by everyone, it does not fulfill the prophecy of Daniel 7:23, that the fourth kingdom "shall devour the whole earth, and shall tread it down, and break it in pieces." This would require figurative interpretation of prophecy far beyond any correspondence to the facts of either prophecy or history.

Far better is the interpretation which does honor to the text and justifies belief in its accuracy as prophetic revelation. This point of view, which is quite common in the Old Testament, is that the present church age is not included in the Old Testament prophetic foreviews. The first and second comings of Christ are frequently spoken of in the same breath, as for instance in Isaiah 61:1-2, which Christ expounded in Luke 4:18-19.

Significantly, Christ quoted only the portion dealing with His first coming and stopped in the middle of a sentence because the last part of the sentence related to His second advent, separated from the first coming by more than nineteen hundred years. In a similar way, in his prophetic vision, Daniel takes human history up to the first coming of Christ when the Roman Empire was in sway, and then leaps to the end of the age when, in fulfillment of prophecy, the fourth empire will be revived and suffer its fatal judgment at the hands of Christ at His second coming to the earth. This interpretation, though not without its problems, allows an accurate and detailed interpretation of this prophecy and is genuinely predictive.

Even Leupold, who may be classified as a conservative amillenarian, states,

> Why does the sequence of historical kingdoms in this vision extend no farther than the Roman whereas we know that many developments came after the Roman Empire and have continued to come before the judgment? We can venture only opinions under this head, opinions that we believe are reasonable and conform with the situation as it is outlined. One suggestion to be borne in mind is the fact that the prophets, barring the conclusion of chapter 9 in Daniel, never see the interval of time lying between the first and second coming of Christ. In the matter of history, therefore, Daniel does not see beyond Christ's days in the flesh and perhaps the persecution as it came upon the early church.[69]

If Daniel 7 had concluded with verse 14, it is probable, with the help of the book of Revelation and other scripture passages, that a reasonable explanation could be made of the text. In view of the complexity and importance of the prophecy, the chapter continues, however, to give the reader a divinely inspired interpretation. It should be borne in mind that when a symbol is interpreted, while the symbol is obviously parabolic and figurative, the interpretation should be taken literally. Accordingly, the explanation can be taken as a factual exegesis of the truth involved in the vision.

The Interpretation of the Four Beasts

7:15-18 I Daniel was grieved in my spirit in the midst of my body, and the visions of my head troubled me. I came near unto one of them that stood by, and asked him the truth of all this. So he told me, and made me know the interpretation of the things. These great beasts, which are four, are four kings, which shall arise out of the earth. But the saints of the most High shall take the kingdom, and possess the kingdom for ever, even for ever and ever.

Having recited in detail the main features of the vision, Daniel now proceeds to give his own reaction and the interpretation given him in answer to his question. Having such a vision in the midst of the night must have been a terrifying experience, as it is obvious to Daniel that he had seen a panorama of tremendous events to come. Like Nebuchadnezzar in chapter 2, Daniel, although a prophet, is troubled by his lack of understanding of the vision. He was grieved in his spirit and troubled by the visions of his head.

By being "grieved" Daniel indicates his distress; by "spirit" he refers to his whole personality. The expression *in the midst of my body*, literally "in the midst of the sheath," compares the soul in the body to a sword in its sheath. Although the expression is peculiar, it is not without parallel as Keil states, "The figure here used, *'in the sheath'* (E.V. 'in the midst of my body'), by which the body is likened to a sheath for the soul, which as a sword in its sheath is concealed by it, is found also in Job xxvii. 8, and in the writing of the rabbis (cf. Buxt. *Lex. talm. s. v.*). It is used also by Pliny, vii. 52."[70]

Writers like Driver and Montgomery[71] find some difficulty with this, but in the main agree with Keil. The Septuagint changes the text to read, "on this account,"[72] but this is not really necessary. Daniel is merely summarizing his extreme concern, affecting spirit and body, and caused by the "visions of my head" (cf. Dan 7:1).

In verse 16, Daniel becomes an actor in the scene by addressing a question to one who stands by, generally considered to be an angel. When Daniel inquired concerning what truth was being revealed by this vision, the interpreter made known the meaning of his vision. Although this aspect of the vision increases the critical questions of those who do not accept Daniel as a sixth-century prophetic book, because Daniel could not himself interpret the vision, there is nothing unusual about this situation. A similar account is found in Genesis 28 when God speaks to Jacob on the occasion of his vision. In Exodus 3, God speaks to Moses out of the burning bush. Conversation with people seen in visions occurs in Ezekiel's vision of the new temple (Eze 40-48), in the visions of Zechariah (Zec 1-6). Almost exact parallels can be found in the book of Revelation where frequently John in the experience of a vision is given the interpretation of what he saw. Revelation 20 involves not only the vision but its God-given interpretation. In Revelation 21:9, one of the seven angels explains to John the new Jerusalem. Daniel has the same experience of a vision plus its explanation in Daniel 8, Daniel 10, and Daniel 12. This is not an abnormal situation.

The interpreter of Daniel's vision first of all gives a general interpretation in verses 17 and 18. In the verses which follow in answer to Daniel's question, more details are given. The summary statement in verse 17 is that the great beasts represent four kings which shall arise out of the earth. Liberal scholars have criticized the fact that the verse states twice that the beasts were four, and Charles states, "The words 'which are four' are omitted by the Septuagint. They are certainly unnecessary; for the seer knows perfectly well the number of the kingdoms."[73] The repetition of the number, however, is to make clear that the four beasts, each individually, represent a king. The "four kings" obviously refer to four kingdoms, as the beasts represent both a king and a kingdom.

Criticism has also been directed at the statement "shall arise out of the earth," as if this were a conflict with the four beasts coming out of the sea (Dan 7:3). Charles, for instance, says, ". . . the words 'shall arise out of the earth' are certainly corrupt. According to vii. 3, they arise out of the sea: cf. Rev. xiii. 1, 4, Ezra xi. 1." Charles goes on to say, "By a careful study of the LXX and Theod. we arrive at the following text: 'These great beasts are four kingdoms, which shall be destroyed from the earth.'"[74] What Charles does not take into consideration is that the sea represents symbolically the nations covering the earth, and what is symbolic in Daniel 7:3 is literal in Daniel 7:17.

In verse 18, the interpreter states that "the saints of the most High" shall take and possess the kingdom forever. Although there has been considerable discussion as to the reference of "the saints," it would seem to include the saved of all ages as well as the holy angels which may be described as "the holy ones" (cf. Dan 7:21, 22, 25, 27; 8:24; 12:7; cf. Ps 16:3; 34:9; Jude 14). In *The Wars of the Sons of Light and the Sons of Darkness*, the faithful Jews have celestial warriors mingled with them in their ranks.[75]

The expression in verse 18 that the saints "shall take the kingdom" can also be translated "receive the kingdom" as in most revised versions and in Young's translation.[76] However, Montgomery prefers to translate it, *"shall take over the sovereignty,"*[77] which is probably the preferred meaning in Daniel 5:31. The thought is, as Young expresses it, "They are not to establish or found the kingdom by their own power,"[78] and yet it is more than merely a passive reception. This is implied in the statement that "Darius the Median took the kingdom" (5:31), meaning that he took aggressive steps to establish his control over the kingdom. Daniel 7:18 goes on to emphasize that the saints possess the kingdom forever, contrasting the everlasting character of the fifth kingdom to the preceding kingdoms, which in due time passed away.

The reference to "the most high," from the Aramaic *Elyonin*, is a translation of a plural noun which could mean "high ones" or "high places." Young is correct, however, in identifying this as God, with the plural expressing majesty. The expression is repeated in Daniel 7:22, 25, 27. The expression although similar should not be confused with the "heavenlies" of Ephesians 2:6 referring to the peculiar position of saints in the present age which refers to place or position, not to God Himself. The kingdom possessed by saints of the most High, while eternal in its characteristics and sovereignty, may without difficulty include the millennial kingdom and the eternal rule of God which follows.

DANIEL REQUESTS INTERPRETATION OF THE FOURTH BEAST

7:19-22 Then I would know the truth of the fourth beast, which was diverse from all the others, exceeding dreadful, whose teeth were of iron, and his nails of brass; which devoured, brake in pieces, and stamped the residue with his feet; and of the ten horns that were in his head, and of the other which came up, and before whom three fell; even of that horn that had eyes, and a mouth that spake very great things, whose look was more stout than his fellows. I beheld, and the same horn made war with the saints, and prevailed against them; Until the Ancient of days came, and judgment was given to the saints of the most High; and the time came that the saints possessed the kingdom.

In asking the question concerning the fourth beast, Daniel gives a recapitulation of the particulars which were of immediate concern to him, especially those which distinguished the fourth beast from those which preceded. After the end is introduced in verse 18, when the saints receive the kingdom forever after the destruction of the fourth beast, in verse 19 attention again focuses on the conflict leading up to this and the items requiring explanation. Among these were aspects of the vision described as "exceeding dreadful," that is, items which produced fear, such as the teeth of iron, the nails of bronze (KJV, "brass"), the stamping of the other beasts, the ten horns, the other horn which came up later, the three horns which fell, and the horn which had eyes and a mouth speaking great things and which looked stronger than the other horns. Daniel also adds particulars not previously indicated in his recital of the vision, that the nails were of bronze, that the little horn was stronger than the other horns, that the little horn made war with the saints and prevailed against them (cf. Rev 11:7; 13:7), and that judgment was given to the saints of the most High.

The fact that Daniel is raising questions about the fourth empire rather than the preceding ones has been taken by critical scholars as another proof of the late date for Daniel. They argue that if Daniel actually lived in the sixth century B.C., as conservative scholars maintain, he would have also been very curious about the first three beasts. Montgomery, for instance, states, "The seer's contemporary interest is revealed by his inquisitiveness concerning the last beast and the judgment which hitherto had been hid in figures."[79]

There is really no justification, however, for this argument as the vision given to Daniel obviously emphasized the fourth beast. Whereas only three verses are given to the first three beasts, the remaining twenty-one verses of the chapter concern the fourth beast and his era; and Daniel, in his recital of the vision, uses eight verses to describe the details. If this is genuine prophecy, it is also true that Daniel is being guided providentially to that which is important from God's standpoint. Even from a human standpoint, the end of the ages with the triumph of the saints would be a matter of primary concern to Daniel. The argument of the critics is dissipated by their own premise that even the fourth kingdom was already history at the time a second-century writer recorded it, and in that case Daniel's curiosity would have to be faked in seeking the interpretation of history rather than a prophetic vision. There is no indication whatever in the text that Daniel thought the fourth beast already had been fulfilled in history.

The expression "judgment was given to the saints of the most High" in verse 22 probably means that judgment was given on their behalf or executed for them, rather than to make the saints judges themselves.[80] As Keil states, ". . . not to be rendered, as Hengstenberg thinks (*Beitr* i. p. 274), by reference to 1 Cor. vi. 2: 'to the saints of the Most High the judgment is given,' *i.e.* the function of the judge. This interpretation is opposed to the context, according to which it is God Himself who executes judgment, and by that judgment justice is done to the people of God, *i.e.* they are delivered from the unrighteous oppression of the beast, and receive the kingdom."[81] The reference to "the Ancient of days" is to God as in verses 9 and 13, and is identical to "the most High" as in verses 18, 25, and 27. As in the preceding revelation of the vision, the destruction of the fourth beast and the inauguration of the fifth kingdom from heaven is described as the time when the saints will possess the kingdom, a clear factor pointing to the end of the age and the second coming of Jesus Christ.

THE INTERPRETATION OF THE VISION OF THE FOURTH BEAST

7:23-25 Thus he said, The fourth beast shall be the fourth kingdom upon earth, which shall be diverse from all kingdoms, and shall devour the whole earth, and shall tread it down, and break it in pieces. And the ten horns out of this kingdom are ten kings that shall arise: and another shall rise after them; and he shall be diverse from the first, and he shall subdue three kings. And he shall speak great words against the most High, and shall wear out the saints of the most High, and think to change times and laws: and they shall be given into his hand until a time and times and the dividing of time.

The interpreter of the vision states plainly in verse 23 that the fourth beast represents the fourth kingdom, an earthly kingdom which will be

174

different from the preceding kingdoms and will devour the whole earth, that is, be worldwide in its sway. In the process, it will tread down and break in pieces the preceding kingdoms. By so much, the interpretation eliminates the idea that the fifth kingdom refers to the rule of God in the new heavens and the new earth (Rev 21 and 22) or that it is merely a spiritual kingdom which gradually gains sway by persuasion, such as the kingdom of God in the earth at the present time. By its terminology the interpretation of verses 23-27 demands that, for the fifth kingdom to overcome the fourth, the fifth must be basically a sovereign and political kingdom, whatever its spiritual characteristics. By so much, it also demands that this be a future fulfillment, inasmuch as nothing in history corresponds to this.

The ten horns of the vision in verse 24 are declared to be ten kings that shall arise. They clearly are simultaneous in their reign because three of them are disrupted by the little horn which is another ruler, but not given the title of king here. He also will be different from the first, that is, from the ten horns, and shall subdue three of them.

The endless explanation of critical scholars attempting to find these ten kings in the history of the Grecian Empire or to find them later in Rome, by their very disagreement among themselves demonstrate the impossibility of satisfactorily explaining this verse as past history. If the ten kings are in power at the end of the age, which also seems to be supported by the ten kings of Revelation 13:1; 17:12, it follows that they must be still future. The fact that they appear in the book of Revelation, written long after the fall of the Grecian Empire, plainly relates them to the Roman Empire in its final stage.

Just as there is special emphasis upon the fourth beast in the vision, so in the prophetic interpretation particular attention is given to the little horn, the outstanding personage at the end of the age, who will be destroyed with the inauguration of the kingdom from heaven. He is described as a blasphemer who "shall speak great words against the most High" and as a persecutor of the saints who "shall wear out the saints of the most High." He will also attempt to "change times and laws," that is, to change times of religious observances and religious traditions such as characterize those who worship God. Critics relate this to Antiochus Epiphanes.[82] While Antiochus may foreshadow the activities of the little horn of Daniel 7, the complete fulfillment will be much more severe and extensive.

The duration of the power of the little horn over the saints and the world is described as continuing "until a time and times and the dividing of times." This expression, also found in Daniel 12:7, is incorrectly identified with "the times of the Gentiles" in Luke 21:24 by Montgomery. As

Montgomery points out, however, the normal, traditional explanation is that the expression means three and one-half years. As Montgomery states it, "Essaying an exact interpretation, 'time' may be interpreted as 'year' after the usual interpretation at 4:13 (*q.v.*). The traditional, and by far the most common, understanding of 'times' is as of a dual; the word is pointed as a pl., but the Aram. later having lost the dual, the tendency of M [Massoretic text] is to ignore it in BAram. . . . Accordingly, one plus two plus one-half equals three and one-half years. The term is identical with the half-year week of 9:27 [which] equals three and one-half years."[83]

Although this expression might be difficult if it were not for other Scriptures (cf. Dan 4:25 where *times* equals years), the meaning seems clearly to refer to the last three and one-half years preceding the second advent of Christ, which will bring in the final form of the kingdom of God on earth. The three and one-half year computation is confirmed by the forty-two months, or three and one-half years, in Revelation 11:2 and 13:5, and the 1260 days of Revelation 11:3. Daniel also refers to 1290 days in 12:11 and 1335 days in 12:12 which apparently includes the establishment of the fifth kingdom as well as the destruction of the beast. All of these considerations lend support to the futuristic interpretation of this final period of world history.

THE DESTRUCTION OF THE FOURTH EMPIRE AND THE ESTABLISHMENT
OF THE EVERLASTING KINGDOM

7:26-28   But the judgment shall sit, and they shall take away his dominion, to consume and to destroy it unto the end. And the kingdom and dominion, and the greatness of the kingdom under the whole heaven, shall be given to the people of the saints of the most High, whose kingdom is an everlasting kingdom, and all dominions shall serve and obey him. Hitherto is the end of the matter. As for me Daniel, my cogitations much troubled me, and my countenance changed in me: but I kept the matter in my heart.

As Daniel has previously indicated, the interpreter now confirms the significance of the vision as describing judgment upon the fourth beast and its ruler, the taking away of his power to rule, and how he is destroyed in the end, that is, either at the end or destroyed eternally. At the destruction of the fourth empire, the kingdom then becomes the possession of "the people of the saints of the most High." This does not mean that God will not rule, as verse 14 plainly states that dominion is given to the Son of man, but it does indicate that the kingdom will be for the benefit and the welfare of the saints in contrast to their previous experience of persecution. In contrast to the preceding kingdoms, which terminated abruptly by God's judgment, the final kingdom will be an everlasting kingdom, and in it all powers and peoples will serve and obey God.

Daniel then pens a postscript to the interpretation of the vision, "Hitherto is the end of the matter," or as Montgomery translates it, "At this point the end of the word."[84] Daniel expresses again how his thoughts troubled him, his countenance changed, but he kept the matter in his heart, that is, did not reveal it to others. The thought of the expression, *my countenance changed in me,* is probably what Montgomery indicates, "and my color changed."[85] Thus ends one of the great chapters of the Bible which conservative scholarship recognizes as a panoramic view of future events revealed to Daniel in the sixth century B.C.

The very early suggestion that the fourth empire was Greece, attributed to the *Sibylline Oracles* (Book iii, line 397) which appeared shortly after the Maccabean period in the second century B.C., is cited by Rowley as evidence of early interpretation that the fourth empire was Greece.[86] Rowley also cites a number of other writers who support interpretation of the fourth empire as Greece before the rise of the modern critical school.[87] Nevertheless, it is true that, until the rise of modern critical interpretation, the majority view was that the fourth kingdom is Rome. There is really nothing in chapter 7 of Daniel to alter the conclusion that the fourth empire is Rome, that its final state has not yet been fulfilled, and that it is a genuine prophetic revelation of God's program for human history. In a modern world, when attention is again being riveted upon the Middle East, and Israel is once again back in the land, these items become of more than academic interest, because they are the key to the present movement of history in anticipation of that which lies ahead.

8

THE VISION OF THE RAM AND THE GOAT

Two important factors mark Daniel 8 as the beginning of a new section. First, beginning with this chapter, the language returns to Hebrew instead of the Aramaic used by Daniel from 2:4 through 7:28. Second, the change of language is in keeping with the change in thought introduced by this chapter. From here to the end of Daniel, the prophecy, even though it concerns the Gentiles, is occupied with human history as it relates to Israel. Therefore, although many expositors divide the book of Daniel into two halves (1-6 and 7-12), there are also good reasons for dividing Daniel into three sections (1, 2-7, 8-12).[1]

The first of Daniel's own visions recorded in Daniel 7 is a broad summary of the times of the Gentiles, with emphasis on the climactic events culminating in the second coming of Christ to the earth. Beginning in chapter 8, Daniel's second vision concerns the empires of Persia and Greece as they relate to Israel. Under Persian government, Israelites went back to rebuild their land and their city, Jerusalem. Under Grecian domination, in particular under Antiochus Epiphanes, the city and the temple were again desolated. Daniel 9 presents Israel's history from the time of Ezra and Nehemiah to the inauguration of the kingdom from heaven at the second coming of Christ immediately preceded by the time of great trouble for Israel. Chapters 10-11 reveal the events relating the Persian and Greek Empires to Israel, with emphasis on the Gentile oppression of Israel. The final section, 11:36—12:13, deals with the end of the age, the period of the revived Roman Empire, and the deliverance of Israel. It is fitting that the last five chapters of Daniel should be written in Hebrew, the language of Israel.

THE VISION AT SHUSHAN

8:1-2 In the third year of the reign of king Belshazzar a vision appeared unto me, even unto me Daniel, after that which appeared unto me at the first. And I saw in a vision; and it came to pass, when I saw, that I was at Shushan in the palace, which is in the province of Elam; and I saw in a vision, and I was by the river of Ulai.

178

The second vision of Daniel occurred, according to verse 1, "in the third year of the reign of king Belshazzar," in other words, about two years after the vision of chapter 7. Because it took place in the reign of Belshazzar, it is clear that both chapter 7 and 8 chronologically occur before chapter 5, the night of Belshazzar's feast. Before archeological discoveries confirmed the historical character of Belshazzar, it was common for critical expositors to conclude that the events of chapter 8 occurred immediately before chapter 5. Some recent expositors also follow this interpretation, although there is no ground for it. For instance, A. C. Gaebelein states, "It was the year when the feast of blasphemy was held and Babylon fell. Then God took His faithful servant aside and revealed to him new things concerning the future."[2] Edward Young assumes without evidence the same chronology, stating, "At any rate, this vision occurred shortly before the events of the fatal night of ch. 5."[3] Zöckler also places this chapter "shortly before the end of this king [Belshazzar]."[4]

On the basis of *The Babylonian Chronicle*, it is now known that Nabonidus began his reign in 556 B.C., and apparently Belshazzar became coregent three years later, 553 B.C., when Nabonidus took residence at Teima, as brought out in chapter 5. Belshazzar previously had served in other royal capacities beginning 560 B.C. Accordingly, if the vision of chapter 7 occurred in 553 B.C., the vision of chapter 8 occurred in 551 B.C., or twelve years before Belshazzar's feast in chapter 5. There is, therefore, no support for placing Daniel 8 near the downfall of Babylon as was the customary chronology before *The Babylonian Chronicle* was discovered. A. L. Oppenheim points out that Belshazzar was officially recognized as coregent while also the crown prince. He cites two legal documents dated in the twelfth and thirteenth years of Nabonidus, the king, and Bel-shar-usur, a variation of Belshazzar, the crown prince, for which there is no parallel in cuneiform literature.[5] This confirms beyond question both the role of Belshazzar as coregent and the dating of this vision before 539 B.C., the date of Belshazzar's death, and indicates the probability of the year 551 B.C. as the date of the vision as the sixth year of Nabonidus as well as the third year of Belshazzar.

The vision of chapter 8 is somewhat different in character from that of chapter 7, as it apparently did not occur in a dream or in a night vision. As Young correctly says, "This vision was not a dream vision like that of ch. 7."[6] Keil says in a similar way, "But not in a dream as that was, but while he was awake."[7] Daniel is careful to distinguish not only the character of the vision but its time by adding "after that which appeared unto me at the first," that is, the vision of chapter 7.

Although this much is clear, expositors have differed widely as to whether Daniel was in the palace at Shushan in the province of Elam, by the river Ulai (as v. 2 indicates) or was transported there in vision and actually was in Babylon at the time. Ancient Susa (called Shushan in the King James Version), about 150 miles north of the present head of the Persian Gulf, was situated midway between Ecbatana and Persepolis, and later became one of the main residences of the Persian kings. According to Josephus, Daniel was actually in Elam.* Keil notes that Bertholdt and Rosenmuller interpret Daniel as stating that he is actually in Shushan (Susa). He also notes that Bertholdt uses this to substantiate a charge of error against the pseudo-Daniel.⁹

Most expositors, whether liberal or conservative, understand Daniel 8 to teach that Daniel was actually in Babylon and in vision only was transported to Shushan. Montgomery cites the overwhelming weight of scholarship on this point that Daniel was there only in vision, which is supported by the Syriac version and the Vulgate, and held by John Calvin and many contemporary writers.¹⁰ Ezekiel also was transported in vision, presumably (Eze 8:3; 40:1 ff.).

The question as to whether Babylon at this time controlled ancient Susa is debated but is beside the point; in any case, in the vision Daniel is projected forward into the prophetic future of the Persian and Grecian Empires.

The probability is that Babylon did not control this city or area at this time, and this perhaps accounts for Daniel's astonishment as he contemplated the vision to find that he was in this place rather than at Babylon. The expression *Shushan the palace* reoccurs in historical sections dealing with the Persian Empire (Neh 1:1; Est 1:2, 5; 2:3, 5). By *the palace* is probably meant the king's residence, which was more in the form of a castle or fortress than merely a luxurious building. Shushan the palace, nevertheless, was destined in the Persian Empire to become the capital rather than Babylon. This was unknown at the time that this vision was given to Daniel, although Susa had served as the capital of the Elamites in antiquity; and conservative scholars find a genuine prophetic prediction in this reference to Susa.

Daniel finds it necessary to define in particular the location of this city, something a second-century pseudo-Daniel would not have had to do. Some critics have attempted to prove that Daniel was in error because Elam was probably not a province of Babylon at that time; however, Daniel does not literally say that it was.¹¹ Daniel also mentions that he was by "the river of Ulai." In regard to this stream near ancient Susa, Montgomery states, "The Ulai can best be identified with an artificial

*Josephus is also the source of the story that Daniel built a building at Ecbatana in Media in which later the kings of Media, Persia and Parthis were buried. Cf. Montgomery's discussion on the tomb of Daniel at Susa, and the tradition that Daniel built a tower at Ecbatana (*The Book of Daniel*, pp. 10-11, 325).

canal which connected the rivers Choastes and Coprates and ran close by Susa."[12]

In a word, Daniel finds himself projected in vision to a town little known at that time and unsuspected for future grandeur, but yet destined to be the important capital of Persia, the home of Esther, and the city from which Nehemiah came to Jerusalem. Beginning in 1884, the site of ancient Susa, then a large mound, has been explored and has divulged many archeological treasures. The code of Hammurabi was found there in 1901. The famous palace referred to by Daniel, Esther and Nehemiah was begun by Darius I and enlarged by later kings. Remains of its magnificence can still be seen near the modern village of Shush.[13] This unusual setting described in detail by Daniel in the opening verses of the eighth chapter now becomes the stage on which a great drama is portrayed in symbol describing the conquests of the second and third empires.

THE RAM WITH THE TWO HORNS

8:3-4 Then I lifted up mine eyes, and saw, and, and, behold, there stood before the river a ram which had two horns: and the two horns were high; but one was higher than the other, and the higher came up last. I saw the ram pushing westward, and northward, and southward; so that no beasts might stand before him, neither was there any that could deliver out of his hand; but he did according to his will, and became great.

Daniel, in his vision, sees a ram with two horns which are unequal, one higher than the other, and the higher one growing out of the ram last. As Daniel watches, he sees the ram pushing westward, northward, and southward; but no mention is made of pushing toward the east. No other beast is found to stand before the ram nor was anyone, whether man or beast, able to deliver from his power. As Daniel summarizes it, the ram does according to his will and becomes great.

The interpretation is provided in Daniel 8:20 that the ram is Medo-Persia, with the two horns representing its major kings. The fact that the ram represents both the Median and Persian Empires in their combined states rather than as separate empires is another important proof that the critics are wrong. The critics attempt to prove, on the basis of the reference to Darius the Mede, that Daniel erroneously taught two empires, first a Median and then a Persian. This, of course, is contradicted by history; and critics use this in attempt to prove Daniel in error. The critics, however, attribute to Daniel what he does not teach; and the problem is their own faulty interpretation. As Young puts it, "Neither here or elsewhere does Dan. conceive of an independently existing Median empire."[14] Historically, it was the combination of the Medes and the

Persians which proved irresistible for almost two hundred years, until Alexander the Great came on the scene.[15]

The portrayal of the two horns representing the two major aspects of the Medo-Persian Empire, that is, the Medes and the Persians, is very accurate, as the Persians coming up last and represented by the higher horn were also the more prominent and powerful. The directions which represent the conquests of the ram include all except east. Although Persia did expand to the east, its principal movement was to the west, north and south. It is the accuracy of this portrayal, rather than any alleged inaccuracy, which is embarrassing to the critic who does not want to accept a sixth-century Daniel who wrote genuine prophecy.

In regard to the use of a ram to represent that great empire, Keil observes, "In the *Bundehesch* the guardian spirit of the Persian kingdom appears under the form of a ram with clean feet and sharp-pointed horns, and . . . the Persian king, when he stood at the head of his army, bore, instead of the diadem, the head of a ram."[16] The references to beasts, as Keil states, "represent *kingdoms* and *nations*."[17]

Not only are both the ram and the goat mentioned in the Old Testament as symbols of power, but Cumont has noted that different lands were assigned to the signs of the Zodiac according to astronomical geography. In this view, Persia is thought of as under the zodiacal sign of Aries, the "ram," and Greece as sharing with Syria, the principal territory of the Seleucid monarchy, the zodiacal sign of Capricorn, the "goat." The word *capricorn* is derived from the Latin, *caper*, a goat and *cornu*, a horn.[18] Taken as a whole, as Driver states, "The verse describes the irresistible advances of the Persian arms, especially in the direction of Palestine, Asia Minor, and Egypt, with particular allusion to the conquests of Cyrus and Cambyses."[19]

THE HE GOAT FROM THE WEST

8:5-7 And as I was considering, behold, an he goat came from the west on the face of the whole earth, and touched not the ground: and the goat had a notable horn between his eyes. And he came to the ram that had two horns, which I had seen standing before the river, and ran unto him in the fury of his power. And I saw him come close unto the ram, and he was moved with choler against him, and smote the ram, and brake his two horns: and there was no power in the ram to stand before him, but he cast him down to the ground, and stamped upon him: and there was none that could deliver the ram out of his hand.

Interpreters of Daniel 8 are generally agreed that the he goat or literally, "buck of the goats,"[20] represents the king of Greece, and more particularly the single important horn between its eyes, as also stated in Daniel 8:21, is "the first king," that is, Alexander the Great. All the facts about this goat and his activities obviously anticipate the dynamic role of Alexander. Like Alexander, the he goat comes "from the west on the face of the whole earth," that is, his conquests beginning in Greece move east and cover the entire territory. The implication in the vision, where it states that the he goat "touched not the ground," is the impression of tremendous speed, which characterized the conquest of Alexander. The unusual horn, one large horn instead of the normal two, symbolically represents the single leadership provided by Alexander.

As Daniel considers, the he goat attacks the ram. The ram is identified with the one seen earlier in the vision as standing before the river. An unusual feature of the attack by the he goat is that it is accomplished "in the fury of his power." There was considerable feeling based upon the historical background in which the Persians had attacked Greece earlier in history. Now it was time for Greek retaliation against the Persians. The goat accordingly "moved with choler against him," that is, "in great anger," and butting the ram, breaks the ram's two horns. This symbolically refers to the disintegration of the Medo-Persian Empire with the result that the ram had no power to stand before the he goat. The contest ends with the he goat casting the ram to the ground and stamping upon it.

All of this, of course, was fulfilled dramatically in history. The forces of Alexander first met and defeated the Persians at the Granicus River in Asia Minor in May 334 B.C., which was the beginning of the complete conquest of the entire Persian Empire. A year and a half later a battle occurred at Issus (November 333 B.C.) near the northeastern tip of the Mediterranean Sea. The power of Persia was finally broken at Gaugamela near Nineveh in October 331 B.C.[21]

There is no discrepancy between history, which records a series of battles, and Daniel's representation that the Persian Empire fell with one blow. Daniel is obviously describing the result rather than the details.[22] That the prophecy is accurate, insofar as it goes, most expositors concede. Here again, the correspondence of the prophecy to later history is so accurate that liberal critics attempt to make it history instead of prophecy.

The divine view of Greece is less complimentary than that of secular historians. Tarn gives high praise of Alexander, for instance: "He [Alexander] was one of the supreme fertilizing forces in history. He lifted the civilized world out of one groove and set it in another; he started a new epoch; nothing could again be as it had been. . . . Particularism was replaced by the idea of the 'inhabited world,' the common possession of civilized men. . . . Greek culture, heretofore practically confined to Greeks, spread throughout the world; and for the use of its inhabitants, in place of the many dialects of Greece, there grew up the form of Greek known as the *koine*, the 'common speech.' "[23] Porteous comments on Tarn's praise, "Not a glimmer of all this appears in the book of Daniel."[24] God's view is different from man's.

THE GREAT HORN BROKEN

8:8 Therefore the he goat waxed very great: and when he was strong, the great horn was broken; and for it came up four notable ones toward the four winds of heaven.

As Daniel contemplates in his vision the triumph of the he goat, an unexpected development takes place. The great horn between the eyes of the he goat is broken just when the he goat has reached the pinnacle of its strength. Out of this grows four notable horns described as being "toward the four winds of heaven." Expositors, both liberal and conservative, have interpreted this verse as representing the untimely death of Alexander and the division of his empire into four major sections. Alexander, who had conquered more of the world than any previous ruler, was not able to conquer himself. Partly due to a strenuous exertion, his dissipated life, and a raging fever, Alexander died in a drunken debauch at Babylon, not yet thirty-three years of age. His death left a great conquest without an effective single leader, and it took about twenty years for the empire to be successfully divided.

Practically all commentators, however, recognize the four horns as symbolic of the four kingdoms of the Diadochi which emerged as follows: (1) Cassander assumed rule over Macedonia and Greece; (2) Lysimacus took control of Thrace, Bithynia, and most of Asia Minor; (3) Seleucus took Syria and the lands to the east including Babylonia; (4) Ptolemy established rule over Egypt and possibly Palestine and Arabia Petraea.[25] A fifth contender for political power, Antigonus, was soon defeated. Thus, with remarkable accuracy, Daniel in his prophetic vision predicts that the empire of Alexander was divided into four divisions, not three or less or five or more.

THE EMERGENCE OF THE LITTLE HORN

8:9-10 And out of one of them came forth a little horn, which waxed exceeding great, toward the south, and toward the east, and toward the pleasant land. And it waxed great, even to the host of heaven; and it cast down some of the host and of the stars to the ground, and stamped upon them.

While there is comparatively little disagreement as to the identity of the ram and the he goat, practically all the controversy over this vision has centered on the meaning of the little horn described in verses 9 and 10. According to Daniel's account, the little horn emerges from one of the four notable horns mentioned in verse 8. The horn, small in the beginning, grows "exceeding great" in three directions: toward the south, toward the east and toward the pleasant land. The implication is that the point of reference is Syria, that "the south" is equal to Egypt, and "the east," in the direction of ancient Medo-Persia or Armenia, and "the pleasant land," or "glorious land" referring to Palestine or Canaan, which lay between Syria and Egypt. The original for "pleasant land" actually means "beauty," with the word for "land" supplied from Daniel 11 (cf. Dan 11:16, 41, 45; Jer 3:19; Eze 20:6, 15; Mal 3:12). Actually, the meaning here may be Jerusalem in particular rather than the land in general.

These conquests, of course, are confirmed in the history of Syria, especially under Antiochus Epiphanes, the eighth king in the Syrian dynasty who reigned 175-164 B.C. (1 Macc 1:10; 6:16). In his lifetime, he conducted military expeditions in relation to all of these areas. Montgomery considers the expression "toward the pleasant land" as a gloss "which is absurd when aligned with the given points of the compass, in which the book is remarkably accurate."[26] There is no justification for this deletion from the text, however, as from Daniel's viewpoint in this whole section, the important question is how the times of the Gentiles relate to Israel. The land of Israel indeed became the battle ground between Syria and Egypt, and the setting of some of Antiochus Epiphanes' most significant blasphemous acts against God. According to 1 Maccabees 1:20, Revised Standard Version, Antiochus first invaded Egypt and then Jerusalem: "after subduing Egypt, Antiochus returned in the one hundred and forty-third year. He went up against Israel and came to Jerusalem with a strong force."

As a result of his military conquests, the little horn, representing Antiochus Epiphanes, is said to grow great "even to the host of heaven." He is pictured as casting some of the host and of the stars to the ground and stamping upon them. This difficult prophecy has aroused many technical discussions as that of Montgomery which extends over several pages.[27] If the mythological explanations such as identifying stars with heathen gods or the seven planets is discarded and this is considered genuine prophecy, probably the best explanation is that this prophecy relates to the persecution and destruction of the people of God with its defiance of the angelic hosts who are their protectors, including the power of God Himself. As Leupold says, "That stars should signify God's holy people is not strange when one considers as a background the words that were spoken to Abraham concerning the numerical increase of the people of God, Gen. 15:5; 22:17. To this may be added Dan. 12:3, where a starlike glory is held out to those who "turn many to righteousness." Compare also Matt. 13:43. If the world calls those men and women stars who excel in one or another department of human activity, why should not a similar statement be still more appropriate with reference to God's people?"[28] Leupold considers the host and the stars in apposition, that is, "the host even the stars." That Antiochus blasphemed God and heavenly power as well as persecuted the people of Israel, the people of God, is all too evident from history. Even Driver states, "The stars are intended to symbolize the faithful Israelites: cf. Enoch xlvi. 7."[29]

THE DESOLATION OF THE SANCTUARY

8:11-14   Yea, he magnified himself even to the prince of the host, and by him the daily sacrifice was taken away, and the place of his sanctuary was cast down. And an host was given him against the daily sacrifice by reason of transgression, and it cast down the truth to the ground; and it practised, and prospered. Then I heard one saint speaking, and another saint said unto that certain saint which spake, How long shall be the vision concerning the daily sacrifice, and the transgression of desolation, to give both the sanctuary and the host to be trodden under foot? And he said unto me, Unto two thousand and three hundred days; then shall the sanctuary be cleansed.

Up to Daniel 8:11, it is not difficult to find fulfillment of the vision in the history of the Medo-Persian, Alexandrian, and post-Alexandrian periods. Beginning with verse 11, however, expositors have differed widely as to whether the main import of the passage refers to Antiochus Epiphanes, with complete fulfillment in his lifetime, or whether the passage either primarily or secondarily refers also to the end of the age, that is, the period of great tribulation preceding the second coming of Jesus Christ. The divergence of interpretation is so wide as to be confusing to the student of Daniel. As Montgomery states, verses 11 and 12 "constitute . . . the most difficult short passage of the bk."[30]

If the many divergent views can be simplified, they fall into three general classifications. First, the critical view that Daniel was a second-century forgery written by a pseudo-Daniel regards this prophecy as simply history written after the fact and completely fulfilled in Antiochus Epiphanes. This, of course, has been rejected by the great majority of conservative scholars. Second, the view that this is genuine sixth-century B.C. prophecy, but completely fulfilled historically in Antiochus Epiphanes. Edward J. Young is strongly in favor of this interpretation[31] and speaks in general for many amillenarians who are conservative interpreters. Third, the view that the prophecy is genuine prediction fulfilled historically in the second century B.C., but typical and anticipatory of the final conflict between God and Gentile rulers at the time of the persecution of Israel prior to the second advent of Christ. The third view sometimes confuses the prophetic and typical interpretations or attempts to find dual fulfillment literally of both aspects of the prophecy. The ultimate decision must rest not simply on verses 11 through 14 but on the interpretation of the prophecy given in verses 20-26.

According to verse 11, the little horn, fulfilled in Antiochus Epiphanes historically, magnifies himself even to the prince of the host. By this is meant that he exalted himself up to the point of claiming divine honor, as brought out in his name Epiphanes which refers to glorious manifestation such as belonged to God. His pretentions are similar to the little horn of Daniel 7:8, 20. Antiochus, however, obviously also directed blasphemous opposition against God Himself and to this extent magnified himself against God as well as reaching toward the glory and honor belonging to God.

As a specific illustration and supreme act manifesting this attitude, it is stated that he took away the daily offerings and desecrated the sanctuary. "By him," in verse 11, is literally, "from him," that is, from God. By this is meant that Antiochus stopped the morning and evening sacrifices, taking away from God what were daily tokens of Israel's worship.[32] The expression *daily sacrifices*, from the Hebrew *tamid*, which means "constant," applies to the daily offerings (cf. Ex 29:38 ff.; Num 28:3 ff.). Young, accordingly, feels that it should not be restricted to the morning and evening sacrifices, but that it included all the offerings customarily offered in the temple services.[33]

This is brought out in 1 Maccabees 1:44-49, referring to the command of Antiochus Epiphanes to depart from the worship of the law of Moses, "And the king sent letters by messengers to Jerusalem and the cities of Judah; he directed them to follow customs strange to the land, to forbid burnt offerings and sacrifices and drink offerings in the sanctuary, to profane Sabbaths and feasts, to defile the sanctuary and the priests, to build altars in sacred precincts and shrines for idols, to sacrifice swine and unclean animals, and to leave their sons uncircumcised. They were to make themselves abominable by everything unclean and profane, so that they should forget the law and change all the ordinances. And whoever does not obey the command of the king shall die" (RSV).

Although it is not necessary to take the expression "the place of his sanctuary was cast down" as meaning destruction by Antiochus of the temple itself, it is of interest that in 1 Maccabees 4:42 ff., in connection with the cleansing of the sanctuary, they literally tore down the altar and built a new one, "they also rebuilt the sanctuary and the interior of the temple, and consecrated the courts" (1 Macc 4:48). As Young comments, "Apparently Antiochus did not actually tear down the temple, although eventually he desecrated it to such a point that it was hardly fit for use."[34]

The obvious parallel between the cessation of the daily sacrifice by

Antiochus Epiphanes and that anticipated in Daniel 9:27, which occurs three and one-half years before the second coming of Christ, has led some expositors to find here evidence for reference to the end of the age and not simply to Antiochus. As far as this prophecy is concerned, however, it did have complete fulfillment in Antiochus.

Verse 12 is a recapitulation of Antiochus Epiphanes' activities against God. The statement that *an host was given him* apparently refers to the fact that the people of Israel were under his power with divine permission. The phrase *against the daily sacrifice* can be translated "with the daily sacrifice," that is, the daily sacrifices were also in his power and he was able to substitute a heathen worship. The phrase *by reason of transgression* should be understood as an extension of this, that is, the daily sacrifices are given in his power in order to permit him to transgress against God. The result is that Antiochus "cast down the truth to the ground," that is, the truth of the law of Moses, practiced his activities, and seemingly prospered. Although the translation of this verse is very difficult, conservative scholars generally interpret it to mean that the people of Israel along with their worship are given over to the power of Antiochus Epiphanes with the resulting transgression and blasphemy against God. The extent of departure from the law is indicated in 1 Maccabees 1:44-49 Revised Standard Version.

Having described the nefarious activities of Antiochus Epiphanes, Daniel now records a conversation between two "saints" or "holy ones," apparently angels, concerning the duration of the desecration of the sanctuary. The question is "How long shall be the vision concerning the daily sacrifice, and the transgression of desolation, to give both the sanctuary and the host to be trodden underfoot?"

The answer given in verse 14 has touched off almost endless exegetical controversy. Daniel is informed that the answer to the riddle is "Unto two thousand and three hundred days; then shall the sanctuary be cleansed." The answer is said to be given "unto me," that is, to Daniel rather than to the other angel. Obviously these angels are brought in for Daniel's benefit and the result is that Daniel hears the answer. The interpretation and fulfillment of this passage is to some extent the crux of this entire chapter.

The Seventh Day Adventists understood that the two thousand and three hundred days referred to years which, on the basis of their interpretation, were to culminate in the year 1884 with the second coming of Christ.[35] The year-day theory for all practical purposes was excluded by the fact that Christ did not come in 1884 in any real fulfillment of the anticipation of this interpretation.

If the twenty-three hundred days are to be considered as days, instead of years, two basic alternatives are offered. Many have taken this as twenty-three hundred twenty-four hour days. Because the days are related to the cessation of the evening and morning sacrifices, another theory was that the phrase actually referred to eleven hundred and fifty days, that is, twenty-three hundred evenings and mornings as set forth by Ephraim of Syria and Hippolytus.[36]

Obviously, the interpretation of this difficult time period is determined largely by the expositor's desire to find fulfillment either in history or in parallel prophecies concerning the future. Generally, expositors even of differing schools of eschatological interpretation follow the idea that these are twenty-three hundred literal days. The concept that the period in view is eleven hundred and fifty days also is taken by some to coincide with the three and one-half years of the great tribulation predicted in Daniel 9:27 and elsewhere, even though there is a discrepancy of over one hundred days.

Keil, in his discussion extending over nine pages, concludes,

> A Hebrew reader could not possibly understand the period of 2300 evening-mornings of 2300 half days or 1150 whole days, because evening and morning at the creation constituted not the half but the whole day. Still less, in the designation of time, 'till 2300 evening-mornings,' could 'evening-mornings' be understood of the evening and morning sacrifices, and the words be regarded as meaning that till 1150 evening sacrifices and 1150 morning sacrifices are discontinued. We must therefore take the words as they are, *i.e.*, understand them as 2300 whole days.[37]

Keil supports this by numerous arguments including the fact, "when the Hebrews wished to express separately day and night, the component parts of a day of a week, then the number of both is expressed. They say, *e.g.*, forty days and forty nights (Gen. vii. 4, 12; Ex. xxiv. 18; 1 Kings xix. 8), and three days and three nights (Jonah ii. 1; Matt. xii. 40), but not eighty or six days-and-nights, when they wish to speak of forty or three full days."[38]

If they are literally twenty-three hundred days, what is the fulfillment? The attempts to relate this to the last seven years of the Gentile period referred to in Daniel 9:27 have confused rather than helped the interpretation. Twenty-three hundred days is less than seven years of 360 days, and the half figure of eleven hundred and fifty days is short of the three and one-half years of the great tribulation. Exegetically, a safe course to follow is to find fulfillment in Antiochus Epiphanes, and then proceed to consider what eschatological or unfilled prophecy may be involved.

Innumerable explanations have been attempted to make the twenty-three hundred days coincide with the history of Antiochus Epiphanes. The terminus *ad quem* of the twenty-three hundred days is taken by most expositors as 164 B.C. when Antiochus Epiphanes died during a military campaign in Media. This permitted the purging of the sanctuary and the return to Jewish worship. Figuring from this date backward twenty-three hundred days would fix the beginning time at 171 B.C. In that year, Onias III, the legitimate high priest, was murdered and a pseudo line of priests assumed power. This would give adequate fulfillment in time for the twenty-three hundred days to elapse at the time of the death of Antiochus. The actual desecration of the temple, however, did not occur until December 25, 167 B.C. when the sacrifices in the temple were forcibly caused to cease and a Greek altar erected in the temple. The actual desecration of the temple lasted only about three years. During this period, Antiochus issued coins with the title "Epiphanes," which claimed that he manifested divine honors and which showed him as beardless and wearing a diadem.[39]

Taking all the evidence into consideration, the best conclusion is that the twenty-three hundred days of Daniel are fulfilled in the period from 171 B.C. and culminated in the death of Antiochus Epiphanes in 164 B.C. The period when the sacrifices ceased was the latter part of this longer period. Although the evidence available today does not offer fulfillment to the precise day, the twenty-three hundred days, obviously a round number, is relatively accurate in defining the period when the Jewish religion began to erode under the persecution of Antiochus, and the period as a whole concluded with his death.

The alternate theories produce more problems than they solve. Considering the days as year-days has provided no fulfillment. Using the figure of eleven hundred and fifty days only creates more problems as it does not fit precisely any scheme of events and has a dubious basis. By far the simplest and most honoring to the Scriptures is the solution that the twenty-three hundred days date from 171 B.C. to 164 B.C. This prophecy may safely be said now to have been fulfilled and does not have any further eschatological significance in the sense of anticipating a future fulfillment. As far as Daniel 8:1-14 is concerned, there is no adequate reason for considering it in any other light than that of fulfilled prophecy from the standpoint of the twentieth century. It is adequately explained in the history of the Medo-Persian and Greek empires, and specifically, in the activities of Antiochus Epiphanes.

VISION INTERPRETED IN RELATION TO THE TIME OF THE END

8:15-19 And it came to pass, when I, even I Daniel, had seen the vision, and sought for the meaning, then, behold, there stood before me as the appearance of a man. And I heard a man's voice between the banks of Ulai, which called, and said, Gabriel, make this man to understand the vision. So he came near where I stood: and when he came, I was afraid, and fell upon my face: but he said unto me, Understand, O son of man:

for at the time of the end shall be the vision. Now as he was speaking with me, I was in a deep sleep on my face toward the ground: but he touched me, and set me upright. And he said, Behold, I will make thee know what shall be in the last end of the indignation: for at the time appointed the end shall be.

With the entire vision recorded and, to some extent, already interpreted, Daniel now enters into active participation in the vision and, as in chapter 7, sought an interpretation. According to verse 15, Daniel "sought for the meaning"; and in response to his desire, a personage stood before him described "as the appearance of a man," but obviously an angel. In verse 16, the angel Gabriel is mentioned specifically, and a man's voice is addressed to Gabriel to instruct Daniel in understanding the vision. The man's voice may be that of Michael the Archangel or even the voice of God, but it is not identified in the text. Calvin believes that the man speaking is Christ.[40] Young points out that the word for *man* in verse 15 is *gāber,* similar in sound to Gabriel and denoting strength or power.[41] To this is added *el,* the word for God, to form the name Gabriel.

Of interest is the fact that this is the first mention in the Bible of a holy angel by name. Gabriel is again mentioned in Daniel 9:21 and in Luke 1:19, 26, where he is the messenger to Zacharias, announcing the future birth of John the Baptist, and to the virgin Mary, announcing the coming birth of Jesus Christ. The only other angel in Scripture named, aside from Satan, is Michael, mentioned in Daniel 10:13, 21; 12:1, and in the New Testament in Jude 9 and Revelation 12:7. The restraint of Scripture in naming angels is in contrast to prolific nomenclature of angels in apocalyptic literature outside the Bible.[42]

Because of the whole context of the vision, the powerful presence of Gabriel, and the mysterious voice which may be the voice of Deity, Daniel is afraid, actually panic-stricken, and falls on his face. The situation is not much different from that of John the apostle in Revelation 1 at the tremendous vision of the glorified Christ. The words of Gabriel are reassuring, and he instructs Daniel, using the title *son of man,* and for the first time in the entire chapter indicates that "the time of the end" is in question in relation to the vision.

Although Daniel apparently had been awake in the earlier part of the vision, we now learn that, as Gabriel was speaking, Daniel had fallen into a deep sleep with his face toward the ground. Montgomery translates *I was in a deep sleep* as "I swooned."[43] In any event, it is not a natural sleep but the result of his fear described in verse 17. As in the case of Ezekiel (Eze 1:28—2:2), Daniel is aroused: as stated in verse 18, Gabriel "touched me, and set me upright." Porteous suggests that the expression, *set me upright* (v. 18), "probably means 'made me stand up where I was.'

Daniel is keeping his distance."⁴⁴ In verse 19, Gabriel then begins a further explanation of what he introduced in verse 17 concerning the time of the end, making clear his intention to let Daniel know "what shall be in the last end of the indignation: for at the time appointed the end shall be." In the verses which follow, details of interpretation of the vision are given.

The expression, *the indignation,* judging by the context (cf. Dan 11:36, where it occurs again) here seems to refer to God's anger against Israel. As in the days of Isaiah, when God used Assyria as His chastening rod (Is 10:5, 25), God in His indignation was using for His corrective purposes the tyranny of Antiochus and "lawless men" (cf. 1 Macc 1:11-15) who carried out Antiochus' orders. In any case, the point is that God is permitting the persecution as a chastening of Israel in this instance.

Because of the introduction of the term *the time of the end* (Dan 8:17, 19) and the additional expression in verse 19 of "in the last end of the indignation," many scholars find in this chapter reference to the ultimate consummation of Gentile times at the second advent of Christ. Although an adequate fulfillment can be found of the prophecy through verse 14 in the history of the centuries before Christ, how can these references to the time of the end be understood? The entire matter is complicated by references which clearly relate to the end of the Gentile period in Daniel 9:27 and by the extended passage Daniel 11:35 ff., where again the time of the end is mentioned, with additional references in chapter 12. The expositor has numerous options, each of which has some support from reputable scholarship.

Although a great deal of variation is found in details of interpretation, four major views emerge: (1) the historical view that all of Daniel 8 has been fulfilled; (2) the futuristic view, the idea that it is entirely future; (3) the view based upon the principle of dual fulfillment of prophecy, that Daniel 8 is intentionally a prophetic reference both to Antiochus Epiphanes, now fulfilled, and to the end of the age and the final world ruler who persecutes Israel before the second advent; (4) the view that the passage is prophecy, historically fulfilled but intentionally typical of similar events and personages at the end of the age.

Premillenarians who emphasize historical fulfillment in this chapter invariably agree to typical anticipation. The historical view is supported largely by liberal critics and amillenarians. S. R. Driver, representing liberal criticism, states, for instance, "In ch. viii. there is a 'little horn,' which is admitted on all hands to represent Antiochus Epiphanes, and whose impious character and doings (viii. 10-12, 25) are in all essentials identical with those attributed to the 'little horn' in ch. vii. (vii. 8 *end* 20, 21, 25): as Delitzsch remarks, it is extremely difficult to think that where the description is so similar, two entirely different persons, living in widely different periods of the world's history should be intended."[45]

Driver, identifying the fourth empire of Daniel 7 as the Greek Empire, as liberal critics do in contrast to most conservative expositors, finds the two little horns identical. In keeping with this, he defines the time of the end as meaning from Daniel's standpoint "the period of Antiochus's persecution, together with the short interval consisting of a few months, which followed before his death (xi. 35, 40), that being, in the view of the author, the 'end' of the present condition of things, and the divine kingdom (vii. 14, 18, 22, 27, xii. 2, 3) being established immediately afterwards." Driver goes on, "This sense of 'end' is based probably upon the use of the word in Am. viii. 2, Ez. vii. 2, 'an end is come, the end is come upon the four corners of the land,' 3, 6: cf. also 'in the time of the iniquity of the end,' Ez. xxi. 25, 29, xxxv. 5; and Hab. ii. 3, 'For the vision is yet for the appointed-time [has reference to the time of its destined fulfillment], and it hasteth toward the end.' "[46]

Conservative amillenarians as represented by Edward J. Young, distinguish between the little horns of chapter 7 and chapter 8. In summarizing his view of the identity of the fourth empire, Young writes, "A comparison of the horns of ch. 8 and the little horn of ch. 7 makes it apparent that the two horns are intended to represent different things. Since the horn of ch. 8 evidently stands for Antiochus Epiphanes, it follows that the little horn of ch. 7 does not stand for Antiochus Epiphanes."[47] In a word, Young finds chapter 8 completely fulfilled in history. The principal difficulty with the purely historical view is that it provides no satisfactory explanation of the expression *the time of the end*, the other references in the book of Daniel which use it as the end of the time of the Gentiles, and certain details that are given in the interpretation of the vision.

A second view, in sharp contrast to the historical interpretation, is that which takes the reference to the little horn of chapter 8 as being the same as the little horn of chapter 7 but considers the entire prophecy to be subject to future fulfillment. It is like the liberal critical view in identifying the two horns, but unlike the liberal critical view in relating it to the Roman Empire in the future and not to the Greek Empire of the past. Although only a few writers have taken this position, G. H. Pember takes as "the first clue to the interpretation" the premise: "The vision is no prophecy of Antiochus Epiphanes: the Little Horn is a far more terrible persecutor, who will arise in the last days."[48]

Tregelles argues for the same conclusions, stating, "Further, the four divided kingdoms which formed themselves out of the empire of Alexander were one by one incorporated within the Roman empire, but it is out of one of these kingdoms that the horn of this chapter springs, hence it is clear that he belongs to the Roman earth. Thus the person spoken of in the two chapters are found within the same territorial limits."[49] Tregelles goes on to compare the similarities between the little horn of chapter 7 and the little horn of chapter 8 as well as a description of the final world ruler in Daniel 11:36-45. Tregelles concludes, "The conclusion from all this appears to be inevitable, that the horn of chapter vii and chapter viii are one and the same person."[50]

The majority of premillennial expositors, however, have not followed this view because the Roman Empire is not clearly in view in chapter 8, and, as a matter of fact, there are a number of contradictions. Although the territory involved in the various world empires is often the same, this does not prove that the events are the same or the personages are the same; and this is the crux of the matter which Tregelles ignores. Pusey, for instance, points out, "In the Grecian empire, the little horn issues, not from the empire itself, but from one of its four-fold divisions. . . . Antiochus Epiphanes came out of one of the four kingdoms of Alexander's successors, and that kingdom existed in him, as the fourth horn issued in the little horn. But in the fourth empire, the horn proceeds, not out of any one horn, but out of the body of the empire itself. It *came up among them* [the horns], wholly distinct from them, and destroyed three of them. Such a marked difference in a symbol, otherwise so alike, must be intended to involve a difference in the fact represented."[51]

While there are obvious similarities between the two little horns of chapter 7 and chapter 8, the differences are important. If the fourth kingdom represented by Daniel 7 is Rome, then obviously the third kingdom represented by the goat in chapter 8 is not Rome. Their characteristics are much different as they arise from different beasts, their horns differ in number, and the end result is different. The Messianic kingdom according to Daniel 7 was going to be erected after the final world empire. This is not true of the period following the he goat in chapter 8. The familiar rule that similarities do not prove identity is applicable here. Two men or events may be alike in many respects but are distinguished by one definite dissimilarity. In this case, there are many factors which contrast the two chapters and their contents.

In view of the problems of a purely historical fulfillment on the one hand or a purely futuristic fulfillment on the other, many expositors have been intrigued with the possibility of a dual fulfillment, that is, that a prophecy fulfilled in part in the past is a foreshadowing of a future event which will completely fulfill the passage. Variations exist in this approach with some taking the entire passage as having dual fufillment, and others taking Daniel 8:1-14 as historically fulfilled and Daniel 8:15-17 as having dual fulfillment. This latter view was popularized by the *Scofield Refer-*

ence Bible. Both the 1917 and the 1967 edition interpret chapter 8 as being fulfilled historically in Antiochus, but prophetically, beginning with verse 17, as being fulfilled at the end of the age with the second advent.[52]

Many premillennial writers follow this interpretation. Louis T. Talbot, for instance, writes "When the vision recorded here was given to Daniel, all of it had to do with then prophetic events; whereas we today can look back and see that everything in verses 1-22 refers to men and empires that have come and gone. We read about them in the pages of secular history. But verses 23-27 of the chapter before us have to do with 'a king of fierce countenance' who shall appear 'in the latter time' (v. 23); and he is none other than the Antichrist who is to come. Again, while verses 1-22 have to do with history, yet the men of whom they speak were shadows of that coming 'man of sin,' who is more fully described in the closing verses of the chapter."[53] Talbot varies from the pattern somewhat by finding typical fulfillment in verses 1-22 and futuristic fulfillment in verses 23-26. Strictly speaking, this does not conform to any of the divisions indicated here, but illustrates that the passage gives prophecy in two different senses.

A number of other expositors find chapter 8 dealing with both Antiochus Epiphanes and the future world ruler. Among them are William Kelly,[54] Nathaniel West,[55] and Joseph A. Seiss.[56]

This view is ably summarized by J. Dwight Pentecost. Pentecost gives a most illuminating overall view of chapters 7 through 12 in the following statement: "The key to understanding chapters 7 through 12 of Daniel's prophecy is to understand that Daniel is focusing his attention on this one great ruler and his kingdom which will arise in the end time. And while Daniel may use historical reference and refer to events which to us may be fulfilled, Daniel is thinking of them only to give us more details about this final form of Gentile world power and its ruler who will reign on the earth. In Daniel chapter 8, we have another reference to this one. Daniel describes a king who is going to conquer the Medo-Persian Empire. This is an historical event that took place several centuries after Daniel lived. There was an individual that came out of the Grecian Empire who was a great enemy of the nation Israel. We know him as Antiochus Epiphanes. Antiochus Epiphanes was a ruler who sought to show his contempt for Palestine, the Jews, and the Jewish religion by going to the temple in Jerusalem with a sow which he slaughtered and put its blood upon the altar. This man was known as one who desolated, or 'the desolator.' But this passage in Daniel 8 is speaking not only of Antiochus in his desolation and his desecration of the Temple; it is looking forward to the great desolator who would come, the one who is called 'the little horn' in Daniel 7. In Daniel 8:23 we read of this one and his ministry."[57]

Pentecost summarizes the facts from Daniel 8:23-25 as a description of the beast in that (1) he is to appear in the latter times of Israel's history (Dan 8:23); (2) through alliance with other nations, he achieves worldwide influence (Dan 8:24); (3) a peace program helps his rise to power (Dan 8:25); (4) he is extremely intelligent and persuasive (Dan 8:23); (5) he is characterized by Satanic control (Dan 8:24); (6) he is a great adversary against Israel and the prince of princes (Dan 8:24-25); (7) a direct judgment from God terminates his rule (Dan 8:25).[58]

It may be concluded that many premillennial expositors find a dual fulfillment in Daniel 8: some of them achieve this by a division of the first part of the chapter as historically fulfilled and the last part prophetically future; some regard the whole chapter as having, in some sense, a dual fulfillment historically as well as in the future; but most of them find the futuristic elements emphasized, especially in the interpretation of the vision.

A variation of the view that the last part of the chapter is specifically futuristic is found in the interpretation which has much to commend itself. This variation regards the entire chapter as historically fulfilled in Antiochus, but to varying degrees foreshadowing typically the future world ruler who would dominate the situation at the end of the times of the Gentiles. In any case, the passage intentionally goes beyond Antiochus to provide prophetic foreshadowing of the final Gentile ruler.

THE INTERPRETATION OF THE RAM AND THE ROUGH GOAT

> **8:20-22** The ram which thou sawest having two horns are the kings of Media and Persia. And the rough goat is the king of Grecia: and the great horn that is between his eyes is the first king. Now that being broken, whereas four stood up for it, four kingdoms shall stand up out of the nation, but not in his power.

The interpretation of the ram and he goat vision as given in verses 20-21 makes explicit what has been assumed in preceding exegesis. Most significant is the fact that Media and Persia are regarded as one empire, refuting the liberal notion that Daniel taught the empire of Media was separate from Persia, which liberals use to justify the exegesis that the second and third empires of Daniel 7 were Media and Persia. All agree that history does not support this, and the liberal interpretation assumes that Daniel was in error. Here the matter is made clear by Daniel himself, and it is evident that the critics are guilty of attributing to Daniel something he did not teach. The he goat described as "rough" or shaggy, although called "the king of Grecia," is an obvious reference to the kingdom as a whole, as the great horn between its eyes is identified as the first king. Practically everyone agrees that this is Alexander the Great.

The four kingdoms represented by the four horns which replaced the great horn that was broken are identified as four kingdoms arising from the he goat nation. They are described as not having the power of the great horn. Aside from expositors pressed to relate this to the Roman empire, where there is no reasonable parallel, the four kingdoms are obviously the four generals of Alexander who partitioned his empire as previously noted. Most expositors agree that verses 20-22 have been fulfilled completely in history in connection with the Medo-Persian and Greek empires and the four divisions following Alexander the Great. The exegetical problems arise in the passage which follows.

THE LATTER TIME OF THE KINGDOM

8:23-26 And in the latter time of their kingdom, when the transgressors are come to the full, a king of fierce countenance, and understanding dark sentences, shall stand up. And his power shall be mighty, but not by his own power: and he shall destroy wonderfully, and shall prosper, and practise, and shall destroy the mighty and the holy people. And through his policy also he shall cause craft to prosper in his hand; and he shall magnify himself in his heart, and by peace shall destroy many: he shall also stand up against the Prince of princes; but he shall be broken without hand. And the vision of the evening and the morning which was told is true: wherefore shut thou up the vision; for it shall be for many days.

In this section of Daniel 8, an individual is pictured prophetically who is said to have the following characteristics: (1) he will appear "in the latter time of their kingdom," that is, of the four kingdoms of verse 22; (2) he will appear "when the transgressors are come to the full"; (3) he will be "a king of fierce countenance, and understanding dark sentences," that is, having a strong or bold countenance and able to interpret riddles, a mark of intelligence (1 Ki 10:1); (4) he shall have great power but his power shall be derived from another (either God, Satan, Alexander the Great); (5) he shall accomplish great exploits including destroying Israel, the mighty and holy people; (6) by his policies "he shall cause craft to prosper in his hand," always busy hatching plots (1 Macc 1:16-51), that is, wickedness shall be on the increase; (7) he shall exalt himself, as did Antiochus Epiphanes; (8) by means of a false peace, he shall destroy many people; (9) he shall oppose "the Prince of princes"; (10) in the end "he shall be broken without hand" (Antiochus died of a foul disease), that is, his power shall be destroyed without human intervention. Finally, Daniel is cautioned that the total vision is true, but the understanding of it shall be delayed for many days as well as its fulfillment.

A careful scrutiny of these many points will justify the conclusion that it is possible to explain all of these elements as fulfilled historically in Antiochus Epiphanes. Most of the factors are obvious and the principal difficulty is occasioned by the expression *in the latter time of their kingdom* and in the statement *he shall stand up against the Prince of princes.* Antiochus Epiphanes, of course, did arise in the latter time of the Syrian kingdom. However, the use of other terms such as *the end* in verses 17 and 19, and *the last end of the indignation* in verse 19 are difficult to harmonize with Antiochus Epiphanes.

It is also objected, as expressed by W. C. Stevens, "The time of Antiochus was in the former time of those kingdoms. His day was not even in the latter time of the old Grecian Empire; for he came to his end more than one hundred years before the Grecian Empire ended. The simple solution is that those four kingdoms are to have 'a latter time'; i.e., they are to be again represented territorially as four kingdoms in the last days at the Times of the Gentiles."[59] The expression *the end* frequently occurs in references in Daniel 9:26; 11:6, 27, 35, 40, 45; 12:4, 6, 9, 13.

Another problem is the statement that the king "shall also stand up against the Prince of princes." H. A. Ironside expresses a common viewpoint that the "Prince of princes can be none other than the Messiah; consequently, these words were not fulfilled in the life and death of Antiochus."[60] However, this objection is not unanswerable, because opposition to God, to Israel, and to the Messianic hope in general, which characterized blasphemers of the Old Testament, can well be interpreted as standing up against "the Prince of princes." After all, Christ existed in Old Testament times as God and as the Angel of Jehovah and as the defender of Israel.

Taken as a whole, the principal problem of the passage when interpreted as prophecy fulfilled completely in Antiochus is the allusions to the end of the age. These are hard to understand as relating to Antiochus in view of the larger picture of Daniel 7 which concludes with the second advent of Christ. It is for this reason, as well as for the many details in the passage, that many expositors believe the interpretation goes beyond the vision. If the vision itself of the little horn can be fulfilled in Antiochus Epiphanes, the interpretation given by the angel seems to go beyond Antiochus to the final world ruler.

Some premillennial interpreters, however, convinced of the futuristic character of the interpretation of the vision, identify the personage here as a different future character than the little horn of Daniel 7. The little horn of Daniel 7 is identified as a Roman and a future world dictator, whereas the little horn of Daniel 8 in its futuristic interpretation is understood by them to refer to the king of the north in Daniel 11:6-15, who is also identified with "the Assyrian" (Mic 5:5-6).[61] Contemporary expositors, however, generally interpret these references to Assyria in other prophetic passages as either already fulfilled in the previous invasion of the Holy Land by Assyria or a description of Assyria in the millennial kingdom. These passages then do not become relevant to Daniel 8.

It may be concluded that this difficult passage apparently goes beyond that which is historically fulfilled in Antiochus Epiphanes to foreshadow a future personage often identified as the world ruler of the end time. In many respects this ruler carries on a persecution of Israel and desecration of the temple similar to what was accomplished historically by Antiochus. This interpretation of the vision may be regarded as an illustration of double fulfillment of prophecy or, using Antiochus as a type, the interpretation may go on to reveal additional facts which go beyond the type in describing the ultimate king who will oppose Israel in the last days. He indeed will be "broken without hand" at the time of the second advent of Jesus Christ.

In concluding the interpretation, Gabriel makes plain that the vision will not become immediately understandable to Daniel and that its fulfillment will occupy many days.

Effect on Daniel

8:27 And I Daniel fainted, and was sick certain days; afterward I rose up, and did the king's business; and I was astonished at the vision, but none understood it.

As a result of the tremendous vision given to Daniel and his exhaustion because of it, Daniel records that he fainted and was sick for days thereafter. Upon his recovery, he was able to resume his conduct of the king's business. Jeffrey notes that Daniel by his immediate resumption of his work in the king's service proves that he had been in Babylon all the time, and that his presence in Susa was purely visionary.[62]

The dramatic character of the vision and its tremendous implications, although not understandable to Daniel, remained in his mind. But he could find none that could give him the complete interpretation. It is obvious that the intent of the vision was to record the prophecy for the benefit of future generations rather than for Daniel himself. Unlike the previous instances where Daniel was the interpreter of divine revelation, here Daniel becomes the recorder of it without understanding all that he wrote or experienced.

The emphasis of the eighth chapter of Daniel is on prophecy as it relates to Israel; and for this reason, the little horn is given prominence both in the vision and in the interpretation. The times of the Gentiles, although not entirely a period of persecution of Israel, often resulted in great trial to them. Of the four great world empires anticipated by Daniel,

only the Persian empire was relatively kind to the Jew. As Christ Himself
indicated in Luke 21:24, the times of the Gentiles is characterized by the
treading down of Jerusalem, and the subjugation and persecution of the
people of Israel.

9

THE PROPHECY OF THE
SEVENTY WEEKS

The third vision of Daniel the prophet, following the two preceding visions of chapters 7 and 8, concerns the program of God for Israel culminating in the coming of their Messiah to the earth to reign. Although other major prophets received detailed information concerning the nations and God's program for salvation, Daniel alone was given the comprehensive program for both the Gentiles, as revealed to Daniel in preceding chapters, and for Israel, as recorded in Daniel 9:24-27. Because of the comprehensive and structural nature of Daniel's prophecies, both for the Gentiles and for Israel, the study of Daniel, and especially this chapter, is the key to understanding the prophetic Scriptures. Of the four major programs revealed in the Bible—for the angels, the Gentiles, Israel, and the church, Daniel had the privilege of being the channel of revelation for the second and third of these programs in the Old Testament.

This chapter begins with Jeremiah's prophecy of seventy years of the desolations of Jerusalem and is advanced by the intercessory prayer of Daniel. The chapter concludes with the third vision of Daniel, given through the agency of the angel Gabriel, which provides one of the most important keys to understanding the Scriptures as a whole. In many respects, this is the high point of the book of Daniel. Although previously Gentile history and prophecy recorded in Daniel was related to the people of Israel, the ninth chapter specifically takes up prophecy as it applies to the chosen people.

The Seventy Years of the Desolations of Jerusalem

9:1-2   In the first year of Darius the son of Ahasuerus, of the seed of the Medes, which was made king over the realm of the Chaldeans; In the first year of his reign I Daniel understood by books the number of the years, whereof the word of the Lord came to Jeremiah the prophet, that he would accomplish seventy years in the desolations of Jerusalem.

According to the opening verse of chapter 9, the third vision of Daniel occurred "In the first year of Darius the son of Ahasuerus, of the seed of the Medes." In other words, the events of Belshazzar's feast in chapter 5 occurred between the visions of chapters 8 and 9. It is not clear where chapter 6 fits into this order of events, but it also may well have occurred in the first year of the reign of Darius, either immediately before or immediately after the events of chapter 9. If Daniel's experience at Belshazzar's feast as well as his deliverance from the lions had already been experienced, these significant evidences of the sovereignty and power of God may well have constituted a divine preparation for the tremendous revelation now about to unfold.

The immediate occasion of this chapter, however, was the discovery by Daniel in the prophecy of Jeremiah that the desolations of Jerusalem would be fulfilled in seventy years. The expression *by books* may be understood to mean "in books." Jeremiah the prophet, in addition to his oral prophetic announcements, had written his prophecies in the closing days of Jerusalem before its destruction at the hand of the Babylonians. Although the first record of Jeremiah had been destroyed (Jer 36:23), Jeremiah rewrote it, acting on instructions from the Lord (Jer 36:28). Jeremiah himself had been taken captive by Jews rebelling against Nebuchadnezzar and had been carried off to Egypt against his will to be buried in a strange land in a nameless grave, but the timeless Scriptures which he wrote found their way across desert and mountain to far away Babylon and fell into the hands of Daniel. How long Daniel had been in possession of these prophecies is not known, but the implication is that Daniel had now come into the full comprehension of Jeremiah's prediction and realized that the seventy years prophesied had about run their course. The time of the vision recorded in Daniel 9 was 538 B.C., about 67 years after Jerusalem had first been captured and Daniel carried off to Babylon (605 B.C.).

Jeremiah had prophesied, "This whole land shall be a desolation, and an astonishment; and these nations shall serve the king of Babylon seventy years. And it shall come to pass, when seventy years are accomplished, that I will punish the king of Babylon, and that nation, saith the LORD, for their iniquity, and the land of the Chaldeans, and will make it perpetual desolations" (Jer 25:11-12). Later, Jeremiah added to this prophecy, "For thus saith the LORD, that after seventy years be accomplished at Babylon I will visit you, and perform my good word toward you, in causing you to return to this place. For I know the thoughts that I think toward you, saith the LORD, thoughts of peace, and not of evil, to give you an expected end. Then shall ye call upon me, and ye shall go and pray unto me, and I will hearken unto you. And ye shall seek me, and find me, when ye shall search for me with all your heart. And I will be found of you, saith the LORD: and I will turn away your captivity, and I will gather you from all the nations and from all the places whither I have driven you, saith the LORD; and I will bring you again into the place whence I caused you to be carried away captive" (Jer 29:10-14).

On the basis of these remarkable prophecies, Daniel was encouraged to pray for the restoration of Jerusalem and the regathering of the people of Israel. Daniel, although too old and probably too infirm to return to Jerusalem himself, lived long enough to see the first expedition of pilgrims return. This occurred in "the first year of Cyrus king of Persia" (Ezra 1:1), and Daniel lived at least until "the third year of Cyrus king of Persia" (Dan 10:1) and probably some years longer.

As brought out in the earlier discussion of chapter 6 relative to Darius the Mede, Darius had been appointed by Cyrus as king of Babylon. The assertion of Daniel 9:1 that Darius "was made king over the realm of the Chaldeans," indicates that he was invested with the kingship by some higher authority. This well agrees with the supposition that he was installed as viceroy in Babylonia by Cyrus the Great. This appointment is confirmed by the verb "was made king" (Hebrew *homlak*) which does not seem a proper reference to Cyrus himself. In this connection, it is of interest that in the Behistun Inscription, Darius I refers to his father, Hystaspes, as having been made king in a similar way.

In studying Daniel 9:2, with its reference to "the desolations of Jerusalem," Sir Robert Anderson distinguishes the duration of the captivity from the duration of the desolations of Jerusalem. Anderson states, "The failure to distinguish between the several judgments of the Servitude, the Captivity and the Desolations, is a fruitful source of error in the study of Daniel and the historical books of Scripture."[1]

Anderson goes on to explain that Israel's servitude and captivity began much earlier than the destruction of the temple. Although Anderson's dates are not according to current archeological findings (606 B.C. instead of 605 for the captivity, 589 B.C. instead of 586 for the desolation of the temple, and his date for the decree of Cyrus 536 B.C. instead of 538), in general, his approach to the fulfillment of Jeremiah's prophecy is worthy of consideration. As previously discussed in the exposition of chapter 1, the captivity probably began in the fall of 605 B.C. at which time a few, such as Daniel and his companions and other of the royal children, were carried off to Babylon as hostages. The major deportation did not take place until about seven years later. According to Donald J. Wiseman, the exact date of the first major deportation was March 16, 597 B.C., after the fall of Jerusalem following a brief revolt against Babylonian rule. About 60,000 were carried away at that time.[2]

Jerusalem itself was finally destroyed in 586 B.C.,[3] and this, according to

Anderson, began the desolations of Jerusalem, the specific prophecy of Jeremiah 25:11, also mentioned in 2 Chronicles 36:21 and in Daniel 9:2.

The precise prophecy of Jeremiah 25:11-12 predicts that the king of Babylon would be punished at the end of seventy years. Jeremiah 29:10 predicted the return to the land after seventy years. For these reasons, it is doubtful whether Anderson's evaluation of Daniel 9:2 as referring to the destruction of the temple itself is valid. The judgment on Babylon and the return to the land of course took place about twenty years before the temple itself was rebuilt and was approximately seventy years after captivity beginning in 605 B.C. Probably the best interpretation, accordingly, is to consider the expression *the desolations of Jerusalem*, in Daniel 9:2, as referring to the period 605 B.C. to 539 B.C. for the judgment on Babylon, and the date of 538 B.C. for the return to the land.

This definition of the expression *the desolations of Jerusalem* (Dan 9:2) is supported by the word for "desolations" (*ḥorbôt*) which is a plural apparently including the environs of Jerusalem. The same expression is translated "all her waste places" in Isaiah 51:3 (cf. 52:9). Actually the destruction of territory formerly under Jerusalem control even predated the 605 date for Jerusalem's fall.

Although it is preferred to consider Daniel 9:2 as the period 605 B.C.-539 B.C., Anderson may be right in distinguishing as he does the period of Israel's captivity from the period of Jerusalem's destruction. Zechariah 1:12, referring to God's destruction of the cities of Judah for three score years and ten, may extend to the time when the temple was rebuilt. This is brought out in Zechariah 1:16 where it is stated, "Therefore thus saith the LORD; I am returned to Jerusalem with mercies: my house shall be built in it, saith the LORD of hosts, and a line shall be stretched forth upon Jerusalem." It is most significant that the return took place approximately seventy years after the capture of Jerusalem in 605 B.C., and the restoration of the temple (515 B.C.) took place approximately seventy years after the destruction of the temple (586 B.C.), the latter period being about twenty years later than the former. In both cases, however, the fulfillment does not have the meticulous accuracy of falling on the very day, as Anderson attempts to prove. It seems to be an approximate number as one would expect by a round number of seventy. Hence, the period between 605 B.C. and 538 B.C. would be approximately sixty-seven years; and the rededication of the temple in March of 515 B.C., would be less than seventy-one years from the destruction of the temple in August of 586 B.C.

What is intended, accordingly, in the statement in Daniel 9:2 is that Daniel realized that the time was approaching when the children of Israel could return. The seventy years of the captivity were about ended. Once the children of Israel were back in the land, they were providentially hindered in fulfilling the rebuilding of the temple until seventy years after the destruction of the temple had also elapsed.

Several principles emerge from Daniel's reference to Jeremiah's prophecy. First, Daniel took the seventy years literally and believed that there would be literal fulfillment. Even though Daniel was fully acquainted with the symbolic form of revelation which God sometimes used to portray panoramic prophetic events, his interpretation of Jeremiah was literal and he expected God to fulfill His word.

Second, Daniel realized that the Word of God would be fulfilled only on the basis of prayer, and this occasioned his fervent plea as recorded in this chapter. On the one hand, Daniel recognized the certainty of divine purposes and the sovereignty of God which will surely fulfill the prophetic word. On the other hand, he recognized human agency, the necessity of faith and prayer, and the urgency to respond to human responsibility as it relates to the divine program. His custom of praying three times a day with his windows open to Jerusalem still in desolation revealed his own heart for the things of God and his concern for the city of Jerusalem.

Third, he recognized the need for confession of sin as a prelude to restoration. With this rich background of the prophetic program revealed through Jeremiah, Daniel's own prayer life, and his concern for the city of Jerusalem as the religious center of the nation of Israel, Daniel approaches the task of expressing his confession and intercession to the God of Abraham, Isaac, and Jacob.

Because Daniel, for the first time, used the word LORD or Jehovah in Daniel 9:2, repeating the expression in verses 4, 10, 13, 14, and 20, critics have used this as an argument against the authenticity of this passage and the prayer which follows.[*4]

DANIEL'S PREPARATION FOR PRAYER

9:3-4 And I set my face unto the Lord God, to seek by prayer and supplications, with fasting, and sackcloth, and ashes: And I prayed unto the LORD my God, and made my confession, and said, O Lord, the great and dreadful God, keeping the covenant and mercy to them that love him, and to them that keep his commandments.

Encouraged by his understanding of God's intention to restore Jerusalem, Daniel now seeks to make adequate preparation to present his confessions and petitions to the Lord. Every possible element of preparation is included. First, he declares, "I set my face unto the Lord God." This was a formal beginning in which Daniel turns away from other things to concentrate on his prayer to the Lord. It implies faith, devotion, and worship. His activity in prayer has a specific end expressed by the word *to seek*. It anticipates that he hopes to find ground for an answer to his

*See discussion of Dan 9:15-19, pp. 211-12.

prayers. The attitude of mind and steadfastness of purpose indicated is now supplemented by prayer and supplications, that is, prayer in general and petition specifically. This is accompanied by every known auxiliary aid to prayer: namely, fasting, that he might not be diverted from prayer by food; sackcloth, a putting aside of ordinary garments in favor of rough cloth speaking of abject need; and ashes, the traditional symbol of grief and humility. In a word, Daniel left nothing undone that might possibly make his prayer more effective or more persuasive. While God honors the briefest of prayers, as the experience of Nehemiah 2:4 indicates, effective prayer requires faith in the Word of God, proper attitude of mind and heart, privacy, and unhurried confession and petition. Daniel's humility, reverence, and earnestness are the hallmarks of effective prayer.

In beginning his prayer to the Lord, Daniel relies upon the fact that the majesty of God's person and the greatness of His power are manifested especially in His fulfilling His covenant promises and manifesting mercy to those who love Him and keep His commandments. As Nelson Glueck has brought out in his study of the word "mercy" (*hesed*), the word connotes not only forgiveness but loyalty in keeping His covenant with Israel.[5] This loyalty of God to His covenant is contrasted with the inexcusable disloyalty of the people of Israel. In beginning his prayer, Daniel thus is assured of the greatness of God and the goodness of God. His problem is that the children of Israel have sinned, broken their covenant, and have made themselves liable to the divine judgment which the faithfulness of God must inflict according to His promises.

DANIEL'S PRAYER OF CONFESSION

9:5-14 We have sinned, and have committed iniquity, and have done wickedly, and have rebelled, even by departing from thy precepts and from thy judgments: Neither have we hearkened unto thy servants the prophets, which spake in thy name to our kings, our princes, and our fathers, and to all the people of the land. O Lord, righteousness belongeth unto thee, but unto us confusion of faces, as at this day; to the men of Judah, and to the inhabitants of Jerusalem, and unto all Israel, that are near, and that are far off, through all the countries whither thou hast driven them, because of their trespass that they have trespassed against thee. O Lord, to us belongeth confusion of face, to our kings, to our princes, and to our fathers, because we have sinned against thee. To the Lord our God belong mercies and forgivenesses, though we have rebelled against him; neither have we obeyed the voice of the LORD our God, to walk in his laws, which he set before us by his servants the prophets. Yea, all Israel have transgressed thy law, even by departing, that they might not obey thy voice; therefore the curse is poured upon us, and the oath that is written in the law of Moses the servant of God, because we have sinned against him. And he hath confirmed his words, which he spake against us, and against our judges that judged us, by bringing upon us a great evil: for under the whole heaven hath not been done as hath been done upon Jerusalem. As it is written in the law of Moses, all this evil is come upon us: yet made we not our prayer before the Lord our God, that we might turn from our iniquities, and understand thy truth. Therefore hath the Lord watched upon the evil, and brought it upon us: for the Lord our God is righteous in all his works which he doeth: for we obeyed not his voice.

Having reminded himself of God's covenant and mercy, Daniel begins his prayer of confession. Daniel himself is one of the few major characters of the Old Testament to whom some sin is not ascribed. He is dealing not with his personal sins, but with his identification with the sin of the nation and the collective responsibility which Daniel shares both in promises of blessing and warnings of divine judgment. Daniel does not spare himself or his people in his confession. As John Calvin points out in his exposition, there is a fourfold description of the extent of their sin: first, they *have sinned* (Heb. ḥāṭā'nû), meaning a serious crime or offense; second, they *have committed iniquity*, that is, "acted unjustly"; third, they *have done wickedly*, or "conducted themselves wickedly"; and fourth, sinning in this way, they *have rebelled even by departing from thy precepts*, that is, "become rebellious and declined from the statutes and commandments of God."[6] Moses Stuart notes, "The *climactic* construction of the sentence is palpable. To turn back from obedience to the divine statutes, in the frame of mind which belongs to *rebels*, is the consummation of wickedness, and so Daniel rightly considers it. The variety of verbs employed here, indicates the design of the speaker to confess all sin of every kind in its full extent."[7]

The heinousness of their sin is amplified in verse 6 by the fact that they have disregarded the prophets which God sent to them. This disrespect and disobedience to the prophets characterized all classes of Israel, including their kings, their princes, other leaders referred to as "our fathers," and finally "all the people of the land." Even in such times of revival as during the reign of Hezekiah when the king's messengers went throughout the land calling people to the Passover at Jerusalem, the Scriptures record that many "laughed them to scorn, and mocked them" (2 Ch 30:10). The disregard of the Word of God in Israel's departure from the precepts and judgments as mentioned in verse 5 as well as the disregard of the prophets, "is the beginning of all moral disorders," as Leupold expresses it.[8]

In verses 7-8, Daniel contrasts the righteousness of God and the confusion of face belonging to Israel. God has been righteous in His judgments upon Israel, and in no way does Israel's distress reflect upon the attributes of God adversely. By contrast, Israel's confusion or shame of face which had made them the object of scorn of the nations was their just desert for rebellion against God. Daniel itemizes those who are especially concerned: first, the men of Judah and the inhabitants of Jerusalem, that is, the kingdom of Judah which was carried into captivity by the Babylonians, and second, "all Israel, that are near, and that are far off," that is, also the ten tribes of the kingdom of Israel which were carried off by the Assyrians in 721 B.C. The scattering of the children of Israel "through all the countries which thou hast driven them," was not occasioned by one sin, but by generation after generation of failure to obey the Law or to give heed to the prophets.

In verse 8, those who are ashamed are itemized according to classes of society, that is, "our kings," "our princes," and "our fathers." The judgment of God did not spare any class but was according to their sins and their rebellion. In this passage, as in Daniel's earlier confession, he does not mince words but refers to Israel's trespasses and their sins with no attempt to excuse them.

Frederick A. Tatford summarizes Daniel 9:5-8 in these words, "There was no tautology in the prolific accumulation of expressions he used: it was rather that he sought to express by every possible word the enormity of the guilt and contumacy of himself and his people. They had sinned in wandering from the right, they had dealt perversely in their wilful impiety, they had done wickedly in their sheer infidelity, they had rebelled in deliberate refractoriness, they had turned aside from the Divine commandments and ordinances. Their cup of iniquity was full. Their guilt was accentuated by the fact that prophets had been sent to them with the Divine message and they had refused to listen. All were implicated— rulers, leaders (the term 'fathers' being used, of course, in a metaphorical rather than in a literal sense), and the people. God was perfectly just, but a shameful countenance betrayed their own guilt. Nor was the confusion of face limited to Judah and Jerusalem: it was true of all Israelites throughout the world. Indeed, their scattering was in punishment for their own unfaithfulness to God. Daniel associated himself completely with his people in acknowledging their wrong-doing and freely confessed that their shamefacedness was due to perfectly justified corrections: they had sinned against God."[9]

Having contrasted the righteousness of God to the sins of Israel, Daniel now turns in verse 9 to the contrast of the mercies and forgiveness of God as compared to the sin of Israel. The word *mercies* here is a different word than in Daniel 9:4 and is correctly translated. Although God is a God of righteousness, He is also a God of mercy. It is on this ground, of course, that Daniel is basing his petition. In doing so, he turns from addressing God directly in the second person to speaking of God in the third person, as if to state a truth for all who will hear, a theological fact now being introduced as the basis for the remainder of the prayer. As Stuart observes, "The plur. form of these nouns ["mercies and forgivenesses"] denotes intensity in the manifestation, or the continued and extended exercise of these qualities or attributes."[10]

Over against the reminder of the mercies and forgivenesses of God, Daniel now plunges into recital of the extent of Israel's sin in verses 10-11. Again, Daniel restates the facts that Israel has not obeyed the voice of the Lord their God. They have not walked according to His laws as proclaimed to them by the Lord's servants, the prophets. The word translated "laws" in verse 10 means literally, "instructions" (cf. Is 1:10 ff.). The rebellion was not on the part of a few but "all Israel have transgressed thy law, even by departing." Because of their persistent failure and rebellion against God, the prophesied curse pronounced upon Israel as "written in the law of Moses the servant of God" was applied.

In Deuteronomy 28, for instance, the conditions of blessing and cursing are set forth before Israel in detail. If they obeyed, they would have every blessing, temporal and spiritual, from God. If they disobeyed, God would destroy them and scatter them over the earth. Moses had made perfectly clear that Israel's situation would indeed be desperate if they disobeyed the Lord God. Most of Deuteronomy 28 is devoted to itemizing these curses, concluding with the prophetic warning of the world-wide dispersion of Israel (Deu 28:63-65) and the resultant uncertainty of life and future which would characterize individual Israelites.

How sad are Moses' words: "And it shall come to pass, that as the LORD rejoiced over you to do you good, and to multiply you; so the LORD will rejoice over you to destroy you, and to bring you to nought; and you shall be plucked from off the land whither thou goest to possess it. And the LORD shall scatter thee among all people, from the one end of the earth even unto the other; and there thou shalt serve other gods, which neither thou nor thy fathers have known, even wood and stone. And among these nations shalt thou find no ease, neither shall the sole of thy foot have rest: but the LORD shall give thee there a trembling heart, and failing of eyes, and sorrow of mind: And thy life shall hang in doubt before thee; and thou shalt fear day and night, and shalt have none assurance of thy life: In the morning thou shalt say, Would God it were even! and at even thou shalt say, Would God it were morning! for the fear of thine heart wherewith thou shalt fear, and for the sight of thine eyes which thou shalt see" (Deu 28:63-67). It was to such passages and similar warnings of God to which Daniel referred.

G. E. Mendenhall has shown that the Mosaic covenant in its form has a close parallel in certain suzerainty treaties (i.e., treaties between the Great King and his vassals) of the Hittite Empire. Sanctions are typically supplied in these treaties by a series of blessings and cursings as also illustrated in Leviticus 26:14-39 and Deuteronomy 27-28. Such warnings are witnessed by heaven and earth (cf. Deu 4:26 and Is 1:2) and in their form are similar to many passages in the Old Testament.[11]

In verses 12-14, Daniel itemizes the evil which God had brought upon them as a result of their sin. In thus bringing judgment upon Israel, He had "confirmed his words, which he spake against us, and against our judges that judged us" (cf. Is 1:10-31; Mic 3). Above all, the other terrible judgment was that of the destruction of Jerusalem itself which was the final blow to Israel's pride and security.

Adding to all their earlier sins, Israel in their extremity did not turn to the Lord in prayer: "yet made we not our prayer before the Lord our God, that we might turn from our iniquities, and understand thy truth." Even in the midst of the terrible manifestation of the righteous judgment of God, there was no revival, no turning to God; rulers and people alike persisted in their evil ways. What Daniel is saying is that God had no alternative, even though He was a God of mercy; for when mercy is spurned, judgment is inevitable. Daniel, accordingly, concludes in verse 14, "Therefore hath the Lord watched upon the evil, and brought it upon us: for the Lord our God is righteous in all his works which he doeth: for we obeyed not his voice." Porteous notes that the word *watched*, which can also be translated "keep ready" or "vigilant," is the same word Jeremiah uses when he tells how God was watchful over His word to perform it (Jer 1:12; cf. 31:28; 44:27). Jehovah was being faithful in keeping His word both in blessings and in cursings, which must have encouraged Daniel in anticipating the end of the captivity.[12]

Daniel's Petition for Forgiveness and Restoration

9:15-19 And now, O Lord our God, that hast brought thy people forth out of the land of Egypt with a mighty hand, and hast gotten thee renown, as at this day; we have sinned, we have done wickedly. O Lord, according to all thy righteousness, I beseech thee, let thine anger and thy fury be turned away from thy city Jerusalem, thy holy mountain: because for our sins, and for the iniquities of our fathers, Jerusalem and thy people are become a reproach to all that are about us. Now therefore, O our God, hear the prayer of thy servant, and his supplications, and cause thy face to shine upon thy sanctuary that is desolate, for the Lord's sake. O my God, incline thine ear, and hear; open thine eyes, and behold our desolations, and the city which is called by thy name: for we do not present our supplications before thee for our righteousnesses, but for thy great mercies. O Lord, hear; O Lord, forgive; O Lord, hearken and do; defer not, for thine own sake, O my God: for thy city and thy people are called by thy name.

In his progression of thought, having laid fully the groundwork by confession of sin and recognition of the righteousness and mercies of God, Daniel now turns to the burden of his prayer—that God would, in keeping with His righteousness and according to His mercies, forgive and restore the people of Israel. In presenting his petition, Daniel first of all appeals to the revelation of the power and forgiveness of God in delivering the people of Israel from Egypt. In doing so, God had not only manifested His forgiveness but His power, and had gained "renown" among the nations for the demonstration of His mighty power. The deliverance of the people of Israel from Egypt is, in many respects, the Old Testament standard illustration of the power of God and His ability to deliver His people. By contrast in the New Testament, the resurrection of Jesus Christ is God's standard of power (Eph 1:19-20). In the future millennial reign of Christ, the standard of power will be the regathering of Israel and their restoration to the land (Jer 16:14-15). The three dispersions of Israel from the land and their regathering are among the more important demonstrations of power in relation to Israel. God had allowed them to go into Egypt and delivered them in the Exodus. He had punished them by the captivities, but now Daniel is pleading with Him to restore His people to their land and their city. The future final regathering of Israel in relation to the millennial kingdom will be the final act fulfilling Amos 9:11-15, when Israel will be regathered never to be dispersed again. In both the dispersions and the regatherings, God's righteousness, power, and mercies are evident.

Having introduced the thought of God's deliverance of Israel from the land of Egypt, Daniel is once again overwhelmed by the wickedness of Israel which seems to block the way for the restoration. He injects, "We have sinned, we have done wickedly"—his theme song up to this point in the prayer—but, nevertheless, proceeds to his petition for Israel's forgiveness and restoration.

Stuart summarizes verse 15 in these words, "Here commences the *supplication* of the speaker; at least, this address is preparatory to it. The argument stands thus: 'O God, who in times past hast wrought wonderful deliverances for thy people, and thereby acquired a glorious name —repeat thy wondrous doings, and add to the glory which thou hast already acquired! As thou didst bring us out of exile in Egypt, so bring us out of exile in Babylon.'—*a name, as at the present time, i.e.* such a name, glory, honor, as is attributed to thee even now.—*We have sinned* etc., the deep sensation of penitence forces from the speaker the repetition of confession."[13]

In making his petition in verses 15-19, Daniel addresses God only as *Adonai* and *Elohim* and no longer uses the term *Jehovah* as he did in verses 4-14. Strangely, most commentators have ignored this significant change in address.[14] Montgomery goes so far as to insert the word *Jehovah* in his translation, although he calls attention in his critical apparatus to the actual Hebrew.[15] The explanation seems to be that in using the word *Adonai,* Daniel is recognizing God's absolute sovereignty over him as Lord.

In presenting his petition specifically, Daniel significantly appeals again to the righteousness of the Lord in verse 16. Although anticipating that the hope of the restoration of Israel depended on the mercies of God, Daniel recognized, nevertheless, that it must be "according to all thy righteousness." Here is implied the whole system of reconciliation to God by sacrifice, supremely fulfilled in Jesus Christ. Daniel recognizes that somehow there is no contradiction between the righteousness of God and His mercies and forgiveness. It is also true that the same Scriptures which predict God's judgment upon Israel also predict their restoration, and it would be in keeping with the veracity of God as a covenant-keeping God not only to inflict judgment but to bring in the promised restoration. In verse 16 as in verse 15, in beginning his petition, Daniel argues on the ground that the children of Israel are "thy people" and that his petition has to do with the restoration of Jerusalem which is "thy city," and "thy holy mountain." The appeal is to the fact that restoration will not only be an act of mercy but also that which will bring honor and glory to God and a testimony to the nations before whom Israel now is "a reproach." As Young expresses it, "The prayer is a tragic confession of guilt. Jerusalem should have been the mount unto which all nations would flow, and Israel should have been a light unto the Gentiles, but because of the people's sins, Jerusalem and Israel had become a reproach."[16]

With his petition now grounded on the fact that an answer would be to the glory of God, Daniel now adds one further item, namely, that the sanctuary itself, the place where God met man in sacrifice, was in desolation and that the whole sacrificial system had fallen into disuse because of the destruction of Jerusalem and its temple. Accordingly, in verse 17, he beseeches God to "hear the prayer of thy servant, and his supplications" and, in answer to Daniel's petition, to "cause thy face to shine upon thy sanctuary that is desolate, for the Lord's sake." Ultimately, it was not simply the restoration of Israel which Daniel sought, nor the restoration of Jerusalem or even of the temple, but specifically the sanctuary with its altar of sacrifice and its holy of holies.

The eloquence of Daniel's prayer now reaches its crescendo. How it must have delighted the ears of God to have heard His devoted servant present His petitions. How it must have moved the heart of God to have heard Daniel say, "O my God, incline thine ear, and hear; open thine eyes, and behold our desolations, and the city which is called by thy name: for we do not present our supplications before thee for our righteousnesses, but for thy great mercies." If prayer to God can be called persuasive, Daniel's prayer certainly merits this description. Daniel in his holy life, his careful preparation in approaching God, his uncompromising confession of sin, and his appeal to God's holy character as the One who is both righteous and merciful, illustrates the kind of prayer that God delights to answer. Daniel, led by the Spirit of God, had expressed precisely the prayer that God wanted to hear and wanted to answer.

In closing his prayer, Daniel once again beseeches God to hear, to forgive, to do, to defer not, all for God's own sake, for God's city Jerusalem, for God's people Israel, who are called by the name of the Lord. As Tatford has well said, "The prayer is one of the most remarkable in the pages of Holy Writ."[17]

Although no other portion of the Bible breathes with more pure devotion or has greater spiritual content than this prayer of Daniel, it has been attacked without mercy by the higher critics, of which Charles is an illustration. Acting on the premise that the book of Daniel as a whole is a second-century forgery and not written by Daniel the prophet in the sixth century B.C., exception is taken by the critics to this section of Daniel as a particular proof that the book of Daniel as a whole could not have been written by Daniel the prophet. Charles has seven arguments against accepting this passage as genuine.[18] Leupold representing conservative scholars summarizes the seven arguments of Charles and refutes them adequately.[19]

Montgomery has summarized the objections of the critics. Although making preliminary concessions that the prayer "is a liturgical gem in form and expression, and excels in literary character the more verbose types found in Ezr. and Neh.," he holds "the prayer is of the liturgical type which existed since the Deuteronomic age represented by Solomon's Prayer, I Ki. 8, the prayers of Jer., Jer. 26.32.44, and the prayers in Ezr.-Neh., Ezr. 9, Neh. 1.9." Montgomery goes on to say, "By far the largest part of this prayer consists of language found in those other compositions."[20]

Not all the higher critics, however, accept the explanation that Daniel 9:2-19 is an interpolation not originally in the book. These complicated arguments have been summarized both for and against by Montgomery. He states,

> Von Gall, *Einheitlichkeit*, 123-126, has developed the thesis that Dan.'s prayer is an interpolation, although the rest of his work contends for the practical integrity of the canonical books. He is followed by Mar., Cha. [Marti's *Commentary*, and Charles]. It is patent, as these scholars argue, that the theme of the prayer does not correspond to the context, which would seem to require a prayer for illumination, cf. 2:20 ff., and not a

liturgical confession bearing on the national catastrophe. Further, Dan.'s
prayer for immediate redemption is in contrast to the recognition of the
far distance of that event, 8:26 and end of this chap. It is pointed out
that v. 4a repeats v. 3 and especially that v. 20 is a joint with the main
narrative, which is resumed in v. 21; this would explain the repetition:
"whiles I was speaking and praying and confessing" "whiles I was speaking in prayer." The present writer agrees with Kamp. [Kamphausen] in
finding these arguments inconclusive. The second-century author may
well have himself inserted such a prayer in his book for the encouragement of the faithful, even as the calculation of the times was intended for
their heartening. . . . For an elaborate study of the Prayer, defending its
authenticity and also arguing for its dependence on the Chronicler, x.
Bayer, *Daniel-studien*, Part I. [21]

The critics' argument is based on the false premise that Jeremiah's
seventy years and the seventy weeks of Daniel 9:24-27 are the same. Because Daniel distinguishes these two periods, it is argued that the material
is an interpolation. It is the critics who are wrong, not Daniel. The alleged
copying from a common source on the part of Daniel, Nehemiah, and
Baruch is better explained by the fact that Daniel was written first (sixth
century B.C., not second century) and that Nehemiah and Baruch had
Daniel before them. Again, it is the critics' theories which are the basis
of their argument, and the theories are in error. The critics of Daniel
argue in a circle; assuming a second century date for Daniel, they then
criticize Daniel for not harmonizing with their erroneous premises. The
unity and beauty of this passage is its own defense.

The Coming of the Angel Gabriel

9:20-23 And whiles I was speaking, and praying, and confessing my
sin and the sin of my people Israel, and presenting my supplication before
the Lord my God for the holy mountain of my God; yea, whiles I was
speaking in prayer, even the man Gabriel, whom I had seen in the vision
at the beginning, being caused to fly swiftly, touched me about the time
of the evening oblation. And he informed me, and talked with me, and
said, O Daniel, I am now come forth to give thee skill and understanding.
At the beginning of thy supplications the commandment came forth, and
I am come to shew thee; for thou art greatly beloved: therefore understand the matter, and consider the vision.

While Daniel was offering his petition to the Lord, the answer was already on the way by means of the heavenly messenger, the angel Gabriel.
Daniel implies in verse 20 that the angel was sent at the very beginning
of his prayer. As Daniel expresses it, it was accomplished "whiles I was
speaking, and praying, and confessing my sin and the sin of my people
Israel, and presenting my supplication before the Lord my God for the
holy mountain of my God." According to verse 21, Gabriel touched
Daniel about the time of the evening oblation. It is obvious that the

prayer of Daniel recorded here is only a summary of the actual oral prayer which probably was lengthy and culminated at the time of the evening sacrifice.

The reference to "the man Gabriel" is not a denial that he is an angel, but serves to identify him with the vision of Daniel 8:15-16. The term man (Heb. *'ish*) is also used in the sense of a servant.[22] As brought out in chapter 8, there is an interesting play upon the thought here. Leupold notes: "The term 'Gabriel' means 'man of God,' but with this difference: the first root, *gebher*, means 'man' as the strong one, and the second root, *'el*, means the 'Strong God.' "[23] In other words, the expression *the man Gabriel* could be translated "the servant, the strong one of the strong God." In addition to the identification by the name itself, Daniel adds, "whom I had seen in the vision at the beginning," that is, in chapter 8. Gabriel, according to Daniel, "being caused to fly swiftly," arrived at the time of the evening oblation. The Hebrew for *being caused to fly swiftly* is difficult, as all commentators note, but this seems to be the best possible translation. The thought is that God directed Gabriel to go immediately to Daniel at the beginning of his petition. Although he flew swiftly, he did not arrive until the end of Daniel's prayer.

It is a touching observation that he arrived at the time of the evening oblation. There, of course, had been no evening oblation for half a century since the destruction of the temple in 586 B.C.; but in Daniel's youth, he had seen the smoke rise from the temple site in the afternoon sky with its reminder that God accepts a sinful people on the basis of a sacrifice offered on their behalf. This sacrifice usually began about 3 P.M., and consisted of a perfect yearling lamb offered as a whole burnt offering accompanied by meal and drink offerings, which typified the future sacrifice of Jesus Christ upon the cross as the spotless Lamb of God (Heb 9:14). Daniel does not speak specifically of the sacrifice but only of "the evening oblation," that is, the meal offering and the drink offering. The time of one, of course, was the time of the other. As the time of the evening sacrifice was also a stated time for prayer, Daniel was encouraged also to pray. As God in a sense met the spiritual need of His people at the time of the sacrifice and oblation, so Gabriel was sent by God to meet Daniel's special need at this time and remind him of the mercies of God.

Upon arrival, Gabriel talks with Daniel and states that the purpose of his coming is "to give thee skill in understanding." Although Daniel's prayer was not directed to his own need of understanding God's dealings with the people of Israel, this is the underlying assumption of his entire prayer. God, in a word, wants to assure Daniel of His unswerving purpose to fulfill all His commitments to Israel, including their ultimate restoration. In verse 23, Gabriel confirms what is implied in verse 20 that he was given instructions to go to Daniel early in Daniel's prayer. The commandment apparently came from God Himself, although conceivably he might have been sent by Michael the Archangel. Because of the magnitude of the revelation which follows, however, it is better to ascribe it to God Himself. According to Gabriel's own statement, he had come to show Daniel what was necessary to understand the entire matter of Israel's program, and specifically, to consider the vision of the seventy weeks described in the verses which follow. Gabriel bears witness to the special relationship which Daniel had to the Lord in that he was one "greatly beloved," in many spiritual and moral characteristics like the Apostle John, the disciple whom Jesus loved (Jn 13:23). The long preamble of twenty-three verses leading up to the great revelation of the seventy weeks is, in itself, a testimony to the importance of this revelation. The stage is now set for Gabriel to reveal to Daniel God's purposes for Israel, culminating in the second coming of Christ to establish His kingdom on the earth.

THE REVELATION OF THE SEVENTY SEVENS OF ISRAEL

9:24 Seventy weeks are determined upon thy people and upon thy holy city, to finish the transgression, and to make an end of sins, and to make reconciliation for iniquity, and to bring in everlasting righteousness, and to seal up the vision and prophecy, and to anoint the most Holy.

In the concluding four verses of Daniel 9, one of the most important prophecies of the Old Testament is contained. The prophecy as a whole is presented in verse 24. The first sixty-nine sevens is described in verse 25. The events between the sixty-ninth seventh and the seventieth seventh are detailed in verse 26. The final period of the seventieth seventh is described in verse 27.

Although many divergent interpretations have been advanced in explanation of this prophecy, they may first be divided into two major divisions, namely, the Christological and the non-Christological views.

The non-Christological approach may be subdivided into the liberal critical view and the conservative amillennial view. Liberal critics, assuming that Daniel is a forgery written in the second century B.C., find in this chapter that the pseudo-Daniel confuses the seventy years of Israel's captivity with the seventy sevens of Gabriel's vision. As Montgomery summarizes the matter in the introduction to chapter 9, "Dan., having learned from the Sacred Books of Jer.'s prophecy of the doom of seventy years' desolation for the Holy City, a term that was now naturally drawing to an end (1.2), sets himself to pray for the forgiveness of his people's sin and the promised deliverance (3-19). The angel Gabriel appears to him (20-21), and interprets the years as year-weeks, with detail of the

distant future and of the crowning epoch of the divine purpose (22-27)."[24]
In a word, Montgomery is saying that this is not prophecy at all but is
presented by the pseudo-Daniel as if it were. Whatever fulfillment there
is, is a fulfillment in history already accomplished at the time this Scripture was written. In his extended note on the interpretation of the seventy
weeks, Montgomery in general attempts to support the idea that the details of the prophecy are to a large extent fulfilled in the life and persecutions of Antiochus Epiphanes.[25]

In his summary, Montgomery states,

> The history of the exegesis of the 70 Weeks is the Dismal Swamp of O. T.
> criticism. The difficulties that beset any "rationalistic" treatment of the
> figures are great enough, but the critics on this side of the fence do not
> agree among themselves; but the trackless wilderness of assumptions and
> theories and efforts to obtain an exact chronology fitting into the history of
> Salvation, after these 2,000 years of infinitely varied interpretations, would
> seem to preclude any use of the 70 Weeks for the determination of a
> definite prophetic chronology. As we have seen, the early Jewish and
> Christian exegesis came to interpret that datum eschatologically and found
> it fulfilled in the fall of Jerusalem; only slowly did the theme of prophecy
> of the Advent of Christ impress itself upon the Church, along with the
> survival, however, of other earlier themes. The early Church rested no
> claims upon the alleged prophecy, but rather remarkably ignored it in a
> theological atmosphere surcharged with Messianism. The great Catholic
> chronographers naturally attacked the subject with scientific zeal, but
> their efforts as well as those of all subsequent chronographers (including
> the great Scalinger and Sir Isaac Newton) have failed.[26]

In other words, Montgomery, for all of his scholarship and knowledge of
the history of interpretation, ends up with no reasonable interpretation at
all.

Some conservative scholars have done no better, however, as illustrated
in the commentary of Edward Young. Although treating the Scriptures
with reverence, he finds no satisfactory conclusion for the seventy sevens
of the prophecy and leaves it more or less like Montgomery without a
satisfactory explanation.[27]

The conservative interpretation of Daniel 9:24-27 usually regards the
time units as years. The decision is, however, by no means unanimous.
Some amillenarians, like Young, who have trouble with fitting this into
their system of eschatology consider this an indefinite period of time.
Actually, the passage does not say "years"; and because it is indefinite,
they consider the question somewhat open. Further, as Young points out,
the word *sevens* is in the masculine plural instead of the usual feminine
plural. No clear explanation is given except that Young feels "it was for
the deliberate purpose of calling attention to the fact that the word *sevens*
is employed in an unusual sense."[28]

Most commentators agree that the time unit is not days. Further, the fact that there were seventy *years* of captivity, discussed earlier in the chapter, would seem to imply that years were also here in view. The interpretation of years at least is preferable to days as Young comments, "The brief period of 490 days would not serve to meet the needs of the prophecy, upon any view. Hence, as far as the present writer knows, this view is almost universally rejected."[29] Young finally concludes after some discussion that Keil and Kliefoth are correct when they hold that the word *sevens* does not necessarily mean year-weeks, but "an intentionally indefinite designation of a period of time measured by the number seven, which chronological duration must be determined on other grounds."[30]

With this point of view, Leupold, an amillenarian, also agrees: "Since the week of creation, 'seven' has always been the mark of divine work in the symbolism of numbers. 'Seventy' contains seven multiplied by ten, which, being a round number, signifies perfection, completion. Therefore, 'seventy heptads'—7x7x10—is the period in which the divine work of greatest moment is brought to perfection. There is nothing fantastic or unusual about this to the interpreter who has seen how frequently the symbolism of numbers plays a significant part in the Scriptures."[31]

Some amillenarians, however, use a literal year time unit for the first sixty-nine weeks but an indefinite period for the last seven years, as in the case of Philip Mauro (see pp. 232-37). In view of the precision of the seventy years of the captivity, however, mentioned in the same chapter, the context indicates the probability of a more literal intention in the revelation.

To be added to the non-Christological interpretation of Young is that of orthodox Jewry which concludes that the period ends with the destruction of Jerusalem in A.D. 70. This, of course, also does not give an adequate explanation of the text.

The overwhelming consensus of scholarship, however, agrees that the time unit should be considered years. It is normal for lexicographical authorities in the field of Hebrew to define the time unit as "period of seven (days, years)," and "*heptad*, weeks."[32]

Otto Zöckler, Professor of Theology in the University of Greifswald in Prussia in the 19th century, argued at length from the internal evidences within Daniel that the Hebrew term translated "week" denotes a period of seven years:

> This cannot possibly denote seventy weeks in the ordinary sense, or 490 days; for the number has an obvious relation to the seventy years of Jeremiah, v. 2, and the brief limit of 490 days is not suited to serve as a mystical paraphrase of the period of three and a half years. Moreover, according to the descriptions in chapters vii. and viii., the three and a

half years were throughout a period of suffering and oppression, while in
v. 25 et seq. the latter and more extended subdivision (amounting to
sixty-two weeks) of the seventy weeks is characterized as being comparatively free from sufferings. Finally, the three and a half years evidently reappear in v. 27, in the form of the "half-week" during which the
sacrifices and oblations were to cease, etc.: and this undeniable identity
of the small fraction at the end of the seventy weeks with the three and a
half years of tribulation, heretofore described, removes it beyond the
reason of doubt that the seventy weeks are to be regarded as *seventy
weeks of years*, and therefore as an *amplification* of the seventy years of
Jeremiah.°[33]

In view of the great variety of opinions which find no Christological
fulfillment at all in this passage, the interpreter necessarily must approach
the Christological interpretation with some caution. Here again, however, diversity of opinion is found even though there is general agreement
that the prophecy somehow relates to the Messiah of Israel. Christological
interpretations divide again into two major categories. All Christological
interpretations tend to interpret the first sixty-nine sevens as literal. The
division comes on the interpretation of the seventieth seven. Amillenarians
generally regard the seventieth seven as following immediately after the
sixty-ninth seven and, therefore, is already fulfilled in history. The other
point of view regards the seventieth seven as separated from the earlier
sequence of years and scheduled for fulfillment in the future in the seven
years preceding the second advent of Christ. Although many minor
variations can be found, the principal question in the Christological interpretation of this text concerns the nature of fulfillment of the last seven
years.

In the Christological interpretation of Daniel 9:24-27, it is generally
assumed that the time units indicated are years. The English word
"weeks" is misleading as the Hebrew is actually the plural of the word for
seven, without specifying whether it is days, months, or years. The only
system of interpretation, however, that gives any literal meaning to this

---

°Zöckler adds, "Such a prophetic or mystical transformation of the seventy years into
many periods of seven years each is not unparalleled in the usage of the ancients; cf.,
e.g., the remarks of Mark Varro in Aul. Gellius, *N.A.* III., 10: '*Se jam undecimam
annorum hebdomadem ingressum esse et ad eum diem septuaginta hedomadas lib-
rorum conscripsisse;*' also Aristotle, *Polit.*, Vii 6; Censorin., *de die natali*, C. 14. It
was, however, peculiarly adapted to the prophet's purpose, and was especially intel-
ligible to his readers, inasmuch as the Mosaic Law (Lev. xxv.2, 4 et seq.; xxvi.34, 35,
43; cf. 2 Chron. xxxvi. 21) had designated every seventh year as a sabbath of the
land, and had introduced the custom of dividing the years into hebdomads, which
thus became familiar to every individual in the Jewish nation during all subsequent
ages. The thought that instead of seventy years, seventy times seventy were to elapse
before the theocracy should be restored in all its power and significance, and that,
consequently, an extended period of delay should precede the advent of the Messianic
era, is 'an integral feature in the mode of conception which prevails throughout the
book' (Kranichfeld)" ("The Book of the Prophet Daniel," in *Commentary on the
Holy Scriptures*, 13:194).

prophecy is to regard the time units as prophetic years of 360 days each according to the Jewish custom of having years of 360 days with an occasional extra month inserted to correct the calendar as needed. The seventy times seven is, therefore, 490 years with the beginning at the time of "the commandment to restore and to build Jerusalem" found in verse 25 and the culmination 490 years later in verse 27. Before detailing the events to be found in the first 483 years (sixty-nine times seven), the events between the sixty-ninth seven and the seventieth seven, and the final seven years, Daniel gives the overall picture in verse 24. Careful attention must be given to the precise character of this important foundational prophecy.

The prophetic period of time in question is declared to be "determined." This involves the assumption of a comprehensive plan of God in which future events are rendered certain and conceived of as a part of an overall plan which is being executed by God.

A very important aspect of the prophecy given at the start is that the period of time in question relates to "thy people" and "thy holy city." Even in ruins, Jerusalem remains the city set apart in the heart of God (cf. 9:20) and Daniel shared this love for the city which is central in God's program for His kingdom both in the past and the future. Unlike the prophecies of Daniel 2, 7, and 8, which primarily related to the Gentiles, this chapter is specifically God's program for the people of Israel, as Daniel would obviously interpret it. To make this equivalent to the church composed of both Jews and Gentiles is to read into the passage something foreign to the whole thinking of Daniel. The church as such has no relation to the city nor to the promises given specifically to Israel relating to their restoration and repossession of the land.

Once it has been established that the prophecy relates to the people of Israel and the holy city Jerusalem, six important purposes of God are clearly discerned in verse 24: (1) "to finish the transgression"; (2) "to make an end of sins"; (3) "to make reconciliation for iniquity"; (4) "to bring in everlasting righteousness"; (5) "to seal up the vision and prophecy"; and (6) "to anoint the most Holy."

These six items, to be completed in the seventy sevens of Daniel 9:24, are comprehensive in nature. Some expositors, like Young, attempt to find three negative results, namely, "to finish the transgression," "to make an end of sins," and "to make reconciliation for iniquity." By contrast, the positive accomplishments would be "to bring in everlasting righteousness," "to seal up the vision and prophecy," and "to anoint the most Holy." This obviously is an arbitrary division, because "to make reconciliation for iniquity" is a positive rather than a negative act and, on the contrary, "to seal up the vision and prophecy" is probably negative instead of positive.[34] The preferable approach is to take each on its own merits.

The first three, however, do deal with sin named in three ways: "the transgression," "sins," and "iniquity." Although a great variety of interpretations are possible, as the text itself does not explain the terminology, the general idea can be ascertained. In the period of the seventy sevens, first will be a program to finish the transgression. The expression *to finish* is derived from the *piel* verb form of the root *kālâ* meaning "to finish" in the sense of bringing to an end. The most obvious meaning is that Israel's course of apostasy and sin and wandering over the face of the earth will be brought to completion within the seventy sevens. The restoration of Israel which Daniel sought in his prayer will ultimately have its fulfillment in this concept.

The second aspect of the program, "to make an end of sins," may be taken either in the sense of taking away sins or bringing sin to final judgment.[35] Due to a variation in textual reading, another possibility is to translate it "to seal up sin."*

Keil translates this aspect, "to seal up sin," and states, "The figure of the sealing stands here in connection with the shutting up in prison. Cf. ch. vi. 18, the king for greater security sealed up the den into which Daniel was cast. Thus also God seals the hand of man that it cannot move, Job xxxvii. 7, and the stars that cannot give light, Job ix. 7. . . . The sins are here described as sealed, because they are altogether removed out of the sight of God."[36]

The final explanation may include all of these items because the eschatological conclusion of Israel's history does indeed bring an end to their previous transgressions, brings their sin into judgment, and also introduces the element of forgiveness.

The third aspect of the program, "to make reconciliation for iniquity," seems to be a rather clear picture of the cross of Christ in which Christ reconciled Israel as well as the world to Himself (2 Co 5:19). As far as the Old Testament revelation of reconciliation is concerned, lexicographers and theologians have understood the Hebrew word *kippēr* when used in relation to sin to mean to "cover," to "wipe out," to "*make . . . as harmless, non-existent,* or *inoperative, to annul*" (so far as God's notice or regard is

---

*The King James Version bases its translation *to make an end* on the *Kere* reading *lᵉhātēm*, the *hiphil* infinitive of *tāmam*, meaning, "to finish, complete, perfect." All the ancient versions follow this reading with the exception of Theodotion. The *Kethib* reading, followed by Keil, is *lahtōm*, the *qal* infinitive of *hātam* meaning "to seal, to seal up." The textual confusion is due to easy interchange of letters. Since *lahtōm*, "to seal up (the vision)," is found in the next line, it seems plausible to suppose that the scribe responsible for the *Kethib* reading was influenced by this word. In short, the *Kere* reading is the preferred reading, as followed in the King James Version, that is, "to make an end" or "to finish sins."

concerned), to *withdraw from God's sight*, with the attached ideas of *reinstating in His favour, freeing from sin*, and *restoring to holiness*."[37]

While the basic provision for reconciliation was made at the cross, the actual application of it is again associated with the second advent of Christ as far as Israel is concerned, and an eschatological explanation is possible for this phase as well as an historic fulfillment.

George N. H. Peters relates Christ's sacrifice to the kingdom specifically:

> Following the Word step by step, it will be found that the sacrifice forms *an eternal basis* for the Kingdom itself. For it constitutes the Theocratic King a Saviour who now saves from sin without violation or lessening of the law, He having died "the just for the unjust," and even qualifies Him as such a King, so that in virtue of His obedience unto death He is given authority over all enemies, and to restore all things. . . . The sacrifice affects the restoration of the Jewish nation; but when the happy time comes that they shall look upon Him whom they have pierced, faith in that sacrifice shall also in them bring forth the peaceable fruits of righteousness. The allegiance of the nations, and all of the Millennial and New Jerusalem descriptions are realized as *resultants* flowing from this sacrifice being duly appreciated and gratefully, yea joyfully, acknowledged. It is out of *the inexhaustible fountain* from whence the abundant mercies of God flow to a world redeemed by it.[38]

The fourth aspect of the program is "to bring in everlasting righteousness." There is a sense in which this also is accomplished by Christ in His first coming in that He provided a righteous ground for God's justification of the sinner. The many Messianic passages, however, which view righteousness as being applied to the earth at the time of the second coming of Christ may be the ultimate explanation. Jeremiah, for instance, stated, "Behold, the days come, saith the LORD, that I will raise unto David a righteous Branch, and a King shall reign and prosper, and shall execute judgment and justice in the earth. In his days, Judah shall be saved, and Israel shall dwell safely: and this is his name whereby he shall be called, THE LORD OUR RIGHTEOUSNESS" (Jer 23:5-6). The righteous character of the Messianic kingdom is pictured in Isaiah 11:2-5 (cf. Is 53:11; Jer 33:15-18).

The fifth aspect of the program, "to seal up the vision and prophecy," is probably best understood to mean the termination of unusual direct revelation by means of vision and oral prophecy. The expression *to seal up* indicates that no more is to be added and that what has been predicted will receive divine confirmation and recognition in the form of actual fulfillment. Once a letter is sealed, its contents are irreversible (cf. 6:8). Young applies this only to the Old Testament prophet,[39] but it is preferable to include in it the cessation of the New Testament prophetic gift seen both in oral prophecy and in the writing of the Scriptures. If the seventieth week is still eschatological, it would allow room for this interpretation which Young, attempting to interpret the entire prophecy as fulfilled, could not allow.

The sixth aspect of the prophecy, "to anoint the most Holy," has been referred to the dedication of the temple built by Zerubbabel, to the sanctification of the altar previously desecrated by Antiochus (1 Macc 4:52-56), and even to the new Jerusalem (Rev 21:1-27).[40] Young suggests that it refers to Christ Himself as anointed by the Spirit.[41] Keil and Leupold prefer to refer it to the new holy of holies in the new Jerusalem (Rev 21:1-3).[42] A. C. Gaebelein, expressing a premillennial view, believes the phrase "has nothing whatever to do with Him [Christ], but it is the anointing of the Holy of Holies in another temple, which will stand in the midst of Jerusalem," that is, the millennial temple.[43]

There is really no ground for dogmatism here as there is a possibility that any of these views might be correct. The interpretation of Keil and Leupold that it refers to the holy of holies in the New Jerusalem has much to commend itself. On the other hand, the other items all seem to be fulfilled before the second advent and the seventieth week itself concludes at that time. If fulfillment is necessary before the second advent, it would probably rule out Keil, Leupold, and Gaebelein, although millennial fulfillment could be regarded as a part of the second advent. On the other hand, the six items are not in chronological order and it would not violate the text seriously to have this prophecy fulfilled at any time in relation to the consummation. If complete fulfillment is found in Antiochus Epiphanes as liberal critics conclude or in the first coming of Christ as characterizes amillenarians like Young, this reduces the perspective. If the final seven years is still eschatologically future, it broadens the possibility of fulfillment to the second advent of Christ and events related to it such as the millennial temple. Amillenarians like Leupold, who hold to an indefinite period of time, can extend the final fulfillment to the eternal state.

The Fulfillment of the Sixty-nine Sevens

9:25 Know therefore and understand, that from the going forth of the commandment to restore and to build Jerusalem unto the Messiah the Prince shall be seven weeks, and threescore and two weeks: the street shall be built again, and the wall, even in troublous times.

At the outset of the revelation of the details of the seventy sevens, Daniel is exhorted to know and understand the main facts of the prophecy (cf. Dan 9:22). Calvin understands it as a statement of fact, "Thou shalt know and understand," instead of an exhortation.[44] It is questionable, however, whether Daniel actually understood it. Some of the later aspects of the prophecy of Daniel are clearly not understood by Daniel (Dan 12:8), although the general assurance of God's divine purpose must have comforted Daniel. It is preferable to consider it an exhortation. The history of the interpretation of these verses is confirmation of the fact that this prophecy is difficult and requires spiritual discernment.

The key to the interpretation of the entire passage is found in the phrase "from the going forth of the commandment to restore and to build Jerusalem." The question of the *terminus a quo*, the date on which the seventy sevens begin, is obviously most important both in interpreting the prophecy and in finding suitable fulfillment. The date is identified as being the one in which a commandment to restore and to build Jerusalem is issued.

As the history of the interpretation of this verse illustrates, a number of interpretations are theoretically possible. Young considers the expression *the commandment to restore and to build Jerusalem* to be "the going forth of a word to restore and to build Jerusalem," that is, "This phrase has reference to the issuance of the word, not from a Persian ruler but from God."[45] Young goes on to point out that the expression *the commandment*, which he insists is better translated "a word" (Heb. *dābār;* cf. 2 Ch 30:5) is also found in Daniel 9:23 for a word from God. Young argues, "It seems difficult, therefore to assume that here, two vv. later, another subject should be introduced without some mention of the fact."[*46]

Of course, it is rather obvious that another subject has been introduced in verse 24 and the two commandments are quite different—that of verse 23 having to do with Gabriel being sent to Daniel and verse 25 having to do with the rebuilding of Jerusalem. Young, however, finds that the word of the Lord referred to here in verse 25 is that given to Jeremiah concerning the return of the children of Israel from the captivity, as quoted in Daniel 9:2. This, of course, completely confuses two entirely different prophecies, one having to do with the captivity and the return to Jerusalem, the other having to do with Israel's future after their return. Young himself admits, however, that this explanation simply does not satisfy the passage as the word of the Lord did not go forth in 586 B.C. when Jerusalem was destroyed. As Young states, "However, it is perfectly clear that in 586 B.C., no word went forth to restore and to build Jerusalem."[47] The same objection can be placed against the date 605 B.C., the beginning of the times of the Gentiles.

Most expositors, however, recognize that the word or commandment mentioned here is a commandment of men even though it may reflect the

---

*Brown, Driver, and Briggs, however, allow *dābār* the meaning "word of command," and translate it, *edict* (p. 182).

will of God and be in keeping with the prophetic word. There are at least four decrees concerning the rebuilding of Jerusalem recorded in Scripture: (1) the decree of Cyrus to rebuild the temple (2 Ch 36:22-23; Ezra 1:1-4; 6:1-5); (2) the decree of Darius confirming the decree of Cyrus (Ezra 6:6-12); (3) the decree of Artaxerxes (Ezra 7:11-26); (4) the decree of Artaxerxes given to Nehemiah authorizing the rebuilding of the city (Neh 2:1-8).

All agree that there was a decree to rebuild the temple, given by Cyrus approximately 538 B.C. The question is whether this decree also authorized the rebuilding of the city. The precise wording of the three decrees as recorded in 2 Chronicles 36 and in Ezra seems to deal only with the temple, and the rebuilding of the city was not fulfilled until the time of Nehemiah where the decree recorded in Nehemiah 2:1-8 clearly refers to the city as a whole.

Implication has been drawn from Ezra 4:12-21 that the city walls were rebuilt at that time and that the reference to "a wall in Judah" in Ezra 9:9 signifies completion. There is no evidence that rebuilding the wall was authorized in 457 B.C. A careful examination of these passages will not prove with any clarity that the wall was ever completed or even begun. The accusations of Israel's enemies were largely false, as the evidence indicates explicitly only that they were building a temple. The extent of the ruins of Jerusalem and of the wall twelve years later, indicated in Nehemiah, are such that the best interpretation is to refer them to the destruction of Jerusalem in 586 B.C. Any date earlier than 445 B.C. for rebuilding the wall is based on insufficient evidence.[48]

The amillennial interpretation of this passage, however, has been to consider the decree of Cyrus in 538 B.C. as the decree to rebuild the city and the wall. Although it is granted that 2 Chronicles and Ezra do not authorize the rebuilding of the city, reference is made to the prophecy of Isaiah 44:28 and 45:13, remarkable prophecies given concerning Cyrus one hundred and fifty years before he came on the scene. According to Isaiah 44:28, God "saith of Cyrus, He is my shepherd, and shall perform all my pleasure: even saying to Jerusalem, Thou shalt be built; and to the temple, Thy foundation shall be laid." Additional prophecies are given concerning Cyrus in Isaiah 45:1-4. Although Cyrus is not specifically mentioned, some have taken Isaiah 45:13 as another reference to him, "I have raised him up in righteousness, and I will direct all his ways: he shall build my city, and he shall let go my captives, not for price nor reward, saith the LORD of hosts." Young finds confirmation of this in the statement in Ezra 4:12, where the enemies of Israel accuse the Jews of "building the rebellious and the bad city, and have set up the walls thereof, and joined the foundations." There is also an obscure reference to the fact that God "has given them mercy, to give us a wall in Judah and Jerusalem." This latter reference, however, seems to refer to the temple itself. Young, accordingly, concludes, "It is not justifiable to distinguish too sharply between the building of the city and the building of the temple. Certainly, if the people had received permission to return to Jerusalem to rebuild the temple, there was also implied in this permission to build for themselves homes in which to dwell. There is no doubt whatever but that the people thus understood the decree (cf. Haggai 1:2-4)."⁴⁹

Young, however, completely misses the point of Haggai's prophecy. It is true that the children of Israel had built houses, but apparently they were not in Jerusalem. To let the temple of God lie waste while they lived in comfortable homes was an offense to God; and, therefore, Haggai exhorts them to build the temple. The question whether Jerusalem was rebuilt is answered in the graphic description of Nehemiah, which Young does not mention, which pictures the city in utter ruins (Neh 2:12-15). He describes the walls as broken down, the gates consumed with fire, and the streets so full of debris that his beast which carried him could not get through. In his challenge to the children of Israel, Nehemiah says, "Ye see the distress that we are in, how Jerusalem lieth waste, and the gates thereof are burned with fire: come, and let us build up the wall of Jerusalem, that we be no more a reproach" (Neh 2:17). Further, in Nehemiah 11, the expedient is resorted to of casting lots so that one in ten would have to move to Jerusalem and build a house there (Neh 11:1).

It is rather evident, when all the evidence is in, that Jerusalem was not rebuilt in the sixth century B.C. although the rebuilding of the temple was indeed the first step toward the restoration of Israel and is that which is in view in the prophecies relating to Cyrus and is made explicit in 2 Chronicles 36:22-23 and Ezra 1:1-4. It is most significant that none of the prophecies in 2 Chronicles or Ezra mention the city but only the temple. Accordingly, the best explanation is that the decree relating to the rebuilding of the city itself is that given to Nehemiah in 445 B.C., about ninety years after the first captives returned and started the building of the temple.

Many of the older commentators, such as Dereser, Havernick, Weigl, interpret the reference to the commandment as indicating the royal edict of Artaxerxes Longimanus, who reigned over Persia 465-425 B.C., and who not only commanded the rebuilding of Jerusalem in 445 B.C. but earlier had commissioned Ezra to return to Jerusalem in 457 B.C. (Ezra 7:11-26).⁵⁰ The date 445 B.C. is based on the reference in Nehemiah 2:1 ff. stating that the decree went forth in the twentieth year of Artaxerxes Longimanus. As his reign began in 465 B.C., twenty years later would be

445 B.C. Most scholars, whether conservative or liberal, accordingly, accept the 445 B.C. date for Nehemiah's decree.

Although Young argues his case well, the ultimate decision to some extent has to be determined by the fulfillment of the prophecy as a whole. Young's explanation beginning it with the decree of Cyrus in 538 B.C. does not permit any reasonably literal interpretation of this prophecy. The 483 years which would then begin in 538 B.C., anticipated in the sixty-nine times seven years, would end in the middle of the first century B.C. when there was no significant event whatever to mark its close. In order to make his explanation plausible, Young has to assume that the years are not literal, the interpretation is not exact, and as a matter of fact, the first sixty-nine times seven years would be an indefinite period of time, actually much longer than the period specified. Although enthusiastically espoused, as Young points out, by "Calvin, Kliefoth, Keil, and lately Mauro also,"[51] it makes impossible any exact fulfillment.*

In verse 25, Daniel is introduced to two periods of time which are immediately consecutive, first a period of seven sevens, or forty-nine years, and then a period of sixty-two sevens, or four hundred and thirty-four years. There is no indication clearly given as to the reason for distinguishing between the two periods except that he adds "the streets shall be built again, and the wall, even in troublesome times."

The word translated "wall" (*ḥārûṣ*) is not the normal word for wall (*ḥômâ*). The root *ḥaraṣ* means "to cut, sharpen, decide." The nominal form *ḥārûṣ*, found only here, is rendered by ancient interpreters as "walls." Most modern lexicographers render it "ditch," or "moat." Zöckler comments, "It was not to be a wretched, confused, and scattered, as well as defenceless mass of houses, but was to be arranged in streets, and to be surrounded with a fortified (wall and) ditch."[52]

The first forty-nine-year period does not fit Young's explanation as the period between the decree of Cyrus (538 B.C.) and the decree of Darius (520 B.C.), obviously was not forty-nine years. The best explanation seems to be that beginning with Nehemiah's decree and the building of the wall, it took a whole generation to clear out all the debris in Jerusalem and restore it as a thriving city. This might well be the fulfillment of the forty-nine years. The specific reference to streets again addresses our attention to Nehemiah's situation where the streets were covered with debris and needed to be rebuilt. That this was accomplished in troublesome times is fully documented by the book of Nehemiah itself. Although the precise fulfillment is not a major item and only the barest of details

---

*Calvin states, for instance, "Next, as to the going forth of the edict, we have stated how inadmissible is any interpretation but the first decree of Cyrus, which permitted the people freely to return to their country" (2:219).

are given, the important point seems to be the question of when the sixty-nine sevens actually end. If the *terminus a quo* is 445 B.C., the date of Nehemiah's decree, what is the *terminus ad quem?*

Sir Robert Anderson has made a detailed study of a possible chronology for this period beginning with the well-established date of 445 B.C. when Nehemiah's decree was issued and culminating in A.D. 32 on the very day of Christ's triumphal entry into Jerusalem shortly before His crucifixion. Sir Robert Anderson specifies that the seventy sevens began on the first Nisan, March 14, 445 B.C. and ended on April 6, A.D. 32, the tenth Nisan. The complicated computation is based upon prophetic years of 360 days totaling 173,880 days. This would be exactly 483 years according to biblical chronology.[53] Alva McClain concurs with Anderson.[54]

That Sir Robert Anderson is right in building upon a 360-day year seems to be attested by the Scriptures. It is customary for the Jews to have twelve months of 360 days each and then to insert a thirteenth month occasionally when necessary to correct the calendar. The use of the 360-day year is confirmed by the forty-two months of the great tribulation (Rev 11:2; 13:5) being equated with 1,260 days (Rev 12:6; 11:3). The conclusions reached by Anderson, however, are quite complicated in their argument and impossible to restate simply.[55] While the details of Anderson's arguments may be debated, the plausibility of a literal interpretation, which begins the period in 445 B.C. and culminates just before the death of Christ, makes this view very attractive.

The principal difficulty is Anderson's conclusion that the death of Christ occurred A.D. 32. Generally speaking, while there has been uncertainty as to the precise year of the death of Christ based upon present evidence, most New Testament chronologers move it one or two years earlier, and plausible attempts have been made to adjust Anderson's chronology to A.D. 30.[56] There has been a tendency, however, in recent New Testament chronology to consider the possibility of a later date for the death of Christ, and no one today is able dogmatically to declare that Sir Robert Anderson's computations are impossible. Accordingly, the best explanation of the time when the sixty-nine sevens ended is that it occurred shortly before the death of Christ anticipated in Daniel 9:26 as following the sixty-ninth seven. Practically all expositors agree that the death of Christ occurred after the sixty-ninth seven.

PROPHESIED EVENTS AFTER THE SIXTY-NINTH SEVEN

9:26 And after threescore and two weeks shall Messiah be cut off, but not for himself: and the people of the prince that shall come shall destroy the city and the sanctuary; and the end thereof shall be with a flood, and unto the end of the war desolations are determined.

In summarizing the period of the sixty-nine sevens, the statement is made in verse 25 that the period will be "unto the Messiah the Prince." Most conservative expositors have interpreted this as a reference to Jesus Christ. Montgomery, however, has another explanation: " 'Messiah' is epithet of king, of priest (*cf.* 2 Mac. 1:10), of prophet; and in a spiritual sense of patriarch (Ps. 105:15), and even of Cyrus, who is 'My Anointed,' Is. 45:1. . . . The second term 'prince,' qualifying the first, is used of various officers of rank: as a chief among officials, esp. in the temple *personnel, e.g.* 11:22 of the high priest, *q.v.;* of nobles or princes, *e.g.,* Job 29:10, 31:37; then of royalty, appearing as an early title for the king in Israel, *e.g.,* 1 Sa. 9:16, and also of foreign kings. Hence both terms are ambiguous, and their combination does not assist identification, for which three candidates have been proposed: Cyrus, the 'Anointed' of Is. 45:1; Zerubbabel, the acclaimed Messiah of the Restoration; and his contemporary, the high priest Joshua b. Josedek."[57]

It is obvious that Montgomery is straining to prove a non-Christological interpretation. By far the majority of scholars who accept Daniel as a genuine book find the reference in verse 25 to Jesus Christ. As Young expresses it, "The old evangelical interpretation is that which alone satisfies the requirements of the case. The 'anointed one' is Jesus Christ, who was cut off by His death upon the Cross of Calvary."[58] If this interpretation of verse 25 is correct, it provides the key to verse 26 which states that after "threescore and two weeks," that is, the 7 plus 62 sevens, or after the end of the sixty-ninth seven, the Messiah shall be "cut off." The verb rendered "to cut off" has the meaning, "to destroy, to kill," for example, in Genesis 9:11; Deuteronomy 20:20; Jeremiah 11:19; Psalm 37:9.

The natural interpretation of verse 26 is that it refers to the death of Jesus Christ upon the cross. As this relates to the chronology of the prophecy, it makes plain that the Messiah will be living at the end of the sixty-ninth seventh and will be cut off, or die, soon after the end of it.

The prominence of the Messiah in Old Testament prophecy and the mention of Him in both verses 25 and 26 make the cutting off of the Messiah one of the important events in the prophetic unfoldment of God's plan for Israel and the world. How tragic that, when the promised King came, He was "cut off." The adulation of the crowd at the triumphal entry and the devotion of those who had been touched by His previous ministry were all to no avail. The unbelief of Israel and the calloused indifference of religious leaders when confronted with the claims of Christ combined with the hardness of heart of Gentile rulers to make this the greatest of tragedies. Christ was indeed not only "cut off" from man and from life, but in His cry on the cross indicated that He was forsaken of God. The plaintive cry "My God, my God, why hast thou forsaken me?"

reveals not only the awfulness of separation from God but points also to the answer—the redemptive purpose. Although the additional explanation *but not for himself* is probably best translated, "There is nothing for him," it is nevertheless true that He died for others. Nothing that rightly belonged to Him as Messiah the Prince was given to Him at that time. He had not come into His full reward nor the exercise of His regal authority. He was the sacrificial lamb of God sent to take away the sins of the world. Outwardly it appeared that evil had triumphed.

Although evangelical expositors have been agreed that the reference is to Jesus Christ, a division has occurred as to whether the event here described comes in the seventieth seventh described in the next verse, or whether it occurs in an interim or parenthetical period between the sixty-ninth seventh and the seventieth seventh. Two theories have emerged, namely, the continuous fulfillment theory which holds that the seventieth seven immediately follows the sixty-ninth, and the gap or parenthesis theory which holds that there is a period of time between the sixty-ninth seven and the seventieth seven. If fulfillment is continuous, then the seventieth week is already history. If there is a gap, there is a possibility that the seventieth week is still future. On this point, a great deal of discussion has emerged.

In the interpretation of this passage and the decision on the question of the continuous fulfillment versus the gap theory, the fulfillment of the prophecy again comes to our rescue. The center part of verse 26 states "the people of the prince that shall come shall destroy the city and the sanctuary." Historically the destruction of Jerusalem occurred in A.D. 70 almost forty years after the death of Christ. Although some expositors, like Young,[59] hold that the sacrifices are caused to cease by Christ in His death which they consider fulfilled in the middle of the last seven years, it is clear that this does not provide in any way for the fulfillment of an event thirty-eight years or more after the end of the sixty-ninth seven. Young and others who follow the continuous fulfillment theory are left without any explanation adequate for interposing an event as occurring after the sixty-ninth seven by some thirty-eight years—which, in their thinking, would actually occur after the seventieth week. In a word, their theory does not provide any normal or literal interpretation of the text and its chronology.

The intervention of two events after the sixty-ninth seven which in their historic fulfillment occupied almost forty years makes necessary a gap between the sixty-ninth seven and the beginning of the seventieth seven of at least this length of time. Those referred to as "the people of the prince that shall come" are obviously the Roman people and in no sense do these people belong to Messiah the Prince. Hence it follows that there are two princes: (1) the Messiah of verses 25 and 26, and (2) "the prince that shall come" who is related to the Roman people. That a second prince is required who is Roman in character and destructive to the Jewish people is confirmed in verse 27 (see following exegesis), which the New Testament declares to be fulfilled in relation to the second coming of Christ (Mt 24:15).

The closing portion of verse 26, although not entirely clear, indicates that the destruction of the city will be like the destruction of a flood and that desolations are sovereignly determined along with war until the end. Because of the reference to "the end" twice in verse 26, it would be contextually possible to refer this to the end of the age and to a future destruction of Jerusalem. According to Revelation 11:2, "The holy city shall they tread under foot forty and two months "probably refers to the great tribulation just before the second advent. However, there is no complete destruction of Jerusalem at the end of the age as Zechariah 14:1-3 indicates that the city is in existence although overtaken by war at the very moment that Christ comes back in power and glory. Accordingly, it is probably better to consider all of verse 26 fulfilled historically.

The same expression of an overflowing flood is used to denote warlike hosts who annihilate their enemies in Daniel 11:10, 22, 26, 40 and in Isaiah 8:8. This seems to be a general reference to the fact that from the time of the destruction of the city of Jerusalem, trouble, war, and desolation will be the normal experience of the people of Israel and will end only at "the consummation" mentioned in verse 27, that is, the end of the seventieth seven. History has certainly corroborated this prophecy, for not only was Jerusalem destroyed but the entire civilization of the Jews in Palestine ceased to exist soon after the end of the sixty-ninth seven, and that desolation continued until recent times. The prophesied events of verse 26, like those of verse 25, already have been fulfilled and constitute clear evidence of the accuracy of the prophetic word. The prophecy of verse 25 dealing as it does with the restoration of Jerusalem at the beginning of the seventy sevens, the sixty-two sevens which follow the first seven sevens culminate in the Messiah, and the prediction that the Messiah shall be cut off and Jerusalem destroyed gives the high points in Israel's history and provides the key to understanding this difficult prophecy. In contrast to the rather clear fulfillment of verses 25-26, verse 27 is an enigma as far as history is concerned; and only futuristic interpretation allows any literal fulfillment.

THE SEVENTIETH SEVEN

9:27 And he shall confirm the covenant with many for one week: and in the midst of the week he shall cause the sacrifice and the oblation to cease, and for the overspreading of abominations he shall make it desolate, even until the consummation, and that determined shall be poured upon the desolate.

Although difference of opinion has been observed in the interpretation of Daniel 9:24-26, in the main the question has been whether fulfillment was non-Christological as liberals hold or Christological as most conservative expositors view the passage. Among conservatives, the major division has been between amillennial and premillennial interpretations. The divergence of interpretation comes to a head, however, in verse 27. Here the choice is clearly between literal fulfillment, which requires a futuristic interpretation with a gap between the sixty-ninth and seventieth week, or several other options which admittedly do not provide any clear fulfillment of verse 27.

In opposition to the futuristic interpretation, at least four other views have been advanced: (1) the liberal view that the seventieth seven is fulfilled in events following the Maccabean persecution just as the preceding sixty-nine sevens were; (2) the view of Jewish scholars that the seventieth week is fulfilled in the destruction of Jerusalem in A.D. 70; (3) the view that the seventieth week of Daniel is an indefinite period beginning with Christ but extending to the end, often held by amillenarians such as Young and Leupold;[60] (4) that the seventieth seven is seven literal years beginning with the public ministry of Christ and ending about three and a half years after His death.[61]

Each of the four views which claim fulfillment largely in the past have their supporting arguments, sometimes presented at length. But they have one common failure, which is the Achilles' heel of their interpretation: none of them provides literal fulfillment of the prophecy. The first view, the Maccabean fulfillment, is built on the premise that Daniel is a forgery and prophecy is impossible. The second and third views explain away problems by spiritualization and have no specific chronology. The numerical system of the seventy sevens becomes merely symbolic. The fourth view, that of Philip Mauro, finds literal fulfillment of the first sixty-nine and one-half sevens, but no fulfillment of the climax.

Even Leupold, an amillenarian who considers the seventy sevens as extending to the second coming of Christ (third view), objects to the historic fulfillment of the seventy sevens. He writes, "All they have left for the last week and the consummation of the seventy year-weeks is an unimportant date seven years after Christ's death, when something so unimportant happened that the commentators are at a loss as to what they should point to. That interpretation runs out into sand. No one has yet advanced a halfway satisfactory answer as to why such a termination of glorious work should be selected to close at the computation."[62]

Leupold comes close to the premillennial interpretation as he identifies "the prince that shall come" of verse 26 with the one who is related to the covenant in verse 27. He states, "The person under consideration as making the covenant is . . .·the Antichrist."[63] Keil, after a lengthy discussion, presents the same view as Leupold; that is, the one making the covenant is the Antichrist. Keil concludes, "Therefore the thought is this: That [an] ungodly prince shall impose on the mass of the people a strong covenant that they should follow him and give themselves to him as their God."[64]

The determination of the antecedent of *he* in verse 27 is the key to the interpretation of the passage. If the normal rule be followed that the antecedent is the nearest preceding possibility, it would go back to the *prince that shall come* of verse 26. This is the normal premillennial interpretation which postulates that the reference is to a future prince who may be identified with the Antichrist who will appear at the end of the interadvent age just before the second coming of Christ. This interpretation is also followed by amillenarians such as Keil and Leupold, as well as by Zöckler.[65]

A number of other interpretations, however, have been advanced. Montgomery believes that the reference is to Antiochus Epiphanes, in keeping with his interpretation that the prophecy was fulfilled in the second century B.C. He states, "The historical background of the sentence so interpreted is clear: the clever diplomacy whereby Ant. made his bargain with the worldly majority, at least of the aristocracy, in Jerusalem. It may be noted that the Jewish comm., Ra. [Rashi], Aez. [Aben Ezra], Jeph. [Jephet], do not hesitate to interpret the covenant as of the treaty between the Jews and the Romans."[66] Montgomery, accordingly, identifies the *he* of verse 25 as *the prince that shall come* of verse 26.

A second view is that *he* refers to Christ. This is supported by Young[67] and Philip Mauro. Mauro states, "If we take the pronoun 'He' as relating to 'the Messiah' mentioned in the preceding verse, then we find in the New Testament Scriptures a perfect fulfillment of the passage, and a fulfillment, moreover, which is set forth in the most conspicuous way. That pronoun *must*, in our opinion, be taken as referring to Christ, because (a) the prophecy is all about Christ, and this is the climax of it; (b) Titus did not make any covenant with the Jews; (c) there is not a word in Scripture about any future 'prince' making a covenant with them."[68]

Mauro, of course, begs the question, for this is the only passage on the seventy sevens of Israel. The question being debated is whether or not verse 27 deals with Christ; and to state dogmatically that "the prophecy is all about Christ" is precisely the matter in question. Nor is it unthinkable that a future ruler would make a covenant with Israel.

A third view has been suggested by Keil, who worded the sentence to read, "One week shall confirm the covenant to many."[69] Keil cites in support not only Theodotion, but Havernick, Hengstenberg, Auberlen, C. von Lengerke, and Hitzig. Keil states, "But this poetic mode of expression is only admissible where the subject treated of in the statement of the speaker comes after the action . . . The confirming of the covenant is not the work of time, but the deed of a definite person."[70] This translation does not seem to have found favor with contemporary expositors.

The difficulty with all these interpretations, as has been pointed out previously, is that there is no seven-year period marked off in any clear way in history which has fulfilled the last unit of seven of Daniel's prophecy. Those who identify *he* as Christ differ as to whether Christ actually confirmed the new covenant of Jeremiah 31:31-37 as Philip Mauro explains it,[71] or as Young interprets it, a reconfirmation of a covenant already in existence, "He shall cause to prevail a covenant for the many."[72]

Ultimately, the question facing every expositor is what interpretation gives the most natural and intelligent exposition of the text. If it is not necessary to consider this literal prophecy, and the time units are not literal, a variety of interpretation immediately becomes possible. If the expositor desires to follow the text meticulously, however, there is really no alternative but to declare the entire seventieth seven future, for there has been no seven-year period fulfilling the events of prophecy, however labored the interpretation. This is usually conceded by those who make the last seven years an indefinite period which allows for still future interpretation.

In summary, it may be concluded that Antiochus Epiphanes does not satisfy the passage for anyone who accepts it as Scripture. Christ does not satisfy the description of verse 27 because there is no seven-year period related to Christ which provides fulfillment for the entire passage. Under these circumstances, the normal antecedent of *he* is *the prince that shall come,* who is not to be identified with Titus but rather with a future enemy of the people of Israel who will bring them into the great tribulation anticipated as still future in the book of Revelation, which was written at least sixty years after the death of Christ and twenty years after the destruction of Jerusalem.

The precise prophecy of verse 27 indicates that the personage in view enters into a covenant relationship *with many,* literally, "with the many," (cf. *many,* literally, "the many," Dan 11:39; 12:2). This is a clear reference to unbelieving Jews who will enter into alliance with *the prince that shall come.* That they are Jews is indicated by *thy people* in verse 24. If the preceding chronology is understood to involve literal years, this should also be a seven-year period. In a word, the prophecy is that there will be a future compact or covenant between a political ruler designated as *the prince that shall come* in verse 26 with the representatives of the Jewish people. Such an alliance will obviously be an unholy relationship and ultimately to the detriment of the people of Israel, however promising it may be at its inception.

According to the prophecy, in the middle of the seven-year period the one who confirms the covenant "shall cause the sacrifice and oblation to cease," that is, all the bloody and non-bloody sacrifices. This could not refer to Jesus Christ at His death on the cross as Philip Mauro insists,[73] because, as a matter of fact, the sacrifices did not cease until A.D. 70, some forty years later. The sacrifices were not stopped by Christ but by the Roman soldiers who destroyed the temple. Contemplated in this prophecy is a yet future event following the type of the desecration of the temple by Antiochus Epiphanes but beginning the great tribulation of which Christ spoke in Matthew 24:15-26, obviously future from Christ's point of view, and, therefore, not the desecration by Antiochus in the second century B.C.

According to the prophecy of Christ, there will be a clear-cut event referred to as the abomination of desolation similar to the language of 9:27, which will occur in the period just preceding the second advent. Christ said, "When ye therefore shall see the abomination of desolation, spoken of by Daniel the prophet, stand in the holy place, (whoso readeth, let him understand:) then let them which be in Judea flee into the mountains: . . . For then shall be great tribulation, such as was not since the beginning of the world to this time, no, nor ever shall be" (Mt 24:15-16, 21). The fulfillment of this prophecy necessarily involves the reactivation of the Mosaic sacrificial system in a temple in Judea. The present occupation of Jerusalem by Israel may be a preparatory step to the re-establishment of the Mosaic system of sacrifices. Obviously, sacrifices cannot be stopped and a temple cannot be desecrated unless both are in operation.

The last part of verse 27 seems to describe the desecration of the temple in the words "for the overspreading of abominations he shall make it desolate, even until the consummation, and that determined shall be poured upon the desolate." The expression *the overspreading of abominations* is better translated "upon the wing of abominations," or as Leupold suggests, "upon the wing of abominable idols."[74] The Hebrew is rendered "abomination of desolation" in 1 Maccabees 1:54; Matthew 24:15; Mark 13:14 and is supported by the most ancient translations including the Septuagint, Theodotion, and the Vulgate. The identification of the expression in Daniel 9:27 with these other references as well as Daniel 11:31 and 12:11 make the meaning here clear. Many fantastic explanations have been given of the use of the word *wing*. Keil after Kliefoth takes the wing as reference " 'to idolatry with its abominations, because that shall be the power which lifts upward the destroyer and desolator, carries him, and moves with him over the earth to lay waste' (Klief.)."[75] Young gives a preferable view after disposing of many other suggestions when he states, "The word apparently refers to the pinnacle of the temple which has become so desecrated that it no longer can be regarded as the temple of the Lord, but as an idol temple. . . . The wing of the temple (Matt. 4:5; Luke 4:8) is the summit of the temple itself."[76]

The word *abomination* used by Christ in Matthew 24:15 may be an allusion to Antiochus in Daniel 11:31, but in Daniel 12:11, it clearly refers to the future stopping of the daily sacrifices, forty-two months before the second advent of Christ. The 1,290 days, actually forty-three months, seem to extend beyond the second advent to the beginning of the millennial kingdom. That which Antiochus did in a small way in the second century B.C. will become a worldwide persecution of Israel and a stopping of their sacrifices in the future great tribulation. According to Revelation 13, the future world ruler of the time of the great tribulation will not only take to himself absolute political power but will demand the worship of the entire world, will blaspheme the true God, and persecute the saints (Rev 13:4-7). His period of great power will terminate at the second advent of Christ. Like the desolation of Daniel 9:27, which is going to continue until the consummation, the desolation according to this passage will continue until the consummation pictured dramatically in Revelation 19 when the beast and the false prophet are cast into the lake of fire. This will be the terminus ad quem of the seventy sevens of Daniel and coincides with the second advent of Jesus Christ to the earth.

In summary, it may be concluded that Daniel's great prophecy of the seventy sevens comprehends the total history of Israel from the time of Nehemiah in 445 B.C. until the second coming of Jesus Christ. In the first period of seven sevens, the city and the streets are rebuilt. In the second period of sixty-two sevens which follows, the Messiah appears and is living at the conclusion of the period. In the parenthesis between the sixty-ninth seven and the seventieth seven, at least two major events take place: the cutting off of the Messiah (the death of Christ) and the destruction of Jerusalem in A.D. 70. Actually, the whole present age intervenes.

The final period of seven years begins with the introduction of a covenant relationship between the future "prince that shall come" and "the many," the people of Israel. This covenant is observed for the first half of the future seven-year period; then the special liberties and protections granted Israel are taken away; and Israel becomes persecuted in their time of great tribulation. The beginning of the last three and one-half years of the seventy sevens of Daniel is marked by the desecration of the future temple, the stopping of the sacrifices, and the desolation of the Jewish religion. It is this period referred to by Christ as the great tribulation in Matthew 24:15-26.

The culmination of the entire prophecy of the seventy weeks is the second advent of Jesus Christ which closes the seventieth seventh of Israel as well as the times of the Gentiles pictured in Daniel's prophecies of the four great world empires. For most of the period, the two great lines of prophecy relating to the Gentiles and Israel run concurrently, and both end with the same major event—the second advent of Jesus Christ, when oppressed Israel is delivered and the oppressor, the Gentile, is judged. With Israel today back in the land, the fulfillment of these prophecies may not be too long distant.

10

THE VISION OF THE GLORY OF GOD

THE FINAL THREE CHAPTERS of the book of Daniel record an extensive revelation of the prophetic future which is without parallel anywhere else in Scripture. As Leupold has expressed it, "There is hardly anything in the Bible that is just like these chapters, especially like chapter 11. The word, the vision, and minute prediction are combined in a manner that is found nowhere else in the Scriptures."[1] The entire content of chapter 10, for instance, is introductory, indicating the extensive character of the prophecy to follow. The introduction actually extends through the first verse of chapter 11. The next section, 11:2—12:4, is divided into two major divisions. The first, 11:2-35, deals with the immediate future, from Darius to Antiochus; and the second, 11:36—12:4, with the far future, the end times just before the second advent of Christ. A final message and revelation is given to Daniel in 12:5-13. The last three chapters constitute the fourth vision of Daniel which gathers together the significant threads of prophecy, especially as they relate to the Holy Land and to the people of Israel.

THE SETTING OF DANIEL'S FOURTH VISION

10:1 In the third year of Cyrus king of Persia a thing was revealed unto Daniel, whose name was called Belteshazzar; and the thing was true, but the time appointed was long: and he understood the thing, and had understanding of the vision.

Almost every detail of the first verse of this chapter has been subject to debate in commentaries. The date of the vision, "In the third year of Cyrus king of Persia" (536 B.C.), has been attacked as a discrepancy as compared with Daniel 1:21 where Daniel is said to have "continued even unto the first year of king Cyrus." As was noted in the exposition of chapter 1, Daniel 1:21 does not say that Daniel died or terminated his career in the first year of king Cyrus but that he continued until this important event which introduced the kingdom of the Medes and the Persians. Although the Septuagint changes the statement in Daniel 10:1 to "the first year," this is a needless harmonization.[2]

Critical objection has also been leveled at the expression *Cyrus king of*

Persia. Montgomery, with many liberal critics, holds, "The designation of Cyrus as 'king of Persia' was not contemporary usage; the Pers. king was entitled 'the king,' 'the great king,' 'king of kings,' or after his conquest of the Babylonian empire 'king of Babel,' 'king of the lands'; Dr. [Driver], *Int.*, 345 *f.* Cyrus was 'the Persian king' only later acc. to Hellenistic use."[3] Although scholars agree that Cyrus was not normally called by the simple designation "king of Persia" under ordinary circumstances until later, at least one contemporary usage of the term has been found.[4] And, after all, why should not Cyrus be called "king of Persia" even if it was not the ordinary way of referring to him? Young states flatly, "This designation of Cyrus was contemporary usage (despite M [Montgomery])."[5] After all, why should the scriptural designation have to conform precisely to ancient usage? The statement is quite clear and pinpoints the time of the vision.

It was in this third year of Cyrus king of Persia, late in Daniel's career, about seventy-two years after he had been carried away as a youth to Babylon, that "a thing," better translated, "a word," that is, a revelation, was revealed to Daniel. By way of identification, his Babylonian name Belteshazzar, is given, to make clear that he is the same Daniel who was so named by Nebuchadnezzar seventy years before.

The general nature of the revelation is described in the verses which follow. Daniel first affirms that the "thing" or word was true, as might be expected of a revelation from God. The second fact concerning the prophecy as translated in the King James Version is that "the time appointed was long." This exceedingly difficult expression has called for considerable comment. The Hebrew here, *sābā' gādôl*, has been variously translated "great warfare"[6] or "a great task"[7] or, more freely, "involved great suffering."[8] The implication is that the period in view is a long and strenuous one involving great conflict and trouble for the people of God.

In contrast to the previous visions, Daniel states that "he understood the thing, and had understanding of the vision." The previous visions had left questions in Daniel's mind which were not fully resolved, although he had faithfully recorded what he had seen and heard. It is doubtful whether Daniel completely understood all the vision which followed, but at least he comprehended its general characteristics and was not left in a state of perplexity, for instance, as indicated in Daniel 8:27 where he was physically sick as a result of the extensive vision given to him. The introductory statement is sufficient, however, to alert the reader that a tremendous revelation is about to be presented.

Daniel's Preparation for the Vision

10:2-3 In those days I Daniel was mourning three full weeks. I ate

no pleasant bread, neither came flesh nor wine in my mouth, neither did
I anoint myself at all, till three whole weeks were fulfilled.

In preparation for the great revelation to follow, Daniel spent three
weeks in mourning during which he did not eat the dainties of the king's
table, abstained from flesh and wine, and also did not anoint himself at
all. *Pleasant bread* is literally, "bread of pleasures, of desires," in contrast
to *bread of affliction* (Deu 16:3), that is, the unleavened bread which was
eaten during the Passover. During this period, Daniel apparently partook
of basic nourishment and water but followed a meager diet. What was
the occasion of this experience of self-inflicted fasting?

The duration of the period is obviously three weeks composed of days
in contrast to the seventy "weeks" of Daniel 9:24-27. Although Leupold
resists the idea that the Hebrew expression here, literally, "three weeks of
days," is used in contrast to Daniel 9, that may be precisely the point;
that is, Daniel wants to make clear that normal days are in view in this
prophecy. Practically everyone agrees that twenty-one days is the resulting sense.[9] In any case, the three weeks included the normal week for the
Passover season, as can be learned by comparison with Daniel 10:4: Passover occurred in the first month, the fourteenth day, and was followed by
seven days in which unleavened bread was eaten.

The occasion for Daniel's fasting probably was his concern for the pilgrims who had returned to Jerusalem two years before, anticipated in his
prayer in Daniel 9. As the book of Ezra makes plain, the children of
Israel had encountered great difficulty in getting settled in the land. Although the altar had been set up and the foundation of the temple laid
(Ezra 3), the work had been suspended because of opposition by the
people of the land (Ezra 4:1-5, 24). All of this was a great concern to
Daniel, for his primary purpose in encouraging the expedition had been
the restoration of the temple as well as the city of Jerusalem.

Humanly speaking, there was ground for anxiety. But Daniel did not
understand that the seventy years of the captivity which expired with the
return of the exiles in Ezra 1 did not fulfill the seventy years of the
desolation of Jerusalem and the temple. This required an additional
twenty years (the difference between 605 B.C., the first deportation of the
Jews, and 586 B.C., the date of the destruction of Jerusalem). From God's
point of view, things were moving exactly on schedule. In a sense, the
vision which followed was a reply to Daniel's questions concerning God's
purposes for the future of Israel in relation to the Gentiles. These purposes involved a far more extensive program than that fulfilled in the
book of Ezra and Nehemiah. While the saints of God may justly be concerned over what seems to be a defeat of God's purpose, the suffering
saint should never forget the majesty of the sovereignty of God which

ultimately proves "that all things work together for good to them that love God" (Ro 8:28). From the divine viewpoint, while we should pray, we should be delivered from anxiety—as Paul stated many years later (Phil 4:6-7). The period of fasting, however, constituted a divine preparation for the revelation. No doubt, abstinence from all but absolutely necessary food and drink, and the omission of anointing oil—indicative of his grief for the affliction of Israel (Amos 6:6; 2 Sa 14:2)—helped to ready Daniel for his great experience.

DANIEL'S GLORIOUS VISION OF GOD

10:4-6 And in the four and twentieth day of the first month, as I was by the side of the great river, which is Hiddekel; then I lifted up mine eyes, and looked, and behold a certain man clothed in linen, whose loins were girded with fine gold of Uphaz: his body also was like the beryl, and his face as the appearance of lightning; and his eyes as lamps of fire, and his arms and his feet like in colour to polished brass, and the voice of his words like the voice of a multitude.

According to verse 4, the time of the vision was the twenty-fourth day of the first month, that is, April or the month Abib (Ex 23:15), known later in the Old Testament as Nisan (Neh 2:1). Scripture does not reveal when the twenty-one days of mourning began, but it seems clear that they had concluded by the twenty-fourth day of the month. The new year was normally begun with a festival of two days celebrating the advent of the new moon (1 Sa 20:18-19, 34),[10] and it was of course unsuitable for him to fast while that joyous festival continued. Daniel probably had observed the Passover on the fourteenth day and the Feast of Unleavened Bread which followed from the fifteenth day to the twenty-first. If the vision came to Daniel immediately after his twenty-one days of mourning, his fast must have begun immediately after the new moon celebration, concluding just before the vision was given to him.

The place of the vision is declared to be "by the side of the great river, which is Hiddekel." Here we learn for the first time that Daniel did not accompany the pilgrims who returned to Jerusalem, although this is implied in the earlier verses of chapter 10. Liberal scholars attempt to turn this into an argument against the historicity of Daniel, assuming that he would automatically return to his native land as soon as permitted. As Young points out, however, if Daniel was merely a fictitious character, an ideal created by a writer in the Maccabean period, it would have been far more natural to have pictured him returning triumphantly to his native land. Young concludes, "The fact that Dan. does not return to Palestine is a strong argument against the view that the book is a product of the Maccabean age."[11] The obvious explanation of Daniel's failure to return is that he was quite old, probably eighty-five years of age, and, according to chapter 6, had been given a prominent place in the government and was not free to leave as were the others. Probably he could do Israel more good by remaining at his post than by accompanying them in the limitations of his age to Palestine.

The statement that the vision occurred by Hiddekel, or the river Tigris, has also been subject to criticism on two counts. First, the question has been raised whether this should be considered a literal and geographic statement or part of the vision. In Daniel 8, Daniel's vision "was by the river of Ulai," but the context makes plain that he is only there in vision not in reality. In chapter 10, however, the context and narrative makes plain that he is actually by the Tigris River, as the following verses relate how the men who were with him but did not see the vision fled. Liberal scholars like Montgomery, however, consider the reference to "the great river" a contradiction with the specification "Hiddekel" or the Tigris River, as the Euphrates River is normally called "the great river." Montgomery, accordingly, regards this "as an early gloss" in the text, with the only alternative that "otherwise we must attribute a solecism or gross error to the writer."[12] The Syriac version substitutes "Euphrates," for "Hiddekel." All of this, however, is quite arbitrary as there is no reason why the Tigris should not also be called a great river; and if that expression uniformly referred to the Euphrates, it would be all the more strange for a copyist to insert, "Hiddekel." Conservative scholars generally agree that the river is the Tigris.[13] The probability is that Daniel had come to this geographic area in connection with his duties as a chief administrator of the government. No great amount of travel need be assumed here because just above Babylon the Euphrates and Tigris are only about thirty-five miles apart.

In this situation, Daniel records that he had a vision of a glorious man. Daniel describes the man as clothed in linen, his loins girded with fine gold, his body having an appearance of beryl, or chrysolite. His face had the appearance of lightning, his eyes as flaming torches, his arms and feet like polished brass, and his voice sounded like the words of a multitude. All commentators agree that the personage was not a man, but either a glorious angel or a theophany, that is, an appearance of God Himself.

Leupold, after considerable discussion, concludes that the personage is a mighty angel on the fact that he requires the help of Michael, mentioned in verse 13, which would not be true of deity. If an angel, it may have been Gabriel, who appeared to Daniel in chapter 8. However, Leupold prefers to identify him with an unknown angel of equal stature with Michael.[14] Young notes that Hengstenberg identified him as Michael and that the Jews considered the figure an angel.[15]

Although there is room for debate even among conservative scholars, the evidence seems more in favor of considering this a theophany. In this case, the man of 10:5-6 is to be distinguished from the angel of 10:10-14 as well as Michael mentioned in 10:13. Although mighty angels are frequently difficult to distinguish from God Himself, as in other visions such as those in Ezekiel and Revelation, the similarity between the man described in 10:5-6 and the glorified Christ in Revelation 1:13-15 has led conservative expositors such as Young and Keil to consider the man a genuine theophany or an appearance of Christ as the Angel of Jehovah.[16]

The description of Daniel attributes to the man in the vision a glorious appearance. The linen was probably the fine white linen which characterized garments of the priests (cf. Ex 28:39-43). In other instances, linen forms the clothing of heavenly visitors (cf. Eze 9:2-3, 11; 10:2, 6-7). The angels at the tomb of Christ are described as having long white garments of brilliant character without specifying that they are linen (Mk 16:5; Lk 24:4; Jn 20:12; cf. Ac 1:10). The girdle was probably also linen embroidered with fine gold. The reference to the "fine gold of Uphaz," has only one other similar reference in the Bible (Jer 10:9), and it is not clear whether Uphaz is geographic or poetic. No clear identification has ever been made, although some have equated Uphaz with Ophir (Is 13:12) on the basis that this word is substituted for Uphaz in a Syriac version of Jeremiah 10:9.[17] It is sufficient to consider the girdle as being embroidered with fine gold of unusual quality.

The appearance of the body as a jewel called "beryl" from the Hebrew *tarshish* is translated "chrysolite" in the Septuagint and is considered by Driver as a topaz. He states, "the topaz of the moderns—a flashing stone, described by Pliny as 'a transparent stone with a refulgence like that of gold.' "[18] The same stone seems to be mentioned in Exodus 28:20 and Ezekiel 1:16; 10:9. It is called *tarshish* as if originating in Spain.[19] Porteous identifies it as the yellow jasper.[20] The impression given to Daniel was that the entire body of the man in the vision was like a gigantic transparent jewel reflecting the glory of the rest of the vision.

The description of the face illumined as it were by lightning, with eyes as flaming torches, is quite similar to the reference to Christ in Revelation 1:14-16. The polished brass of the arms and feet is similar to the "feet like unto fine brass" of Christ (Rev 1:15). And the lightning compares to the countenance of Christ likened to the sun in brilliance in Revelation 1:16, also to similar references in Ezekiel 1:13-14. Accompanying the visual image of glory was the mighty sound of the voice of a multitude, apparently not words which could be understood, but giving the impression of great power (cf. Rev 1:15). As Driver expresses it, "An impressive, but inarticulate, sound seems to be what the comparison is intended to suggest."[21] The total impression upon Daniel, described in the verses which follow, must have been tremendous and similar to that of John the apostle when he saw the glorified Christ (Rev 1:17).

EFFECT OF THE VISION ON DANIEL

10:7-9 And I Daniel alone saw the vision: for the men that were with me saw not the vision; but a great quaking fell upon them, so that they fled to hide themselves. Therefore I was left alone, and saw this great vision, and there remained no strength in me: for my comeliness was turned in me into corruption, and I retained no strength. Yet heard I the voice of his words: and when I heard the voice of his words, then was I in a deep sleep on my face, and my face toward the ground.

The vision which Daniel saw was apparent only to him and not to the men who accompanied him. The situation was somewhat similar to that of the men who accompanied Paul on the road to Damascus (Ac 9:7; 22:9), except that here the men saw and heard nothing but apparently sensed something which gave them great fear. When those who accompanied Daniel fled to hide themselves, Daniel was left alone as he states in verse 8. The failure of the men to see the vision, however, can hardly be attributed simply to their lack of spiritual perception as Leupold suggests.[22] Undoubtedly, Daniel alone of the group was spiritually qualified to receive a vision, but the choice of the recipient of the vision was made by divine will and those who accompanied Daniel were not allowed to see the vision which was intended for Daniel only.

The fact that the men did not see the vision and fled makes clear that this is an actual event which occurred near the Tigris River and that Daniel is not there merely in vision. Those who accompanied Daniel were not part of the vision itself, and their departure opened the way for Daniel's further experience alone.

The sight of the vision affected Daniel physically, robbing him of normal physical strength; and his normal appearance of health, described as "my comeliness," was affected in a way similar to the appearance of Christ in Isaiah 52:14, the Hebrew of *corruption* (Dan 10:8) and *marred* (Is 52:14) coming from the same root.

Although apparently rendered immobile by his lack of strength, Daniel was still able to hear "the voice of his words"; but this only increased his incapacity, and he fell in a swoon with his face toward the ground (cf. Ex 19:16-22). Daniel's experience illustrates the difficulty of mortal, sinful man, even a prophet like Daniel, of encountering the glory of God, in relation to which the holiest of men come short (Ro 3:23). It was in this posture of weakness and semiconsciousness that Daniel was to be strengthened to receive additional revelation.

DANIEL'S STRENGTH RESTORED BY AN ANGEL

10:10-11 And, behold, an hand touched me, which set me upon my knees and upon the palms of my hands. And he said unto me, O Daniel, a man greatly beloved, understand the words that I speak unto thee, and stand upright: for unto thee am I now sent. And when he had spoken this word unto me, I stood trembling.

In verse 10, Daniel records that in his extremity a hand touched him, raising him sufficiently so that now he was resting on his hands and knees. If the original vision was a theophany or an appearance of God, it is evident that this is another personage, probably an angel. It is said that the angel "set me upon my knees," literally translated, "shook me up upon my knees." The action was much like arousing one from sleep.

The angel addresses Daniel and gives him the title, "a man greatly beloved." Although God loves the entire world so much that He provided His Son as its Savior, certain individuals, because of their special relationship to God, are the objects of unusual divine love. David, in spite of his sins, was sought of the Lord as "a man after his own heart" (1 Sa 13:14; Ac 13:22); and John the apostle was "one of his disciples, whom Jesus loved" (Jn 13:23). As a parent loves all of his children but may love one or more in a special way, so the heart of God responds to those who love Him most.

The angel then exhorts Daniel to understand his message and to stand upright to receive it, for this was the purpose of the angel's coming to Daniel. Upon this exhortation, Daniel is able to stand upright although trembling. The message of the angel naturally tended to reassure Daniel that God's purpose in giving him the vision was gracious and loving, and Daniel had nothing to fear.

THE PURPOSE OF THE ANGEL'S VISIT

10:12-14 Then said he unto me, Fear not, Daniel: for from the first day that thou didst set thine heart to understand, and to chasten thyself before thy God, thy words were heard, and I am come for thy words. But the prince of the kingdom of Persia withstood me one and twenty days: but, lo, Michael, one of the chief princes, came to help me; and I remained there with the kings of Persia. Now I am come to make thee understand what shall befall thy people in the latter days: for yet the vision is for many days.

Daniel is further encouraged by the exhortation, "Fear not, Daniel." To allay the fears of Daniel still further, the angel informs him that from the very beginning of his intercession, three weeks before, God had undertaken to answer his prayers and send the angelic messenger to him. What a reassurance it is that when one comes to God as Daniel did, setting his heart to understand and chastening himself before God, one may expect Daniel's experience of the response of God that his words were heard and the messenger dispatched. The delay is explained in verse 13 as being occasioned by the opposition of "the prince of the kingdom of Persia" who "withstood me one and twenty days." This "prince" is not the king of the kingdom of Persia but rather the angelic leader of Persia, a fallen angel under the direction of Satan, in contrast to the angelic prince Michael who leads and protects Israel. That the angel described as "the prince" of Persia is a wicked angel is clear from the fact that his opposition to the angelic messenger to Daniel is given as the reason for the delay of twenty-one days.

All during the period of Daniel's fasting and prayer, a spiritual conflict was underway. This was resolved by the coming of Michael described as "one of the chief princes" (cf. Dan 10:21; 12:1; Jude 9; Rev 12:7). Michael seems to be the most powerful of the holy angels, and with his assistance the messenger to Daniel is released to fulfill his mission. The statement *I remained there with the kings of Persia* may be translated, "I was left there with the kings of Persia," meaning, that having been delivered from the prince of Persia, the angelic messenger was permitted to go on his way unattended.

Driver suggests that the phrase *and I remained there* actually means "I was superfluous there," inasmuch as Michael, who was more powerful, had relieved him. The Hebrew word translated "I remained" (*nôtartî*, from *yātar*) does not properly signify "to remain behind" but "to remain over, to be superfluous." Driver says of Daniel 10:13, "*I was left over there beside the kings* (i.e., I had nothing more to do)."[23]

Zöckler refutes Calvin and others who understand the conflict of the angel as being with an earthly king rather than an angelic being. Calvin says, "If we weigh these words too judiciously, we shall readily conclude, that the angel fought rather against the king of the Persians than for him."[24] Zöckler supports the idea that this is angelic warfare on the basis of the following considerations:

(1) in chap. xi.5, where [*sar*] is unquestionably employed in the latter sense, the connection is entirely different from the character of the present passage, where the [*hassārîm*] which immediately follows obviously denotes *angelic princes*; (2) the Persian kings, on the other hand, are termed [*malkê pārās*] at the end of the verse; (3) the idea of an angel's conflict with a *human* king seems very inappropriate; (4) the angel Michael was Israel's 'prince,' *i.e.*, guardian angel, according to v. 21; chap. xii.1; and corresponding to this, the prince of Persia who is here noticed, and the prince of Graecia mentioned in v. 20, were, without doubt, the *angels* of Persia and Javan respectively; (5) the idea of guardian angels over entire realms, whether friendly or hostile in their disposition toward the theocracy, is attested by various Old-Test. parallels, particularly by Isa. xxiv.21

. . .; Isa. xlvi.2; Jer. xlvi.25; xlix.3 (where the gods of the heathen nations take the place of the guardian angels); Deut. xxxii.8; and Psa. xcvi.4, lxx.; also Bar. iv.7 and Ecclus. xvii.17 . . .—to say nothing of New-Test. passages, such as I Cor. viii.5; x.20 et seq.[25]

Although the entire subject of the unseen struggle between the holy angels and the fallen angels is not clearly revealed in the Scriptures, from the rare glimpses which are afforded, as in this instance, it is plain that behind the political and social conditions of the world there is angelic influence—good on the part of the holy angels, evil on the part of the angels under satanic control. This is the struggle to which Paul referred in Ephesians 6:10-18.

Keil interprets the expression, "I remained there with the kings of Persia," as meaning that a victory of major character was won against the demonic forces which had previously controlled the kingdom of Persia, and the subsequent result was that the kingdom of Persia now would become the object of divine direction through angelic ministry. He understands the plural of "kings of Persia" to indicate all the kings of Persia which followed. Keil states, "The plural denotes, that by the subjugation of the demon of the Persian kingdom, his influence not merely over Cyrus, but over all the following kings of Persia, was brought to an end, so that the whole of the Persian kings became accessible to the influence of the spirit proceeding from God and in advancing the welfare of Israel."[26]

Leupold summarizes the correct interpretation in these words,

> Bad angels, called demons in the New Testament, are, without a doubt, referred to here. In the course of time, these demonic powers gained a very strong influence over certain nations and the government of these nations. They became the controlling power. They used whatever resources they could muster to hamper God's work and to thwart His purposes. . . . We get a rare glimpse behind the scene of world history. There are spiritual forces at work that are far in excess of what men who disregard revelation would suppose. They struggle behind the struggles that are written on the pages of history.[27]

The fact that the angelic messenger needed the help of Michael, however, refutes Young's interpretation that the speaker is the Angel of Jehovah or the Lord Himself.[28] While even an important angel might need the help of Michael, it is hardly acceptable that Christ in the Old Testament, prior to the incarnation, would need angelic help to gain a victory over a fallen angel. The circumstances seem to indicate that this must be an angel, not a theophany, and, therefore, be distinguished from the theophany of 10:5-6.

The angelic messenger now explains to Daniel that his purpose in coming is to make Daniel understand what would befall "thy people," that is, Israel, "in the latter days." The angel explains that much time is involved in the vision.

The expression *in the latter days* is an important chronological term related to the prophetic program which is unfolded in the book of Daniel. As previously considered in the exposition of Daniel 2:28, this phrase is seen to refer to the entire history of Israel beginning as early as the predictions of Jacob who declared to his sons "that which shall befall you in the last days" (Gen 49:1) and extending and climaxing in the second coming of Jesus Christ to the earth. The latter days view the entire history of Israel as culminating in the climax of the second advent and the establishment of the earthly kingdom.

Daniel's concern for his people, which probably occasioned his three weeks' fast and prayer, is now to be somewhat relieved by a specific revelation in addition to that already given in Daniel 9:24-27. The particulars of the vision include the experiences of Israel in the time of Antiochus Epiphanes and culminate in the great tribulation just before the second advent. Although Daniel probably did not understand the details, he could be reassured that God had a plan which ended in the ultimate victory of divine power. Although the prophecies made clear that there were powerful forces at work against Israel, which would inflict upon them much suffering and loss, in the end the power of God would triumph and Israel would be exalted as a nation.

DANIEL AGAIN STRENGTHENED BY THE ANGEL

10:15-17 And when he had spoken such words unto me, I set my face toward the ground, and I became dumb. And, behold, one like the similitude of the sons of men touched my lips: then I opened my mouth, and spake, and said unto him that stood before me, O my lord, by the vision my sorrows are turned upon me, and I have retained no strength. For how can the servant of this my lord talk with this my lord? for as for me, straightway there remained no strength in me, neither is there breath left in me.

Daniel's weakness once again overwhelms him. Speechless, he turns his face to the ground. Calvin, refuting the notion that Daniel here is repenting his prophetic office, states, "By becoming prostrate on the ground, he manifested his reverence, and by becoming dumb, displayed his astonishment."[29] Whether or not Daniel actually fell to the ground is not clearly stated in verse 15, but the effect may well be what Calvin intimates.

Once again Daniel experiences strengthening from God. Whether or not the personage described as "one like the similitude of the sons of men" is a theophany, that is, Christ as the Angel of Jehovah, or is another angel is not clear. Probably it is another angelic messenger. Upon being strengthened and having his ability to speak restored, Daniel again confesses his weakness and lack of strength. His sorrows, or pains, as well as his weakness had returned with the additional vision. Daniel goes on to explain that he has difficulty in talking because he lacks both strength and breath. Montgomery suggests that *breath* should be "spirit."[30] But Daniel's problem was physical rather than lack of spirit. All of this made it difficult for Daniel as expressed in his statement, "How can the servant of this my lord talk with this my lord?" As Charles interprets it, "The sense then is 'how can so mean a servant of my lord talk with so great a one as my lord?' "[31] Daniel was in great difficulty in carrying on normal conversation with the angelic messenger.

DANIEL STRENGTHENED FOR THE THIRD TIME

> **10:18-19** Then there came again and touched me one like the appearance of a man, and he strengthened me, and said, O man greatly beloved, fear not: peace be unto thee, be strong, yea, be strong. And when he had spoken unto me, I was strengthened, and said, Let my lord speak; for thou hast strengthened me.

For the third time in this chapter, Daniel is strengthened supernaturally by one who comes and touches him. Leupold believes that the same angel mentioned in verse 10 and following is the one who strengthens Daniel in each instance.[32] However, in view of the plurality of angelic ministry, there is no special reason why Daniel should not have the ministry of more than one angel. The description of verse 16, as well as the description of verse 18, would be unnecessary if only one angel was involved. The context of verses 18 and 19, however, seems to link this angel as the one who addressed Daniel in verses 11-12.

The angel again exhorts Daniel with the reassuring salutation, "O man greatly beloved," to not be afraid, to receive peace from God, and to be strong. Daniel was then strengthened and was able to say, "Let my lord speak; for thou hast strengthened me."

The detail given to this experience of Daniel leaves the impression that the revelation to follow must be of tremendous character, as indeed it is. The triple strengthening of Daniel in this agonizing experience has sometimes been compared to that of the Lord's temptation in the Garden of Gethsemane (Mt 26:39-44; Mk 14:35-41; Lk 22:39-44).[33] In both cases, an angel is the source of strength (Lk 22:43). This is the last time in this vision where Daniel requires additional strength to be administered by the angel.

THE ANGELIC REVELATION INTRODUCED

> **10:20-21** Then said he, Knowest thou wherefore I come unto thee? and now will I return to fight with the prince of Persia: and when I am

249

gone forth, lo, the prince of Grecia shall come. But I will show thee that which is noted in the scripture of truth: and there is none that holdeth with me in these things, but Michael your prince.

The stage now having been set for the great revelation to follow, the angel poses the question once again, "Knowest thou wherefore I come unto thee?" Critics have found fault with these concluding verses of chapter 10 as needlessly repetitious and confusing.[34] Montgomery is sure that the text here is faulty. Such criticism, however, does not take into consideration Daniel's weak and confused state. It would be quite natural after Daniel's experience of swooning and being unable to speak, now to consider the purpose of the angelic message. The angel reveals that he is obligated to return to "fight with the prince of Persia" and by implication, later with "the prince of Grecia." This also has been assailed as unnecessary, due to the previous victory; but the implication is that there is constant warfare in spiritual victory, and this would require the further attention of the angel. The mention of both Persia and Greece also directs our attention to the second and third major empires which are involved in the prophecies of Daniel 11:1-35. From this we can learn that, behind the many details of prophecy relating to the history of this period, there is the unseen struggle between angelic forces that the will of God may be accomplished.

An unusual phrase is found in verse 21, *the scripture of truth*. This term is literally "the writing of truth" (*ketāb 'ĕmet*), a reference to God's record of truth in general, of which the Bible is one expression. The facts to be revealed are already in God's record and are now to become part of the Holy Scriptures. The plan of God is obviously greater than that which is revealed in the Bible itself.

Verse 21 is introduced by "But" (*'ăbāl*) which is a strong adversative particle which serves to introduce the antidote to the fears for the theocracy cited in verse 20. The angelic conflict, great though it is, is subject to "the writing of truth," translated "the book of truth" in most modern English versions. Zöckler comments, "Properly, 'in a book of truth,' *i.e.*, in a Divine document upon which 'the yet unrevealed (Deut. xxxii. 34) fortunes of nations (Rev. v. 1) as well as of individuals (Psa. cxxxix. 60) in the future are entered' (Hitzig). Cf. the books of judgment in chap. vii. 10 and also the term [*'ĕmet*] in chap. xi. 2, which briefly comprehends the contents of the book of truth."[35]

Concerning the "writing of truth," Jeffrey notes, "In the Talmud (Rosh-ha-Shana 16 b) we read how on New Years Day the books were opened and fates recorded. These tablets in the book are frequently mentioned in Jubilees and the Testaments of the Twelve Patriarchs, and in the Prayer of Joseph preserved in Origen, *Philocalia* xxiii, 15 we read, 'For I have read in the tablets of heaven all that shall befall you and your sons.' "[36] The sovereignty of God reflected in His plan revealed in the Scriptures is Daniel's assurance in this hour of uncertainty and need. To this basis for faith, the angelic messenger refers.

In regard to the coming revelation and the spiritual struggle it records, the angelic messenger has been given unusual responsibility which is exceeded only by Michael, described as "your prince." Daniel in this way is reminded of the special angelic ministry which God had provided him all through life and especially in this present period of detailed divine revelation. The entire experience of Daniel in this chapter is on the one hand a reminder of human weakness and insufficiency, and on the other, of divine enablement which will strengthen Daniel for his responsible task of recording this great revelation. The fact that an entire chapter is devoted to this preparation makes clear that the revelation to follow is important in the consummation of God's purposes in the world.

11

WORLD HISTORY FROM DARIUS TO
THE TIME OF THE END

THE LONG INTRODUCTION of chapter 10 to the fourth and final vision given to Daniel is followed in chapter 11 by the revelation of important events beginning with Darius the Mede (539 B.C.) and extending to the last Gentile ruler in the time of the end. Chapter 11 naturally divides into two major sections. The first, verses 1-35, describes the major rulers of the Persian Empire and then gives in great detail some of the major events of the third empire following Alexander the Great, concluding with Antiochus Epiphanes (175-164 B.C.). The entire period from the death of Antiochus Epiphanes to the time of the end is skipped over with no reference to events of the present church age, and the second section, verses 36-45, deals with the last Gentile ruler who will be in power when Christ comes in His second advent. This is followed in chapter 12 by further prophecy of the last 1335 days, a period including the great tribulation, the second advent, and the beginning of the fifth or millennial kingdom. Probably no other portion of Scripture presents more minute prophecy than Daniel 11:1-35, and this has prompted the sharpest attack of critics seeking to discredit this prophetic portion.

Interestingly enough, it was the eleventh chapter of Daniel with its detailed prophecy of about two hundred years of history that prompted the heathen philosopher Porphyry (third century A.D.) to attack the book of Daniel as a forgery. In his study, Porphyry established the fact that history corresponded closely to the prophetic revelation of Daniel 11:1-35, and the correspondence was so precise that he was persuaded that no one could have prophesied these events in the future. Accordingly, he solved the problem by taking the position that the book of Daniel was written after the events occurred, that is, it was written in the second century B.C. This attack prompted Jerome to defend the book of Daniel and to issue his own commentary, which for over one thousand years thereafter was considered the standard commentary on the book of Daniel. As Wilbur Smith has said, "The most important single work produced by the Church Fathers on any of the prophetic writings of the Old Testament, com-

252

menting upon the original Hebrew text, and showing a complete mastery of all the literature of the Church on the subjects touched upon to the time of composition, is without question St. Jerome's Commentary on the Book of Daniel."[1]

The controversy between Jerome and Porphyry has characterized discussion of the book of Daniel ever since, as has been noted in earlier discussion. Here, however, the lines are clearly drawn as the prophecy is detailed and specific, and fulfillment has already occurred. Daniel 11:1-35 is either the most precise and accurate prophecy of the future, fully demonstrating its divine inspiration, or as Porphyry claimed, it is a dishonest attempt to present history as if prophesied centuries earlier. Modern critics of Daniel have not gone much beyond the basic premise of Porphyry, namely, that such detailed prophecy is impossible, and, therefore, absurd and incredible.[2]

Farrar, expressing the critics' point of view in a modern setting, introduces his chapter on Daniel 11 with this summary:

> If this chapter were indeed the utterance of a prophet in the Babylonian Exile, nearly four hundred years before the events—events of which many are of small comparative importance in the world's history—which are here so enigmatically and yet so minutely depicted, the revelation would be the most unique and perplexing in the whole Scriptures. It would represent a sudden and total departure from every method of God's providence and of God's manifestations of His will to the mind of the prophets. It would stand absolutely and abnormally alone as an abandonment of the limitations of all else which has ever been foretold.[3]

Leupold observes that Farrar's criticism was answered long before he made it by Hengstenberg and others who cite numerous passages in the Bible of detailed prophecy which at least support the idea that prophecy can be detailed and specific.[4]

A case in point is the whole subject of Messianic prophecy which predicted the coming of Christ with hundreds of details. The Median conquest of Babylon as a result of the drying up of the Euphrates River and the Babylonian drunken feast is anticipated in detail in Jeremiah 50-51 (note especially 50:38; 51:32, 36, 39, 57). Other illustrations include Isaiah 13:17-18; 21:1-10. In a similar way, prophecies concerning Syria, Phoenicia, Tyre, Gaza, Askelon, Ashdod, and the Philistines are given in Zechariah 9:1-8. Actually, however, proof texts are not needed, as the issue is a clear-cut question as to whether God is omniscient about the future. If He is, revelation may be just as detailed as God elects to make it; and detailed prophecy becomes no more difficult or incredible than broad predictions.

Keil attempts to mediate between the skeptic and the position that this is detailed prophecy by distinguishing between prediction of details and prophecy in general. Accordingly, he considers it unimportant whether the details of the prophecy precisely correspond to history as only the general fact that world kingdoms will not endure and in the end the people of God will be delivered constitutes the burden of this passage. Keil states,

> Accordingly, the revelation has this as its object, to show how the heathen world-kingdoms shall not attain to an enduring stability, and by their persecution of the people of God shall only accomplish their purification, and bring on the end, in which, through their destruction, the people of God shall be delivered from all oppression and be transfigured. In order to reveal this to him (that it must be carried forward to completion by severe tribulation), it was not necessary that he should receive a complete account of the different events which would take place in the heathen world-power in the course of time, nor have it especially made prominent that their enmity shall first come to a completed manifestation under the last king who should arise out of the fourth world-kingdom.[5]

In making this concession to the critics, Keil concedes far more than the record requires. If the text is properly interpreted, the alleged historical errors fade; and Daniel's record stands accurate and complete, although not without problems of interpretation such as are true in any prophetic utterance. The expositor of this portion of Scripture has no convenient compromise between the two diverse views. Either this is genuine prophecy or it is not. The fact that it corresponds so closely to history should be, instead of a basis for criticism, a marvelous confirmation that prophecy properly understood is just as accurate as history. As has been previously pointed out, the attack on the prophecies of Daniel always fall short. The fulfillment of the complete revelation anticipates a situation yet future and could not be considered history even from the point of view of an alleged second-century Daniel.

In attempting the difficult exegesis of this portion, the general principle should be observed that prophecy, as far as it goes, is accurate, but that prophecy is selective. The revelation does not contain all the history of the period nor name all the rulers. It is not always possible to determine why some facts are included and others excluded. But the total picture of struggle and turmoil which characterized the period of the third empire is portrayed by special reference to Antiochus Epiphanes, who is given more space than any other ruler in this chapter because of the relevance of his activities to the people of Israel.

FOUR IMPORTANT KINGS OF MEDO-PERSIA

11:1-2 Also I in the first year of Darius the Mede, even I, stood to confirm and to strengthen him. And now will I show thee the truth.

254

> Behold, there shall stand up yet three kings in Persia; and the fourth
> shall be far richer than they all: and by his strength through his riches he
> shall stir up all against the realm of Grecia.

The opening verse of chapter 11 is often considered the closing verse
of chapter 10. In it, the angel, seen in 10:18, declares his support to confirm and strengthen Darius the Mede from the very beginning of his
reign in Babylon. The statement that the angel "stood" in verse 1 is
probably used in *sensu bellico s. militari*, that is, standing as in a military
conflict against the enemy, as in 10:13. His stand is usually taken as
being in support of Darius the Mede, "to confirm and strengthen him,"
but it is possible that "him" refers not to Darius the Mede—for the angel
must fight *against* the prince of Persia (10:13)—but to Michael, the prince
of Israel, on whose side he contends (10:21). In the first year of Darius
the Mede when the world power passed from the Babylonian to the Medo-
Persian, the angel stood by Michael, the guardian of Israel, until he
succeeded in turning the new kingdom from hostility to favor toward
Israel. The story of chapter 6 demonstrates that efforts were made in the
first year of Darius to make him hostile toward Israel. But God sent His
angel on that occasion and shut the lions' mouths (Dan 6:22). The
miraculous deliverance by the angel caused Darius the Mede to reverse
his policies to favor Israel (6:24-27). The beginning of the second great
empire with the fall of Babylon in chapter 5 was, then, more than a
military conquest or triumph of the armies of the Medes and Persians.
It was a new chapter in the divine drama of angelic warfare behind the
scenes, and the change was by divine appointment.

The survey of history provided in the opening verses of chapter 11
fixes the prophecy as dealing with a period later than Nebuchadnezzar's
dream but coinciding with the prophecy of chapter 8 of the ram and he
goat. Porteous expresses it this way:

> The survey of history begins at a slightly later point than in Nebuchad-
> nezzar's dream (ch. 2) and in Daniel's vision of the beasts (ch. 7), but
> at the same point as in Daniel's vision of the ram and the he-goat (ch.
> 8). In fact, we are now given the amplification in detail of that vision,
> the various kings appearing *in propria persona* and no longer disguised
> as horns of heraldic beasts. Like Macbeth in the witches' cave, Daniel
> is supposedly permitted to see king after king appearing on the stage of
> history, strutting out his part and making way for his successor.[6]

With the passing of the Babylonian Empire, the natural question arose
concerning the future of the Medo-Persian Empire. Concerning this, the
angel announces, "And now will I show thee the truth," that is, the truth
of what will come to pass in the future (cf. "the scripture of truth,"
10:21). Daniel is informed that there will be three kings in Persia to be

followed by a fourth far richer and greater than the others, who shall use his strength and riches to "stir up all against the realm of Grecia." The identity of these four kings has, of course, been disputed; and Montgomery uses the many different combinations and explanations as an evidence of the incredibility of this prophecy.[7]

The most natural explanation, however, is that the four kings are the first four Persian rulers in addition to Darius the Mede, the point being that later Persian rulers were unimportant and in a state of decline. Assuming that all four kings are still future, Darius the Mede and Cyrus, known as Cyrus II (550-530 B.C.), are probably excluded. Note that the prophecy states, "Behold, there shall stand up yet three kings in Persia" or, as the New Berkeley Version translates, "three more kings shall arise in Persia," that is, in the future. The prophecy came to Daniel in the third year of Cyrus (10:1). The four kings would then be Cambyses (529-522 B.C., not mentioned in the Old Testament), Pseudo-Smerdis (522-521 B.C.), Darius I Hystaspes (521-486 B.C., Ezra 5, 6), and Xerxes I (486-465 B.C., Ezra 4:6). This identification has the advantage of taking Persian kings in order, climaxing with Xerxes I who led the great expedition against Greece. Xerxes represents, on the one hand, the acme in the development of Persian power, and, on the other hand, the beginning of its dissolution. Another conservative interpretation eliminates Pseudo-Smerdis, who reigned only briefly, and adds after Xerxes I, Artaxerxes I (465-424 B.C., Ezra 7:11-26) as the fourth ruler. However, according to the prophecy, the fourth ruler is the one who contends against Greece, which was not true of Artaxerxes I.

According to Daniel, the climax of Persian rulers came with Xerxes I who in secular history used his great riches and a period of some four years to gather a great army amounting to hundreds of thousands, one of the largest armies in the ancient world. The expedition which he launched in 480 B.C. against Greece was disastrous, however, and Xerxes never recovered. The Ahasuerus of Esther 1 may be identified with Xerxes I, and the ill-fated expedition against Greece may have occurred between chapters 1 and 2 of Esther. Details on the Persian Empire are not given here because these are covered adequately in the books of Ezra, Nehemiah, and Esther, insofar as they related to the people of Israel and the plan of God, and these records are supplemented by the prophetical books Haggai, Zechariah, and Malachi. The revelation turns immediately to details of the third empire not given elsewhere in the Word of God.

The Rise and Fall of Alexander the Great

11:3-4 And a mighty king shall stand up, that shall rule with great dominion, and do according to his will. And when he shall stand up, his kingdom shall be broken, and shall be divided toward the four winds of heaven; and not to his posterity, nor according to his dominion which he ruled: for his kingdom shall be plucked up, even for others beside those.

One of the by-products of the attack on Greece by Xerxes I is that he incurred the undying hatred of Greece. Montgomery and some critics believe this is the ultimate meaning of "he shall stir up all" in verse 2. Montgomery translates it, " 'and he will stir up all, namely (?) the kingdom of Greece,' " and comments, "But the point is not that he made war against Greece (as far as Asia was concerned, Persia remained mistress, *n.b.*, the Peace of Callias 449 B.C.), but rather that the world was aroused against the king."[8] Although there may be question whether this translation is justified, the facts are that Alexander the Great in conquering the Persian Empire was repaying Xerxes I. Alexander the Great was indeed "a mighty king" which Leupold translates "a hero-king"[9] and the remaining description fits Alexander the Great perfectly. He indeed had great dominion and was absolute ruler who did "according to his will."

As previously revealed, in Daniel 8:8, Alexander died prematurely. The expression in verse 4, *when he shall stand up*, may be translated "while he was growing strong," that is, while still ascending in power. Another rendering, perhaps more normal Hebrew, is "and as soon as he shall have stood up," indicating the brief duration of Alexander's reign. The word *stood* has the same military connotation as in the preceding verses.

The angel predicts to Daniel that his kingdom shall be broken and divided to the four winds of heaven. This was fulfilled literally in that his kingdom was shattered after his death and not only divided to the four winds, but divided among his four generals. Alexander's empire was not given to his posterity. Hercules, the son of Alexander at the time of his death, whose mother was Barsina, was murdered by Polysperchon. Young Alexander, born posthumously of Roxana, was murdered in 310 B.C. The empire of Alexander the Great, after it fell into the hands of his four generals, did not preserve the glory and power it had in Alexander's day. The strong central rule which had characterized it passed with the death of Alexander. This event, recorded in Daniel's prophecy written about 539 B.C., was fulfilled when Alexander died in 323 B.C.

PTOLEMY I SOTER AND SELEUCUS I NICATOR

11:5 And the king of the south shall be strong, and one of his princes; and he shall be strong above him, and have dominion; his dominion shall be a great dominion.

Beginning in verse 5, the struggle between the various kings of the south, that is Egypt, and the kings of the north, that is Syria, begin and are traced by Daniel in this prophecy to the time of Antiochus IV Epiph-

257

anes (175-164 B.C.), a period of about 150 years. In verse 8, the king of the south is identified as Egypt, and the Septuagint translates *south* as "Egypt" throughout this passage. Syria is not mentioned by name, as at the time of Daniel's writing, no such nation existed and such a reference would be confusing. In tracing the struggles between Egypt and Syria, the prophecy is selective and not all the rulers are mentioned, but usually the identification is clear.

The king of the south in verse 5 is probably Ptolemy I Soter (323-285 B.C.). The one referred to as "he shall be strong above him" is the king of Syria, Seleucus I Nicator (312-281 B.C.). These rulers took the title of king in 306 B.C. Seleucus had fled from Antigonus of Babylon and was temporarily associated with Ptolemy I. They combined their strength and defeated Antigonus, thus paving the way for Seleucus to gain control of the entire area from Asia Minor to India; and in time, he became stronger than Ptolemy who ruled Egypt. Hence the Scripture says that Seleucus "shall be strong above him [Ptolemy] and have dominion; his dominion shall be a great dominion." This is qualified by the statement in the preceding verse, "not according to his dominion which he ruled." The emergence of Ptolemy as ruler of Egypt and Seleucus as ruler of Syria and surrounding territory laid the basis for these two lines of rulers in their respective countries and also set up a situation where they became rivals. The king of the south was also strong, as verse 5 indicates. The expression *one of his princes* probably refers to Seleucus described in the clause which follows. A possible translation is "and one of his princes shall be stronger than he."[10]

MARRIAGE OF THE DAUGHTER OF EGYPT TO THE KING OF SYRIA

11:6 And in the end of years they shall join themselves together; for the king's daughter of the south shall come to the king of the north to make an agreement: but she shall not retain the power of the arm; neither shall he stand, nor his arm: but she shall be given up, and they that brought her, and he that begat her, and he that strengthened her in these times.

The expression *in the end of years* means "after a lapse of several years" (cf. 2 Ch 18:2; Dan 11:8, 13). In the passage of time, it was natural that there would be intermarriage for political reasons between Egypt and Syria, and such is pictured in verse 6. The participants were the king of the south, Ptolemy II Philadelphus (285-246 B.C.) and his daughter, Berenice, who was married to Antiochus II Theos (261-246 B.C.) about 252 B.C. Passed over without mention is Antiochus I Soter (281-261 B.C.). The marriage was consummated at the demand of Ptolemy Philadelphus who required Antiochus to divorce his own wife, Laodiceia (or Laodice), in order to facilitate this marriage. His intent was to provide a basis of agreement, literally, "to make a straightening" between the two nations. As verse 6 indicates, however, the union was not successful in that "she shall not retain the power of the arm," that is, physical or political power, and neither of the male participants prospered. As it was indicated: "neither shall he stand, nor his arm; but she shall be given up, and they that brought her, and he that begat her, and he that strengthened her in these times." "He that strengthened her," means, "he that obtained her in marriage." Within a few years of the marriage, Ptolemy died; and Antiochus then took back his wife, Laodiceia. To gain revenge, however, Laodiceia murdered her husband as well as his Egyptian wife, Berenice, and the infant son of Antiochus and Berenice. The reference to "he that begat her" is, of course, to Ptolemy II whose death precipitated the murders which followed.

PTOLEMY EUERGETES AND SELEUCUS CALLINICUS

11:7-9 But out of a branch of her roots shall one stand up in his estate, which shall come with an army, and shall enter into the fortress of the king of the north, and shall deal against them, and shall prevail: and shall also carry captives into Egypt their gods, with their princes, and with their precious vessels of silver and of gold; and he shall continue more years than the king of the north. So the king of the south shall come into his kingdom, and shall return into his own land.

Subsequent to the events of verse 6, a new king of Egypt known as Ptolemy III Euergetes (246-221 B.C.) succeeded in prevailing militarily over the king of the north, Seleucus Callinicus (247-226 B.C.); and, as the prophecy indicates, he entered "into the fortress of the king of the north," carried into Egypt princes as hostages, some of their idols, and their precious vessels of silver and gold. The expression *out of a branch of her roots*, literally, "the sprouting of her roots," signifies lineage, the immediate ancestry of Berenice. The person referred to is consequently the son of her parents, her own brother, Ptolemy III Euergetes, the successor of Ptolemy Philadelphus.

The Hebrew word translated "princes" (11:8) can be rendered "molten images," and the transportation of the idols indicates the total subjugation of the northern kingdom (cf. Is 46:1-2; Jer 48:7; 49:3; Hos 10:5).[11] In commemoration of his deed, Ptolemy Euergetes erected the monument *Marmor Adulitanum*, which boasts that he subjugated Mesopotamia, Persia, Susiana, Media, and all the countries as far as Bactria. The expression *shall continue more years than the king of the north* is best understood as meaning, "he shall refrain some years from the king of the north" (ASV), that is, "refrain from attacking the king of the north" (RSV).

Verse nine is probably better rendered "And he shall come into the realm of the king of the south, but he shall return into his own land" (ASV, also RSV). The actor is the king of the north, just mentioned in the previous verse, rather than the king of the south.

Jerome, in his commentary, provides this description of the conquest by Ptolemy Euergetes:

> He came up with a great army and advanced into the province of the king of the North, that is Seleucus Callinicus, who together with his mother Laodice was ruling in Syria, and abused them, and not only did he seize Syria, but also took Cilicia and the remoter regions beyond the Euphrates and nearly all of Asia as well. And then, when he heard that a rebellion was afoot in Egypt, he ravaged the kingdom of Seleucus and carried off as booty forty thousand talents of silver, and also precious vessels and images of the gods to the amount of two and a half thousand. Among them were the same images which Cambyses had brought to Persia at the time when he conquered Egypt. The Egyptian people were indeed devoted to idolatry, for when he had brought back their gods to them after so many years, they called him Euergetes (Benefactor). And he himself retained possession of Syria, but he handed over Cilicia to his friend, Antiochus, that he might govern it, and the provinces beyond the Euphrates he handed over to Xanthippus, another general.[12]

The precise accuracy of the prophecy written by Daniel three hundred years before it happened has occasioned the attack of the critics, but actually its accuracy is a support for the accuracy of scriptural prophecy as a whole.

Verse 9 as translated in the King James Version seems to imply that the king of the south returns to his own land. A better translation, however, would indicate that he, Seleucus Callinicus, is the subject of the verb *shall come into his kingdom* and refers to the fact that Seleucus several years after the Egyptian invasion was able to mount a return attack on Egypt about 240 B.C. Seleucus, however, was defeated completely and was forced to "return into his own land."[13] This, of course, was only the beginning of the seesaw battle between the two nations. The inclusion of this background material leads up to the important point, which is the burden of the prophecy in verses 10-19—the ascendancy of Syria over Egypt and the return of the Holy Land to Syrian control. This set the stage for the persecutions of Israel under Antiochus Epiphanes, which is the major concern of verses 21-35 of this prophecy.

THE STRUGGLE BETWEEN SELEUCUS AND ANTIOCHUS III THE GREAT AGAINST PTOLEMY PHILOPATOR

11:10-19 But his sons shall be stirred up, and shall assemble a multitude of great forces: and one shall certainly come, and overflow, and pass through: then shall he return, and be stirred up, even to his fortress.

And the king of the south shall be moved with choler, and shall come forth and fight with him, even with the king of the north: and he shall set forth a great multitude; but the multitude shall be given into his hand. And when he hath taken away the multitude, his heart shall be lifted up; and he shall cast down many ten thousands: but he shall not be strengthened by it. For the king of the north shall return, and shall set forth a multitude greater than the former, and shall certainly come after certain years with a great army and with much riches. And in those times there shall many stand up against the king of the south: also the robbers of thy people shall exalt themselves to establish the vision; but they shall fall. So the king of the north shall come, and cast up a mount, and take the most fenced cities: and the arms of the south shall not withstand, neither his chosen people, neither shall there be any strength to withstand. But he that cometh against him shall do according to his own will, and none shall stand before him: and he shall stand in the glorious land, which by his hand shall be consumed. He shall also set his face to enter with the strength of his whole kingdom, and upright ones with him; thus shall he do: and he shall give him the daughter of women, corrupting her: but she shall not stand on his side, neither be for him. After this shall he turn his face unto the isles, and shall take many: but a prince for his own behalf shall cause the reproach offered by him to cease; without his own reproach he shall cause it to turn upon him. Then he shall turn his face toward the fort of his own land: but he shall stumble and fall, and not be found.

Although Seleucus Callinicus was unsuccessful in his attack on Egypt, his successors described as "his sons" proved to be more successful. Seleucus III (226-223 B.C.) came to an untimely end, having perished in battle in Asia Minor, but the task was ably carried on by Antiochus III the Great (223-187 B.C.). Because of the passing of Seleucus, the plural of the first part of verse 10 is changed to the singular. Antiochus the Great was able to mount several campaigns against Egypt; and largely because of the indolence of the Egyptian ruler, Ptolemy Philopator (221-203 B.C.), he restored to Syria the territory as far south as Gaza.

The approach of the armies this near Egypt proper aroused the Egyptian ruler, who assembled a large army to combat Antiochus (11:11). In 217 B.C., Antiochus met the Egyptian army at the Palestinian border at Raphia. The Egyptian army was directed by Ptolemy accompanied by his sister-wife, Arsinoe.[14] There were about 70,000 soldiers on each side. The battle resulted in a complete victory for Egypt (11:11-12); and as Jerome comments, "Antiochus lost his entire army and was almost captured as he fled to the desert."[15] The prophecy was fulfilled that the multitude of the Syrians was given into the hand of the Egyptians. However, a peace had to be arranged because Antiochus had managed to escape. As verse 12 indicates, the Egyptian monarch was too indolent to pursue his advantage; and although the battle was disastrous for the

Syrians, it tended to bring peace between the two nations, at least temporarily.[16]

Meanwhile, Antiochus turned his attention to conquests in the east, in which he was quite successful, gathering strength and wealth. In the period 212-204 B.C. he advanced east to the borders of India and as far north as the Caspian. Ptolemy Philopator and his queen died mysteriously in 203 B.C. and were succeeded by their infant son, Ptolemy V Epiphanes.

In 201 B.C., Antiochus managed to assemble another great army and again began a series of attacks on Egypt, as described in verse 13-16. The expression *the robbers of thy people* (11:14) refers to persons who violate law and justice; hence, they are "robbers," or "men of violence" (RSV). As Zöckler says, "The oracle refers to the league against Egypt, into which a large number of Jews entered with Antiochus the Great, and to their participation in his warlike operations against that country, e.g., in his attacks on the garrison which the Egyptian general Scopas had left in the citadel of Jerusalem."[17] Zöckler comments: "The theocratic writer sternly condemns this partial revolt to the Syrians as a criminal course or as common robbery, because of the many benefits conferred on the Jewish state by the earlier Ptolemies."[18]

The reference *to establish the vision* is probably a prophecy of the afflictions of the Jews under Antiochus Epiphanes already recorded in Daniel 8 and 9. These troubles appropriately can be regarded as a consequence of the revolt of the Egyptians against Syria. Encouraged by the rising power of Rome which threatened Syria, Egypt fought back. The Egyptian armies led by Scopas were defeated at Paneas, near the headwaters of the Jordan River. Antiochus III subsequently forced Scopas to surrender at Sidon, referred to as "the most fenced cities," literally "a city of fortifications," which the Seleucid king captured in 199-198 B.C. This victory resulted in the Syrian occupation of all Palestine as far south as Gaza. The allusion to "the arms at the south shall not stand" is to the unsuccessful attempt by three Egyptian leaders, Eropas, Menacles, and Damoyenus to rescue the besieged Scopas from Sidon. Threatened by Rome, however, Antiochus effected a diplomatic settlement with Egypt by marrying his daughter Cleopatra to the young king, Ptolemy V Epiphanes in 192 B.C. In so doing, he fulfilled the prophecy "he shall give him the daughter of women, corrupting her: but she shall not stand on his side, neither be for him." The expression *corrupting her* may mean "to ruin the land,"[19] that is, Antiochus the Great purposed by this betrothal of his young daughter to the seven-year old Ptolemy to ruin his former opponent and present ally. As Young states, "In this stratagem, however, Antiochus fails, because Cleopatra constantly sides with her husband over against her father."[20]

In this series of events, the prophecies of verses 13-17 are accurately fulfilled. Antiochus the Great begins to suffer reverses, however, as indicated in verse 18, where "prince for his own behalf" refers to the Roman consul Lucius Scipio Asiaticus, who, as Young expresses it, "brought about the defeat of Antiochus."[21] The reference to "the reproach offered by him," refers to Antiochus' scornful treatment of the Roman ambassadors at a meeting in Lysimachia, when he said contemptuously, "Asia did not concern them, the Romans, and he was not subject to their orders."[22]

This defeat came about in the following manner. Having successfully sustained his conquest against Egypt by defeating Scopas, Antiochus then turned his attention to the threat from the west and attempted to equal the conquests of Alexander the Great by conquering Greece. In this he was notably unsuccessful, being defeated in 191 B.C. at Thermopylae north of Athens and again in 189 B.C. at Magnesia on the Maeander River southeast of Ephesus by soldiers of Rome and Pergamum under the leadership of the Roman general Scipio. This fulfilled the prophecies of verses 18 and 19, and from an historic viewpoint, was important in removing from Europe the control by Asiatic governments. This paved the way for Roman expansion later.[23]

Antiochus the Great, who could have gone down in history as one of the great conquerors of the ancient world if he had been content to leave Greece alone, instead fulfilled the prophecy of verse 19 in that he had to return to his own land, defeated and broken. He was killed trying to plunder a temple in Elam. From the standpoint of the history of Israel, this was important because Antiochus the Great was followed by Seleucus IV Philopator (187-175 B.C.), who in turn was succeeded by Antiochus IV Epiphanes (175-164 B.C.), the notorious persecutor of the Jews described in detail in Daniel 11:21-35. In these prophecies, properly interpreted, is an accurate prophetic picture of this period, which would be remarkable even if it was history. As prophecy, it bears the unmistakable imprint of divine inspiration.

SELEUCUS PHILOPATOR, THE RAISER OF TAXES

11:20 Then shall stand up in his estate a raiser of taxes in the glory of the kingdom: but within few days he shall be destroyed, neither in anger, nor in battle.

The Seleucid king ruling between the times of Antiochus the Great and Antiochus Epiphanes, Seleucus IV Philopator, is mentioned here for his oppression by taxation of the people of Israel. Because of the rising power of Rome, he was forced to pay tribute to the Romans of a thousand talents annually.[24] In order to raise this large amount of money, Seleucus had to tax all the lands under his domain, including special taxes from the Jews secured by a tax collector named Heliodorus (2 Mac 3:7) who took treasures from the temple at Jerusalem.[25] As Zöckler points out, "Soon after Heliodorus was dispatched to plunder the temple, Seleucus Philopator was suddenly and mysteriously removed. This explains the statement, 'within a few days he shall be destroyed' (11:20), possibly by poison administered to him by the same Heliodorus."[26] This set the stage for the terrible persecutions by Antiochus Epiphanes which followed.

THE RISE OF ANTIOCHUS IV EPIPHANES

11:21-23 And in his estate shall stand up a vile person, to whom they shall not give the honour of the kingdom: but he shall come in peaceably, and obtain the kingdom by flatteries. And with the arms of a flood shall they be overflown from before him, and shall be broken; yea, also the prince of the covenant. And after the league made with him he shall work deceitfully: for he shall come up, and shall become strong with a small people.

Beginning with verse 21, a major section of this chapter is devoted to a comparatively obscure Syrian ruler who was on the throne from 175 to 164 B.C., previously alluded to as the "little horn" (Dan 8:9-14, 23-25). He reigned in the days of the decline of the Syrian power and the rise of Rome to the west, and only his death in 164 B.C. prevented his humiliation by Rome. From the standpoint of Scripture and the revelation by the angel to Daniel, this was the most important feature of the entire third empire. The reasons for the prominence of Antiochus IV Epiphanes were his desecration of the Jewish temple and altar, and his bitter persecution of the Jewish people. As is true of the entire section beginning with chapter 8, Gentile dominion is viewed primarily from its relationship to the progress of the Jewish nation. By comparison with Seleucus IV Philopator, his predecessor, he is described as "a vile person." The title Epiphanes, meaning "glorious," was a title which Antiochus gave himself, in keeping with his desire to be regarded as god. The description here given is God's viewpoint of him because of his immoral life, persecution, and hatred of the people of God. His life was characterized by intrigue, expediency, and lust for power in which honor was always secondary.

The expression *to whom they shall not give the honour of the kingdom* has reference to the fact that he seized the throne rather than obtaining it honorably. At the time his predecessor died, there were several possible candidates for the throne. Probably the most legitimate ruler would have been Demetrius, the young son of his brother Seleucus IV, who at the time was being held in Rome as a hostage by the Romans. There was also a younger son of Seleucus IV, also by name of Antiochus, who was still a baby in Syria. Antiochus IV, the brother of Seleucus IV, was in

Athens at the time of his brother's death. There he received word that his brother Seleucus had been murdered by Heliodorus, as prophesied in Daniel 11:20, "he shall be destroyed, neither in anger, nor in battle." Montgomery describes this as dying " 'with his boots on,' a disgrace to a king; *cf.* Saul's death."²⁷

Posing as the guardian of young Antiochus who was in Syria, Antiochus IV Epiphanes proceeded to Antioch where by various intrigues, referred to in verse 21 as "he shall come in peaceably, and obtain the kingdom by flatteries," he secured the throne. Meanwhile, young Antiochus was murdered by Andronicus, whom Antiochus IV then put to death, although it is possible that Antiochus himself had laid the whole plot. Heliodorus, who had murdered Seleucus IV, was not able to secure the throne and disappeared. Antiochus IV was therefore secure on his throne and began an active life of military conquest and intrigue in his struggle for power against both Egypt and Rome.

Verse 22 speaks of military activity including several campaigns against Egypt. The prophecy does not attempt to be specific but describes in general how armies on various occasions were destroyed as by a flood and "shall be broken." The reference to "the arms of a flood" may refer to military forces rather than a natural flood.° In other words, he shall be victorious over his enemies. The forces which he overwhelmed include, as Zöckler states, "in part the troops of Heliodorus, whom Antiochus routed with the assistance of his Pergamenian allies, and in part the Egyptian forces which sought to deprive him of Coele-Syria soon after his accession to the throne."†²⁸ When Antiochus learned that the Egyptians were about to attack him, he invaded Egypt in 170 b.c. and defeated the Egyptians in a battle which occurred between Mt. Casius and Pelusium, an area on the southeast sea coast of the Mediterranean Sea halfway between Gaza and the Nile delta.²⁹ The battle area is today called Ras Baron.

The reference to the "prince of the covenant" prophesies the murder of the high priest Onias, which was ordered by Antiochus in 172 b.c., and indicates the troublesome times of his reign. The high priest bore the title "prince of the covenant" because he was de facto the head of the theocracy at that time. In 11:28 and 11:32 the "covenant" is used for the Jewish state.

°ASV, "And the overwhelming forces shall be overwhelmed from before him." RSV, "Armies shall be utterly swept away before him."

†In support of this Zöckler quotes Hitzig as follows, "For after the death of Cleopatra (v. 17), Eulaus and Lenaeus, the guardians of her son, Ptolemy Philometor, demanded the cession of Coele-Syria, the dowry which had hitherto been refused (Polyb. XXVIII. 1; Diodor., *Leg.* 18, p. 624 Wess.; Livy, XLII. 49). Antiochus, on the other hand, would not acknowledge that his father had promised such a dowry (Polyb., XXVIII. 17), and therefore refused to grant it" (F. Hitzig, *Kurzgefasstes exeget.* Handbuch zum A. T.; 10th pamphlet, *Das Buch Daniel,* Leipsig, 1850).

Verse 23 described his various leagues with other nations, especially with Egypt which involved considerable intrigue and deceit. At the time, there was a contest for power between two of Antiochus' nephews, Ptolemy Philometor and Ptolemy Euergetes for control of Egypt. Antiochus supported Ptolemy Philometor, but only for his own gain. Out of it, Antiochus became stronger himself.

ANTIOCHUS' GROWTH IN POWER

11:24-26 He shall enter peaceably even upon the fattest places of the province; and he shall do that which his fathers have not done, nor his fathers' fathers; he shall scatter among them the prey, and spoil, and riches: yea, and he shall forecast his devices against the strong holds, even for a time. And he shall stir up his power and his courage against the king of the south with a great army; and the king of the south shall be stirred up to battle with a very great and mighty army; but he shall not stand: for they shall forecast devices against him. Yea, they that feed of the portion of his meat shall destroy him, and his army shall overflow: and many shall fall down slain.

Always active to enlarge his kingdom, either by military devices or intrigue, Antiochus, according to verse 24, like his fathers, robbed the richest places of the country under his control. The prediction *He shall enter peaceably* means that he attacked the enemy "in a time of security" or "peace," when the enemy did not expect him. Unlike his father, Antiochus IV did not use his wealth secured in this way for personal advantage so much as to buy favor with others and to secure their cooperation. The expression *he shall scatter among them the prey, and spoil, and riches* indicates this distribution of the wealth he had secured. According to 1 Maccabees 3:30, "He feared that he might not have such funds as he had before for his expenses and for the gifts which he used to give more lavishly than preceding kings" (RSV).

Among his military maneuvers were several expeditions against Egypt which are indicated in verse 25. Which of the several expeditions this represents is of no importance, as this prophecy is simply describing in general the characteristics of the reign of Antiochus IV. The outcome of the battle was that the king of Egypt was defeated as indicated in the statement *but he shall not stand*, referring to the king of the south. Even those who should have supported him conspired against him as revealed in verse 26. The result was that, generally speaking, Antiochus was victorious over the Egyptians.

THE WICKEDNESS OF ANTIOCHUS

11:27-28 And both these kings' hearts shall be to do mischief, and they shall speak lies at one table; but it shall not prosper: for yet the end shall be at the time appointed. Then shall he return into his land with great riches; and his heart shall be against the holy covenant; and he shall do exploits, and return to his own land.

The struggle between Syria and Egypt, however, led to various agreements which did not prosper. Neither the rulers of Egypt nor Syria were honorable in their agreements as indicated in verse 27, "they shall speak lies at one table; but it shall not prosper." As the last part of verse 27 makes clear, in spite of all his intrigue, Antiochus was fulfilling prophecy on schedule.

Antiochus, returning from Egypt with great riches, began to manifest his hatred against the people of Israel and his covetousness in relation to the wealth of the temple. This is indicated in the statement, *His heart shall be against the holy covenant.**

Antiochus Opposed by Rome Persecutes the Jews

11:29-31 At the time appointed he shall return, and come toward the south; but it shall not be as the former, or as the latter. For the ships of Chittim shall come against him: therefore he shall be grieved, and return, and have indignation against the holy covenant: so shall he do; he shall even return, and have intelligence with them that forsake the holy covenant. And arms shall stand on his part, and they shall pollute the sanctuary of strength, and shall take away the daily sacrifice, and they shall place the abomination that maketh desolate.

In another expedition against Egypt, "at the time appointed," that is, by God, he managed to capture Ptolemy Philometor but was finally forced to evacuate Egypt because he failed to take the city of Alexandria.[30] His success was not as great as in former expeditions, as stated, "It shall not be as the former, or as the latter." Still another invasion of Egypt occurred about 168 B.C. Here, however, he was met near Alexandria by a Roman consul, Gaius Popillius Laenas, who summarily demanded that he leave Egypt at the pain of being attacked by Rome. The Roman consul is reported to have drawn a circle about the king and told him that his decision had to be reached before he stepped out of the circle. Rather than risk a war with Rome, Antiochus, although greatly displeased, withdrew from Egypt immediately and conceded Egypt to Roman power. Prophetically, this is indicated in verse 30 by the statement *for the ships of Chittim shall come against him,* usually taken as a symbolic representation of Roman power which came from the west past Chittim (also spelled Kittim), a reference to the island of Cyprus which was to the west of his kingdom. The fleet of Laenas sailed to Egypt after the Roman victory over Perseus of Macedon near Pydna south of Thes-

*A detailed description of the violent atrocities and murder of thousands of Jews by Antiochus while marching through Judea is found in 1 Maccabees 1:20-28 and 2 Maccabees 5:11-17.

267

salonica (June 22, 168 B.C.). In the Septuagint, the expression *the ships of Chittim* is translated "the Romans," giving the sense if not the exact translation.

Disgruntled by his defeat in Egypt at the hands of Rome, Antiochus Epiphanes seems to have vented his wrath upon the Jewish people as intimated in verse 30 in the expression, "have indignation against the holy covenant." The history of the period is given in 1 and 2 Maccabees. The added statement *and have intelligence with them that forsake the holy covenant* indicates his affiliation with those who sided with Antiochus, who became his favorites and proteges (cf. 1 Mac 2:18; 2 Mac 6:1).

In the process of his opposition to the Jews, Antiochus polluted the holy altar in the temple by offering a sow upon the altar and forbidding the continuance of the daily sacrifices (cf. 1 Mac 1:44-54). He also issued orders that the Jews should cease their worship and erected in the holy place an idol, probably the image of Zeus Olympius. This represents placing "the abomination that maketh desolate," mentioned in verse 31 to which Christ referred in Matthew 24:15. The parallel prophecy in Daniel 8:23-25 covers the same series of incidents.

This desecration of the temple, in opposition to the Jewish faith, precipitated the Maccabean revolt which was cruelly suppressed by Antiochus with tens of thousands of Israelites perishing. The entire series of incidents, however, including the persecution of Israel, the desecration of their temple, and the stopping of the daily sacrifice, although fulfilled historically in Antiochus' persecution of Israel, is also prophetic of the future persecution of Israel which will result in the great tribulation. The reference in Matthew 24:15 where Christ is describing the beginning of the great tribulation is linked to the desecration of the temple by Antiochus as being similar in kind. Antiochus thus becomes a type of the future man of sin and his activities foreshadow the ultimate blasphemous persecution of Israel and the desecration of their temple.

The Resulting Persecutions of Israel

11:32-35 And such as do wickedly against the covenant shall he corrupt by flatteries: but the people that do know their God shall be strong, and do exploits. And they that understand among the people shall instruct many: yet they shall fall by the sword, and by flame, by captivity, and by spoil, many days. Now when they shall fall, they shall be holpen with a little help: but many shall cleave to them with flatteries. And some of them of understanding shall fall, to try them, and to purge, and to make them white, even to the time of the end: because it is yet for a time appointed.

The continued opposition of Antiochus to the Jewish faith is prophesied in verse 32, indicating how he attempts to corrupt them; but the strong reaction of the Jewish people is indicated in the expression *but the people that do know their God shall be strong, and do exploits.* The resulting conflict, however, brought much harm on the people of Israel; and though it caused to some extent a spiritual revival, many were killed, as indicated in verse 33. Some of the Jews succumbed to the flattery of the king and defected from their fellow Jews as they revolted against Antiochus. It was a time of purging and separation of the true from the false, of those who were courageous from those who were fainthearted.

Zöckler quotes Fuller to indicate the various processes used to purify the Jews, "Not only the pretended adherents to Jehovah's party to separate themselves from His sincere followers, but the latter themselves, incited thereto by the example of steadfastness and self-denial furnished by their martyrs, shall cast out from themselves everything that is impure; and they shall succeed in gaining over all those who share their convictions in their hearts, but have been hindered by fear and timidity from avowing an open connection with them. In like manner, a Nicodemus and a Joseph of Arimathaea were induced by the very death of Christ on the cross to confess their allegiance to him.—Thus Antiochus attempts to annihilate the party among the Jews that is devoted to its God, but succeeds only in contributing to its purifying."[31]

The purging process is indicated in verse 35 to continue "to the time of the end." It is clear from this reference that the persecutions of Antiochus are not the time of the end, even though they foreshadow them. The mention of "the time of the end" in verse 35 is notice, however, that from verse 36 on, the prophecy leaps the centuries that intervene to the last generation prior to God's judgment of Gentile power and its rulers. Beginning in verse 36, prophecy is unfolded that is as yet unfulfilled.

The amazingly detailed prophecies of the first thirty-five verses of this chapter, containing as they do approximately one hundred and thirty-five prophetic statements, all now fulfilled, constitute an impressive introduction to the events that are yet future, beginning in verse 36. Critics who on the one hand assail this chapter as being so accurate that it could not possibly be written before the event, and on the other hand attempt to find discrepancies which support their contention that the pseudo-Daniel is a poor historian, actually are arguing on both sides of the question at the same time. The fact is that there is no supported evidence which can contradict any statement made in these thirty-five verses. The contention that it cannot be prophetic because of its accuracy involves assumptions which would undermine the entire prophetic Scriptures. From the divine viewpoint, the accuracy of this prophetic word is supporting evidence that prophecy yet unfulfilled will have the same precise fulfillment in the future. This is especially relevant to the futuristic aspect of this vision of Daniel beginning in Daniel 11:36.

THE KING OF THE END TIME

11:36 And the king shall do according to his will; and he shall exalt himself, and magnify himself above every god, and shall speak marvellous things against the God of gods, and shall prosper till the indignation be accomplished: for that that is determined shall be done.

Beginning with verse 36, a sharp break in the prophecy may be observed, introduced by the expression *the time of the end* in verse 35. Up to this point, the prophecy dealing with the Persian and Grecian Empires has been fulfilled minutely and with amazing precision. Beginning with verse 36, however, an entirely different situation obtains. No commentator claims to find precise fulfillment in the remainder of this chapter. Although Zöckler and others attempt to relate Daniel 11:36-45 to Antiochus, many students of Scripture have recognized from antiquity that another king must be in view. Ibn-Ezra, for example, identified this king with Constantine the Great; Rashi and Calvin referred him to the Roman Empire as a whole; and Jerome, Theodoret, and Luther, among others, identified him with the New Testament Antichrist.[32] In contrast to the preceding section, there is no specific correspondence to history. Accordingly, scholars who regard this as genuine Scripture, usually regard this section as future and unfulfilled.

As E. B. Pusey has noted, "Even the Jews in S. Jerome's time looked upon this prophecy as having still to receive its fulfillment."[33] In reference to Daniel 11:36, Jerome comments,

"The Jews believe that this passage has reference to the Antichrist, alleging that after the small help of Julian a king is going to rise up who shall do according to his own will and shall lift himself up against all that is called god, and shall speak arrogant words against the God of gods. He shall act in such a way as to sit in the Temple of God and shall make himself out to be God, and his will shall be prospered until the wrath of God is fulfilled, for in him the consummation will take place. We, too, understand this to refer to the Antichrist."[34]

Earlier Jerome had pointed out that Antiochus was merely a foreshadowing of the Antichrist, "Just as the Savior had Solomon and the other saints as types of His advent, so also we should believe that the Antichrist very properly had as a type of himself the utterly wicked king, Antiochus, who persecuted the saints and defiled the Temple."[35]

Although many variations of interpretation exist, in general, interpretations of Daniel 11:36-45 fall into three major categories: (1) that it is a further historic or prophetic account fulfilled in Antiochus Epiphanes;

(2) that it is fiction, that is, the wishful thinking of the author which does not correspond to history precisely; (3) that it is genuine prophecy as yet unfulfilled.

Liberal critics, following the thesis that Daniel was written by a second-century B.C. writer, almost uniformly hold that this section was fulfilled in the life and death of Antiochus Epiphanes.[36] Even liberal scholars, however, agree that this section is not nearly as accurate as the earlier portion. Although finding it an accurate forecast of Antiochus' death—in regarding the passage as a prophecy of the king's catastrophic end, as Montgomery holds—liberals also admit as Montgomery does, "but it cannot, with those conservative theologians, be taken in any way as an exact prophecy of the actual events of his ruin. The alleged final victorious war with Egypt, including the conquest of Cyrenaica and Ethiopia, in the face of the power of Rome and the silence of secular history, is absolutely imaginary."[37] In other words, even liberal scholars, who find the earlier section so remarkably accurate that they hold it as history rather than prophecy, admit a sharp difference in the latter section beginning in verse 36 as not corresponding to history. This is the reason why conservative scholars have rejected the historical interpretation and, with due regard to the inspiration of Scripture, expect a future fulfillment.

The second possibility, that the passage is fiction, does not seem to have seriously attracted even the liberal scholar, preferring as he does to identify it with Antiochus Epiphanes. Other competing interpretations, such as those that compare the passage to Constantine the Great, Omar ibn El-Khattab, the Roman Empire (Calvin), the Pope of Rome, the Papal system, or Herod the Great (Mauro), all cited by Young, are not generally considered live options today.[38]

Because of the completely unsatisfactory explanation of an historical fulfillment of verses 36-45 in contrast with the precise fulfillment of the earlier portion, conservative expositors relate this passage to the climax of history culminating in the second advent of Christ. This, of course, is in keeping with the total tenor of Daniel's prophecies which characteristically have their climax in the end of the interadvent age and the triumph of the kingdom of heaven which the Son of man will accomplish when He returns. The passage, therefore, is to be considered as contemporaneous with the climax of chapter 2, the destruction of the image, and the destruction of the little horn of Daniel 7, a period described in the book of Revelation, chapters 6-19. The king described in verses 36-39 of Daniel 11 and the events of the subsequent verses therefore have nothing to do with the second century B.C., and are entirely future and unfulfilled.

Among conservative scholars, however, two differing identifications of

the king of verse 36 are given. The common identification is that offered
by J. N. Darby that the king of Daniel 11:36 is none other than the Antichrist, who is an unregenerate Jew living in Palestine at the end time but
in league with the Roman world ruler. Darby, although not emphasizing
the racial background of this king, identifies him with the man of sin of
2 Thessalonians 2:3-10 and with the false prophet of Revelation 13:11-
18.[39] A. C. Gaebelein offers the same interpretation with more specific
emphasis on the Jewish character of this ruler as a false Messiah acceptable to the Jewish people.[40] The principal support for this point of view
is found in the expression of verse 37 "neither shall he regard the God
of his fathers," which is identified as the God of Israel. Further, it is
assumed that Jewish people will not accept even a false Messiah unless
he is Jewish in background. As an apostate, he disregards his fathers'
God, the hope of the Messiah, and instead honors the Roman world
dictator as god.

A better identification of the king, the second identification, however,
is to relate him to the Roman world ruler, the same individual as the
little horn of Daniel 7 and the beast out of the sea of Revelation 13:1-10.
Upon careful consideration, the evidence in support of Darby's identification is seen to be insufficient, and the second view is preferred.

According to verse 36, the king is an absolute ruler who "shall do
according to his will." If this is the great tribulation, as intimated in
Daniel 12:1, when the Roman ruler is a world ruler, it is difficult to con-
template any other ruler who could be absolute in authority, especially
in an area so close to the center of Roman power as Palestine. There can
be only one king who does absolutely according to his will in this period,
and this must be the world ruler which according to Daniel 7:23 "shall
devour the whole earth, and tread it down, and break it in pieces."
Although other rulers will be associated with him, such as the ten horns
of Revelation 17:12 and the false prophet of Revelation 13:11-18, none
of these can be described as absolute rulers.

Further evidence is found in the fact that he not only assumes complete
political rule but also the role of God. According to verse 36, "he shall
exalt himself, and magnify himself above every god." In his claim for
deity, which he demands that all recognize at the pain of death (Rev
13:15), he clearly asserts his supremacy over all others. To describe a
ruler in Palestine during this time under these extravagant terms would
be incongruous with the total situation. According to verse 36, he shall
also blaspheme against the true God and prosper for a time until he
comes to his end.

Liberal interpreters cite this verse as evidence of identification of this
passage with Antiochus Epiphanes, for it is well established that Antio-

chus claimed qualities belonging to God as manifested in the coins of his realm and in the title of Epiphanes itself, which he considered as stating that he manifested the powers of God. Montgomery states, for instance, "but Epiphanes took his godhead very seriously. He was the first to assume 'Theos' on his coins, and the addition of 'Manifest' (practically 'incarnate') indicated his self-identification with Deity, he was not merely a god like his forebears. The ever-increasing obsession of godhead appears from the sequence of his coins."[41] The identification of this passage with Antiochus, however, breaks down as the prophecy unfolds in succeeding verses. If this is indeed the end time, just before the second advent of Christ, the description of the king fits only one person, namely, the Roman who "shall prosper till the indignation be accomplished," that is, his blasphemous course be fulfilled.

The Final World Religion

11:37-39 Neither shall he regard the God of his fathers, nor the desire of women, nor regard any god: for he shall magnify himself above all. But in his estate shall he honour the God of forces: and a god whom his fathers knew not shall he honour with gold, and silver, and with precious stones, and pleasant things. Thus shall he do in the most strong holds with a strange god, whom he shall acknowledge and increase with glory: and he shall cause them to rule over many, and shall divide the land for gain.

One of the more important arguments supporting the conclusion that this king is a Jew is found in the opening phrase of verse 37, "neither shall he regard the God of his fathers." As Gaebelein states, "The King, Antichrist shall not regard the God of his fathers. Here his Jewish descent becomes evident. It is a Jewish phrase 'the God of his fathers' and beside this, to establish his fraudulent claim to be the King Messiah, he must be a Jew."[42] Gaebelein and others upholding this view, however, overlook a most decisive fact that the word for "God" here is *Elohim*, a name for God in general, applying both to the true God and to false gods. If the expression had been the usual one when referring to the God of Israel, *the Jehovah of his fathers*, the identification would be unmistakable. Very frequently in Scripture, the God of Israel is described as Jehovah, "the LORD God" of their fathers (cf. Ex 3:15-16; 4:5; Deu 1:11, 21; 4:1; 6:3; 12:1; 26:7; 29:25; Jos 18:3; Judg 2:12; 2 Ki 21:22; 1 Ch 29:20; 2 Ch 7:22; 11:16; 13:18; 15:12; 19:4; 20:6; 21:10; 24:24; 28:9; 29:5; 30:7, 19; 34:33; 36:15; Ezra 7:27; 8:28). Although Daniel uses "God (*Elohim*) of my fathers" in Daniel 2:23 in view of this common usage elsewhere in Scripture, for Daniel to omit the word Jehovah or LORD, (KJV) in a passage where a specific name for the God of Israel would be necessary, becomes significant. The expression should be rendered "the gods of his fathers," that is, any god, as most revisions translate it.

In keeping with the blasphemous character of this king who magnifies himself above every god, he disregards whatever deities his fathers worshiped. In keeping with the general word for god, *Elohim*, the expression, "*the gods of his fathers*," becomes a general reference to any deities whether pagan or the true God.

In keeping with his disregard for former deities, he does not pay respect to what is called "the desire of women." This expression has been regarded as a reference to a specific pagan goddess such as Ewald's identification with Tammuz-Adonis which Montgomery states has "come to be generally adopted" since Bevan.[43]

Bevan in his discussion states, "'*The Desire of women*' must, to judge by the context, be some object of women. Most modern interpreters, following Ephraim Syrus, explain this as a reference to the goddess Nanaia, whose temple in Elymais the king endeavoured to plunder shortly before his death. But to this view there are two objections. Firstly, the attack upon the temple of Nanaia cannot have been heard of in Judaea till the year 164 B.C. Secondly, there is no reason why Nanaia should be designated as the Desire of women. Even if her worship was, as has been supposed, of a voluptuous character, this would scarcely give rise to such an appellation. It appears, therefore, much more probable that Ewald is right in explaining the Desire of women as Tammuz (Adonis), whose cult had been popular in Syria from time immemorial, especially amongst women (Ezek. viii. 14)."[44] Others, like Young after Keil,[45] consider it the normal love or desire for women which is natural to men, meaning that this king is inhuman in his disregard of women.

Although Daniel is not specific, a plausible explanation of this passage, in the light of Daniel's Jewish background, is that this expression, *the desire of women*, is the natural desire of Jewish women to become the mother of the promised Messiah, the seed of the woman promised in Genesis 3:15. The expression then becomes a symbol of the Messianic hope in general. As Gaebelein expresses it, "Still more interesting is the statement 'he shall not regard the desire of women.' The Lord Jesus Christ is here in view. The word 'desire' is in the same construct form in Hebrew (*hemdat*) as in Haggai 2:7 and I Samuel 9:20, indicating that the noun following 'desire' is subjective not objective; hence it means "desired by women," not a desire for women. Pious Jewish women in Pre-messianic times had one great desire, they wanted to be mothers, with a view to Him, who is the promised seed of the woman. His birth was desired by these godly mothers of Israel. This King then hates God and hates His blessed Son, the Lord Jesus Christ."[46]

Although none of the explanations can be proved beyond question, as Daniel is not specific, it is quite clear that this king would be opposed to the Messianic hope; and from Daniel's point of view, this would be important. In other words, he would disregard the gods of the past as well as the promised Son of God who is to come from heaven.

Although the blasphemous character of this ruler is evident, the prophecy continues that he shall not "regard any god: for he shall magnify himself above all." His blasphemy is twofold: that of rejection of the true God as well as all false gods, and that of the assumption of deity to himself. Although Antiochus Epiphanes had some aspirations of being recognized as having divine qualities, even the liberal scholars who attempt historic fulfillment in him in relation to this passage are embarrassed by the sweeping statement that is made. There is no extrascriptural proof that Antiochus went this far, and the futuristic interpretation makes far more sense.

Although ascribing deity to himself, the characteristics of his theology are explained in verse 38. In the place that God occupies in other men's thinking, this king is stated to "honour the God of forces," or as it is better translated, "the god of fortresses." This god is stated to be peculiarly different from the gods which his fathers knew, and the revelation continues, "a god whom his fathers knew not shall he honour with gold, and silver, and with precious stones, and pleasant things." Here again, the liberal scholar is embarrassed by the extensive claim that is made which far exceeds anything true of Antiochus Epiphanes. There was nothing unusual about his claims to divine qualities which many previous rulers have shared, and his confidence in armed might certainly was no different from that of other rulers. How then is this "god of fortresses" different from any previous deities?

Those who, like Gaebelein, identify this king as an apostate Jew at the end of the age, are likewise embarrassed as "the god of fortresses" then has to be identified with the Roman world ruler. As Gaebelein states, "The one whom he will honour is none other than the first beast, the little horn."[47] If this is intended, however, as an identification, it is a strange one and quite different from any other identification of the Roman ruler in Scripture. The worship of a man as God has many parallels in history and would not be distinctive.

Although all expositors necessarily must use their judgment in determining the identification of this description, what will be completely different about the world religion at the end time will be (1) the complete destruction of all previous religions symbolized in Revelation 17:16 and (2) the worship of the world ruler without reference to any other divine power except that of Satan. For this world ruler, already claiming to be God, to acknowledge something as supreme clearly indicates that "the god of fortresses" is not a person but the power to make war, symbolized in the word *fortress*. Examining all other passages relating to the end time, it becomes evident that the sole confidence of the final world ruler is in military power, personified as "the god of war," or "god of fortresses." In other words, he is a complete materialist in contrast to all previous religions and all previous men who claimed divine qualities. This is blasphemy to the ultimate, the exaltation of human power and attainment. He is Satan's masterpiece, a human being who is Satan's substitute for Jesus Christ, hence properly identified as the Antichrist.

His activities, in keeping with his complete materialism, are characterized by warfare and his honoring those who honor him. Those cooperating are given subsidiary rule expressed in the phrase, "he shall cause them to rule over many," and he "shall divide the land for gain," that is, shall reapportion territories in keeping with his desire for conquest. As far as the record goes, Antiochus did not divide lands among those who defected to him, and nothing of this sort is indicated in the passages which report his briberies (1 Mac 2:18; 3:30 ff.). This would be an important omission in the history of Antiochus if he is in view in this prophecy.

Taking the passage Daniel 11:36-39 as a whole, it is apparent that the revelation provides an incisive analysis of the combination of materialism, militarism, and religion, all of which will be embodied in the final world ruler. The situation in the last third of the twentieth century is rather amazing in the light of this revelation of the consummation of human history. Already active in the world is the promotion of a world church and a world religion which will have its culmination first in the symbolic harlot of Revelation 17, the earlier form of the world religion, and then will be replaced by the worship of this king as the final form of world religion.

The rise of communism in our modern world, although often regarded as primarily a political movement, is actually a practical extension of philosophic materialism which knows no deity, no supernatural God, and religiously is similar to the materialism of this final world ruler. When the twin forces of communism and world religion are combined in this king, a third force evident in the modern world also will come to its culmination, namely, the present trend toward world government, of which the United Nations may be a foreshadowing. This portion of Daniel, in the light of contemporary trends, becomes an illuminating prophetic commentary on the ultimate end of these present forces in the world which will unite the political, religious, and materialistic philosophies of our day in one man who is Satan's nomination for king of kings and lords of lords. The apex of this development will be reached in the last half of Daniel's seventieth week, the three and a half years of the great tribulation, immediately preceding the second advent of Jesus Christ. However, his world government is assailed by catastrophic judgments from God portrayed in Revelation 6-18, and the inherent difficulties of ruling the entire globe come to their fruition in a final world war of which the closing portion of Daniel 11 furnishes a description.

THE FINAL WORLD WAR ERUPTS

11:40-43 And at the time of the end shall the king of the south push at him: and the king of the north shall come against him like a whirlwind, with chariots, and with horsemen, and with many ships; and he shall enter into the countries, and shall overflow and pass over. He shall enter also into the glorious land, and many countries shall be overthrown: but these shall escape out of his hand, even Edom, and Moab, and the chief of the children of Ammon. He shall stretch forth his hand also upon the countries: and the land of Egypt shall not escape. But he shall have power over the treasures of gold and of silver, and over all the precious things of Egypt: and the Libyans and the Ethiopians shall be at his steps.

The time of the end introduced in verse 35 is again mentioned in the opening portion of verse 40 to make clear that the military struggle here is that which will characterize the end of the age. The general nature and location of the warfare is also specified. The king mentioned in 11:36-39 is now attacked by "the king of the south" and "the king of the north." Earlier in this chapter, the king of the south is uniformly Egypt and refers to the warfare of the third and second centuries B.C. which has already been fulfilled. Here the king of the south is clearly the leader of a political and military force that comes from the south of the Holy Land, but the probability is that it involves much more than only Egypt and can be identified as the African army. There is no mention whatever of such campaigns in the Maccabean books or by Livy, Polybius, and Appian. No such warfare is described in history.

The king of the north, identified as Syria in the prophecies fulfilled in the second and third centuries B.C., is obviously more than the small territory possessed by Syria at that time and probably includes all the political and military force of the lands to the north of the Holy Land; hence the term could include Russia as well as related countries.

A natural question is the relation of this struggle to the battle described in Ezekiel 38-39, where a great military force coming from the north attacks the land of Israel. The context in Ezekiel describes the time as a period of peace for Israel (Eze 38:8, 11, 14), which probably is best identified as the first half of Daniel's seventieth week when Israel is in covenant relationship with the Roman ruler and protected from attack. This period of peace is broken at the midpoint of the seventieth week when the Roman ruler becomes a world ruler, and the great tribulation begins with its persecution of Israel.

The chronology of Daniel 11:36-39 refers to the period of world rule, and, therefore, is later than Ezekiel 38 and 39. Hence, it may be concluded that the battle described here, beginning with verse 40, is a later development, possibly several years later than the battle described in Ezekiel. If a Russian force is involved in the phrase, "the king of the north," it would indicate that, in the period between the two battles, Russia is able to reassemble an army and once again participate in a military way in this great war. In any event, this battle is quite different from that of Ezekiel as, according to the Ezekiel prediction, the invader comes only from the north, whereas in this portion, the Holy Land is invaded both from the north and south, and later from the east.

In the light of the previous context, where the king is pictured as an absolute ruler, coinciding with other Scriptures picturing a world government at this time (Dan 7:23; Rev 13:7), the war is in the nature of a rebellion against his leadership and signifies the breaking up of the world government which previously had been in power. The initial nature of the battle is quite clear.

A major exegetical problem is the reference in verse 40 to "and he shall enter into the countries, and shall overflow and pass over." The question is whether "he" refers to the king of the south, the king of the north, or the former world ruler who is defending his empire. In the light of the context which follows, it is preferable to take the "he" as referring to the king of 11:36, the world ruler.

The identification of the subject of the action of verse 41 and following as the king of 11:36 seems to be most in keeping with the entire tenor of this passage which presents the last world ruler. Alternative suggestions have been made, which would greatly alter the meaning of this passage. Among the views, several may be mentioned. The liberal interpretation is that this refers to the historic struggles of Antiochus Epiphanes with Egypt; but any comparison of the predictions here with actual events of the closing of the reign of Antiochus presents serious difficulties, and even the liberals have to accuse their pseudo-Daniel of being guilty of historical inaccuracies.[48] Actually, there is no correspondence to history here.

If the futuristic interpretation is accepted, a number of options are possible. If the ruler of 11:36 is only a minor character and not a world ruler, it would open the way for regarding this war to be merely an intersectional conflict as H. A. Ironside interprets it.[49] In this case, this entire passage does not refer to the world ruler. Another view is to identify the king of the north as the Antichrist and the future world ruler.

This is the position of Edward Young, who states, "The two opponents are the Anti-christ and the king of the South, who begins the battle by pushing or butting (cf. 8:4) against his enemy."[50]

The best interpretation, however, is that the main actor, the king of 11:36, is to be identified with the final great world ruler. Leupold supports this view and considers the entire section to indicate a defeat of the invading armies and the triumph of the king until the end. Leupold writes, "The variety of the resources that are to be employed against the Antichrist indicate how great his power must be at the latter end— 'chariots, horsemen, and many ships.' But the Antichrist will not be slow to repel the attack. He himself shall 'come into these lands,' that is, the lands of those who have assailed him, and 'shall sweep along and pass through.' "[51] The major revelation here, therefore, is that the king of 11:36, although engaged in bitter struggle, continues to dominate the situation until he comes to his end at the second coming of Jesus Christ.

His counterattack on those who have assailed him results in his entering into their countries, occupying "the glorious land," referring to the Holy Land and many other countries including Egypt. It appears, however, that he does not completely restore the situation, as it is stated that Edom and Moab and the children of Ammon escape (11:41). His victory is such that he is able to increase greatly his treasures of gold and silver and obtain precious things from Egypt. From this point on, however, his authority is supported only insofar as his military campaigns are able to occupy various countries. His world empire, apparently originating in a decree which at that time was not contested, no longer remains intact.

THE FINAL BATTLES

11:44-45 But tidings out of the east and out of the north shall trouble him: therefore he shall go forth with great fury to destroy, and utterly to make away many. And he shall plant the tabernacles of his palace between the seas in the glorious holy mountain; yet he shall come to his end, and none shall help him.

To add to the difficulties encountered by the king, occasioned by the invasion from the north and the south, now word is received of a gigantic army from the east and another invasion from the north. It is clear that the warfare extends over a period of time and that more than one battle is involved. The tidings out of the east probably refer to the gigantic invasion described in Revelation 9:13-21; cf. 16:12. Here, according to Revelation 9:16, an army of two hundred million men cross the Euphrates and descend upon the Holy Land. Although such an army is staggering in its size and many commentators consider the number symbolic rather than literal, in the present population explosion of Asia, an army of two hundred million is no longer impossible. Red China alone claims to have a militia numbering two hundred million today.[52] Even if this number be regarded as symbolic, it must certainly represent a gigantic army.

At the same time, another invasion is reported from the north. Against both of these invaders, the king launches counterattacks which result in many perishing; and he succeeds in establishing his tent-palace "between the seas in the glorious holy mountain," best understood as being a reference to Jerusalem situated between the Mediterranean Sea and the Dead Sea. Actually, the struggle goes on without cessation right up to the day of the second advent of Christ as brought out in Zechariah 14:1-4. Daniel does not dwell upon details in the climax of this struggle.

In spite of his victories in a military way, the last world ruler, according to Daniel, "shall come to his end, and none shall help him." The liberal interpretation relating this to Antiochus simply does not fit the passage, as Antiochus died in battle in Media, and nothing significant immediately followed his death. If this is indeed the time of the end and this is the final world ruler of the times of the Gentiles, the best identification is to refer his doom to the second advent of Christ and the destruction of the beast and the armies described in Revelation 19:17-21. According to that passage, the king and the false prophet associated with him are cast alive into the lake of fire. The armies which had assembled to contend against each other but had united in opposition to Christ in His second advent are destroyed. That the time of the second advent is in view is brought out clearly in the next chapter where the time of the end is made definitely to include the great tribulation and the resurrection of the dead described in Revelation 20:4-6.

Taken as a whole, Daniel 11:36-45 is a description of the closing days of the times of the Gentiles, specifically, the great tribulation with its world ruler, world religion, and materialistic philosophy. In spite of its satanic support, the world government fragmentizes into sectional disputes and a great world war which climaxes with the second advent of Christ. This brings the time of the Gentiles to a close with the destruction of the wicked rulers who led it. Further details are added in the next chapter.

12

THE TIME OF THE END

THE MATERIAL DESCRIBED as the fourth vision of Daniel beginning in chapter 10 has its climax in the great tribulation and the resurrection which follows, mentioned in the early verses of chapter 12. This is also the high point in the book of Daniel itself and the goal of Daniel's prophecies relating both to the Gentiles and to Israel. It is comparable to Revelation 19, the high point of the last book of the Bible.

All commentators agree that the chapter division at this point is unfortunate as the narrative of chapter 11 naturally extends through the first three verses of chapter 12. As Porteous expresses it,

> The first four verses of chapter 12 are the completion of the long section which began with chapter 10. They give in remarkably brief compass and restrained language the writer's expectation of what the divinely appointed end would be like. It would be climax of which Israel would be the centre, as is shown by the fact that Michael, the patron angel of Israel, is to play the decisive part on God's behalf. The great tribulation will come to a head but Israel will escape, all those in Israel, that is to say, whose names are written in the book of life (Ps. 69.29; Ex. 32.32; cf. the later passages Phil. 4.3; Rev. 3.5). God already knows His own.[1]

Added to the previous revelation are the important disclosures (1) that the time of the end has a special relationship to "the children of thy people," that is, Israel, (2) that Israel will experience at that time a special deliverance to be realized by those in Israel who worship God, and (3) that the doctrine of resurrection which climaxes the time of the end is the special hope of those who are martyred.

The entire section from Daniel 11:36 to 12:3 constitutes a revelation of the major factors of the time of the end which may be summarized as follows: (1) a world ruler, (2) a world religion, (3) a world war, (4) a time of great tribulation for Israel, (5) deliverance for the people of God at the end of the tribulation, (6) resurrection and judgment, and (7) reward of the righteous. All of these factors are introduced in this section. Added elsewhere in the Scriptures are the additional facts that this time of the end begins with the breaking of the covenant by "the prince that shall come" (Dan 9:26-27); that the "time of the end" will last for three and one-half years (Dan 7:25; 12:7; Rev 13:5); that the time of the end is the same as the time of Jacob's trouble and the great tribulation (Jer 30:7; Mt 24:21). Many additional details are supplied in Revelation 6-19.

The fact that the opening section of chapter 12 is obviously eschatologically future, constitutes a major embarrassment to liberals who attempt to find Antiochus Epiphanes in 11:36-45. Chapter 12, which is naturally connected to the preceding section, clearly does not refer to Antiochus Epiphanes but to the consummation of the ages and the resurrection and reward of the saints. Nowhere does the attempt to make Daniel entirely history fail more miserably than here, as the detailed exegesis of these verses demonstrates.

THE GREAT TRIBULATION

12:1 And at that time shall Michael stand up, the great prince which standeth for the children of thy people: and there shall be a time of trouble, such as never was since there was a nation even to that same time: and at that time thy people shall be delivered, every one that shall be found written in the book.

The opening phrase of chapter 12, *and at that time*, makes clear that this passage is talking about the same period of time as the previous context, that is, "the time of the end" (11:40). The action here in verse 1 is not subsequent to the preceding events but coincides with them chronologically. Chapter 11 had dealt primarily with the political and religious aspects of the time of the end. Chapter 12 relates this now to the people of Israel. Here is stated in clear terms that this is the time of trouble for the people of Israel, "such as never was since there was a nation even to that same time." To take the expression *the children of thy people* in any other sense than that of Israel is to ignore the uniform meaning of *thy people* throughout the book of Daniel. The people involved are *a nation*, that is, the nation Israel.

The unprecedented time of trouble here mentioned is a major theme of both the Old and New Testament. As early as Deuteronomy 4:30, it was predicted that "in the latter days" the children of Israel would be "in tribulation." Jeremiah had referred to it as "the time of Jacob's trouble," in his lament, "Alas! for that day is great, so that none is like it: it is even the time of Jacob's trouble, but he shall be saved out of it" (Jer 30:7).

Christ described the great tribulation as beginning with "the abomination of desolation, spoken of by Daniel the prophet" (Mt 24:15), a reference to the breaking of the covenant and desecration of the temple in Daniel 9:27. Christ's warning to the children of Israel at that time was that they should "flee into the mountains," not taking time to secure clothes or food. Christ graphically described the period in these words, "For then shall be great tribulation, such as was not since the beginning of the world to this time, no, nor ever shall be. And except those days should be shortened, there should no flesh be saved: but for the elect's sake those days shall be shortened" (Mt 24:21-22).

This description of the time of the end confirms Daniel's revelation that the time of the end will be a period of trouble such as the world has never known, trouble of such character that it would result in the extermination of the human race if it were not cut short by the consummation, the second coming of Jesus Christ. This is made clear from a further study of Revelation 6-19, where the great catastrophes which overtake the world in the breaking of the seals, the blowing of the trumpets, and the emptying of the vials of divine judgment decimate the world's population. All of these Scriptures agree that there is no precedent to this end-time trouble. Even liberal expositors find it impossible to harmonize Daniel 12:1 with the persecutions of Antiochus Epiphanes in the second century B.C.

As Keil has observed,

> . . . the contents of ver. 1 do not agree with the period of persecution under Antiochus. That which is said regarding the greatness of the persecution is much too strong for it. . . . Though the oppression which Antiochus brought upon Israel may have been most severe, yet it could not be said of it without exaggeration, that it was such a tribulation as never had been from the beginning of the world. Antiochus, it is true, sought to outroot Judaism root and branch, but Pharaoh also wished to do the same by his command to destroy all the Hebrew male children at their birth; and as Antiochus wished to make the worship of the Grecian Zeus, so also Jezebel the worship of the Phoenician Hercules, in the place of the worship of Jehovah, the national religion in Israel.[2]

Numerous other allusions in Scripture to this period indicate that it is indeed a time of supreme trial for Israel. Zechariah 13:8 declares of this period, "And it shall come to pass, that in all the land, saith the LORD, two parts therein shall be cut off and die; but the third shall be left therein." Zechariah goes on to picture the refining process until the people of Israel acknowledge the Lord as their God. The very next verses describe the final struggle for Jerusalem and the second advent of Christ which delivers Israel. This time of trouble is parallel to the warfare described in Daniel 11:40-45.

In their distress, the children of Israel are especially aided by Michael, the archangel (Jude 9). As the head of the holy angels, Michael is given the special responsibility of protecting the children of Israel. Although

283

Calvin preferred the interpretation that Michael was the person of Christ,[3] there is no justification for confusing Michael and Christ. Earlier in Daniel itself, mention was made of Michael in Daniel 10:13-21, where Michael participated in the angelic warfare which had prevented the messenger from reaching Daniel promptly. Michael was indeed a "great prince" among the angels whose activity is especially directed to the children of Israel in their time of great trouble.

Because of the purpose of God and the ministry of Michael, it is revealed to Daniel that "at that time thy people shall be delivered, every one that shall be found written in the book." This obviously refers to the end of the tribulation, at which time some of the children of Israel, who by miraculous divine protection had been preserved, will be delivered from their persecutors (Dan 7:18, 27). The repeated reference to "thy people," twice in one verse, seems to limit this to the people of Israel, rather than to all the saints as Young and Leupold interpret it, after Calvin.[4] This is in keeping with the whole tenor of Daniel which deals with Israel as Daniel's people. The deliverance will not extend to all Israel in that unbelieving or apostate Israel is excluded; and even here, it refers only to those actually living at the time of the return of Christ as many others may be martyred. The prophecy assures, however, that in spite of satanic efforts to exterminate the people of Israel, a godly remnant will be ready to greet their Messiah when He returns (Zec 12:10; 13:8-9). The people of Israel who have endured the times of the Gentiles ever since the days of Nebuchadnezzar will be delivered "at that time," an expression repeated twice in this verse.

The reference to "every one that shall be found written in the book" conveys the thought that those delivered have their names inscribed in the book of life (Ex 32:32, 33; Ps 69:28; Rev 13:8; 17:8; 20:15; 21:27). At the second coming of Christ, not every individual Israelite is spiritually prepared for His return, as Ezekiel 20:33-38 makes clear, describing the purging out of the rebels in Israel at the time of the second advent. Although Israel as a nation will be delivered from their persecutors (Ro 11:26), individual Israelites will still face the searching judgment of Christ as to their spiritual preparation to enter the kingdom. For Jew as well as Gentile, the issue will be whether they have eternal life.

THE RESURRECTIONS

12:2 And many of those who sleep in the dust of the earth shall awake, some to everlasting life, and some to shame and everlasting contempt.

As a climax to the time of tribulation described in the preceding context, verse 2 reveals that there will be a resurrection from the dead. Both

liberal and conservative expositors consider the main thrust of this passage the promise of ultimate bliss for the righteous who suffer in the
preceding period of tribulation. As Montgomery expresses, "The end of
the godless tyrant must have its positive foil in the bliss of the righteous;
so the elder apocalypses concluded, e.g., Eze. 38:39, Joel 4 (3)."[5]

Bevan, who labors to connect this passage with Antiochus, nevertheless
states,

> Verse 2 introduces the resurrection of the dead. To what extent this
> belief existed among the Jews in pre-Maccabean times, cannot here be
> discussed, but this is in any case the earliest passage where the belief is
> unambiguously set forth. Here, however, the resurrection is far from
> being universal; it includes "many," not all, of the dead. That only
> Israelites are raised is not expressly stated, but appears probable from the
> context. . . . Those who awake are divided into two classes, corresponding
> to the division in chap. xi.32.[6]

Montgomery quotes Bevan with approval.[7] Although Montgomery is
right that the doctrine of resurrection is the hope of saints in trial, he
and Bevan are wrong that this is the earliest passage where this belief is
revealed clearly. It is clear that Abraham had confidence in resurrection
from the dead in offering Isaac (Gen 22:5; Heb 11:19). Job, who probably lived before Moses, stated his faith in the well known passage, "For
I know that my redeemer liveth, and that he shall stand at the latter day
upon the earth: And though after my skin worms destroy this body, yet
in my flesh shall I see God" (Job 19:25-26). Isaiah, who lived more than
a century before Daniel, predicted that dead men would live again and
that their bodies should rise (Is 26:19). Hosea, a contemporary of Isaiah,
predicted, "I will ransom them from the power of the grave, I will redeem
them from death" (Ho 13:14). Even the resurrection of Christ is predicted in the words, "My flesh also shall rest in hope. For thou wilt not
leave my soul in hell; neither wilt thou suffer thine Holy One to see
corruption" (Ps 16:9-10). Here Daniel is not revealing something new
but what has always been the hope of the saints. This, of course, is enlarged in the New Testament with the added truth of the rapture of living
saints.

Although both liberal and conservative scholars generally agree that
resurrection is in view in this passage, because of the wording of the
prophecy, questions have risen concerning (1) the character of the event,
(2) the time of the event, and (3) the inclusion of the event. Interpretation of the passage has been affected by the general eschatological position of the interpreter; normally premillenarians interpret the passage
somewhat differently from amillenarians.

Strange to say, some premillenarians, although conservative in their general interpretation, have questioned whether this passage actually teaches resurrection. A. C. Gaebelein, for instance, states flatly, "Physical resurrection is not taught in the second verse of this chapter. . . . We repeat, the passage has nothing to do with physical resurrection. Physical resurrection is however used as a figure of the national revival of Israel in that day."[8] William Kelly takes precisely the same position when he says, "The verse is constantly applied to the resurrection of the body; and it is true that the Spirit founds the figure, which is here used to foreshadow the revival of Israel, upon that resurrection. But it can be shewn that it has not the least reference to a bodily resurrection, either of us or of Israel."[9] Even H. A. Ironside concurs with this teaching stating, "The second verse does not, I believe, speak of an actual physical resurrection, but rather of a moral and national one. . . . It is the same kind of language that is used both in Isaiah 26:12-19 and Ezekiel 37. . . ."[10]

The motivation behind this interpretation is their zeal not only to support in general the premillennial interpretation of Scripture and the restoration of the nation Israel at the second coming of Christ, but especially to harmonize this passage with their teaching that Old Testament saints are raised at the time of the rapture of the church before the tribulation and hence would not be raised here at a later time. Most contemporary premillenarians, who are also pretribulationists, believe that this approach is unnecessary and actually misinterprets the passage.

Robert Culver, for instance, in commenting on Gaebelein states, "The thing so utterly unacceptable about this is that Gaebelein adopts the very 'spiritualizing' or 'symbolizing' principle of interpretation which our opponents adopt—and that in the midst of a passage where everything else is esteemed (by Gaebelein and all Premillennialists) to be literal, not figurative. He does with this passage precisely what the Postmillennialists and Amillennialists do with reference to a first resurrection in Revelation 20."[11]

It is significant that expositors who spiritualize the resurrection of Daniel 12:2 interpret the first part of the verse as applying to Israel's restoration, but they pass over the last part of the verse referring to those who awake to shame and everlasting contempt. Certainly the wicked are literally raised from the dead for their final judgment (Rev 20:12-13), and the same verb must mean resurrection for the righteous as well. The meaning of *awake* must be resurrection in both instances. It is not necessary to press this passage out of its natural meaning in order to support premillennialism, and there is nothing in this passage that contradicts pretribulationism either if understood normally. Nor does a proper understanding of this passage contradict a national restoration of Israel at the second coming of Christ. This is taught in many other prophetic passages also.

What is presented here is that those who have died will be raised from the dead to join those living in this period of restoration. Israelites who survive the tribulation and who are the objects of the divine deliverance prophesied in Romans 11:26 will be joined by the Old Testament saints who are raised from the dead. This will occur after the great tribulation, at the second coming of Christ. Actually, there is no passage in Scripture which teaches that the Old Testament saints will be raised at the time the church is raptured, that is, before the final tribulation. It is preferable, therefore, to consider their resurrection as occurring at the same time as the restoration of the living nation with the result that resurrected Israel and those still in their natural bodies who are delivered at the second coming of Christ will join hands and ministries in establishing Israel in the land in the millennial kingdom which follows the second advent. Accordingly, the exegesis of this passage which interprets it as revealing an actual resurrection at the time of the second coming of Christ is preferable. At the same time, those who have died in the great tribulation just preceding will also be raised as taught in Revelation 20:4-6.

If this is a genuine resurrection, what is the timing of the event? Here the distinction in interpretation arises from the differing point of view of the amillennial and postmillennial interpretations. Amillenarians like Leupold and Edward Young, with some qualification, consider this a general resurrection preceding the eternal state which follows.[12] However, some scholars not committed to premillennialism admit that this is not a general resurrection. J. M. Fuller considers this "not the last and general resurrection, but a partial one which precedes that, and is confined to Daniel's nation."[13] Young, while holding that the ultimate meaning is a general resurrection by implication, says, ". . . the Scripture at this point is not speaking of a general resurrection. . . ."[14]

Premillenarians, however, believe that the hope of a thousand-year kingdom on earth after the second coming of Christ is clearly taught in many Old Testament and New Testament passages and the resurrection of the wicked is placed at the close of the millennium. How can the premillennial point of view be harmonized with this verse?

Some help is afforded in understanding Daniel 12:2 by appealing to more accurate translations. Actually the Hebrew seems to separate sharply the two classes of resurrection. Tregelles following earlier Jewish commentators translated verse 2, "And many from among the sleepers of the dust of the earth shall awake; these shall be unto everlasting life; but those the rest of the sleepers, those who do not awake at this time, shall be unto shame and everlasting contempt."[15] Robert Culver defends this translation by finding support in commentaries by Seiss, and Nathaniel West.[16]

There is obviously no problem in the resurrection of the righteous at the second coming of Jesus Christ as premillenarians and amillenarians generally agree on this point. By the beginning of the millennial kingdom, all the righteous dead already have been raised. Pretribulationists believe that the church, the saints of the present age, are raised before the tribulation; and if Old Testament saints are not raised before the tribulation, they will be raised after the tribulation, prior to the millennial kingdom. Hence, there is no conflict with the statement of the righteous being raised at this time.

The problem arises, however, in that the passage states that the resurrection will extend to "some to shame and everlasting contempt." Here, premillenarians appeal to the clear distinction provided in Revelation 20 which states, after revealing the resurrection of the righteous, "But the rest of the dead live not again until the thousand years were finished. This is the first resurrection" (v. 5). The resurrection of the wicked, the second resurrection, is revealed in Revelation 20:12-13. If the resurrection of Revelation 20:5 and that of 20:12-13 are actual resurrections, fulfilling the prophecy of the resurrection of Daniel 12, it makes very clear that there will be more than one resurrection. The confident assertion of amillenarians such as Leupold that, "A dual resurrection is taught nowhere in the Scriptures"[17] is a judgment which ignores obvious distinctions in the Bible.

First of all, Jesus Christ rose from the dead, as even amillenarians agree. His resurrection is unquestionably separated in time from the final resurrection. At the time of the resurrection of Christ, a token resurrection of saints occurred as stated in Matthew 27:52-53, "And the graves were opened; and many bodies of the saints which slept arose, and came out of the graves after his resurrection, and went into the holy city, and appeared unto many." This also appears to be a genuine resurrection. If the pretribulational position is correct, there is also a resurrection of the church prior to the great tribulation. In any event, a natural and normal interpretation of Revelation 20 would indicate that the resurrection of the righteous occurred at the beginning of the thousand years and the resurrection of the wicked at the end of the thousand years (Rev 20:12-14). Only by spiritualizing this passage and making the first resurrection the new birth of the believer—rather ridiculous in the context of Revelation 20:4 which speaks of martyred dead—can a genuine separation of the resurrection of the righteous and the wicked be denied.

Accordingly, premillenarians consider the revelation to Daniel as a statement of fact that after the great tribulation and the second coming of Christ many, of both the righteous and of the wicked, will be raised. It is not at all unusual for the Old Testament in prophecy to include events separated by a considerable span of time as if they concurred in immediate relation to each other. The passing over of the entire present age—the period between the first and second advents of Christ—in such passages as Isaiah 61:1-2 is familiar to all expositors of the Old Testament. Here is another illustration. The righteous will be raised according to this interpretation as a reward for their faith and faithfulness, but the wicked who die are warned concerning their final judgment. The setting off of the many who awake, into two classes by inference assumes that there will be two resurrections with different destinies. Although this passage does not teach premillennialism expressly, it is not out of harmony with the premillennial interpretation.

In the understanding of this passage, a further difficulty arises in the use of the term *many*. Here, expositors are divided as to whether the word means precisely what it indicates, that is, "many, but not all," or whether the word is here used in the sense that all will be raised.

Leupold argues at some length that *many* means as a matter of fact in this passage "all." He states, "There are also other instances where 'many' and 'all' are used interchangeably, the one emphasizing the fact that there are numerically *many*, the other the fact that *all* are involved."[18] Leupold goes on to cite Matthew 20:28; 26:28; and Romans 5:15, 16 as cases in point.[19]

The fact is, however, that while in some cases *all* may also be "many," it is also true that in some cases *many* is not "all." Here, the precise expositor would prefer to let the text stand for itself, and the text does not say "all." Although interpreting *many* as "all" would be natural exegesis for amillenarians, it is of interest that Edward Young, also an amillenarian, does not take this position. He says,

> We should expect the text to say *all*. In order to escape the difficulty, some expositors have taken the word *many* in the sense of *all*. However, this is forced and unnatural. The correct solution appears to be found in the fact that the Scripture at this point is not speaking of a general resurrection, but rather is setting forth a thought that the salvation which is to occur at this time will not be limited to those who are alive, but will extend also to those who lost their lives. . . . The words, of course, do not exclude the general resurrection, but rather imply it. Their emphasis, however, is upon the resurrection of those who died during the period of great distress.[20]

Even Bevan states, as previously quoted, "Here, however, the resurrection is far from being universal; it includes 'many,' not all, of the dead. That only Israelites are raised is not expressly stated, but appears probable from the context."[21]

From the standpoint of the pretribulational interpretation of prophecy, which holds to a resurrection of the church before the tribulation and therefore as preceding this resurrection, this passage can be taken quite literally. As a matter of fact, if the pretribulationists are correct, there will be an extensive resurrection of the righteous at this point when Christ returns to reign. Although it would be too much to say that this confirms pretribulationism, it harmonizes with this interpretation precisely. At the same time, Young is probably correct that the hope of resurrection is especially extended to the martyred dead of the tribulation who are given special mention in Revelation 20:4.

The Reward of the Righteous

12:3 And they that be wise shall shine like the brightness of the firmament; and they that turn many to righteousness as the stars for ever and ever.

Following the resurrection of the righteous, their faithfulness in witness will be rewarded. It is significant that no mention is made of the punishment of the wicked. Their resurrection will not occur until a thousand years later, according to Revelation 20; and the final judgment at the great white throne will include the judgment of those who wickedly opposed Christ at His second advent and who will be destroyed according to Revelation 19:17-21. The main point of Revelation 20 is that the saints, whether living or dead, may look forward to a glorious reward at the conclusion of the great tribulation when Christ returns.

From verse 2, it is learned that they will receive everlasting life. As Young states, "This is the first occurrence of this expression in the OT."[22] In addition to receiving eternal life itself, those who are among the resurrection to everlasting life will be rewarded by glorification. They are described as "wise" in that they were able to see through the unbelief and wickedness of their generation and put their confidence in the unseen eternal values of their faith. They behaved themselves wisely; that is, they were obedient to God. Because of this, their reward is that they will shine with the same glory as the heavens and fulfill the same function to "declare the glory of God" (Ps 19:1). In a natural Hebrew parallelism, they are also described as having turned "many to righteousness." The lot of those who have influenced others to faith will also be to shine as the stars forever. In the background are the particular references to the fact that "they that understand among the people shall instruct many" (Dan 11:33), fulfilled in the second century B.C., and reference to "them of understanding" mentioned in Daniel 11:35, living in the same period.

To limit this, however, to those in the reign of Antiochus is unjustified, as they are illustrations of faithful saints in all ages.

Keil has summarized the teaching of this passage in these words: "The salvation of the people, which the end shall bring in, consists accordingly in the consummation of the people of God by the resurrection of the dead and the judgment dividing the pious from the godless, according to which the pious shall be raised to eternal life, and the godless shall be given up to everlasting shame and contempt. But the leaders of the people who, amid the wars and conflicts of this life, have turned many to righteousness, shall shine in the imperishable glory of heaven."[23]

The Conclusion of the Revelation

12:4 But thou, O Daniel, shut up the words, and seal the book, even to the time of the end: many shall run to and fro, and knowledge shall be increased.

After experiencing the broad expanse of the revelation—beginning as it did with the kings of Persia, extending through the Maccabean period, then leaping to the end of the age and the great tribulation, and including the resurrections and reward of the righteous—Daniel is now instructed to "shut up the words, and seal the book." In this statement, it is made plain that the revelation, although enlightening and reassuring even to Daniel, was not intended primarily to interpret these events to him alone. The prophecies thus revealed were to have primary application to those living in "the time of the end." In fact, the entire revelation, even the portions already fulfilled through Daniel 11:35, are designed to help those seeking to trust in the Lord in their affliction at the climax of the age. It is significant that in the twentieth century, even though twenty-five hundred years have elapsed, the prophecies of Daniel have never been more relevant to an attempt to understand the course of history and impending future events.

The close of verse 4 with its statement, "many shall run to and fro, and knowledge shall be increased," is difficult to translate; and commentators have not been agreed as to its precise meaning. The familiar interpretation that this phrase refers to increased travel in modern days certainly makes sense, as never in the history of the world has there been more travel. However, in the context the search for knowledge seems to be the main idea. Montgomery interprets it in the light of Amos 8:12, "And they shall wander from sea to sea, and from the north even to the east, they shall run to and fro to seek the word of the LORD, and shall not find it."[24] John Calvin translated it, "Many shall investigate, and knowledge shall increase."[25] Leupold interprets the verse to mean, "Many shall diligently peruse it, and knowledge shall be increased."[26] In the Hebrew the word for "knowledge" is *hadda'at*, literally, "the knowledge," that is, understanding of this long prophecy. Some consider the sentence as referring to the eyes of a reader running "to and fro" in reading the Word of God (cf. 2 Chr 16:9). Whether or not physical wandering and travel is involved, the implication is that attempts to understand the truth will require considerable effort.

Young agrees with Montgomery in finding the key in Amos 8:12 and states, "The verb appears to describe a vain travelling about in order to discover knowledge."[27] As Young goes on to explain, what the angel is saying to Daniel is that for the immediate future, attempts to understand these prophecies will be in vain, but in the time of the end, when these prophecies will become especially pertinent, additional understanding will be given. Accordingly, it is not too much to say that a twentieth-century interpreter of Daniel may understand these prophecies with greater clarity and be able to relate them to history in a way that was impossible in the sixth century B.C. There is also the intimation that the ceaseless search for knowledge by men will often go unrewarded either because they do not look in the right place for it, or because their time and circumstance does not justify their understanding of prophecy that does not immediately concern them. No doubt, those living in the time of the end will have far greater understanding of these things than is possible today.

How Long Until the Time of the End

12:5-8 Then I, Daniel, looked and, behold, there stood other two, the one on this side of the bank of the river, and the other on that side of the bank of the river. And one said to the man clothed in linen, which was upon the waters of the river, How long shall it be to the end of these wonders? And I heard the man clothed in linen, which was upon the waters of the river, when he held up his right hand and his left hand unto heaven, and sware by him that liveth for ever, that it shall be for a time, times, and an half; and when he shall have accomplished to scatter the power of the holy people, all these things shall be finished. And I heard, but I understood not: then said I, O my Lord, what shall be the end of these things?

At the conclusion of the vision Daniel, still observing the scene by the side of the river as in chapter 10, observes two individuals, one on one side of the river and the other on the other. It may be assumed that the river is the Hiddekel (10:4), that is, the Tigris, its more modern name. The individuals whom Daniel observes are probably angelic creatures, in keeping with his experiences in chapter 10. One of these asks the obvious question in the light of the great prophecies which have just preceded, "How long shall it be to the end of these wonders?" In verse 7, reference is made to "the man clothed in linen," apparently the same one described in verses 5 and 6 of chapter 10.

As Daniel observes, the man clothed in linen holds up his right hand and his left to heaven and swears "by him that liveth for ever," no doubt a reference to God, that the time factor involved in the time of the end is "for a time, times, and an half." Although the second angel does not participate in this revelation, it may be in keeping with the concept of two witnesses as establishing a point (Deu 19:15; 31:28; 2 Co 13:1). The fact that the one making the statement raises both hands indicates the solemnity of the oath. Ordinarily, only one hand was raised (Gen 14:22; Deu 32:40). The message is obviously delivered on behalf of God and, to some extent, parallels the thought of Deuteronomy 32:40.[28]

The revelation is further solemnized by the fact that the angel stands by the bank of the river, and the particular word for river is the word ordinarily used for the Nile River. As Young states, "There must be a reason for the choice of the word translated *stream*. As already indicated, it is the common designation for the Nile river. Possibly, it is deliberately employed here to remind Dan. that just as the Lord had once stood over Egypt, the world-nation which was hostile to God's people, so now does He stand over the world kingdom, represented symbolically by the Nile stream, actually the Tigris, ready again to deliver His people."[29]

What is the meaning of the phrase *a time, times, and an half*. This expression, also occurring in Daniel 7:25, apparently refers to the last period preceding the second coming of Christ which brings conclusion to the time of the end. Montgomery, although a liberal scholar, correctly stated the meaning when he wrote, "Here, v. 7, it is in the terms of 7:25, with the Heb. equivalent of the Aram. there; i.e., three and a half years."[30] In other words, it is the last half of the seven-year period of Daniel 9:27 which culminates in the second advent. The expression *time,* is considered a single unit; *times,* as equivalent to two units; and *an half,* a half unit. Adding these units amounts to three and one-half. Obviously, this expression would be obscure if it were not for added light given in other passages and the further revelation given in this chapter. When the three and a half years are fulfilled in them, as the prophecy states, "He shall have accomplished to scatter the power of the holy people," that is, it will be the period of terrible persecution of the people of Israel. The verb translated "scatter" means "to shatter," allowing the translation, "when (they) finish shattering the hand (fig. for *power*) of the holy people."[31] When the persecution has run its course in God's time, and "all these things shall be finished," the time of the end will be concluded.

Although Daniel heard the prophecy plainly, he states in verse 8 that he did not understand it. Daniel rephrases the original question asked by the angel in verse 6, and addresses the angel with the words, "O my Lord, what shall be the end of these things?" Daniel is stating his bewilderment in his effort to understand the revelations given concerning the consummation of the time of the end.

THE CONCLUDING EXPLANATION OF THE ANGEL

12:9-13 And he said, Go thy way, Daniel: for the words are closed up and sealed till the time of the end. Many shall be purified, and made white, and tried; but the wicked shall do wickedly: and none of the wicked shall understand; but the wise shall understand. And from the time that the daily sacrifice shall be taken away, and the abomination that maketh desolate set up, there shall be a thousand two hundred and ninety days. Blessed is he that waiteth, and cometh to the thousand three hundred and five and thirty days. But go thou thy way till the end be: for thou shalt rest, and stand in thy lot at the end of the days.

In verse 9, Daniel is once again informed that the revelation given to him will not be completely understood until the time of the end. Daniel is not rebuked for his curiosity, as it is only natural to ask the questions which he raised. The primary purpose of the revelation, however, was to inform those who would live in the time of the end. The confirming interpretation of history and prophecy fulfilled would be necessary before the final prophecies could be understood.

However, in partial answer to Daniel's question, which concerned the purpose of the events revealed, the prophet is informed in verse 10 that the time of the end will have a twofold result: first, it will result in the purification of the saints; second, it will manifest the true character of the wickedness of the human heart. Likewise, understanding the events of the time of the end will be possible for "the wise" who "shall understand," but "none of the wicked shall understand." The understanding of prophecy peculiarly requires spiritual insight and the teaching of the Holy Spirit. Even though the Scriptures describe in great detail the time of the end, it is obvious that the wicked will not avail themselves of this divine revelation; but it will be a source of comfort and direction to those who are true believers in God. Divine revelation is often given in such a way that it is hid to the wicked even though it is understandable by those spiritually minded.

In verses 11 and 12, two important revelations are given by way of clarification of the duration of the time of the end. According to verse 11, a period of 1,290 days will elapse from the time that the daily sacrifice is taken away until the time of the end is consummated. The time that the daily sacrifice is taken away is equated with "the abomination that maketh desolate." This expression originating in the revelation of Daniel 9:27 has reference to the stopping of sacrifices in the middle of the seven-year period. The predicted event had its corresponding anticipation in the desolation of the temple by Antiochus Epiphanes in the second century B.C. (Dan 8:11-14). That this event is future and not a reference to the historic desecration by Antiochus is apparent from the prophecy of Christ in Matthew 24:15 where "the abomination of desolation, spoken of by Daniel the prophet," is given as a sign of the great tribulation. From these passages, it is obvious that the last three and a half years of the time of the end is in view.

Seiss summarizes this interpretation as follows,

> Nor shall this state of things be only for a few days, weeks or months, but for full three and a half years. In not less than six different places, and in almost as many different ways, is this declared in the prophecies, including both Testaments. It is for "a time and times and the dividing of time" (Dan. vii.25)—"It shall be for a time, times, and a half" (xii.7)—"the holy city shall be tread underfoot forty and two months" (Rev. xi.2)—"the woman fled into the wilderness, a thousand two hundred and three-score days"—for "a time, and times, and half a time" (xii.6, 14)—"and power was given him to continue forty and two months" (xiii.5). All these passages refer to one and the same period of oppression and trouble under the Antichrist, and in each instance the measure is three and a half years, dating from the breaking of the league and the suspension of the daily offering to the destruction of the monster by the revelation of Jesus Christ. Our Lord ministered on earth three and a half years, and the Antichrist shall enact his Satanic ministry for the same length of time.[32]

The three and a half years of Daniel 9:27, however, are normally taken to be three and a half years or forty-two months of thirty days each, following the custom of the Jews. This would be only 1,260 days. The duration of the great tribulation as forty-two months is confirmed by Revelation 11:2; 13:5, which is considered equivalent to the "time, times, and an half" of Daniel 7:25 and 12:7. Why then are thirty days added to the 1,260 days? This question is further complicated by verse 12 which states that there is a special blessing for the one who attains to the 1,335 days. This is still another forty-five days beyond the limit of verse 11.

Although Daniel does not explain these varying durations, it is obvious that the second coming of Christ and the establishment of His millennial kingdom requires time. The 1,260 day period or precisely forty-two months of thirty days each, can be regarded as culminating with the second advent itself. This is followed by several divine judgments such as the judgment of the nations (Mt 25:31-46), and the regathering and judgment of Israel (Eze 20:34-38). These great judgments beginning with the living on earth and purging out of unbelievers who have worshiped the beast, although handled quickly, will require time. By the

1,335 days, or seventy-five days after the second advent, these great judgments will have been accomplished and the millennial kingdom formally launched. Those who attain to this period are obviously those who have been judged worthy to enter the kingdom. Hence, they are called "blessed."

In any case, there is no justification for the attempts to link this with Antiochus Epiphanes as Montgomery does.[33] Even Zöckler admits, "The troubled events of the Maccabean period, which might deserve notice as the points of the beginning and the end of the historical equivalent of the three and a half years, do not present a satisfactory reason for such vacillating predictions; for the exact period required cannot be found in that epoch, however its limits may be fixed."[34] Here, as throughout the book of Daniel, the expression *the time of the end* is the end of Gentile power, which obviously extends beyond the present age to the second advent as anticipated in the prophecy of Christ in Matthew 24:15-31. The whole approach of the liberal scholar attempting to treat Daniel as history and not prophecy, breaks down when the comprehensive nature of Daniel's prophetic foreview is understood. The explanation of the additional time required to complete the transfer from the time of the end to the time of the fifth kingdom no doubt did not help Daniel much. But in the light of New Testament revelation, it provides the background for the transition from the great tribulation to the kingdom of peace and righteousness on earth.

Anticipating that Daniel would not completely understand these additional revelations, the angel informs him, "But go thou thy way till the end be." The angel predicts that Daniel will "rest," that is, die, and "stand in thy lot at the end of the days," that is, be resurrected in the resurrection of Daniel 12:2 and participate in the glorious triumph of Christ as the millennial kingdom is inaugurated. Inasmuch as resurrected saints are declared to reign with Christ (e.g., Rev 5:10), it is conceivable that Daniel, who reigned under Nebuchadnezzar and Darius the Mede, will be allocated a future executive responsibility in the kingdom of Christ on earth for which his earthly experience could constitute a preparation.

This concluding revelation of Daniel's prophecy, acting as a capstone on all the preceding tremendous revelations, establishes the book of Daniel as the greatest and most comprehensive prophetic revelation of the Old Testament. Its counterpart in the New Testament in the book of Revelation provides the final word of God concerning the prophetic program of the ages. In the light of world conditions today, which would seem to anticipate the fulfillment of Daniel's time of the end, it is possible to understand Daniel today as never before in history. The hour may not be far distant when faithful saints in the midst of trial in the great tribulation will turn to these pages of Scripture and find in them the strength and courage to remain true even though it mean a martyr's death.

For Christians living in the age of grace and searching for understanding of these difficult days which may be bringing to a close God's purpose in His church, the book of Daniel, as never before, casts a broad light upon contemporary events foreshadowing the consummation which may not be far distant. If God is reviving His people Israel politically, allowing the church to drift into indifference and apostasy, and permitting the nations to move toward centralization of political power, it may not be long before the time of the end will overtake the world. Many who look for the coming of the Lord anticipate their removal from the earth's scene before the final days of the time of the Gentiles are fulfilled.

When the plan of God has run its full course, it will be evident then with even more clarity than at present that God has not allowed a word to fall to the ground. As Christ said while on earth, "Till heaven and earth pass, one jot or one tittle shall in no wise pass from the law, till all be fulfilled" (Mt 5:18).

NOTES

INTRODUCTION

1. Cf. H. C. Leupold, *Exposition of Daniel,* p. 8.
2. Cf. ibid., pp. 5-7.
3. Robert Dick Wilson, "Book of Daniel," *ISBE* 2:783.
4. J. Barton Payne, "Book of Daniel," *Zondervan Pictorial Bible Dictionary,* p. 198.
5. Ralph Alexander, Abstract of "Hermeneutics of Old Testament Apocalyptic Literature," doctor's dissertation, p. 1.
6. Ibid.
7. Cf. H. H. Rowley, *The Relevance of the Apocalyptic,* pp. 29-55; and Stanley B. Frost, *Old Testament Apocalyptic,* pp. 178-209.
8. Cf. W. J. Martin, "Language of the Old Testament," *The New Bible Dictionary,* pp. 712-13.
9. William H. Brownlee, *The Meaning of the Qumran Scrolls for the Bible,* p. 36.
10. S. R. Driver, *The Book of Daniel,* pp. lix-lx.
11. Martin, p. 712; cf. Wilson, 2:784.
12. Gleason L. Archer, Jr., *A Survey of Old Testament Introduction,* pp. 377-78.
13. Cf. Robert D. Culver, *Daniel and the Latter Days,* pp. 95-104; and Carl August Auberlen, *The Prophecies of Daniel and the Revelations of St. John,* pp. 27-31.
14. Wilson, 2: 783-84.
15. Cf. ibid., p. 784.
16. Cf. ibid., p. 787.
17. Jerome, *Commentary on Daniel,* pp. 15-16.
18. Thomas S. Kepler, *Dreams of the Future,* pp. 32-33.
19. Merrill F. Unger, *Unger's Bible Dictionary,* p. 238.
20. James A. Montgomery, *A Critical and Exegetical Commentary on the Book of Daniel,* p. 3.
21. Ibid., p. 2.
22. James B. Pritchard, ed., *Ancient Near Eastern Texts Relating to the Old Testament,* pp. 149-55.
23. Cf. W. A. Criswell, *Expository Sermons on the Book of Daniel,* 1: 54.
24. Charles Boutflower, *In and Around the Book of Daniel,* pp. 287-88.
25. Brownlee, p. 30.
26. Jacob M. Myers, *The Anchor Bible, I Chronicles,* pp. LXXXVII ff.
27. Raymond K. Harrison, *Introduction to the Old Testament,* p. 1118.
28. Wilson, 2:785.
29. Leupold, p. 143.
30. Robert Dick Wilson, "The Aramaic of Daniel," in *Biblical and Theological Studies,* p. 296.
31. Edwin M. Yamauchi, *Greece and Babylon,* pp. 17-24.
32. Robert Dick Wilson, *Studies in the Book of Daniel,* 402 pp.
33. Alexander, abs. p. 2.
34. Cf. Rowley, pp. 56-57.
35. Cf. Montgomery, pp. 84 ff.; and Archer, pp. 380-81.

CHAPTER 1

1. J. A. Montgomery, *A Critical and Exegetical Commentary on the Book of Daniel,* pp. 113-16.

2. Carl Frederick Keil, *Biblical Commentary on the Book of Daniel*, p. 60.
3. Jack Finegan, *Handbook of Biblical Chronology*, p. 202.
4. Hayim Tadmor, "Chronicle of the Last Kings of Judah," *Journal of Near Eastern Studies* 15:227.
5. D. J. Wiseman, *Chronicles of the Chaldean Kings*, pp. 20-26.
6. H. C. Leupold, *Exposition of Daniel*, pp. 47-54.
7. Finegan, pp. 194-201.
8. Edwin R. Thiele, *Mysterious Numbers of the Hebrew Kings*, p. 166.
9. Leupold, pp. 54-55.
10. Keil, pp. 62-71.
11. Edward J. Young, *The Prophecy of Daniel*, p. 38.
12. Siegfried H Horn, *Seventh Day Adventist Dictionary of the Bible*, p. 83.
13. Young, p. 39.
14. Flavius Josephus, *The Works of Flavius Josephus*, p. 222.
15. Young, p. 39.
16. Montgomery, p. 119.
17. Robert H. Charles, *The Book of Daniel*, p. 7.
18. A. L. Oppenheim, "Babylonian and Assyrian Historical Texts," in *Ancient Near Eastern Texts Relating to the Old Testament*, p. 308.
19. Montgomery, p. 127.
20. Leupold, p. 62. See Montgomery, pp. 127-28 for a complete discussion; cf. Brown, Driver, and Briggs, *Hebrew and English Lexicon to the Old Testament*, p. 834.
21. Young, p. 42.
22. The privilege of sitting at the king's table is discussed by Roland de Vaux, *Ancient Israel, Its Life and Institutions*, pp. 120-23.
23. Young, p. 274.
24. Leupold, p. 64.
25. Keil, p. 79; Young, p. 43.
26. Keil, p. 79.
27. Cf. Young, p. 43.
28. Ibid.
29. Cf. Leupold, p. 65.
30. Ibid.; cf. Montgomery, p. 128.
31. Montgomery, pp. 128-29; Brown, Driver, and Briggs, p. 567; Horn, p. 724.
32. Young, p. 43.
33. Keil, pp. 79-80.
34. Keil, p. 80.
35. Young, p. 45.
36. Ibid.
37. Montgomery, p. 131.
38. Cf. Leupold, p. 70; Keil, p. 81.
39. Young, pp. 45-46.
40. Montgomery, p. 131.
41. Young, p. 46; cf. Montgomery, p. 132.
42. John Calvin, *Commentaries on the Book of the Prophet Daniel*, 1:105.
43. Calvin, 1:112.
44. Keil, p. 83.
45. Young, pp. 52-53.
46. Charles, p. 12.

CHAPTER 2

1. Samuel P. Tregelles, *Remarks on the Prophetic Visions in the Book of Daniel*, p. 6.
2. D. J. Wiseman, *Chronicles of the Chaldean Kings (626-556 B.C.)*, p. 25.
3. Ibid.
4. Ibid., p. 26.
5. H. C. Leupold, *Exposition of Daniel*, p. 81.
6. Ibid., p. 82.
7. E. J. Young, *The Prophecy of Daniel*, pp. 55-56; and S. R. Driver, *The Book of Daniel*, p. 17. Cf. previous discussion of Dan 1:1.

8. Wiseman, pp. 25 ff.; E. R. Thiele, *The Mysterious Numbers of the Hebrew Kings*, pp. 159 ff.; and J. Finegan, *Handbook of Biblical Chronology*, p. 38.
9. J. A. Montgomery, *A Critical and Exegetical Commentary on the Book of Daniel*, pp. 140-41.
10. R. D. Wilson, *Studies in the Book of Daniel*, 402 pp.
11. For support for the pluperfect see P. Paul Jouon, S. J., *Grammaire de l' Hebreu Biblique*, p. 322, para. 118 *d.*
12. Leupold, p. 83.
13. Montgomery, p. 141.
14. Geoffrey R. King, *Daniel*, p. 49.
15. Leupold, p. 75.
16. Ibid., p. 76.
17. Young, p. 57. *See also* p. 51.
18. See Leupold's discussion, pp. 83-86; and Young, pp. 271-73.
19. Cf. Young, pp. 58-59; and Leupold, pp. 86-88.
20. K. A. Kitchen, "The Aramaic of Daniel," in *Notes on Some Problems in the Book of Daniel*, eds. D. J. Wiseman, et al., p. 31.
21. Ibid., p. 32.
22. Franz Rosenthal, *A Grammar of Biblical Aramaic*, pp. 59, 76.
23. C. F. Keil, *Biblical Commentary on the Book of Daniel*, pp. 90-92.
24. Leupold, p 89.
25. Young, p. 60.
26. Ibid.
27. Young, p. 60; Montgomery, pp. 145-47.
28. Driver, p. 20.
29. Leupold, p. 90.
30. Keil, p. 89.
31. Young, p. 62.
32. Ibid., p. 63.
33. Montgomery, pp. 149-50.
34. Keil, p. 96.
35. Brown, Driver, and Briggs, *Hebrew and English Lexicon to the Old Testament*, p. 933.
36. Montgomery, p. 156.
37. W. H. Griffith Thomas, "The Purpose of the Fourth Gospel," *Bibliotheca Sacra* 125:262.
38. Montgomery, p. 157.
39. Leupold, p. 101.
40. Ibid., p. 105.
41. Montgomery, p. 162; cf. discussion by Leupold, pp. 105-6.
42. Driver, p. 26.
43. Ibid.
44. Leupold, p. 105.
45. R. D. Culver, *Daniel and the Latter Days*, p. 107.
46. Ibid., p. 108.
47. Young, p. 71; Keil, p. 102.
48. Keil, p. 102.
49. Ibid., p. 103.
50. Leupold, p. 110.
51. Ibid.
52. Ibid., pp. 111-12.
53. Keil, p. 104.
54. Young, p. 72.
55. Ibid., p. 73.
56. Eric W. Heaton, *The Book of Daniel*, p. 131, cf. pp. 169-72.
57. Young, pp. 73-74.
58. Frederic W. Farrar, *The Book of Daniel*, pp. 154-160; cf. Leupold, pp. 115-16.
59. Leupold, p. 117; Wilson, pp. 128-295.
60. Wilson, p. 264.
61. Leupold, p. 119.
62. Young, p. 77.
63. Cf. Young's discussion, pp. 76-77; and Montgomery, pp. 167-68.
64. Montgomery, p. 167.

65. Ibid.
66. Keil, p. 108.
67. Montgomery, p. 176.
68. Keil, pp. 108-9.
69. Henry A. Ironside, *Lectures on Daniel the Prophet,* pp. 36-37.
70. Arno C. Gaebelein, *The Prophet Daniel,* p. 31.
71. Keil, p. 109.
72. Ibid.
73. King, p. 72.
74. Ibid., pp. 72-73.
75. Ibid., p. 73.
76. Ibid., pp. 75-76.
77. Culver, pp. 115-20.
78. Ibid.
79. Leupold, p. 121.
80. Young, p. 78.
81. Ibid.
82. Josephus, "Jewish Antiquities," in *Josephus,* 6:476-77.
83. Young, pp. 81-82.

Chapter 3

1. S. P. Tregelles, *Remarks on the Prophetic Visions in the Book of Daniel.*
2. R. D. Culver, *Daniel and the Latter Days.*
3. G. R. King, *Daniel,* p. 78.
4. For a full discussion see C. F. Keil, *Biblical Commentary on the Book of Daniel,* pp. 114-15.
5. H. C. Leupold, *Exposition of Daniel,* pp. 136-37.
6. Ibid., p. 137; cf. E. J. Young, *The Prophecy of Daniel,* pp. 83-85; and Keil, pp. 118-19.
7. J. A. Montgomery, *A Critical and Exegetical Commentary on the Book of Daniel,* p. 195.
8. Cf. Leupold, p. 137; and Keil, p. 119.
9. Young, p. 85.
10. Ibid.
11. Ibid., p. 86.
12. Montgomery, pp. 199-200.
13. K. A. Kitchen, "The Aramaic of Daniel," in *Notes on Some Problems in the Book of Daniel,* p. 43. For entire discussion see pp. 35-50.
14. Keil, pp. 120-21.
15. G. L. Archer, Jr., *A Survey of Old Testament Introduction,* p. 375.
16. Concerning Greek loan words, see Kitchen, pp. 44-50. Of particular interest is the presence of a Greek money term, *stater,* in the Aramaic papyri from Egypt in documents of c. 400 B.C.
17. R. D. Wilson, *Biblical and Theological Studies,* p. 296. Cf. Leupold, p. 143; also the discussion on "The Greek Words in Daniel" in Edwin M. Yamauchi's, *Greece and Babylon,* pp. 17-24.
18. William F. Albright, *From the Stone Age to Christianity,* p. 259.
19. Leupold, p. 143.
20. Ibid.
21. T. C. Mitchell and R. Joyce, "The Musical Instruments in Nebuchadnezzar's Orchestra," in *Notes on Some Problems in the Book of Daniel,* pp. 19-27.
22. Yamauchi, pp. 17-24.
23. For a complete description of these instruments see Leupold, pp. 144-45; Mitchell and Joyce, pp. 19-27; and Keil, pp. 122-24.
24. Keil, p. 124; cf. Leupold, p. 145.
25. Keil, p. 124.
26. Montgomery, p. 202.
27. Cf. the account of a young slave being thrown into a furnace, cited by Emil G. Kraeling, *Rand McNally Bible Atlas,* p. 323.
28. Montgomery, pp. 205-7; F. Rosenthal, *A Grammar of Biblical Aramaic,* p. 40.
29. Cf. Montgomery, pp. 208-9; and Rosenthal, pp. 24, 84.

30. Young, p. 90.
31. Montgomery, p. 208.
32. Leupold, p. 153.
33. King, p. 85.
34. R. H. Charles, *The Book of Daniel*, p. 35.
35. Rudolph Kittel, *Biblia Hebraica*, 2:1270.
36. Leupold, p. 159.
37. Ibid., pp. 163-64.

CHAPTER 4

1. H. C. Leupold, *Exposition of Daniel*, p. 204.
2. Cf. R. H. Charles, *The Book of Daniel*, p. 39; and J. A. Montgomery, *A Critical and Exegetical Commentary on the Book of Daniel*, pp. 220-23; 247-49.
3. Charles, p. 37.
4. Ibid.
5. Montgomery, pp. 247-49.
6. Ibid., p. 222.
7. Cf. Leupold, pp. 170-71.
8. Ibid., p. 173.
9. E. J. Young, *The Prophecy of Daniel*, p. 99; Montgomery, pp. 225-26.
10. Leupold, p. 176; S. R. Driver, *The Book of Daniel*, p. 48.
11. Driver, p. 48, citing his "Hebrew Authority," in *Authority and Archeology*, pp. 137-38.
12. Young, p. 99; cf. Driver, p. 48.
13. Leupold, p. 178.
14. Montgomery, pp. 229-30.
15. Norman W. Porteous, *Daniel: A Commentary*, p. 68.
16. Young, p. 101.
17. Cf. ibid., pp. 101-2; Leupold, p. 180; and Montgomery, pp. 228-30.
18. C. F. Keil, *Biblical Commentary on the Book of Daniel*, p. 150.
19. Montgomery, pp. 231-32.
20. Keil, pp. 148-51.
21. Ibid., p. 154.
22. Young, p. 106.
23. Leupold, p. 190.
24. For further discussion of this, see Leupold, pp. 194-96.
25. Montgomery, pp. 243-44.
26. Leupold, p. 201.
27. Keil, p. 159.
28. Young, p. 112.
29. Raymond Harrison, *Introduction to the Old Testament*, pp. 1116-17.
30. Frank M. Cross, *The Ancient Library of Qumran and Modern Biblical Studies*, pp. 123-24; cf. Millar Burrows, *More Light on the Dead Sea Scrolls*, p. 400, and David N. Freedman, "The Prayer of Nabonidus," *Bulletin of the American Schools of Oriental Research* 145:31-32. For a conservative evaluation, see Raymond K. Harrison, *Introduction to the Old Testament*, pp. 1117-21.
31. Montgomery, p. 245.
32. Young, p. 113.

CHAPTER 5

1. Eusebius, *Praeper. Ev.* ix. 41, cited by C. F. Keil, *Biblical Commentary on the Book of Daniel*, p. 164.
2. See Raymond P. Dougherty, *Nabonidus and Belshazzar*.
3. James A. Montgomery, *A Critical and Exegetical Commentary on the Book of Daniel*, p. 249.
4. E. J. Young, *The Prophecy of Daniel*, p. 115.
5. Cf. H. C. Leupold, *Exposition of Daniel*, p. 210; and George A. Barton, *Archaeology and the Bible*, p. 481 ff.
6. H. H. Rowley, "The Historicity of the Fifth Chapter of Daniel," *Journal of Theological Studies* 32:12.

7. N. W. Porteous, *Daniel: A Commentary*, p. 76.
8. For further discussion of this problem, see Young, pp. 115-19; Keil, pp. 162-79; and Leupold, pp. 208-14. Cf. the interesting discussion of Belshazzar by C. Boutflower, *In and Around the Book of Daniel*, pp. 114 ff.
9. Keil, pp. 165-76.
10. Leupold, pp. 208-13.
11. Ibid., p. 214. See also Keil, p. 179, citing Athenaeus, as does Young, p. 118.
12. M. E. L. Mallowan, "Nimrud," in *Archaeology and Old Testament Study*, p. 62.
13. Athenaeus, *Deipnosophistae* IV, 145.
14. Ibid., p. 165.
15. Keil, pp. 174-75.
16. Leupold, p. 211.
17. Edward B. Pusey, *Daniel the Prophet*, p. 346. See also Leupold, pp. 216-17, who discusses this quotation from Pusey.
18. Otto Zöckler, *Daniel, Commentary on the Holy Scriptures*, p. 126.
19. Keil, p. 181.
20. Herodotus, *History of the Persian Wars*, 1:178-83.
21. Cf. Merrill F. Unger, *Unger's Bible Dictionary*, pp. 115-16; and T. G. Pinches, "Babel, Babylon," in *International Standard Bible Encyclopedia*, 1:350. For a map of Babylon in sixth century B.C., see D. J. Wiseman, "Babylon," in *The New Bible Dictionary*, pp. 117-20. For pictures and further details, see R. K. Harrison, "Babylon," in *The Zondervan Pictorial Bible Dictionary*, pp. 89-93.
22. Cf. Montgomery, p. 253, citing Koldewey, *Das wieder erstehende Babylon;* and E. G. Kraeling, *Rand McNally Bible Atlas*, p. 327.
23. Keil, pp. 182-83.
24. Ibid., p. 184.
25. F. Rosenthal, *A Grammar of Biblical Aramaic*, p. 71.
26. R. H. Charles, *The Book of Daniel*, pp. 57-59; cf. Keil, pp. 184-85.
27. Keil, p. 185; Leupold, pp. 224-25.
28. Montgomery, p. 258.
29. Arthur Jeffery, "The Book of Daniel, Introduction and Exegesis," in *The Interpreter's Bible*, 6:426.
30. G. R. King, *Daniel*, p. 148.
31. Young, p. 124.
32. Cf. Montgomery, pp. 262-64.
33. Charles, pp. 57-59; Keil, p. 126.
34. Young, pp. 125-26.
35. Ibid., p. 126; cf. Montgomery, pp. 263-64.
36. Leupold, p. 235.
37. Herodotus, 1:190-91.
38. Keil, pp. 171-72.
39. J. B. Pritchard, ed., *Ancient Near Eastern Texts Relating to the Old Testament*, pp. 315-16.
40. John C. Whitcomb, Jr., *Darius the Mede*, p. 73.

CHAPTER 6

1. H. H. Rowley, *Darius the Mede and the Four World Empires in the Book of Daniel*, p. 8.
2. D. J. Wiseman, "Some Historical Problems in the Book of Daniel," in *Notes on Some Problems in the Book of Daniel*, pp. 9-18.
3. Rowley, pp. 30-36.
4. Ibid., pp. 37-43.
5. Ibid., pp. 19-29.
6. Ibid., pp. 12-18.
7. R. D. Wilson, *Studies in the Book of Daniel*, pp. 128 ff.
8. Rowley, p. 19.
9. J. C. Whitcomb, Jr., *Darius the Mede*.
10. Wiseman, p. 14.
11. K. A. Kitchen, *Ancient Orient and the Old Testament*, pp. 30 ff.
12. J. A. Montgomery, *A Critical and Exegetical Commentary on the Book of Daniel*, p. 269.

13. Ibid.
14. Ibid., pp. 269-70.
15. Ibid., p. 270.
16. F. Rosenthal, *A Grammar of Biblical Aramaic*, p. 96.
17. E. J. Young, *The Prophecy of Daniel*, p. 134.
18. Moses Stuart, *A Commentary on the Book of Daniel*, p. 171.
19. C. F. Keil, *Biblical Commentary on the Book of Daniel*, p. 216.
20. Rosenthal, p. 81. For further discussion, see Montgomery, pp. 277-78.
21. Montgomery, p. 278.
22. Ibid.

Chapter 7

1. For an outline study of Daniel's view of world history by the author, see *The Nations in Prophecy*, pp. 53-60.
2. C. F. Keil, *Biblical Commentary on the Book of Daniel*, p. 245.
3. Ibid., pp. 245-46.
4. H. H. Rowley, *Darius the Mede and the Four World Empires in the Book of Daniel*, p. 179.
5. D. J. Wiseman, "Some Historical Problems in the Book of Daniel," in *Notes on Some Problems in the Book of Daniel*, p. 10.
6. James A. Montgomery, *A Critical and Exegetical Commentary on the Book of Daniel*, p. 88.
7. Ibid., p. 282.
8. Ibid., pp. 88-89.
9. Ibid., p. 88.
10. Rowley, p. 179.
11. D. J. Wiseman, "Belshazzar," in *The New Bible Dictionary*, p. 139.
12. R. D. Culver, *Daniel and the Latter Days*, pp. 95-104.
13. C. A. Auberlen, *The Prophecies of Daniel and the Revelations of St. John*.
14. Montgomery, p. 282.
15. Arthur Jeffrey, "The Book of Daniel," in *The Interpreter's Bible*, p. 452.
16. Keil, p. 222.
17. Ibid.
18. Ibid., pp. 222-23.
19. H. C. Leupold, *Exposition of Daniel*, pp. 284-85.
20. For a study of the prophecies concerning Babylon, see Walvoord, *The Nations in Prophecy*, pp. 61-69.
21. Leupold, p. 287.
22. Rowley, p. 67.
23. Ibid.
24. Ibid.
25. The radical textual emendations of H. L. Ginsberg (*Studies in Daniel*, chap. 2, pp. 5 ff.), have been successfully disposed of by H. H. Rowley ("The Unity of the Book of Daniel," in *Hebrew Union College Annual* 23:233-73, and *The Servant of the Lord and Other Essays on the Old Testament*, pp. 250 ff.).
26. Leupold, pp. 289-90.
27. For a summary of the biblical references to and prophecies about the Medo-Persian empire, see Walvoord, *The Nations in Prophecy*, pp. 70-75.
28. Montgomery, p. 283.
29. Rowley, *Darius the Mede*, pp. 138-60.
30. R. H. Charles, *The Book of Daniel*, p. 68.
31. Rowley, pp. 144-45.
32. Ibid., pp. 145-46.
33. S. R. Driver, *The Book of Daniel*, p. 82.
34. Jerome, *Commentary on Daniel*, p. 74.
35. E. J. Young, *The Prophecy of Daniel*, p. 145.
36. Leupold, p. 292.
37. For a summary of Daniel's prophecies about Greece, see Walvoord, *The Nations in Prophecy*, pp. 76-82.
38. Young, pp. 145-46.
39. J. Calvin, *Commentaries on the Book of the Prophet Daniel*, 2:18-19; Jerome, p. 75.

40. Keil, p. 293.
41. Young, p. 146.
42. Leupold, p. 287.
43. For a summary of the history of Rome, see Walvoord, *The Nations in Prophecy,* pp. 83-87.
44. Rowley, p. 71.
45. Ibid., p. 93.
46. Leupold, pp. 297-98.
47. Young, p. 293.
48. Cf. ibid.
49. Cf. ibid., p. 290.
50. Cf. Young, pp. 275-94; and Leupold, pp. 298-99.
51. Young, pp. 148-50.
52. Leupold, p. 308.
53. G. L. Archer, Jr., *A Survey of Old Testament Introduction,* p. 384.
54. A. C. Gaebelein, *The Prophet Daniel,* p. 77.
55. Leupold, p. 305.
56. Young, p. 152.
57. Rowley, p. 87.
58. Montgomery, p. 302.
59. Driver, p. 87.
60. N. W. Porteous, *Daniel: A Commentary,* p. 110.
61. Driver, p. 88.
62. Cf. Young, p. 154; and Leupold, p. 307.
63. Driver, p. 88.
64. Keil, p. 236.
65. Young, p. 155; Montgomery, pp. 317-24.
66. Young, pp. 155-56.
67. Edward Gibbon, *The Decline and Fall of the Roman Empire,* 2:1441.
68. Ibid., p. 1458.
69. Leupold, pp. 313-14.
70. Keil, pp. 237-39.
71. Driver, p. 89; Montgomery, p. 306.
72. Driver, p. 89.
73. Charles, p. 79.
74. Ibid.
75. T. H. Gaster, *The Dead Sea Scriptures,* p. 275.
76. Young, p. 157.
77. Montgomery, p. 307.
78. Young, p. 158.
79. Montgomery, p. 309.
80. Ibid.; Driver, p. 91.
81. Keil, p. 240.
82. Driver, p. 92; cf. also Montgomery, pp. 311-12.
83. Montgomery, p. 312.
84. Ibid., p. 316.
85. Ibid.
86. Rowley, *Darius the Mede,* p. 70.
87. Ibid., p. 71.

Chapter 8

1. Cf. R. D. Culver, *Daniel and the Latter Days,* pp. 95-104.
2. A. C. Gaebelein, *The Prophet Daniel,* p. 94.
3. E. J. Young, *The Prophecy of Daniel,* p. 165.
4. Otto Zöckler, "The Book of the Prophet Daniel," in *A Commentary on the Holy Scriptures,* 13:171; cf. pp. 33-34.
5. A. L. Oppenheim, "Belshazzar," in *The Interpreter's Dictionary of the Bible,* 1:379-80.
6. Young, p. 165.
7. C. F. Keil, *Biblical Commentary on the Book of Daniel,* p. 285.

8. J. A. Montgomery, *The Book of Daniel*, p. 325. Cf. Josephus, *The Works of Flavius Josephus*, p. 320.
9. Keil, p. 285.
10. Montgomery, pp. 325-26.
11. S. R. Driver, *The Book of Daniel*, p. 111.
12. Montgomery, p. 327.
13. Cf. M. F. Unger, *Unger's Bible Dictionary*, pp. 1022-23.
14. Young, p. 178.
15. For a brief history of Medo-Persia, see Walvoord, *The Nations in Prophecy*, pp. 70 ff.
16. Keil, p. 290.
17. Ibid., p. 291.
18. F. Cumont, "La plus Ancienne geographie astrologique," *Klio* 9:263-73.
19. Driver, p. 113.
20. H. C. Leupold, *Exposition of Daniel*, p. 339.
21. Young, p. 169; cf. Walvoord, *The Nations in Prophecy*, pp. 76 ff.
22. Young, p. 169.
23. William W. Tarn, *Alexander the Great*, 1:145-46.
24. N. W. Porteous, *Daniel: A Commentary*, p. 123.
25. Young, p. 169; Leupold, p. 344; Montgomery, pp. 332-33.
26. Montgomery, p. 333.
27. Ibid., pp. 333-35.
28. Leupold, p. 346.
29. Driver, p. 116.
30. Montgomery, p. 335.
31. Young, pp. 165 ff.
32. Montgomery, pp. 335-36.
33. Young, p. 172.
34. Ibid.
35. Uriah Smith, *The Sanctuary and the Twenty-three Hundred Days of Daniel 8:14*, p. 119.
36. Young, p. 173.
37. Keil, p. 304.
38. Ibid., pp. 303-4.
39. See D. H. Wheaton, "Antiochus," in *The New Bible Dictionary*, pp. 41-42.
40. J. Calvin, *Commentaries on the Book of the Prophet Daniel*, 2:112.
41. Young, p. 175.
42. For extrascriptural mention of angels, see Montgomery, p. 345.
43. Ibid., p. 346.
44. Porteous, p. 128.
45. Driver, p. 99.
46. Ibid., p. 121. Bracketed material in the original.
47. Young, p. 288.
48. George H. Pember, *The Great Prophecies of the Centuries Concerning Israel and the Gentiles*, pp. 289-90; cf. Clarence Larkin, *The Book of Daniel*, p. 165.
49. S. P. Tregelles, *Remarks on the Prophetic Visions in the Book of Daniel*, p. 82.
50. Ibid., p. 83.
51. E. B. Pusey, *Daniel the Prophet*, p. 135.
52. Cyrus I. Scofield, ed., *Scofield Reference Bible*, p. 913, and *New Scofield Reference Bible*, p. 911.
53. Louis T. Talbot, *The Prophecies of Daniel*, p. 143.
54. William Kelly, *Lectures on the Book of Daniel*, p. 132.
55. Nathaniel West, *Daniel's Great Prophecy*, p. 103.
56. Joseph A. Seiss, *Voices from Babylon: Or the Records of Daniel the Prophet*, p. 221.
57. J. Dwight Pentecost, *Prophecy for Today*, pp. 82-83.
58. J. D. Pentecost, *Things to Come*, pp. 332-34. These points are a summary of an extended discussion.
59. William C. Stevens, *The Book of Daniel*, p. 125.
60. H. A. Ironside, *Lectures on Daniel the Prophet*, p. 150.
61. Cf. Ironside, pp. 147-51; and A. C. Gaebelein, pp. 111-13.
62. A. Jeffrey, "Daniel," in *The Interpreter's Bible*, 6:483.

CHAPTER 9

1. Robert Anderson, *The Coming Prince,* p. iii.
2. Cited by Wilbur M. Smith, "Jerusalem," in *Zondervan Pictorial Bible Dictionary,* p. 421.
3. Cf. D. F. Payne, "Jerusalem," in *The New Bible Dictionary,* p. 616.
4. Cf. R. H. Charles, *The Book of Daniel,* pp. 96-97. Cf. also N. W. Porteous, *Daniel: A Commentary,* p. 137.
5. Nelson Glueck, *Hesed in the Bible.*
6. J. Calvin, *Commentaries on the Prophet Daniel,* 2:150.
7. M. Stuart, *A Commentary on the Book of Daniel,* p. 258.
8. H. C. Leupold, *Exposition of Daniel,* p. 384.
9. Frederick A. Tatford, *The Climax of the Ages,* p. 150.
10. Stuart, pp. 259-60.
11. G. E. Mendenhall, *Law and Covenant in Israel and the Ancient Near East.*
12. Porteous, p. 138.
13. Stuart, p. 261.
14. J. A. Montgomery, *A Critical and Exegetical Commentary on the Book of Daniel,* pp. 366-68; E. J. Young, *The Prophecy of Daniel,* pp. 188-89; Leupold, pp. 390 ff.
15. Montgomery, p. 369.
16. Young, p. 188.
17. Tatford, p. 155.
18. Charles, pp. 96-102.
19. Leupold, pp. 395-99.
20. Montgomery, p. 361.
21. Ibid., pp. 362-63.
22. Leupold, p. 400.
23. Ibid.
24. Montgomery, pp. 358-59.
25. Ibid., pp. 390-401.
26. Ibid., pp. 400-1.
27. Young, pp. 220-21.
28. Ibid., p. 195.
29. Ibid., p. 196.
30. Keil, p. 339; Young, p. 196.
31. Leupold, p. 409.
32. Brown, Driver, and Briggs, *A Hebrew and English Lexicon of the Old Testament,* p. 988.
33. O. Zöckler, "The Book of the Prophet Daniel," in *Commentary on the Holy Scriptures,* 13:194.
34. Cf. Young, p. 197.
35. Young, pp. 198-99; C. F. Keil, *Biblical Commentary on the Book of Daniel,* p. 342.
36. Keil, p. 342.
37. S. R. Driver, "Propitiation," in *A Dictionary of the Bible,* 4:131.
38. George N. H. Peters, *The Theocratic Kingdom,* 3:455-56.
39. Young, p. 200.
40. Cf. Young, pp. 200-1.
41. Ibid., p. 201.
42. Keil, p. 349; Leupold, pp. 414-16.
43. A. C. Gaebelein, *The Prophet Daniel,* p. 133.
44. Calvin, 2:219.
45. Young, p. 201.
46. Ibid.
47. Ibid., p. 202.
48. For a brief explanation of the earlier view beginning the seventy weeks in 457 B.C., see G. L. Archer, Jr., *A Survey of Old Testament Introduction,* p. 387; J. B. Payne, "Daniel," *Zondervan Pictorial Bible Dictionary,* p. 198; J. B. Payne, *The Theology of the Older Testament,* p. 521.
49. Young, p. 203.
50. M. F. Unger, *Unger's Bible Dictionary,* p. 94.
51. Young, p. 203.
52. Zöckler, p. 199.

53. Anderson, p. 128.
54. Alva J. McClain, *Daniel's Prophecies of the Seventy Weeks,* p. 20.
55. Cf. Glenn R. Goss, "The Chronological Problems of the Seventy Weeks of Daniel," doctor's dissertation.
56. Leslie P. Madison, "Problems of Chronology in the Life of Christ," doctor's dissertation.
57. Montgomery, pp. 378-79.
58. Young, p. 207.
59. Ibid., pp. 208 ff.
60. Young, pp. 208 ff.; Leupold, pp. 431-40.
61. Philip Mauro, *The Seventy Weeks and the Great Tribulation,* pp. 70 ff.
62. Leupold, pp. 436-37.
63. Ibid., p. 431.
64. Keil, p. 367.
65. Ibid., p. 373; Leupold, p. 431; Zöckler, p. 202.
66. Montgomery, p. 385.
67. Young, p. 209.
68. Mauro, p. 81.
69. Keil, p. 365.
70. Ibid.
71. Mauro, pp. 81-83.
72. Young, p. 208. Orig. in italics.
73. Mauro, p. 83.
74. Leupold, p. 431.
75. Keil, p. 372.
76. Young, p. 218.

Chapter 10

1. H. C. Leupold, *Exposition of Daniel,* p. 441.
2. For discussion from the liberal point of view, see J. A. Montgomery, *A Critical and Exegetical Commentary on the Book of Daniel,* pp. 137-39; 404-5.
3. Ibid., p. 405.
4. Leupold, p. 442.
5. E. J. Young, *The Prophecy of Daniel,* p. 223. Young cites in support several articles by Robert Dick Wilson, such as "The Title 'king of Persia' in the Scriptures," *Princeton Theological Review,* 15:90-145 and "Royal Titles in Antiquity: An Essay in Criticism," *Princeton Theological Review,* 2:257-82; 465-97; 618-64; 3: 55-80; 238-67; 422-40; 558-72.
6. Cf. Young, p. 223; Leupold, p. 443.
7. Montgomery, p. 404.
8. Leupold, p. 443.
9. Ibid., p. 446.
10. Ibid., p. 447.
11. Young, p. 223.
12. Montgomery, p. 407.
13. C. F. Keil, *Biblical Commentary on the Old Testament,* p. 409; Leupold, p. 447; Young, p. 224. Contrast Montgomery, p. 407.
14. Leupold, pp. 447-48.
15. Young, p. 225.
16. Keil, p. 409; Young, p. 225.
17. Montgomery, p. 408.
18. S. R. Driver, *The Book of Daniel,* p. 154.
19. Ibid.; Leupold, p. 449.
20. N. W. Porteous, *Daniel, A Commentary,* p. 152.
21. Driver, p. 155.
22. Leupold, p. 450.
23. Brown, Driver, and Briggs, *A Hebrew and English Lexicon of the Old Testament,* p. 451.
24. J. Calvin, *Commentaries on the Book of Daniel,* 2:252.
25. O. Zöckler, "The Book of the Prophet Daniel," in *Commentary on the Holy Scriptures,* p. 228.

26. Keil, p. 419.
27. Leupold, pp. 457-58.
28. Young, p. 227.
29. Calvin, 2:257.
30. Montgomery, p. 413.
31. R. H. Charles, *The Book of Daniel,* p. 116.
32. Leupold, p. 463.
33. Ibid., p. 464.
34. Cf. Montgomery, pp. 416-18.
35. Zöckler, p. 231.
36. A. Jeffrey, "The Book of Daniel," in *The Interpreter's Bible,* 6:510.

CHAPTER 11

1. W. M. Smith, Introduction to *Commentary on Daniel,* by Jerome, p. 5.
2. For an interesting study of Porphyry, see W. A. Criswell, *Expository Sermons on the Book of Daniel,* 1:19 ff.
3. F. W. Farrar, *The Book of Daniel,* p. 299.
4. H. C. Leupold, *Exposition of Daniel,* pp. 471-73.
5. C. F. Keil, *Biblical Commentary on the Book of Daniel,* p. 429.
6. N. W. Porteous, *Daniel: A Commentary,* p. 156.
7. J. A. Montgomery, *A Critical and Exegetical Commentary on the Book of Daniel,* p. 423.
8. Montgomery, p. 424.
9. Leupold, p. 476.
10. See discussion of this point by Young, p. 234.
11. Brown, Driver, and Briggs, *Hebrew and English Lexicon of the Old Testament,* p. 651.
12. Jerome, *Commentary on Daniel,* p. 123.
13. O. Zöckler, *Daniel: Commentary on The Holy Scriptures,* p. 242.
14. Montgomery, p. 433.
15. Jerome, p. 124.
16. E. J. Young, *The Prophecy of Daniel,* p. 238.
17. Cf. original account by Josephus, *Works of Flavius Josephus,* pp. 354-56.
18. Zöckler, p. 244.
19. Brown, Driver, and Briggs, p. 1008.
20. Young, p. 240.
21. Ibid.
22. Cf. Polyb. 18. 34; and Livy, 33. 19, 38, 40, as cited by Zöckler, p. 246.
23. Cf. Montgomery, pp. 434-35.
24. Leupold, p. 492.
25. Ibid., p. 493.
26. Zöckler, p. 246, citing Appian, *Syr.* C. 45.
27. Montgomery, p. 445.
28. Zöckler, p. 247.
29. Cf. Yohanan Aharoni and Michael Avi-Yonah, *The Macmillan Bible Atlas,* p. 117.
30. Montgomery, pp. 446-47.
31. Zöckler, p. 251, quoting John M. Fuller, *An Essay on the Authenticity of the Book of Daniel.*
32. Zöckler, p. 251.
33. E. B. Pusey, *Daniel the Prophet,* p. 139.
34. Jerome, *Commentary on Daniel,* p. 136.
35. Ibid., p. 130.
36. Montgomery, pp. 464 ff.
37. Ibid., p. 465.
38. Young, pp. 246-47.
39. John N. Darby, *Studies on the Book of Daniel,* pp. 107-14.
40. A. C. Gaebelein, *The Prophet Daniel,* pp. 180-95.
41. Montgomery, p. 461.
42. Gaebelein, p. 188.
43. Montgomery, pp. 461-62.
44. Anthony A. Bevan, *A Short Commentary on the Book of Daniel,* pp. 196-97.

45. Keil, pp. 464-65; Young, p. 249. Leupold holds a similar view, pp. 515-16.
46. Gaebelein, p. 188.
47. Ibid.
48. Cf. Montgomery, pp. 464-67.
49. H. A. Ironside, *Lectures on Daniel*, pp. 222-23.
50. Young, p. 251.
51. Leupold, p. 521.
52. *Time*, May 21, 1965, p. 35.

CHAPTER 12

1. N. W. Porteous, *Daniel, A Commentary*, p. 170.
2. C. F. Keil, *Biblical Commentary on the Old Testament*, pp. 477-78.
3. J. Calvin, *Commentaries on the Book of the Prophet Daniel*, 2:369.
4. E. J. Young, *The Prophecy of Daniel*, p. 255; H. C. Leupold, *Exposition of Daniel*, pp. 528-29; Calvin, 2:371-72.
5. J. A. Montgomery, *A Critical and Exegetical Commentary on The Book of Daniel*, p. 471.
6. A. A. Bevan, *A Short Commentary on The Book of Daniel*, p. 201.
7. Montgomery, ibid.
8. A. C. Gaebelein, *The Prophet Daniel*, p. 200.
9. W. Kelly, *Lectures on the Book of Daniel*, pp. 225-26.
10. H. A. Ironside, *Lectures on Daniel the Prophet*, pp. 231-32.
11. R. D. Culver, *Daniel and the Latter Days*, p. 172.
12. Leupold, pp. 529-532; Young, p. 256.
13. John M. Fuller, *An Essay on the Authenticity of the Book of Daniel*, p. 339.
14. Young, p. 256.
15. S. P. Tregelles, *Remarks on the Prophetic Visions in the Book of Daniel*, p. 162.
16. Culver, p. 175.
17. Leupold, p. 530.
18. Ibid.
19. Ibid.
20. Young, p. 256.
21. Bevan, p. 201.
22. Young, p. 256.
23. Keil, p. 484.
24. Montgomery, pp. 473-74.
25. Calvin, 2:379. Orig. in italics.
26. Leupold, p. 534.
27. Young, p. 258.
28. Cf. Young, p. 259.
29. Ibid.
30. Montgomery, p. 475.
31. Brown, Driver, and Briggs, *Hebrew and English Lexicon of the Old Testament*, p. 658.
32. J. A. Seiss, *Voices from Babylon*, pp. 310-11.
33. Montgomery, p. 477.
34. O. Zöckler, "The Book of the Prophet Daniel," in *Commentary on the Holy Scriptures*, 13:267.

BIBLIOGRAPHY

AHARONI, YOHANAN, and AVI-YONAH, MICHAEL. *The Macmillan Bible Atlas*. New York: Macmillan, 1968.

ALBRIGHT, WILLIAM F. *From the Stone Age to Christianity*. 2d ed. New York: Doubleday, Anchor Books, 1957.

ALEXANDER, RALPH. Abstract of "Hermeneutics of Old Testament Apocalyptic Literature." Doctor's dissertation, Dallas Theological Seminary, 1968.

ANDERSON, ROBERT. *The Coming Prince*. 14th ed. Grand Rapids: Kregel, 1954.

ANDREWS, SAMUEL J. *Christianity and Anti-Christianity*. Chicago: The Bible Inst. Colportage Assn., 1937.

Apocrypha of the Old Testament. Revised Standard Version. New York: Nelson, 1957.

ARCHER, GLEASON L., JR. *A Survey of Old Testament Introduction*. Chicago: Moody, 1964.

ARTHUR, ALEXANDER. *A Critical Commentary on the Book of Daniel*. Edinburgh: Norman MacLeod, 1893.

ATHENAEUS. "The Deipnosophists." In *Athenaeus*, trans. Charles Burton Gulick, vol. 2. Loeb Classical Library. London: Heinemann, 1927-41.

AUBERLEN, CARL AUGUST. *The Prophecies of Daniel and the Revelations of St. John*. Edinburgh: T. & T. Clark, 1857.

AUCHINCLOSS, WILLIAM STUART. *The Only Key to Daniel's Prophecies*. New York: Van Nostrand, 1904.

———. *The Book of Daniel Unlocked*. New York: Van Nostrand, 1905.

AVRAAMIDES, ACHILLES. "The Historicity of Daniel's Record Regarding Belshazzar." Master's thesis, Dallas Theological Seminary, 1961.

BARNES, ALBERT. *Daniel*. Vol. 2. Notes on the Old Testament, ed. Robert Few. Grand Rapids: Baker, 1950.

———. *Notes, Critical, Illustrative, and Practical, on the Book of Daniel*. New York: Leavitt & Allen, 1861.

BARTON, GEORGE A. *Archaeology and the Bible*. Philadelphia: Amer. S. S. Union, 1916.

BEAVAN, E. R. "Syria and the Jews." In *The Cambridge Ancient History*, ed. S. A. Cook, F. E. Adcock, and M. P. Charlesworth, vol. 8. Cambridge: University Press, 1930.

BEVAN, ANTHONY ASHLEY. *A Short Commentary on the Book of Daniel*. Cambridge: University Press, 1892.

BLACH, MATTHEW, and ROWLEY, H. H., eds. *Peale's Commentary on the Bible*. London: Nelson, 1961.

BOUTFLOWER, CHARLES. *In and Around the Book of Daniel*. Grand Rapids: Zondervan, 1963.

BRINKMAN, J. A. "Neo-Babylonian Texts in the Archaeological Museum at Florence." *Journal of Near Eastern Studies* 25 (July 1966):202-9.

BROWN, FRANCIS; DRIVER, S. R.; and BRIGGS, CHARLES A., eds. *A Hebrew and English Lexicon of the Old Testament.* Oxford: Clarendon, 1955.

BROWNLEE, WILLIAM H. *The Meaning of the Qumran Scrolls for the Bible.* New York: Oxford, 1964.

BUBER, MARTIN. *Daniel: Dialogues on Realization.* Trans. Maurice Fredman. New York: Holt, Rinehart, & Winston, 1964.

BULLINGER, ETHELBERT WILLIAM. *The Companion Bible.* 6 vols. London: Oxford, 1910.

BURROWS, MILLAR. *More Light on the Dead Sea Scrolls.* New York: Viking, 1958.

BURTON, ALFRED H. *Hints on the Book of Daniel.* London: Holness, 1903.

CACHEMAILLE, E. P. *The Seventy Weeks and the Messiah.* London: Thynne, 1918.

CALVIN, JOHN. *Commentaries on the Book of the Prophet Daniel.* 2 vols. Trans. Thomas Myers. Edinburgh: Calvin Trans. Soc., 1852.

CARROLL, BENAJAH HARVEY. *Daniel and the Inter-Biblical Period.* An Interpretation of the English Bible, ed. J. B. Cranfill, vol. 11. New York: Revell, 1915.

CLERMONT-GANNEAU. *Journal Asiatique.* 1886.

CHARLES, ROBERT HENRY. *Apocrypha and Pseudipigrapha of the Old Testament in English.* Vol. 2. Oxford: Clarendon, 1913.

———. *The Book of Daniel.* The New Century Bible, ed. Walter F. Adeney. New York: H. Frowde, Oxford U., n.d.

COLTON, T. G. *The Jewish Persecutor; or, A Sketch of the Life and Character of Antiochus Epiphanes.* Boston: Mass. Sabbath School Soc., 1860.

COOPER, DAVID L. *The 70 Weeks of Daniel.* Los Angeles: Biblical Res. Soc., 1941.

CRISWELL, WALLIE AMOS. *Expository Sermons on the Book of Daniel.* Vol. 1. Grand Rapids: Zondervan, 1968.

CROSS, FRANK MOORE. *The Ancient Library of Qumran and Modern Biblical Studies.* Garden City, N.Y.: Doubleday, 1958.

CULVER, ROBERT D. *Daniel and the Latter Days.* Chicago: Moody, n.d.

———. "Daniel." In *The Wycliffe Bible Commentary,* ed. Charles F. Pfeiffer and Everett F. Harrison. Chicago: Moody, 1962.

CUMONT, F. "La Plus Ancienne geographie astrologique," *Klio* 9 (1909):263-73.

DARBY, JOHN NELSON. *Studies on the Book of Daniel.* London: G. Morrish, n.d.

DEANE, H. *The Book of Daniel.* The "Layman's Handy Commentary" Series, ed. Charles John Ellicott, vol. 22. Grand Rapids: Zondervan, 1959.

———. *Daniel: His Life and Times.* New York: A. Randolph, 1888.

DEHAAN, MARTIN RALPH. *Daniel the Prophet.* Grand Rapids: Zondervan, 1947.

DESPREZ, PHILIP F. *Daniel and John.* London: C. K. Paul, 1878.

DE VAUX, ROLAND. *Ancient Israel, Its Life and Institutions.* Trans. John McHugh. New York: McGraw Hill, 1961.

DOUGHERTY, RAYMOND PHILIP. *Nabonidus and Belshazzar.* Yale Oriental Series, vol. 15. New Haven: Yale U., 1929.

DRIVER, SAMUEL ROLLES. *The Book of Daniel.* The Cambiidge Bible for Schools and Colleges. Cambridge: U. Press, 1900.

———. "Hebrew Authority." In *Authority and Archaeology—Sacred and Profane,* ed. David G. Hogarth. London: Murray, 1899.

———. "Propitiation." In *A Dictionary of the Bible,* ed. James Hastings, vol. 4. Edinburgh: T. & T. Clark, 1902.

EWALD, GEORG HEINRICH AUGUST. *Commentary on the Prophets of the Old Testament.* Trans. J. Frederick Smith. Vol. 5. London: Williams & Norgate, 1881.

FARRAR, FREDERIC WILLIAM. *The Book of Daniel, The Expositor's Bible.* Ed. W. Robertson Nicoll. Cincinnati: Jennings & Graham, n.d.

FINEGAN, JACK. *Handbook of Biblical Chronology.* Princeton: Princeton U., 1964.

FREEDMAN, DAVID N. "The Prayer of Nabonidus." *Bulletin of the American Schools of Oriental Research* 145 (Feb. 1957): 31-32.

FROST, STANLEY B. *Old Testament Apocalyptic.* London: Epworth, 1952.

FULLER, JOHN M. *An Essay on the Authenticity of the Book of Daniel.* Cambridge: 1864.

GAEBELEIN, ARNO CLEMENS. *The Prophet Daniel.* New York: Our Hope Publ., 1911.

GASTER, T. H. *The Dead Sea Scriptures.* Garden City, N. Y.: Doubleday, 1956.

GIBBON, EDWARD. *The Decline and Fall of the Roman Empire.* 2 vols. New York: Modern Library, n.d.

GINSBERG, H. LOUIS. *Studies in Daniel.* New York: Jewish Theol. Sem. of Amer., 1948.

GLUECK, NELSON. *Hesed in the Bible.* Trans. Alfred Gottscholk. Ed. Gerald A. LaRue. Cincinnati: Heb. Union Col., 1967.

GOSS, GLENN R. "The Chronological Problems of the Seventy Weeks of Daniel." Doctor's dissertation, Dallas Theol. Sem., 1966.

HARMON, DAVID A. "Problem of the Sixty-nine Weeks of Daniel's Prophecy of the Seventy Weeks." Master's thesis, Dallas Theol. Sem., 1957.

HARRISON, RAYMOND K. "Babylon." In *The Zondervan Pictorial Bible Dictionary,* ed. Merrill C. Tenney. Grand Rapids: Zondervan, 1963.

———. *Introduction to the Old Testament.* Grand Rapids: Eerdmans, 1969.

HEATH, ALBAN. *The Prophecies of Daniel in the Light of History.* London: Covenant Publ., 1941.

HEATON, ERIC WILLIAM. *The Book of Daniel.* Torch Bible Commentaries, ed. John Marsh, Alan Richardson, and R. Gregor Smith. London: SCM, 1956.

HERODOTUS. Vol. 1. Trans. Henry Carey. New York: Harper, 1889.

HINKLEY, WILLARD H. *The Book of Daniel.* Boston: New-Church Union, 1894.

HOFFMANN, JOHANNES FRIEDRICH. *Antiochus IV Epiphanes.* Leipzig: Ackermann & Glaser, 1873.

HORN, SIEGFRIED H. *Seventh-Day Adventist Bible Dictionary.* Washington, D. C.: Review & Herald Publ., 1960.

IRONSIDE, HENRY ALLEN. *Lectures on Daniel the Prophet.* New York: Loizeaux, 1920.

JAMIESON, ROBERT; FAUSSET, A. R.; and BROWN, DAVID. *A Commentary: Critical, Experimental and Practical on the Old and New Testaments.* 6 vols. Grand Rapids: Eerdmans, 1945.

JEFFERY, ARTHUR. "The Book of Daniel, Introduction and Exegesis." In *The Interpreter's Bible*, ed. George A. Buttrick, vol. 6. New York: Abingdon-Cokesbury, 1951.

JEROME. *Commentary on Daniel*. Trans. Gleason L. Archer, Jr. Grand Rapids: Baker, 1958.

JOHNSON, PHILIP C. *The Book of Daniel*. Grand Rapids: Baker, 1964.

JONES, ALEXANDER, ed. *The Jerusalem Bible*. Garden City, N. Y.: Doubleday, 1966.

JOSEPHUS, FLAVIUS. "Against Apion." Trans. H. St. J. Thackeray. In *Josephus*, vol. 1. Loeb Classical Library. London: Heinemann, 1926.

————. "Jewish Antiquities." Trans. Ralph Marcus et al. In *Josephus*, vols. 5-9. Loeb Classical Library. Cambridge: Harvard U., 1926.

————. *The Works of Flavius Josephus*. Trans. William Whiston. Philadelphia: Porter & Coates, n.d.

JOUON, P. PAUL, S. J. *Grammaire de l'Hebreu Biblique*. Rome: Institut Biblique Pontifical, 1947.

KEIL, CARL FRIEDRICH. *Biblical Commentary on the Book of Daniel*. Trans. M. G. Easton. Grand Rapids: Eerdmans, 1955.

KELLY, WILLIAM. *Lectures on the Book of Daniel*. 2d ed. London: G. Morrish, 1881.

KENNEDY, GERALD. "Daniel." In *The Interpreter's Bible*, ed. George A. Buttrick, vol. 6. New York: Abingdon, 1956.

KEPLER, THOMAS S. *Dreams of the Future*. Bible Guides, ed. William Barclay and F. F. Bruce, no. 22. Nashville: Abingdon, 1963.

KING, GEOFFREY R. *Daniel*. Grand Rapids: Eerdmanns, 1966.

KIRK, THOMAS. *Daniel the Prophet*. Edinburgh: A. Elliot, 1906.

KITCHEN, KENNETH ANDERSON. *Ancient Orient and the Old Testament*. Chicago: Inter-Varsity, 1966.

KITTEL, RUDOLF. "The Aramaic of Daniel." In *Notes on Some Problems in the Book of Daniel*, ed. D. J. Wiseman et al. London: Tyndale, 1965.

————. *Biblia Hebraica*. Vol. 2. Stuttgartiae: Priv. Wurtt. Bibelanstalt, 1945.

KRAELING, EMIL GOTTLIEB. "The Handwriting on the Wall." *Journal of Biblical Literature*, 63 (1944): 11-18.

————. *Rand McNally Bible Atlas*. New York: Rand McNally, 1966.

LANG, GEORGE HENRY. *The Histories and Prophecies of Daniel*. 3d ed. London: Oliphants, 1942.

LARKIN, CLARENCE. *The Book of Daniel*. Philadelphia: Rev. Clarence Larkin, Est., 1929.

LEUPOLD, HERBERT CARL. *Exposition of Daniel*. Minneapolis: Augsburg, 1949.

LUCK, G. COLEMAN. *Daniel*. Chicago: Moody, 1958.

LUTHI, WALTER. *Daniel Speaks to the Church*. Trans. John M. Jensen. Minneapolis: Augsburg, 1947.

MADISON, LESLIE P. "Problems of Chronology in the Life of Christ." Doctor's dissertation, Dallas Theol. Sem., 1963.

MALLOWAN, E. L. "Nimrud." In *Archaeology and Old Testament Study*, ed. D. Winton Thomas. Oxford: Clarendon, 1967.

MARTIN, W. J. "Language of the Old Testament." In *The New Bible Dictionary*, ed. J. D. Douglas. Grand Rapids: Eerdmans, 1965.

MAURO, PHILIP. *The Seventy Weeks and the Great Tribulation*. Boston: Scripture Truth Depot, 1923.

McClain, Alva J. *Daniel's Prophecy of the Seventy Weeks.* Grand Rapids: Zondervan, 1940.

Mendenhall, G. E. *Law and Covenant in Israel and the Ancient Near East.* Biblical Colloquium, 1955.

Milik, J. T. " 'Priere de Nabonide' et autres ecrits d'un cycle de Daniel." *Revue Biblique* 63 (July 1956): 407-15.

Mitchell, T. C., and Joyce, R. "The Musical Instruments in Nebuchadnezzar's Orchestra." In *Notes on Some Problems in the Book of Daniel,* ed. D. J Wiseman et al. London: Tyndale, 1965.

Montgomery, James A. *A Critical and Exegetical Commentary on the Book of Daniel.* The International Critical Commentary. Edinburgh: T. & T. Clark, 1964.

Myers, Jacob B. *The Anchor Bible, I Chronicles.* Garden City, N. Y.: Doubleday, 1965.

Newell, Philip R. *Daniel: the Man Greatly Beloved and His Prophecies.* Chicago: Moody, 1962.

Newton, Isaac. *Observations upon the Prophecies of Daniel.* Ed. P. Berthwick. London: James Nisbet, 1831.

Oppenheim, A. Leo. "Belshazzar." In *The Interpreter's Dictionary of the Bible,* ed. George A. Buttrick, vol. 1. New York: Abingdon-Cokesbury, 1962.

Parker, R. A., and Duberstein, Waldo H. *Babylonian Chronology 626 B.C.-A.D. 45.* U. of Chicago, 1942.

Payne, D. F. "Jerusalem." In *The New Bible Dictionary.* ed. J. D. Douglas. Grand Rapids: Eerdmans, 1965.

Payne, J. Barton. "Book of Daniel." In *Zondervan Pictorial Bible Dictionary,* ed. Merrill C. Tenney. Grand Rapids: Zondervan, 1963.

———. *The Theology of the Older Testament.* Grand Rapids: Zondervan, 1962.

Pember, George Hawkins. *The Great Prophecies of the Centuries Concerning Israel and the Gentiles.* London: Hodder & Stoughton, 1895.

Pentecost, J. Dwight. *Prophecy for Today.* Grand Rapids: Zondervan, 1961.

———. *Things to Come.* Findlay, Ohio: Dunham, 1958.

Peters, George Nathaniel Henry. *The Theocratic Kingdom.* 3 vols. Grand Rapids: Kregel, 1952.

Petrie, Arthur. *The Message of Daniel.* Harrisburg: Christian Pubns., 1947.

Pettingill, William L. *Simple Studies in Daniel.* 4th ed. Philadelphia: Phila. Sch. of the Bible, 1920.

Pinches, T. G. "Babel, Babylon." In *The International Standard Bible Encyclopedia,* ed. James Orr. Chicago: Howard-Severance, 1930.

Porteous, Norman W. *Daniel: A Commentary.* Philadelphia: Westminster, 1965.

Prince, J. Dymeley. *A Critical Commentary on the Book of Daniel.* London: Williams & Norgate, 1899.

Pritchard, James B., ed. *Ancient Near Eastern Texts Relating to the Old Testament.* Princeton, N. J.: Princeton U., 1950.

Pusey, Edward B. *Daniel the Prophet.* New York: Funk & Wagnalls, 1885.

Rosenthal, Franz. *A Grammar of Biblical Aramaic.* Wiesbaden: O. Harrassowitz, 1961.

Rowley, Harold Henry. *Darius the Mede and the Four World Empires in the Book of Daniel.* Cardiff, Wales: U. of Wales, 1959.

———. "The Historicity of the Fifth Chapter of Daniel." *Journal of Theological Studies* 32 (Oct. 1930): 12-31.

———. *The Relevance of the Apocalyptic.* 2d ed. London: Lutterworth, 1952.

———. *The Servant of the Lord and Other Essays on the Old Testament.* London: Lutterworth, 1952.

———. "The Unity of the Book of Daniel." In *Hebrew Union College Annual,* vol. 23. London: January 1950.

SAGGS, H. W. F. "Babylon." In *Archaeology and Old Testament Study,* ed. D. Winton Thomas. Oxford: Clarendon, 1967.

———. *The Greatness That Was Babylon.* New York: Hawthorne, 1962.

SCOFIELD, CYRUS I., ed. *New Scofield Reference Bible.* New York: Oxford U., 1967.

———. *Scofield Reference Bible.* New York: Oxford U., 1917.

SEISS, JOSEPH A. *Voices From Babylon: Or the Records of Daniel the Prophet.* Philadelphia: Porter & Coates, 1879.

SHUNK, GEORGE WESLEY. "The Seventieth Week of Daniel." Doctor's dissertation, Dallas Theol. Sem., 1953.

SMITH, R. PAYNE. *Daniel: An Exposition of the Historical Portion of the Writings of the Prophet Daniel.* Cincinnati: Crouston & Curts, n.d.

SMITH, URIAH. *The Sanctuary and the Twenty-three Hundred Days of Daniel 8:14.* Battle Creek, Mich.: Steam Press, 1877.

———. "Thoughts on the Prophecies of Daniel." Part I, pp. 317. In *Daniel and the Revelation.* Washington, D. C.: Review & Herald, 1897.

SMITH, WILBUR M. Introduction to *Commentary on Daniel,* by Jerome. Grand Rapids: Baker, 1958.

———. "Jerusalem." In *The Zondervan Pictorial Bible Dictionary,* ed. Merrill C. Tenney. Grand Rapids: Zondervan, 1963.

STEVENS, WILLIAM C. *The Book of Daniel.* Rev. ed. Los Angeles: Bible House of L. A., 1949.

STUART, MOSES. *A Commentary on the Book of Daniel.* Boston: Crocker & Brewster, 1850.

TADMOR, HAYIM. "Chronicle of the Last Kings of Judah." *Journal of Near Eastern Studies* 15 (Oct. 1956): 227.

TARN, WILLIAM WOODTHROPE. *Alexander the Great.* 2 vols. Cambridge: Cambridge U., 1948.

TALBOT, LOUIS T. *The Prophecies of Daniel.* 3d ed. Wheaton, Ill.: Van Kampen, 1954.

TATFORD, FREDERICK A. *The Climax of the Ages.* London: Marshall, Morgan & Scott, 1953.

———. *God's Program of the Ages.* Grand Rapids: Kregel, 1967.

TCHERIKOVER, VICTOR. *Hellenistic Civilization and the Jews.* Trans. F. Applebaum. Philadelphia: Jewish Pub. Soc. of Amer., 1961.

TERRY, MILTON S. *The Prophecies of Daniel.* New York: Hunt & Eaton, 1893.

THIELE, EDWIN R. *The Mysterious Numbers of the Hebrew Kings.* Chicago: U. of Chicago, 1951.

THOMAS, DAVID WINTON, ed. *Archaeology and Old Testament Study.* Oxford: Clarendon, 1967.

THOMAS, W. H. GRIFFITH. "The Purpose of the Fourth Gospel." *Bibliotheca Sacra* 125 (July-September 1968): 253-62.

Time, May 21, 1965.
TREGELLES, SAMUEL PRIDEAUX. *Remarks on the Prophetic Visions in the Book of Daniel.* 7th ed. London: Sovereign Grace, 1965.
UNGER, MERRILL F. *Unger's Bible Dictionary.* Chicago: Moody, 1957.
———. *The Dead Sea Scrolls.* Grand Rapids: Zondervan, 1957.
———. *Introductory Guide to the Old Testament.* Grand Rapids: Zondervan, 1951.
VINE, WILLIAM EDWYN. *The Roman Empire in the Light of Prophecy.* Glasgow: Pickering & Inglis, n.d.
WALVOORD, JOHN F. *Millennial Kingdom.* Grand Rapids: Dunham, 1959.
———. *The Nations in Prophecy.* Grand Rapids: Zondervan, 1967.
———. "Prophecy and the Deterioration of the Nations." In *The Sure Word of Prophecy,* ed. John W. Bradbury. New York: Revell, 1943.
———. "The Times of the Gentiles." In *Understanding the Times,* ed. William Culbertson and Herman B. Centz. Grand Rapids: Zondervan, 1956.
———. *The Revelation of Jesus Christ.* Chicago: Moody, 1966.
———. *Israel in Prophecy.* Grand Rapids: Zondervan, 1962.
WEST, NATHANIEL. *Daniel's Great Prophecy.* London: "Prophetic News," n.d.
———. *Daniel's Great Prophecy.* New York: Hope of Israel, 1898.
WHEATON, D. H. "Antiochus." In *The New Bible Dictionary,* ed. J. D. Douglas. Grand Rapids: Eerdmans, 1965.
WHITCOMB, JOHN C. JR. *Darius the Mede.* Grand Rapids: Eerdmans, 1959.
WILSON, ROBERT DICK. "The Aramaic of Daniel." In *Biblical and Theological Studies.* New York: Scribner, 1912.
———. "Book of Daniel." In *The International Standard Bible Encyclopedia,* ed. James Orr, vol. 2. Chicago: Howard-Severance, 1930.
———. "Royal Titles in Antiquity: An Essay in Criticism." *Princeton Theological Review* 2 (1904): 257-82; 465-97; 618-64; 3 (1905): 55-80; 238-67; 422-40; 558-72.
———. *Studies in the Book of Daniel.* New York: Putnam, 1917.
———. "The Title 'king of Persia' in the Scriptures." *Princeton Theological Review* 15 (1917): 90-145.
WISEMAN, DONALD J. "Babylon." In *The New Bible Dictionary,* ed. J. D. Douglas. Grand Rapids: Eerdmans, 1965.
———. "Belshazzar." In *The New Bible Dictionary,* ed. J. D. Douglas. Grand Rapids: Eerdmans, 1965.
———. *Chronicles of the Chaldean Kings (626-556 B.C.).* London: Trustees of the Brit. Museum, 1961.
———. "Some Historical Problems in the Book of Daniel." In *Notes on Some Problems in the Book of Daniel,* ed. D. J. Wiseman et al. London: Tyndale, 1965.
WRIGHT, CHARLES H. H. *Daniel and His Prophecies.* London: Williams & Norgate, 1906.
———. *Daniel and Its Critics.* London: William & Norgate, 1906.
YAMAUCHI, EDWIN M. *Greece and Babylon.* Grand Rapids: Baker, 1967.
YOUNG, EDWARD J. *The Prophecy of Daniel.* Grand Rapids: Eerdmans, 1949.
ZÖCKLER, OTTO. "The Book of the Prophet Daniel." In *Commentary on the Holy Scriptures,* ed. John Peter Lange, vol. 13. 1876 ed. Grand Rapids: Zondervan, 1960.

INDEX

Moody Press, a ministry of the Moody Bible Institute, is
designed for education, evangelization and edification.
If we may assist you in knowing more about Christ and
the Christian life, please write us without obligation to:
Moody Press, c/o MLM, Chicago, Illinois 60610.